DREAM SAGA

Volume 1

by
Megumi
Tachikawa

TOKYOPOP

HAMBURG // LONDON // LOS ANGELES // TOKYO

Dream Saga Vol. 1
Created by Megumi Tachikawa

Translation - Emi Onishi
English Adaptation - Solina Wong
Retouch and Lettering - Abelardo Bigting
Production Artist - James Lee
Cover Design - Anna Kernbaum

Editor - Nora Wong
Digital Imaging Manager - Chris Buford
Pre-Press Manager - Antonio DePietro
Production Managers - Jennifer Miller and Mutsumi Miyazaki
Art Director - Matt Alford
Managing Editor - Jill Freshney
VP of Production - Ron Klamert
President and C.O.O. - John Parker
Publisher and C.E.O. - Stuart Levy

A  Manga

TOKYOPOP Inc.
5900 Wilshire Blvd. Suite 2000
Los Angeles, CA 90036

E-mail: editor@TOKYOPOP.com
Come visit us online at www.TOKYOPOP.com

ISBN: 1-59182-774-4

First TOKYOPOP printing: August 2004
10 9 8 7 6 5 4 3 2
Printed in the USA

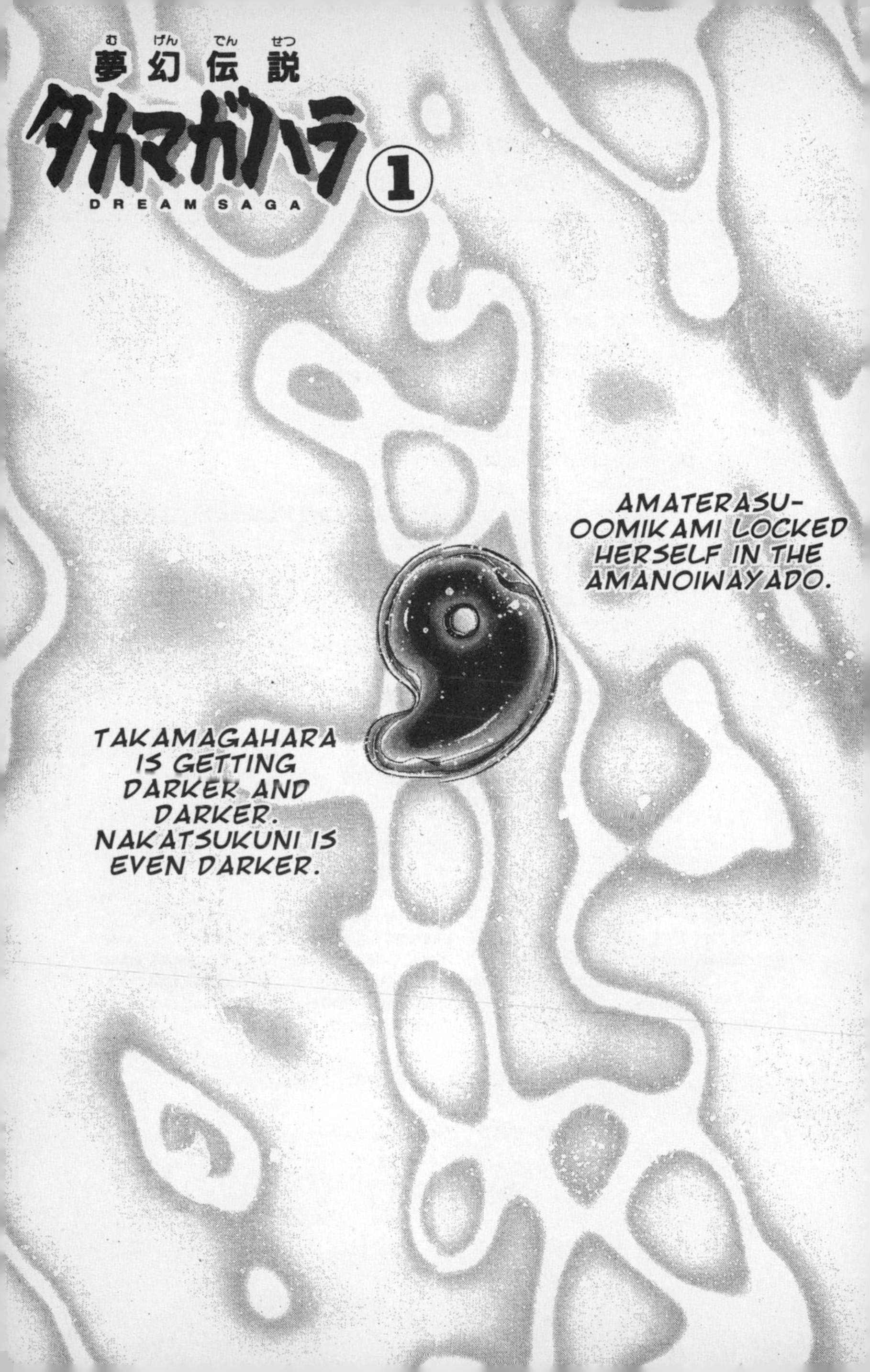
夢幻伝説（むげんでんせつ）
タカマガハラ ①
DREAM SAGA
AMATERASU-OOMIKAMI LOCKED HERSELF IN THE AMANOIWAYADO.
TAKAMAGAHARA IS GETTING DARKER AND DARKER. NAKATSUKUNI IS EVEN DARKER.

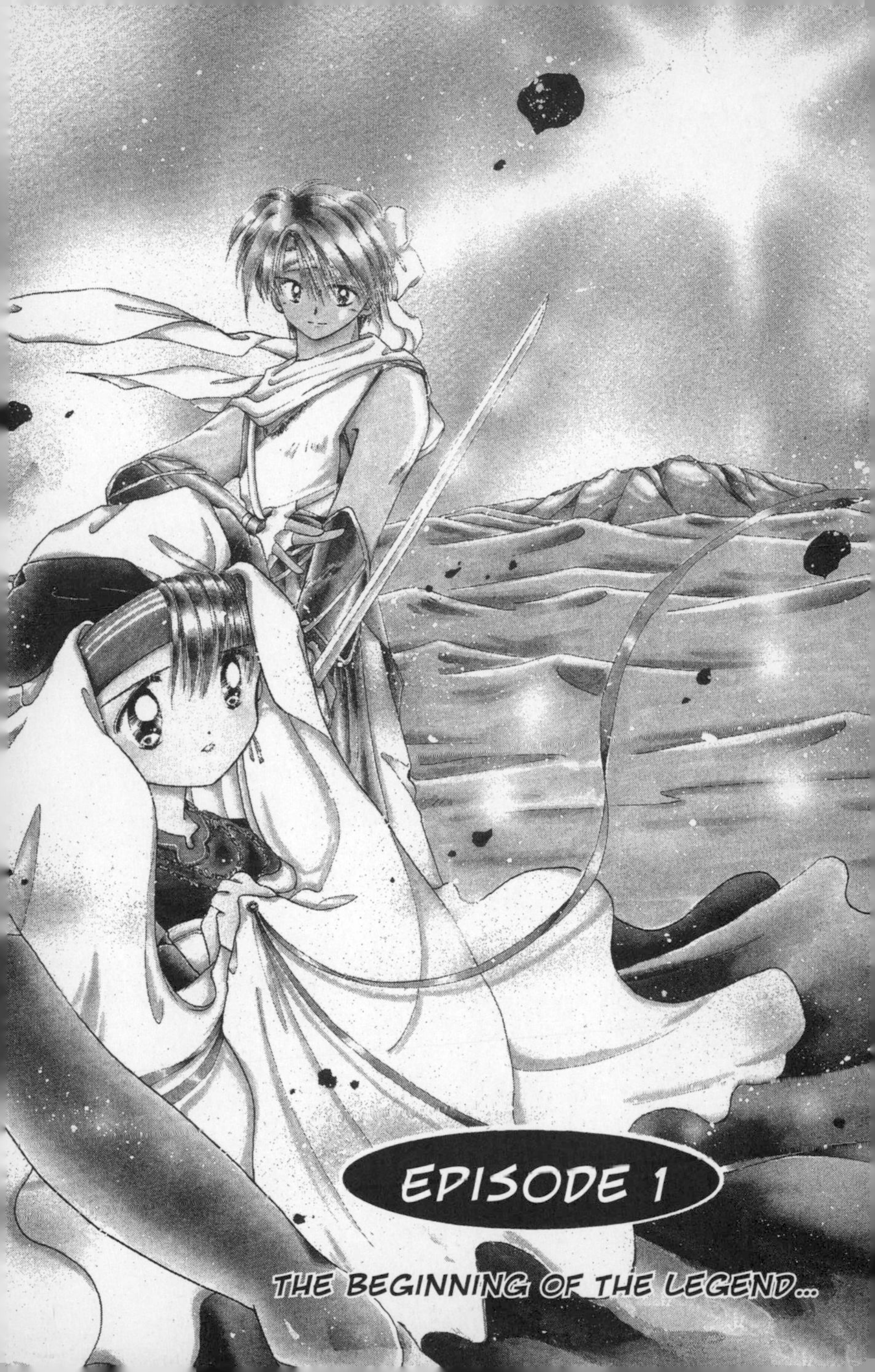
EPISODE 1
THE BEGINNING OF THE LEGEND...

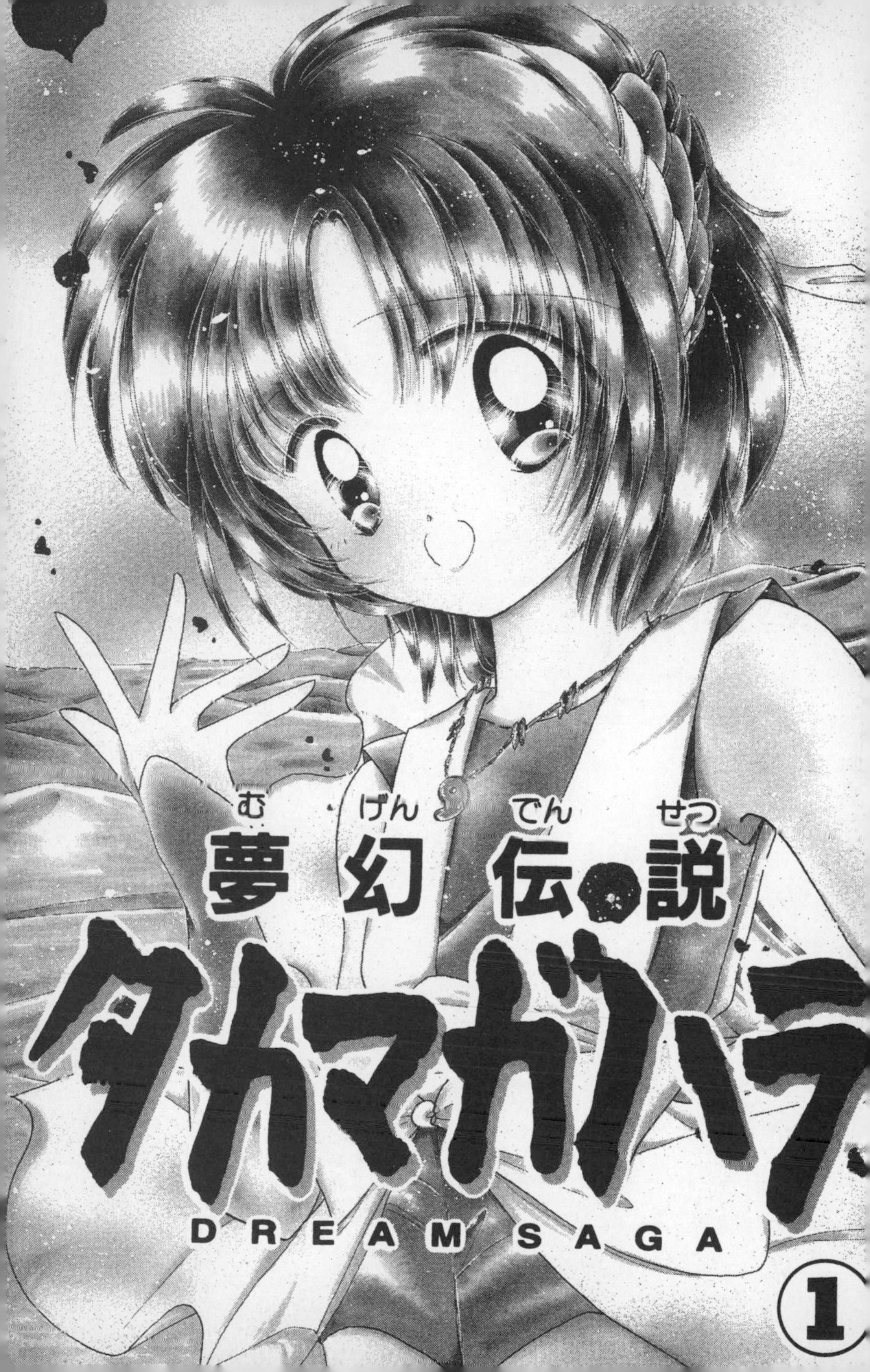
夢幻伝説 (むげんでんせつ)
タカマガハラ
DREAM SAGA
1

Hi! I'm Megumi Tachikawa. Thanks for buying "Dream Saga: Takamagahara" Vol. 1. This is an adventure-fantasy series. Well, at least that's what I have in mind at this point. We'll see what happens! I've wanted to write a story like this for a long time. Ever since I started writing this story, I've received tons of letters from fans telling me their names are "Yuuki" also. There are so many Yuukis around the world, although the Kanji characters of some of your names are a little different. I've been reading all of your letters! I haven't had the chance to write back to all of you, but I wanted you to know that I'm reading every single one of them. So please don't worry! Whether or not your name is Yuuki, I hope you'll enjoy all the "Dream Saga" adventures with Yuuki through this series! Maybe you'll go to Takamagahara in your dreams, too! As always, I want to answer some of your questions in your letters as we go along, so you'll see these sidebars throughout the book. Are you ready? Let's begin our adventure of the Dream Saga Takamagahara!

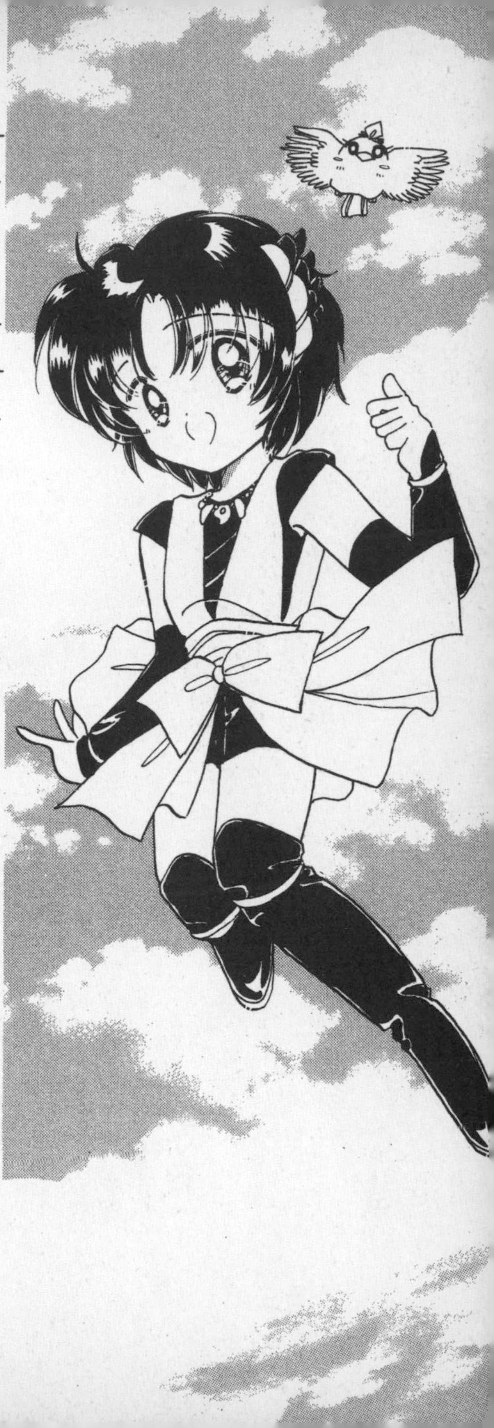

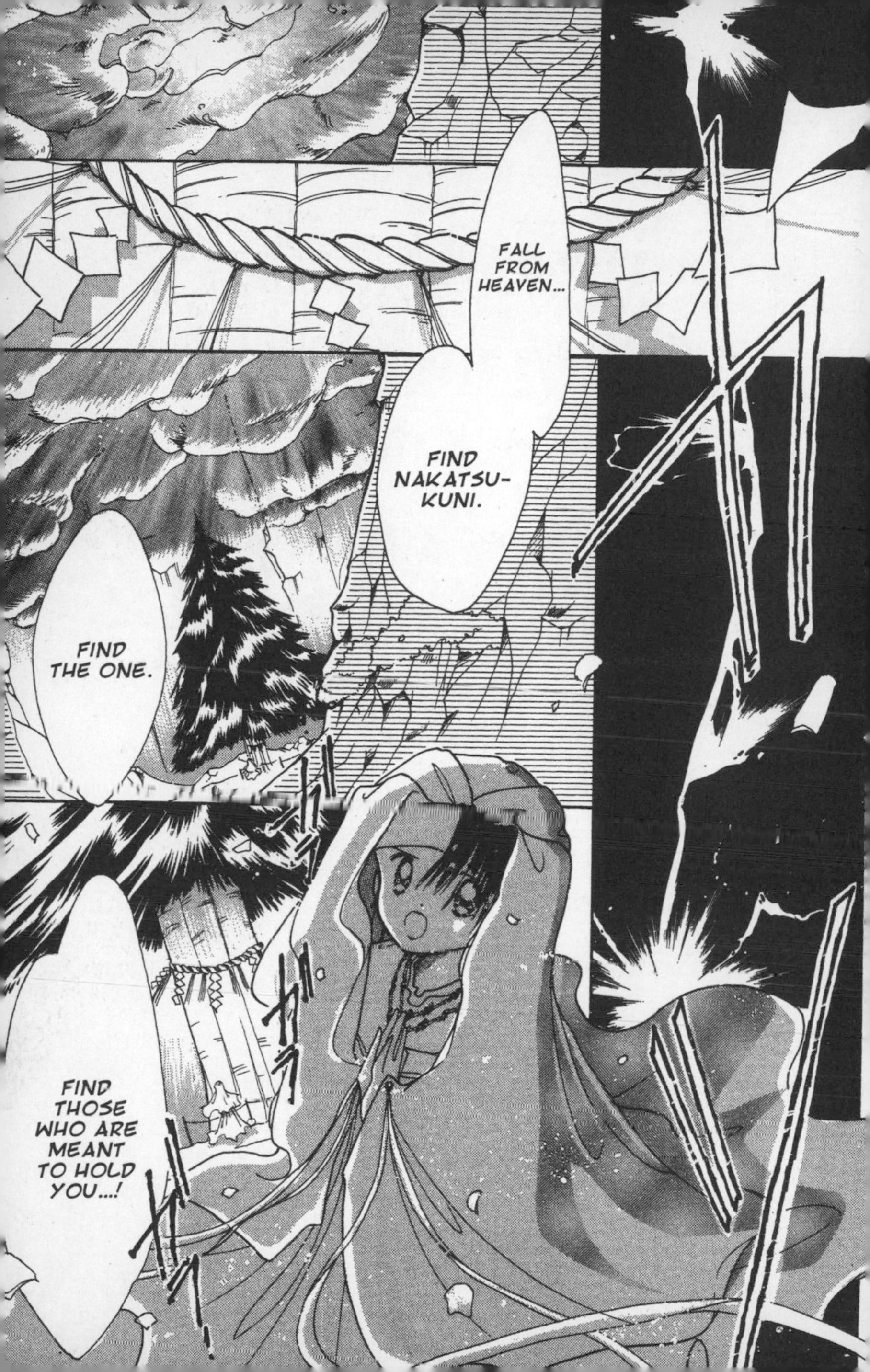
FALL FROM HEAVEN...
FIND NAKATSU-KUNI.
FIND THE ONE.
FIND THOSE WHO ARE MEANT TO HOLD YOU...!

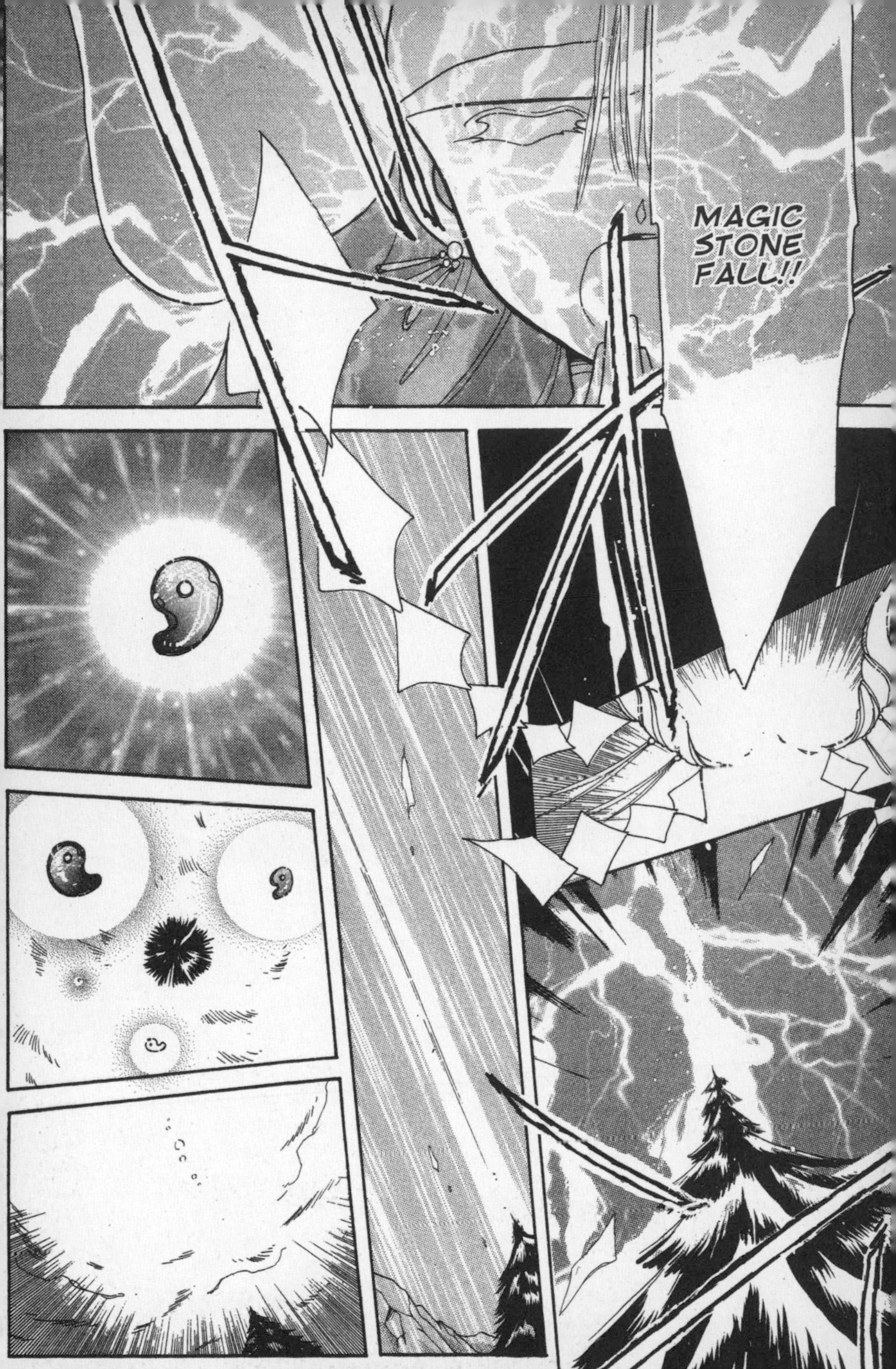
MAGIC STONE FALL!!

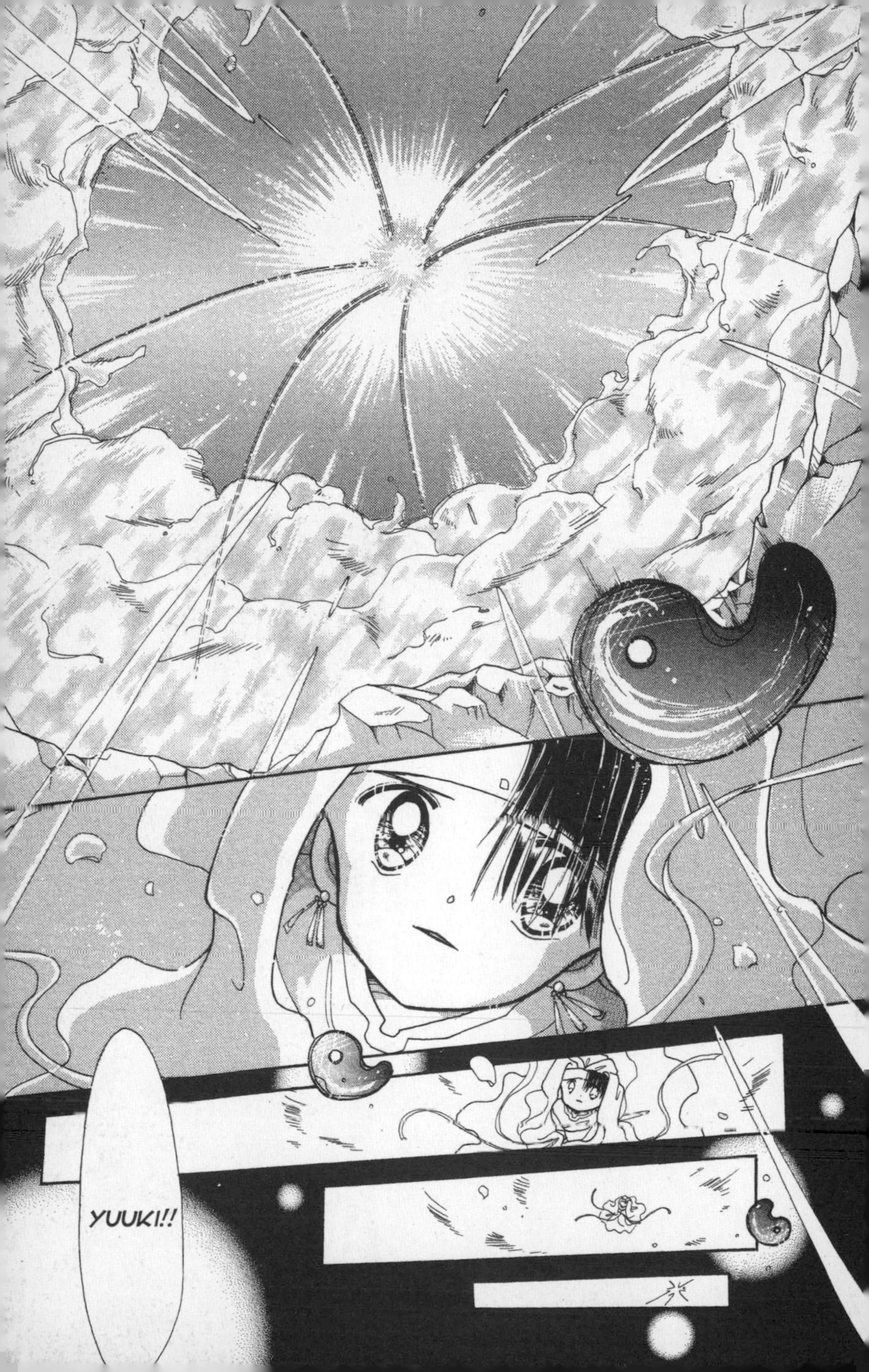
YUUKI!!

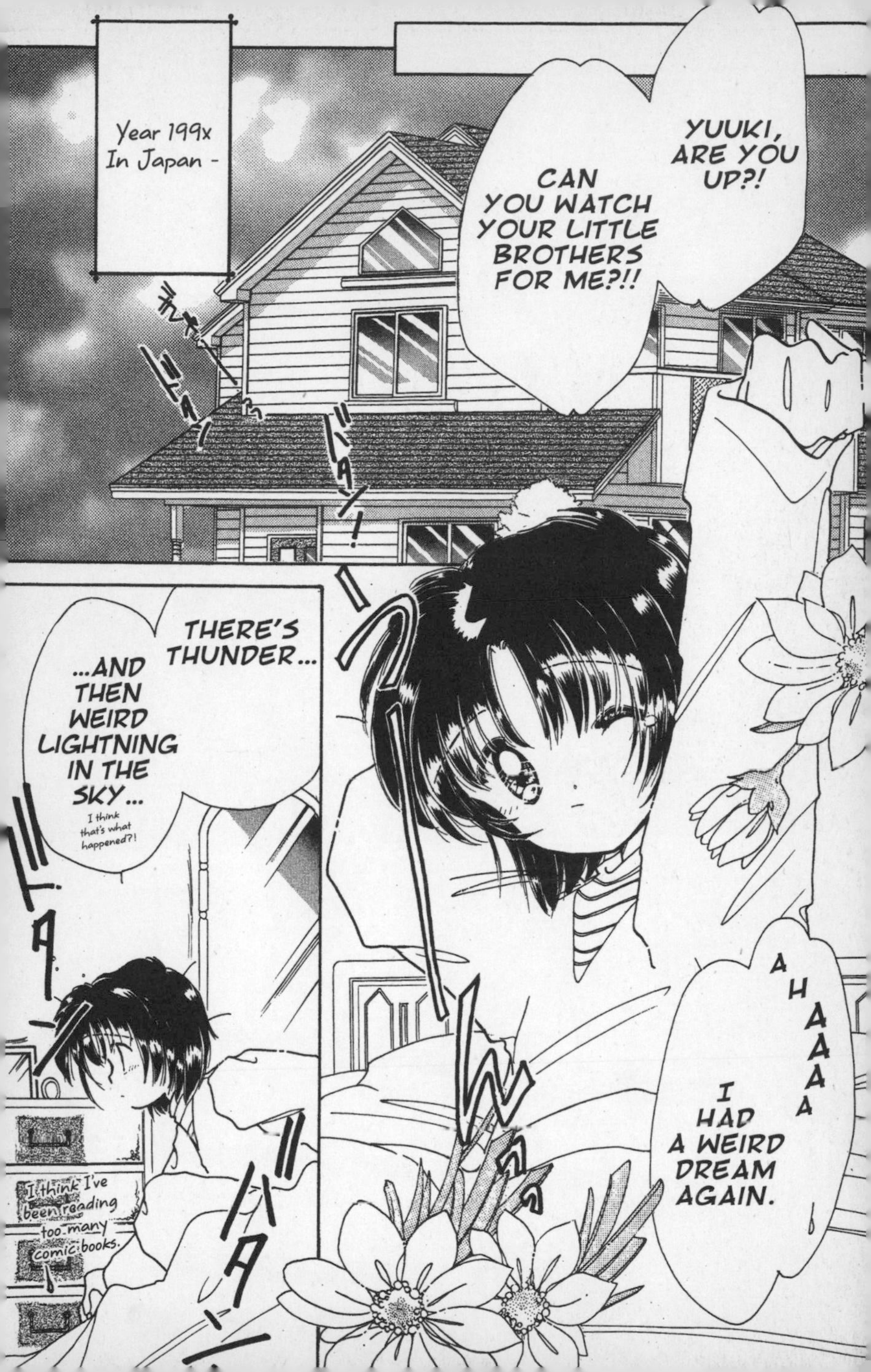
YUUKI, ARE YOU UP?!
CAN YOU WATCH YOUR LITTLE BROTHERS FOR ME?!!
Year 199x In Japan -
AHAAAA
I HAD A WEIRD DREAM AGAIN.
THERE'S THUNDER...
...AND THEN WEIRD LIGHTNING IN THE SKY...
I think that's what happened?!
I think I've been reading too many comic books.

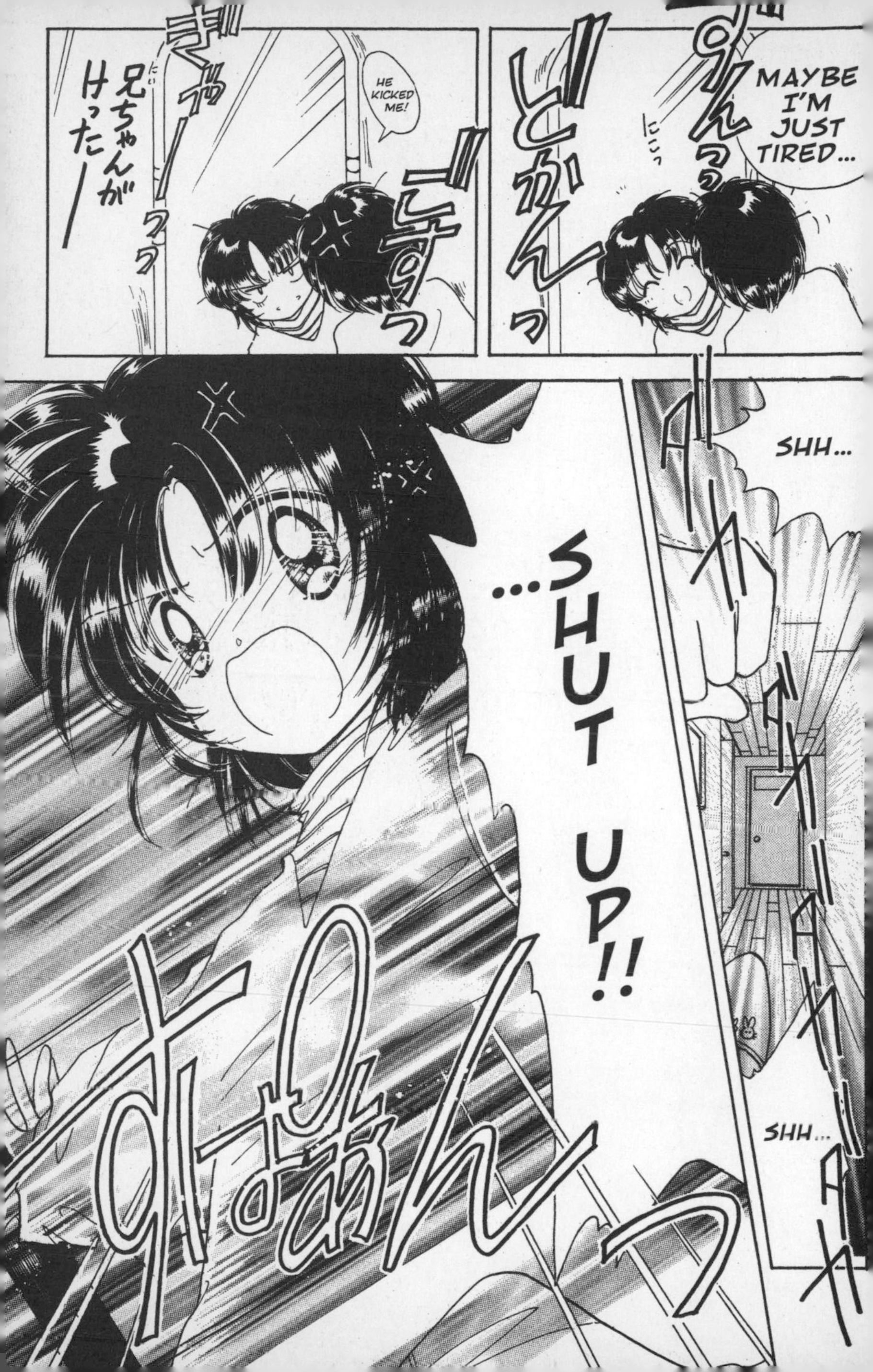
MAYBE I'M JUST TIRED...
ぱんっっ
どかんっ
HE KICKED ME!
ごすっ
ぎゃーっっ
兄ちゃんがけったー
SHH...
SHH...
...SHUT UP!!

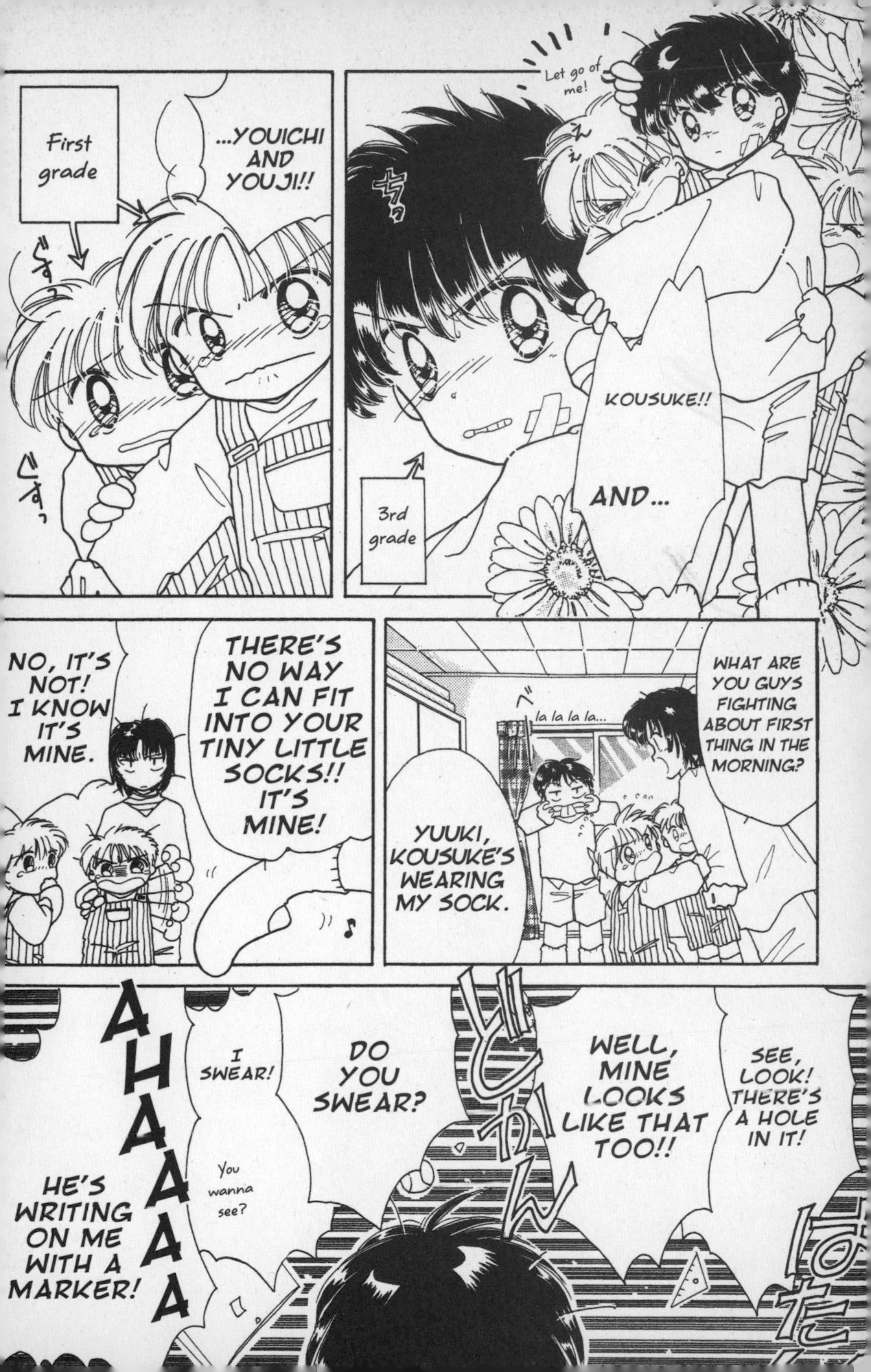
Let go of me!
KOUSUKE!!
AND...
3rd grade
...YOUICHI AND YOUJI!!
First grade
WHAT ARE YOU GUYS FIGHTING ABOUT FIRST THING IN THE MORNING?
la la la la...
YUUKI, KOUSUKE'S WEARING MY SOCK.
THERE'S NO WAY I CAN FIT INTO YOUR TINY LITTLE SOCKS!! IT'S MINE!
NO, IT'S NOT! I KNOW IT'S MINE.
SEE, LOOK! THERE'S A HOLE IN IT!
WELL, MINE LOOKS LIKE THAT TOO!!
DO YOU SWEAR?
I SWEAR!
You wanna see?
AHAAAAA
HE'S WRITING ON ME WITH A MARKER!

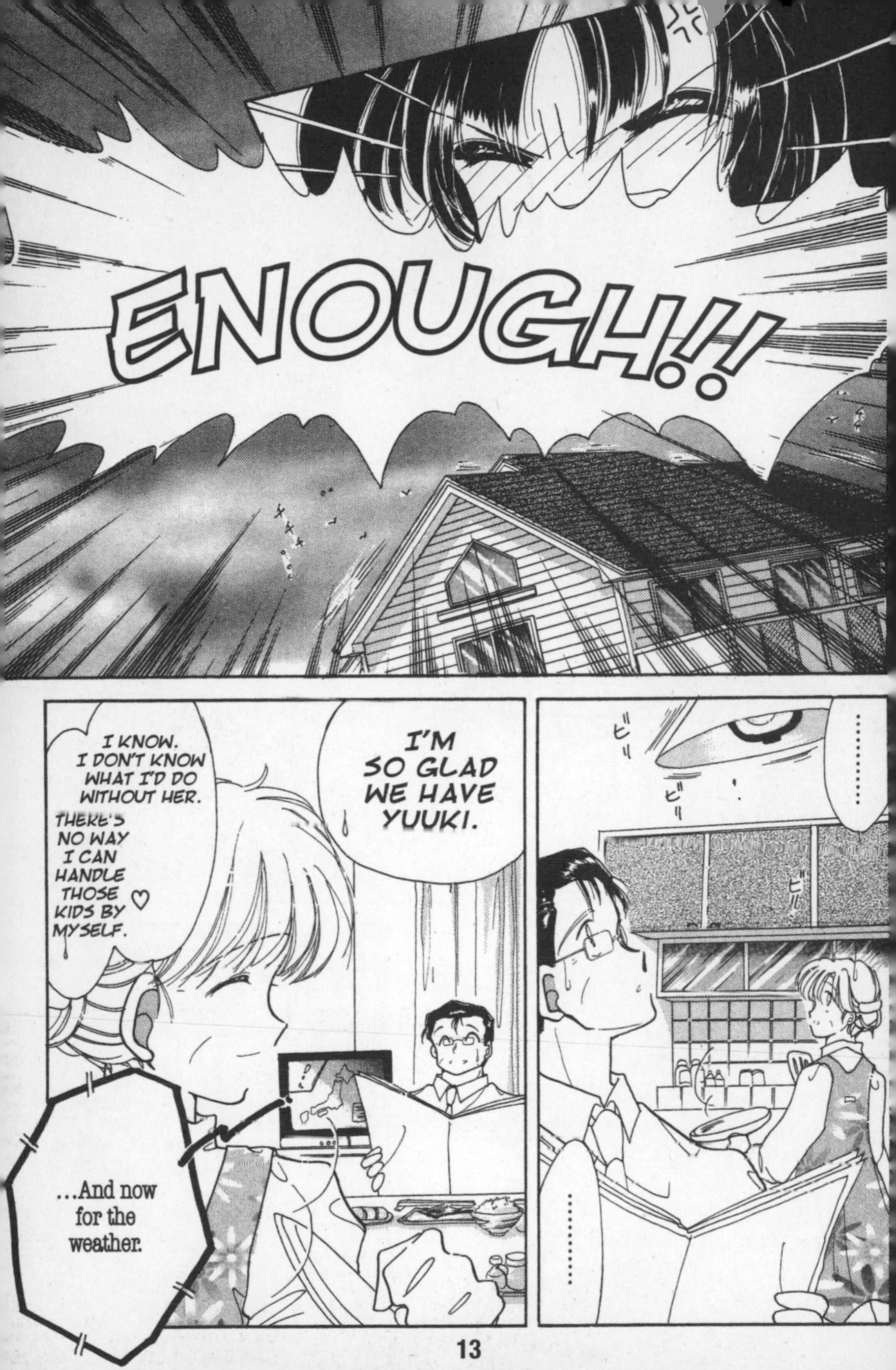
ENOUGH!!
ビリ
ビリ
ビリ
......
......
I'M SO GLAD WE HAVE YUUKI.
I KNOW. I DON'T KNOW WHAT I'D DO WITHOUT HER.
THERE'S NO WAY I CAN HANDLE THOSE KIDS BY MYSELF. ♡
...And now for the weather.

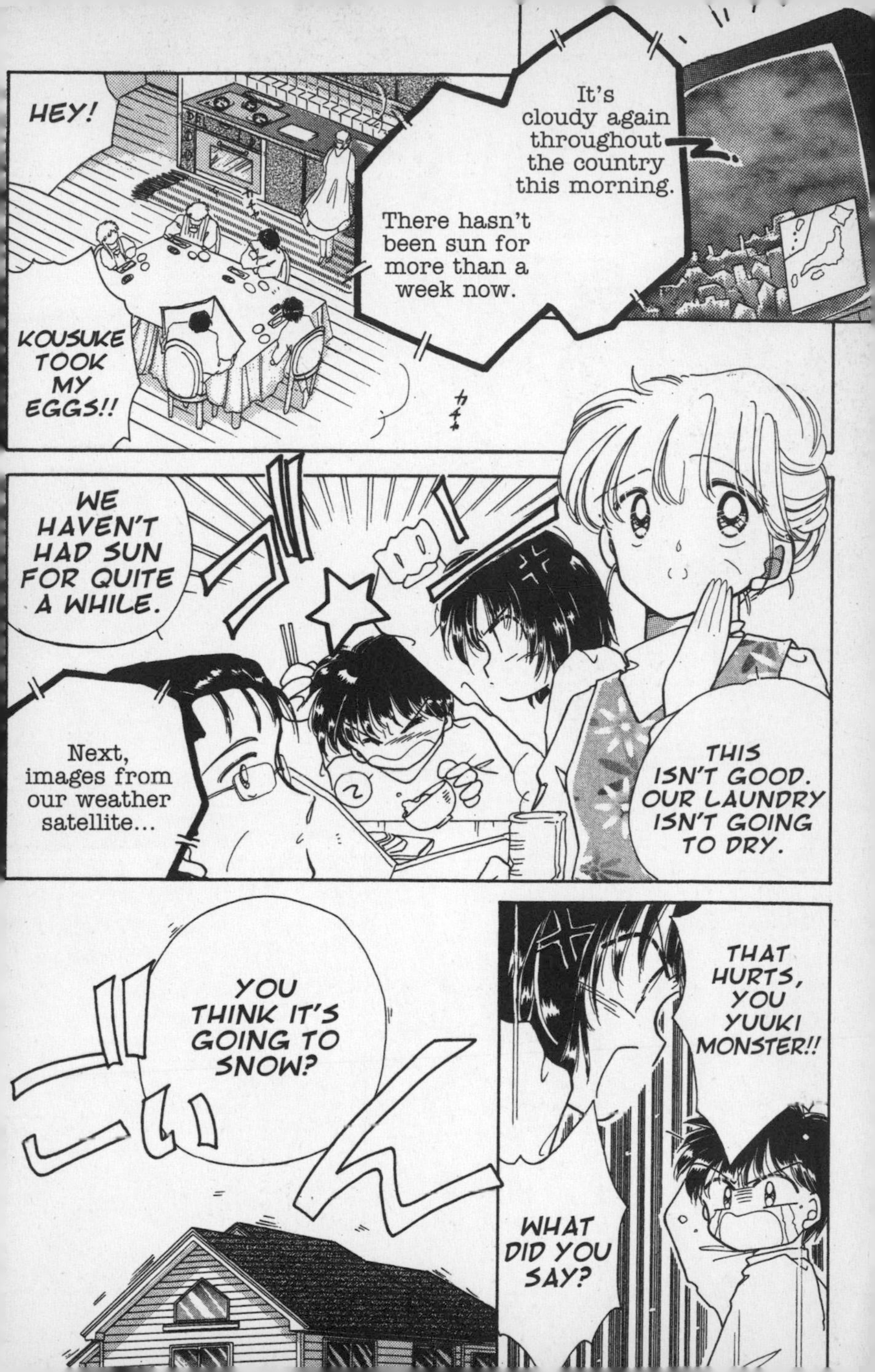
It's cloudy again throughout the country this morning.
There hasn't been sun for more than a week now.
HEY!
KOUSUKE TOOK MY EGGS!!
WE HAVEN'T HAD SUN FOR QUITE A WHILE.
THIS ISN'T GOOD. OUR LAUNDRY ISN'T GOING TO DRY.
Next, images from our weather satellite...
THAT HURTS, YOU YUUKI MONSTER!!
WHAT DID YOU SAY?
YOU THINK IT'S GOING TO SNOW?

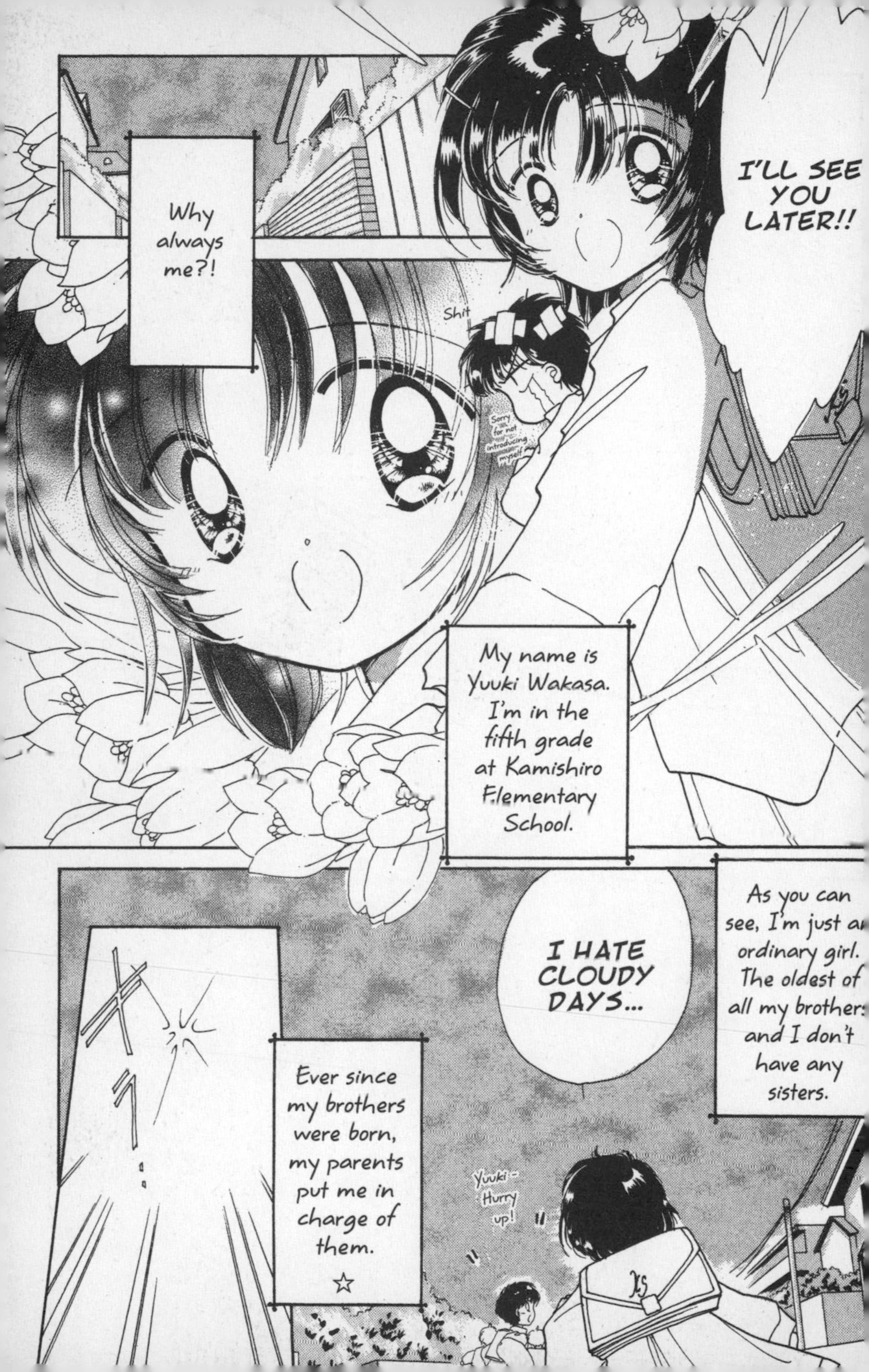
I'LL SEE YOU LATER!!
Shit
Sorry for not introducing myself
Why always me?!
My name is Yuuki Wakasa. I'm in the fifth grade at Kamishiro Elementary School.
As you can see, I'm just a ordinary girl. The oldest of all my brothers and I don't have any sisters.
I HATE CLOUDY DAYS...
Yuuki- Hurry up!
Ever since my brothers were born, my parents put me in charge of them. ☆

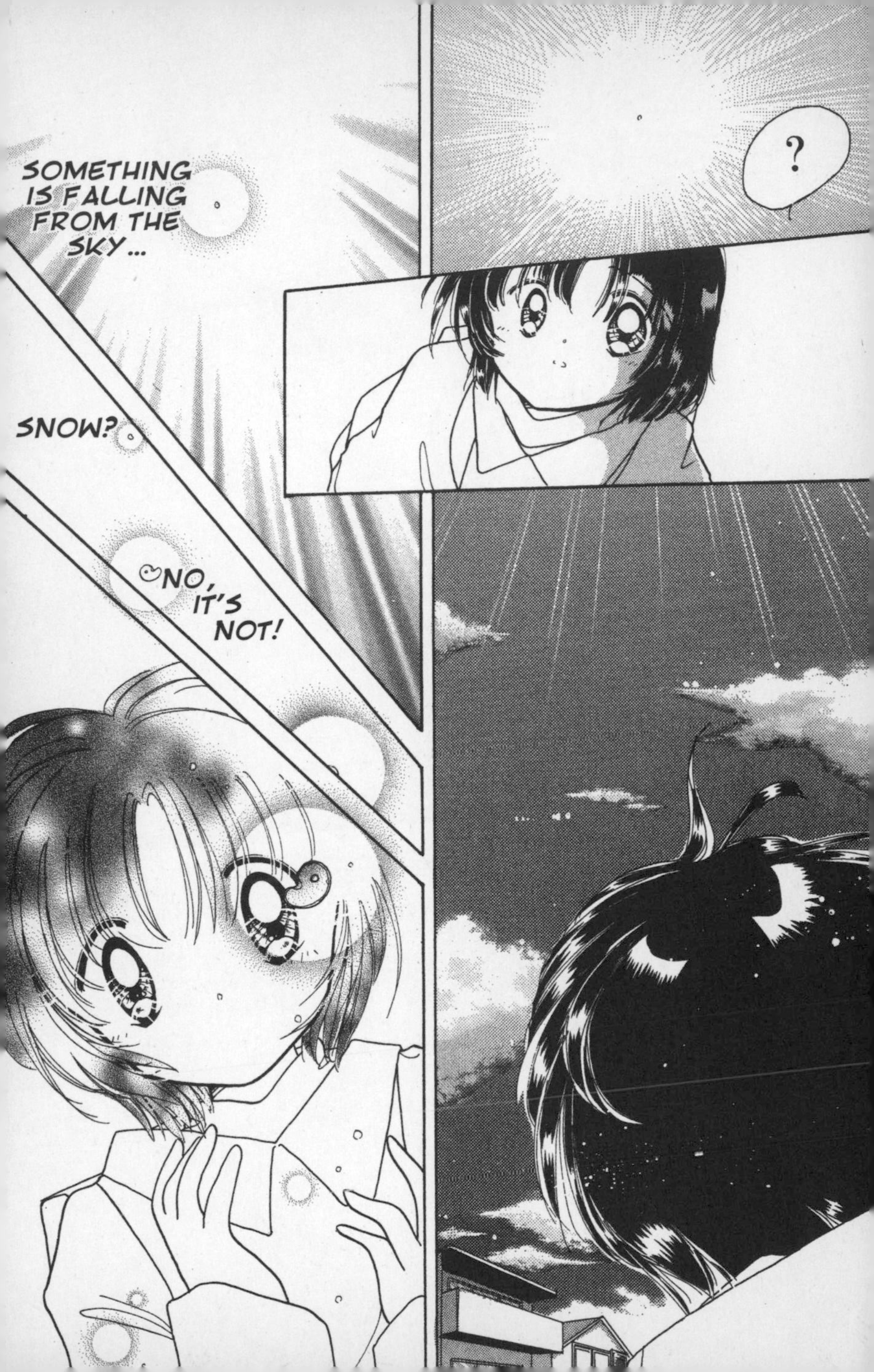
?
SOMETHING IS FALLING FROM THE SKY...
SNOW?
NO, IT'S NOT!

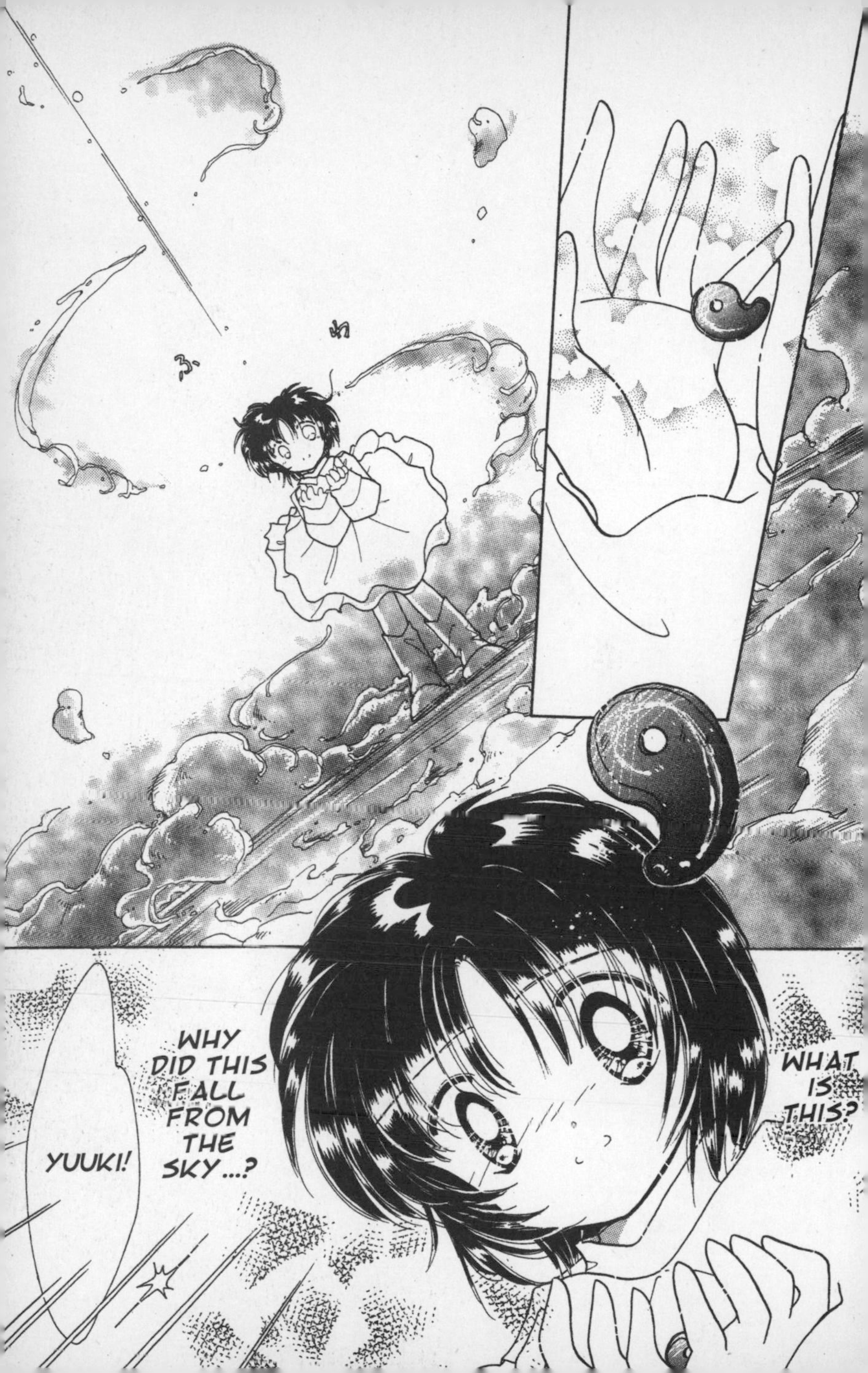
WHAT IS THIS?
WHY DID THIS FALL FROM THE SKY ...?
YUUKI!

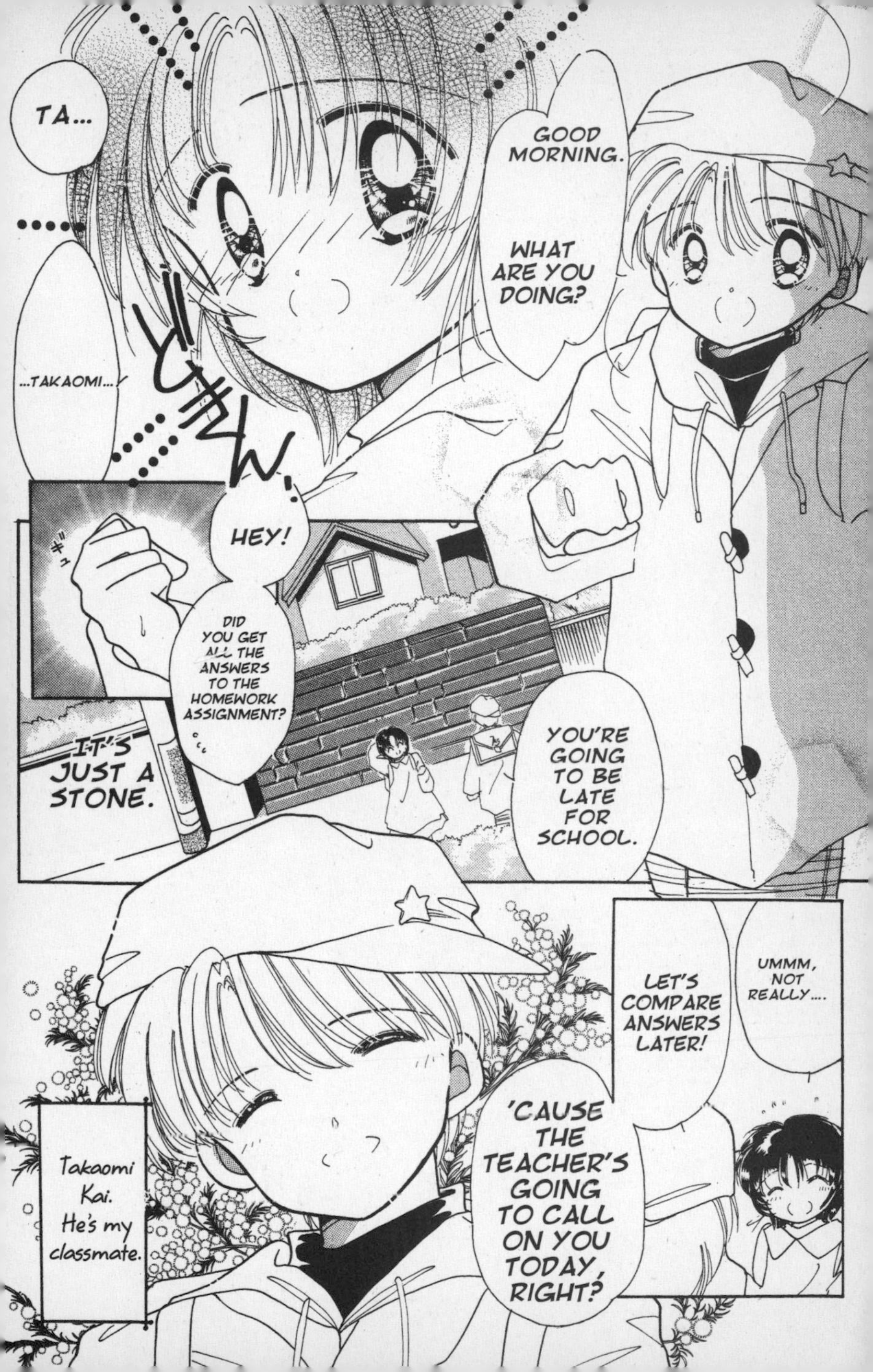
GOOD MORNING.
WHAT ARE YOU DOING?
TA...
...
...TAKAOMI...
YOU'RE GOING TO BE LATE FOR SCHOOL.
HEY!
DID YOU GET ALL THE ANSWERS TO THE HOMEWORK ASSIGNMENT?
IT'S JUST A STONE.
ギュ
UMMM, NOT REALLY....
LET'S COMPARE ANSWERS LATER!
'CAUSE THE TEACHER'S GOING TO CALL ON YOU TODAY, RIGHT?
Takaomi Kai. He's my classmate.

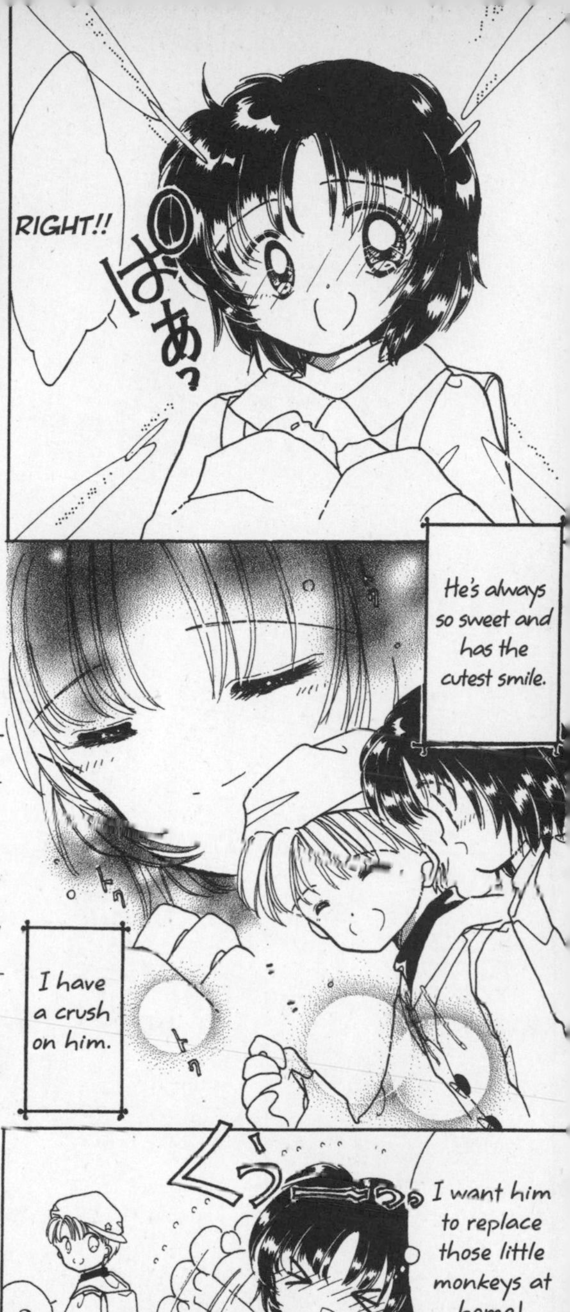
RIGHT!!
ぱあっ
He's always so sweet and has the cutest smile.
I have a crush on him.
くーっ
I want him to replace those little monkeys at home!
?

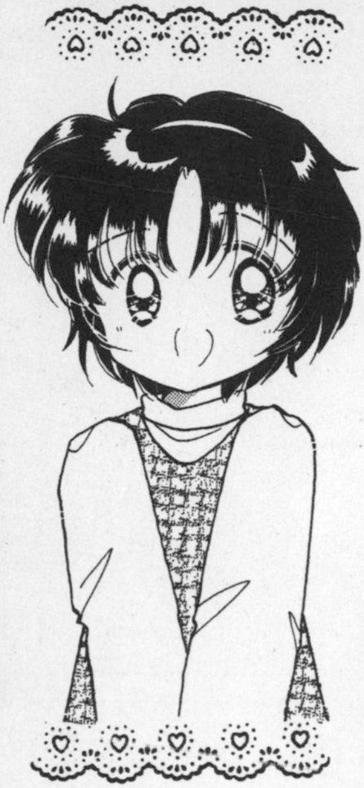

Yuuki Wakasa

Born on January 7. Blood type: B.

I'm the heroine in the story and currently in the fifth grade. I have three younger brothers who I look after. My mother has a pretty laid-back personality, so I'm always helping her with things around the house. I guess that's why I have such a strong personality! When it comes to taking care of my brothers, my biggest weapon is Seiza* and scolding them. I love to save money in my piggy bank. I've had a crush on my classmate Takaomi Kai since the third grade.

* A sitting posture in martial arts to show formality and respect, or a method of punishment.

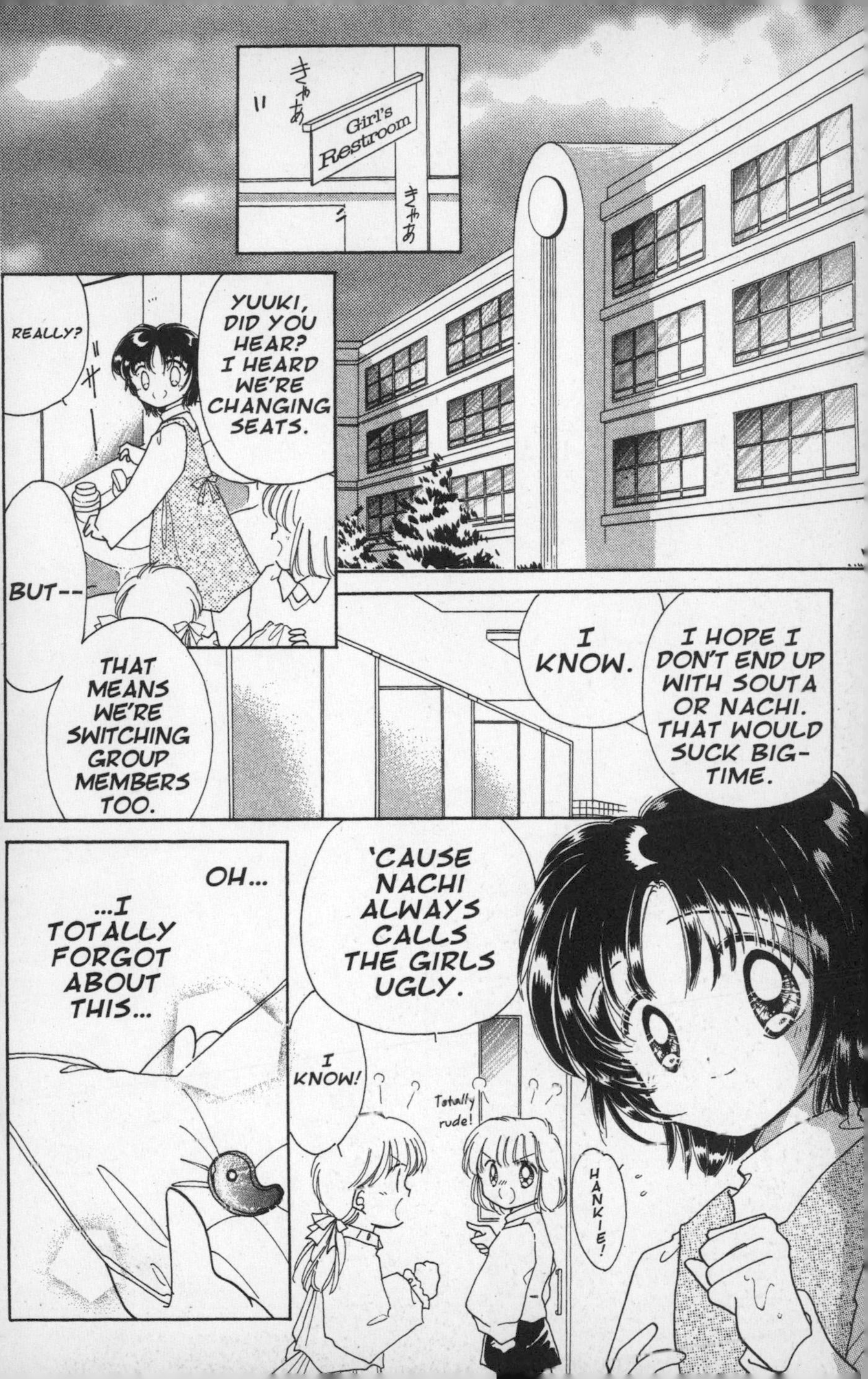
きゃあ
Girl's Restroom
きゃあ
YUUKI, DID YOU HEAR? I HEARD WE'RE CHANGING SEATS.
REALLY?
BUT--
THAT MEANS WE'RE SWITCHING GROUP MEMBERS TOO.
I HOPE I DON'T END UP WITH SOUTA OR NACHI. THAT WOULD SUCK BIG-TIME.
I KNOW.
'CAUSE NACHI ALWAYS CALLS THE GIRLS UGLY.
HANKIE!
Totally rude!
I KNOW!
OH...
...I TOTALLY FORGOT ABOUT THIS...

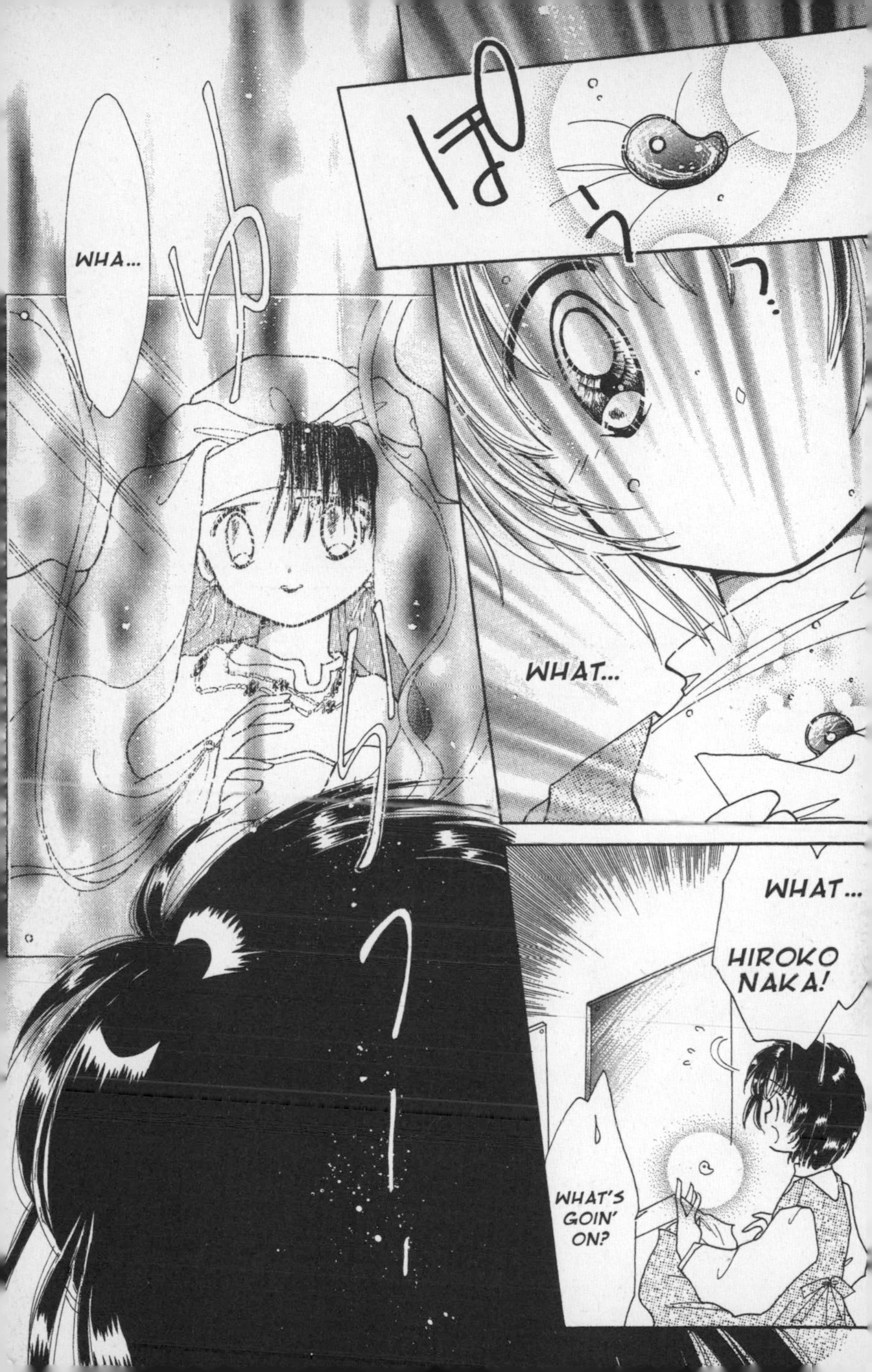
ぽーっ
WHAT...
WHA...
WHAT...
HIROKO NAKA!
WHAT'S GOIN' ON?

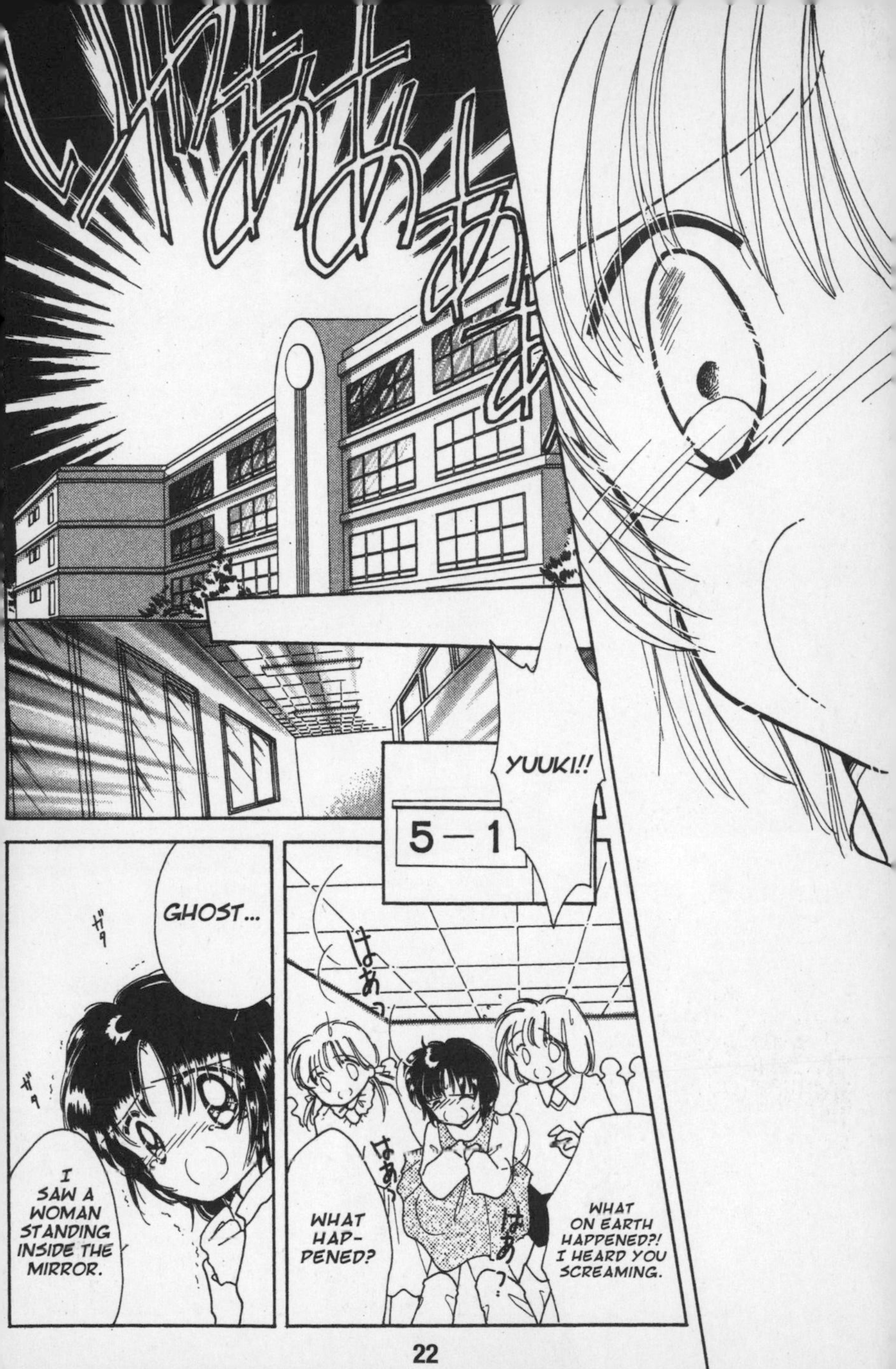
YUUKI!!
WHAT ON EARTH HAPPENED?! I HEARD YOU SCREAMING.
WHAT HAP-PENED?
GHOST...
I SAW A WOMAN STANDING INSIDE THE MIRROR.

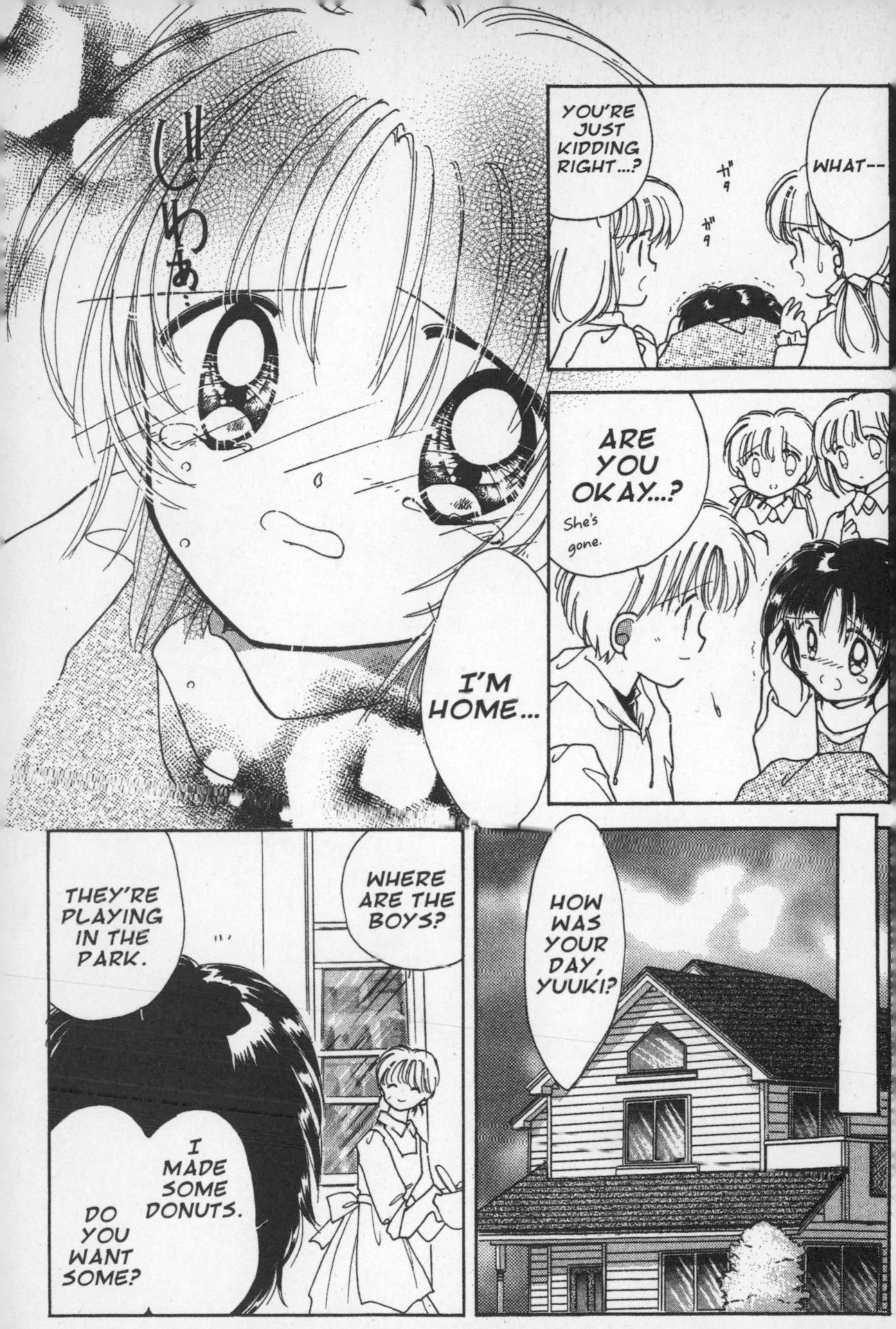
WHAT--
YOU'RE JUST KIDDING RIGHT...?
ガタ
ガタ
ARE YOU OKAY...?
She's gone.
I'M HOME...
HOW WAS YOUR DAY, YUUKI?
WHERE ARE THE BOYS?
THEY'RE PLAYING IN THE PARK.
I MADE SOME DONUTS.
DO YOU WANT SOME?

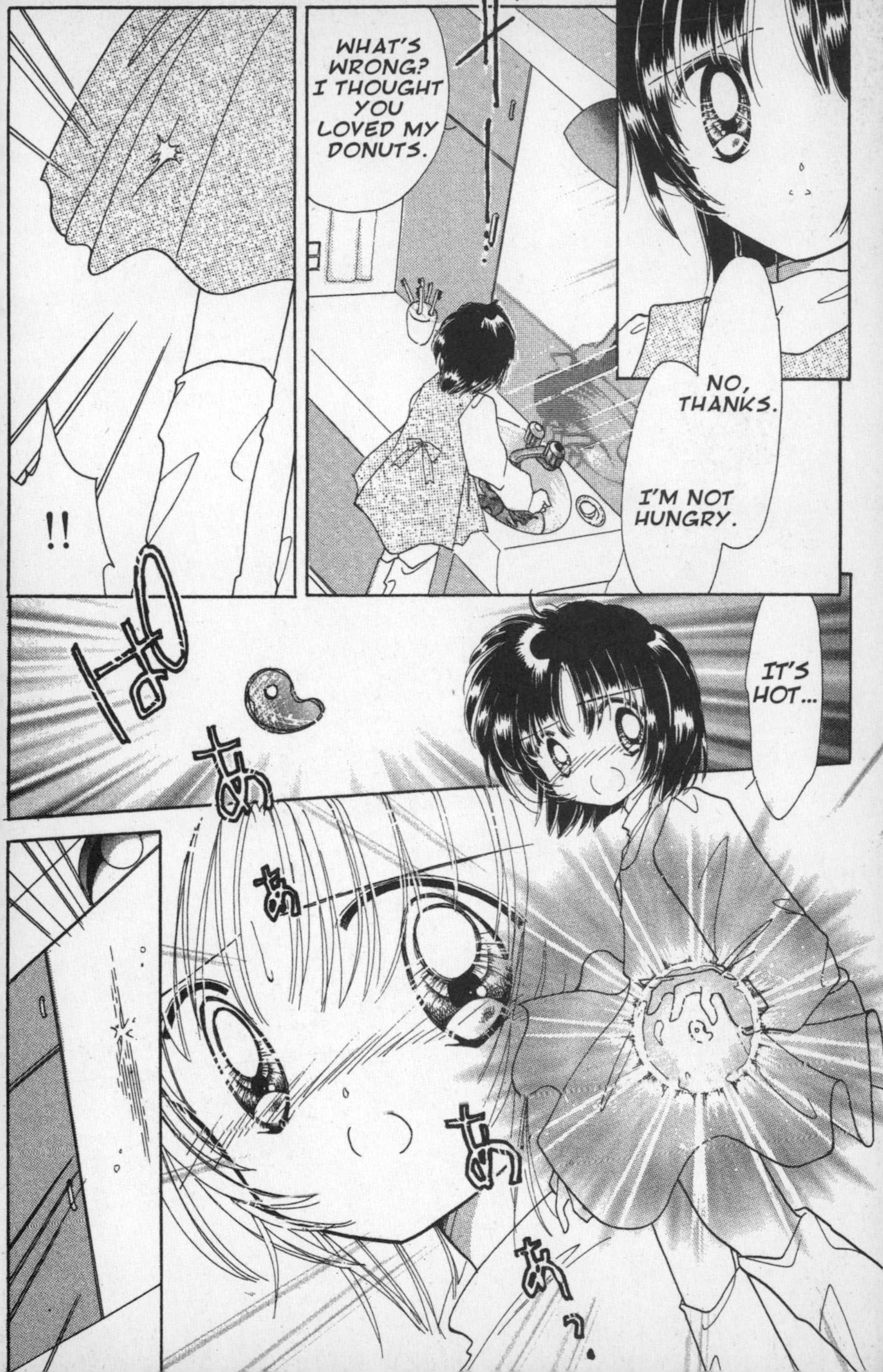
NO, THANKS.
I'M NOT HUNGRY.
WHAT'S WRONG? I THOUGHT YOU LOVED MY DONUTS.
!!
IT'S HOT...

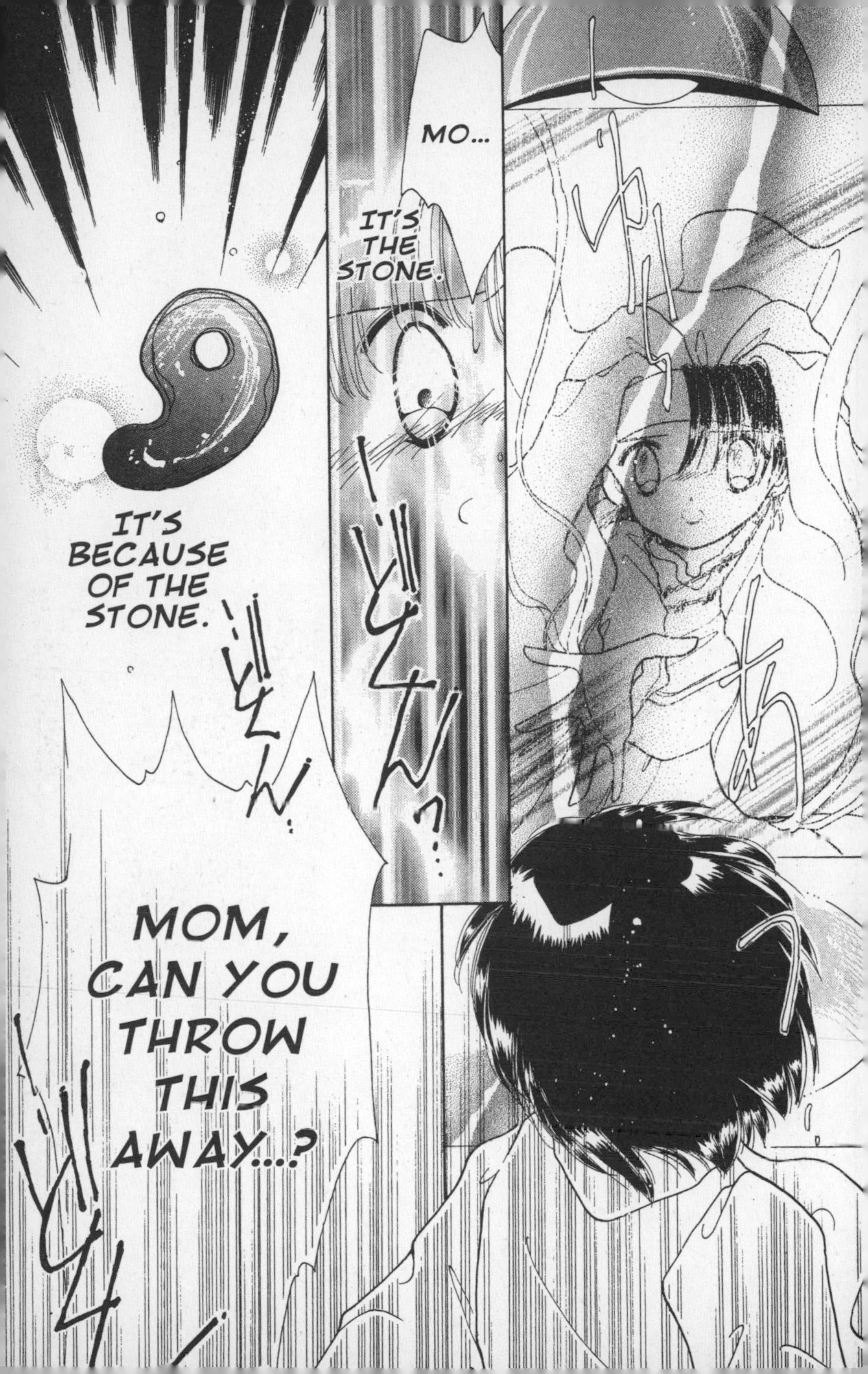
MO...
IT'S THE STONE.
IT'S BECAUSE OF THE STONE.
MOM, CAN YOU THROW THIS AWAY...?

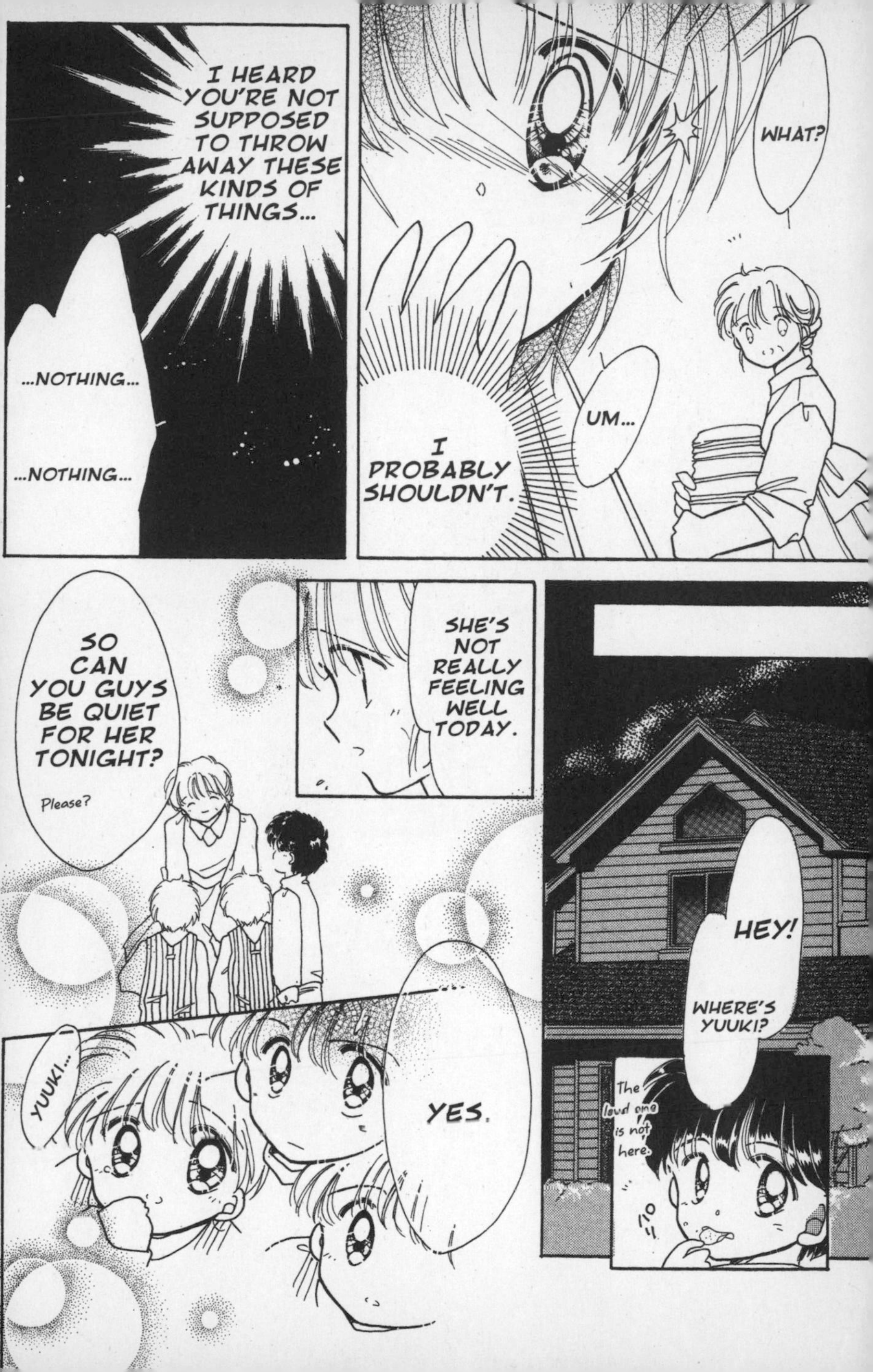
WHAT?
UM...
I PROBABLY SHOULDN'T.
I HEARD YOU'RE NOT SUPPOSED TO THROW AWAY THESE KINDS OF THINGS...
...NOTHING...
...NOTHING...
HEY!
WHERE'S YUUKI?
The loud one is not here.
SHE'S NOT REALLY FEELING WELL TODAY.
SO CAN YOU GUYS BE QUIET FOR HER TONIGHT?
Please?
YES.
YUUKI...

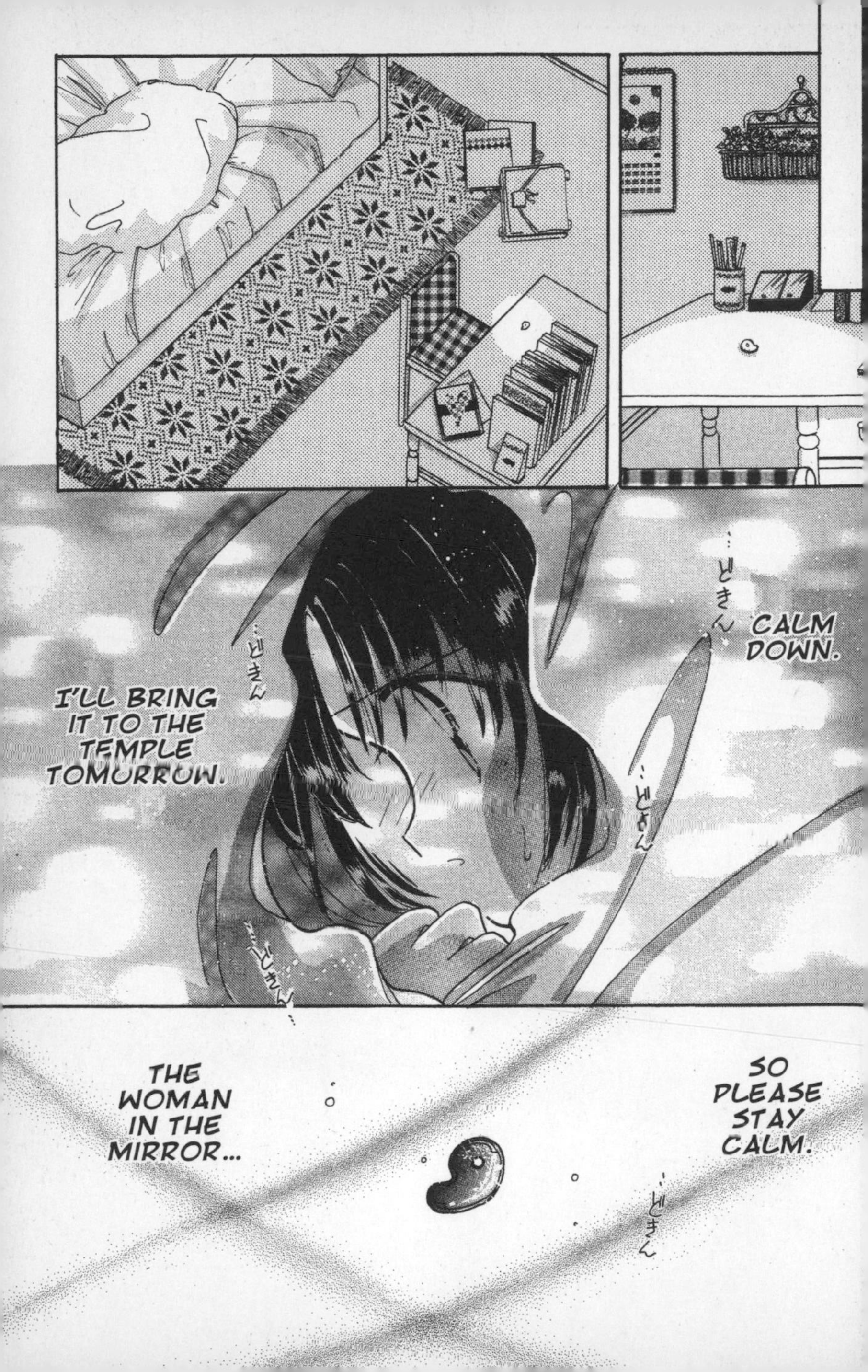

…どきん
CALM DOWN.
…どきん
…どきん
I'LL BRING IT TO THE TEMPLE TOMORROW.
…どきん…
…どきん
SO PLEASE STAY CALM.
THE WOMAN IN THE MIRROR...

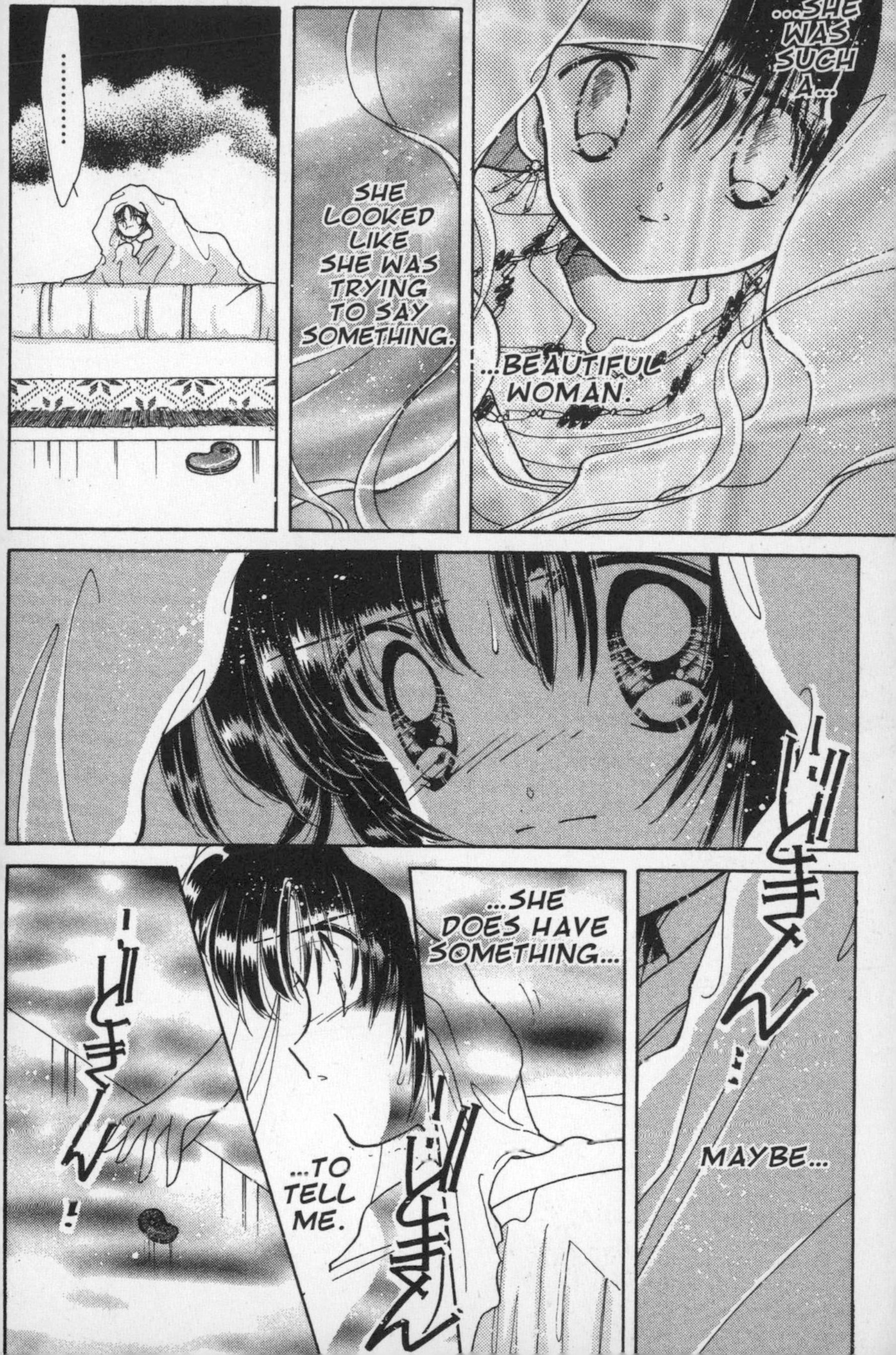

...SHE WAS SUCH A...
...BEAUTIFUL WOMAN.
SHE LOOKED LIKE SHE WAS TRYING TO SAY SOMETHING.
......
どきん
MAYBE...
...SHE DOES HAVE SOMETHING...
...TO TELL ME.
どきん
どきん

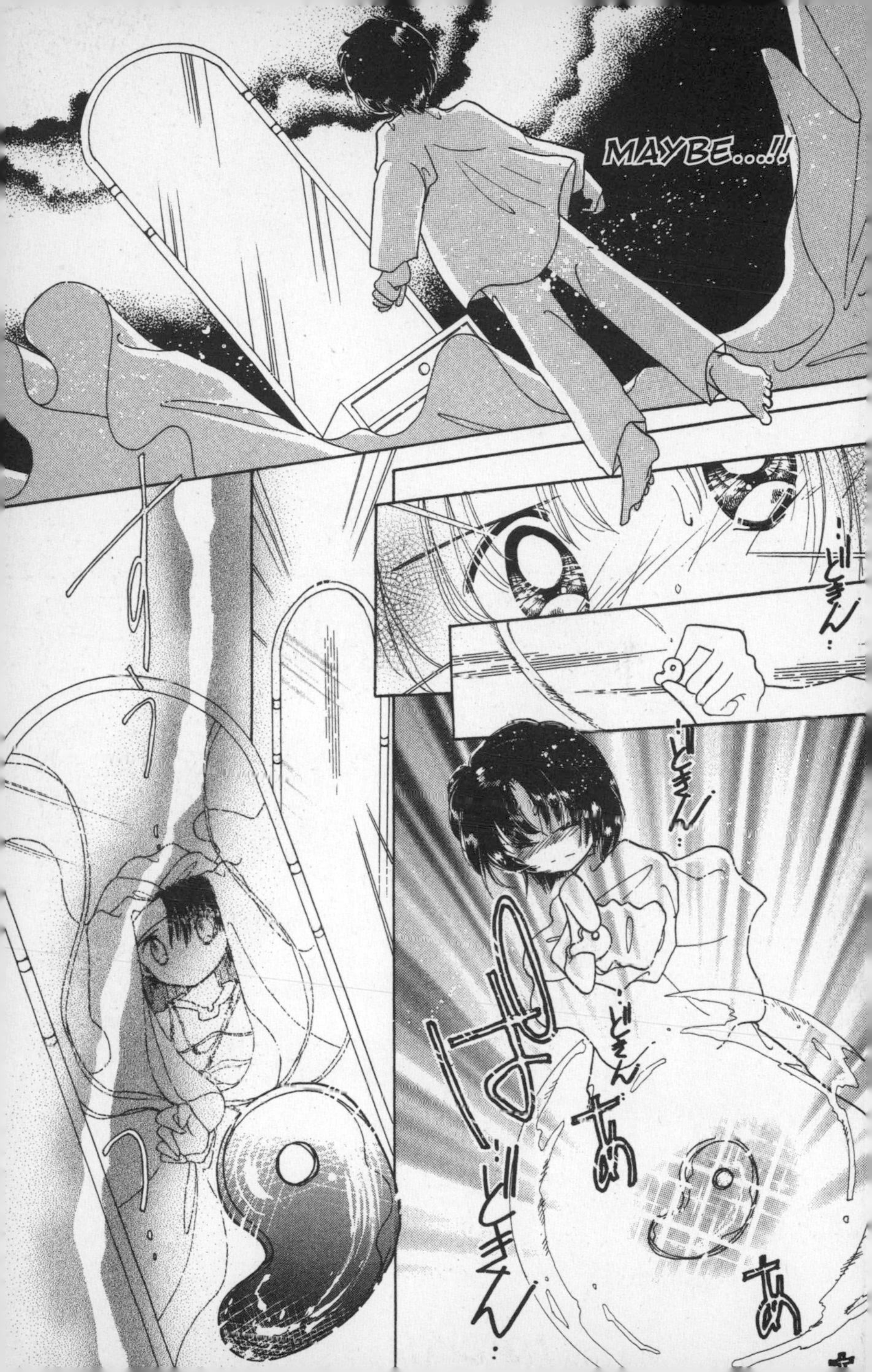
MAYBE...!!
...どきん...
...どきん...
...どきん
ああ
...どきん...
ああ

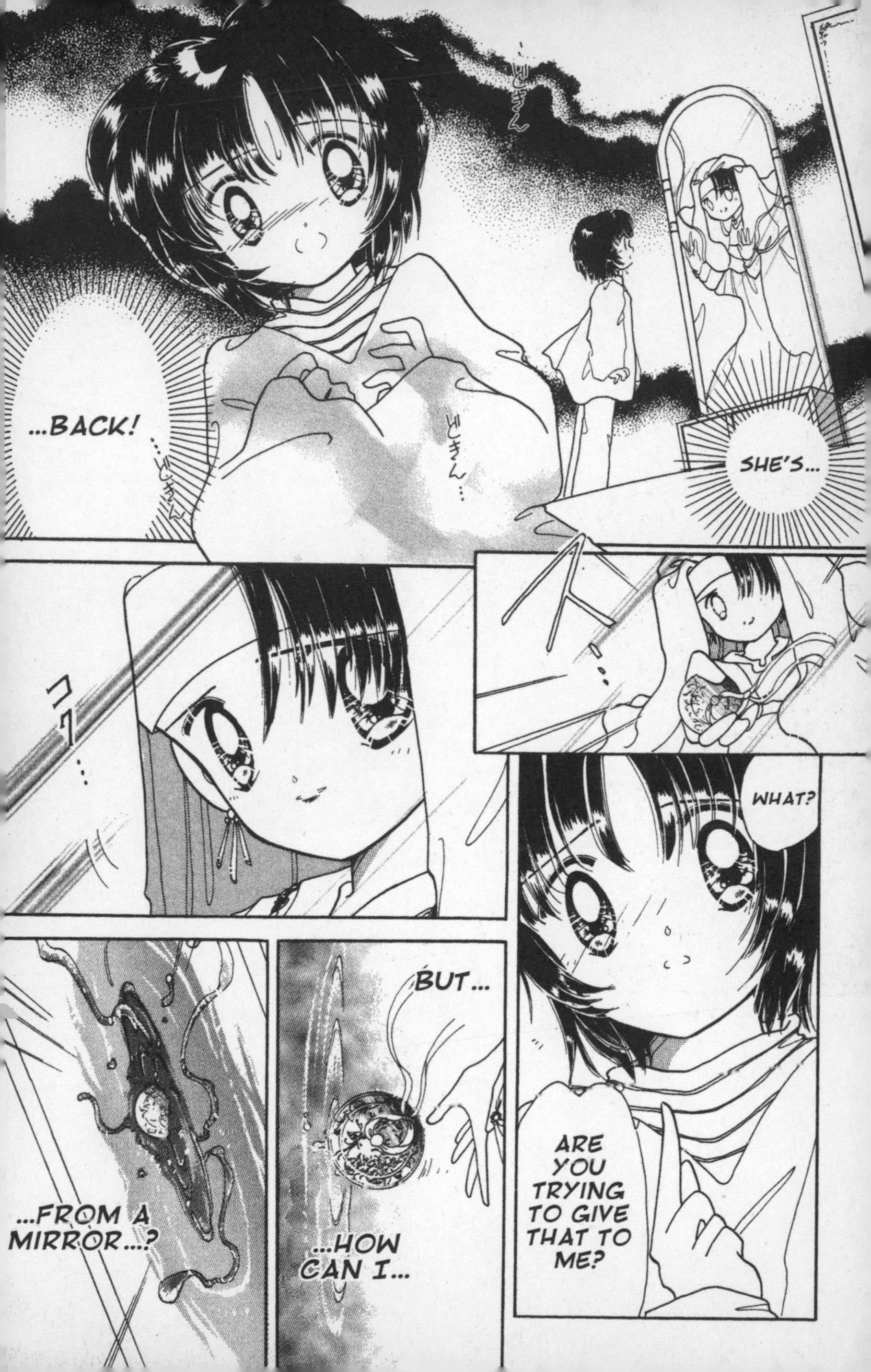
SHE'S...
...BACK!
WHAT?
ARE YOU TRYING TO GIVE THAT TO ME?
BUT...
...HOW CAN I...
...FROM A MIRROR...?

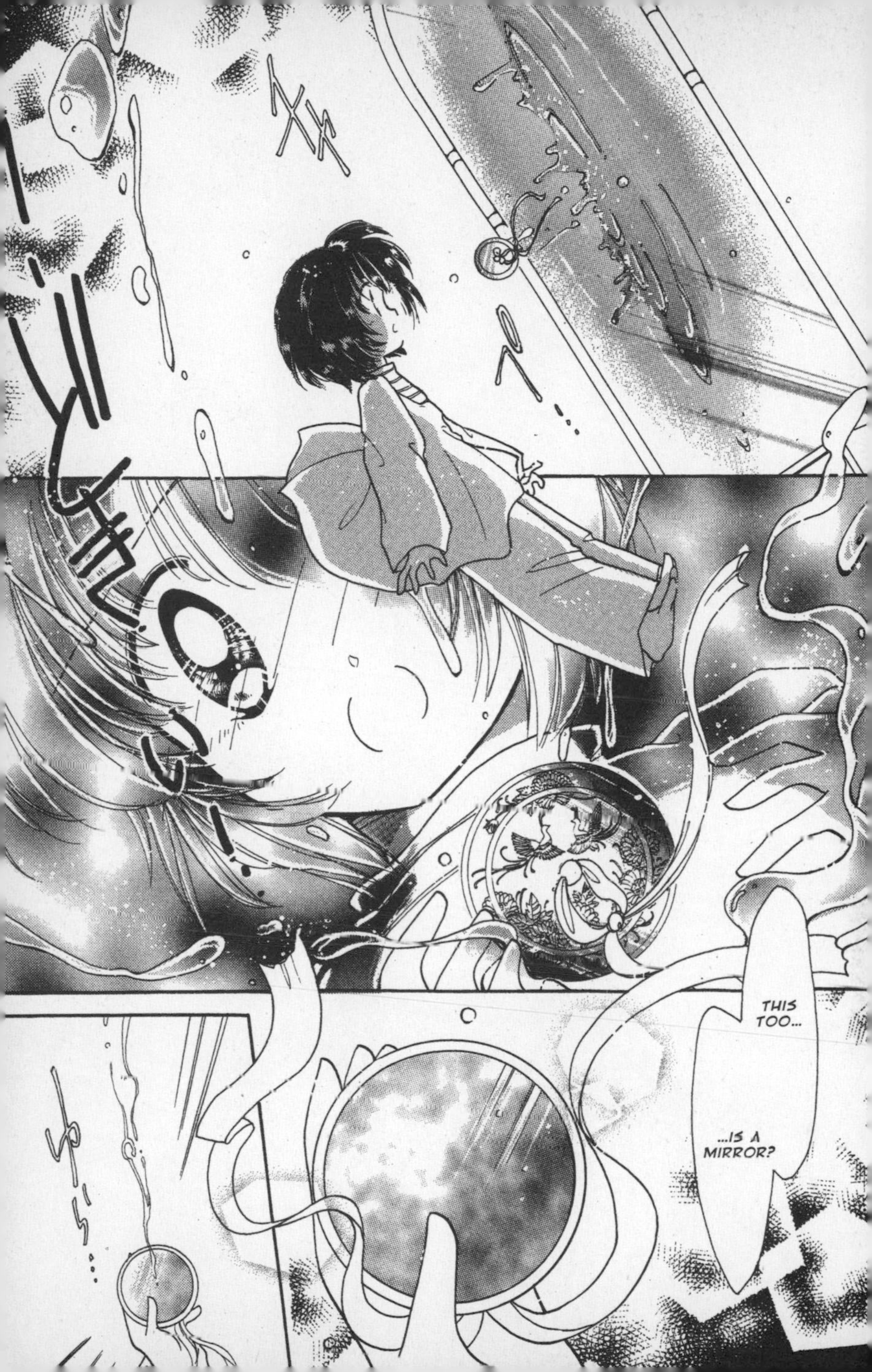
THIS TOO...
...IS A MIRROR?

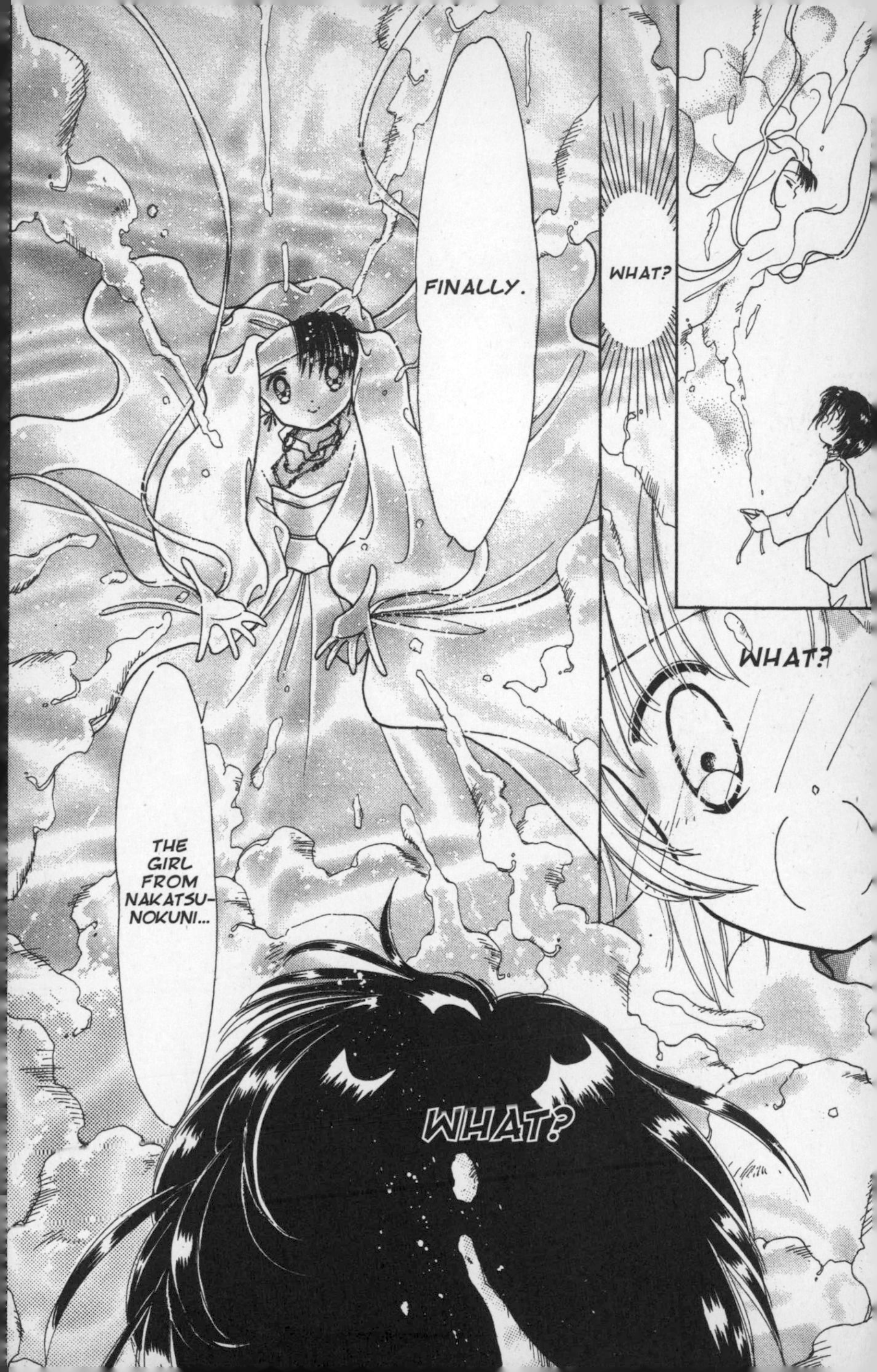
WHAT?
WHAT?
FINALLY.
THE GIRL FROM NAKATSU-NOKUNI...
WHAT?

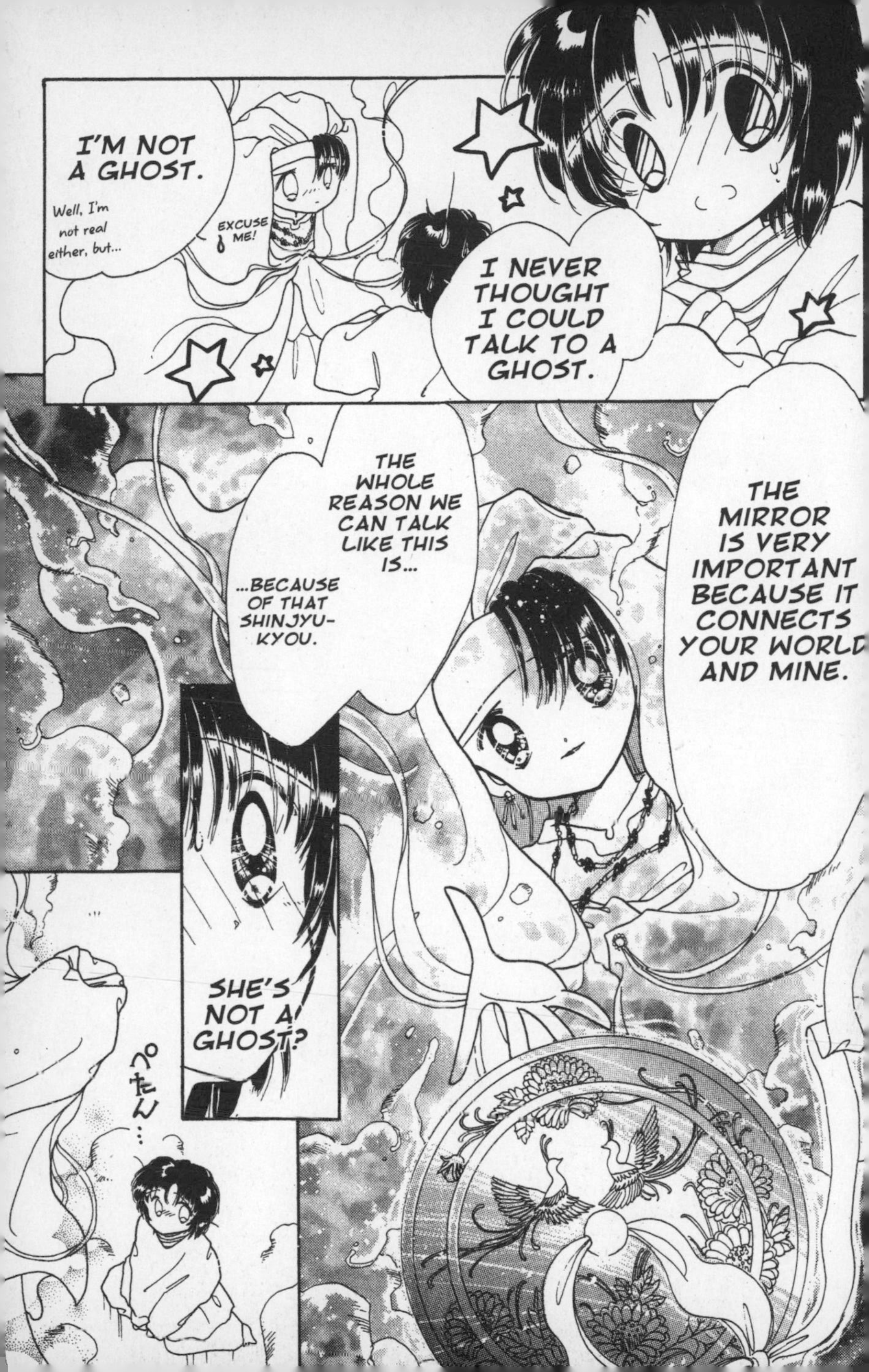
I NEVER THOUGHT I COULD TALK TO A GHOST.
EXCUSE ME!
I'M NOT A GHOST.
Well, I'm not real either, but...
THE MIRROR IS VERY IMPORTANT BECAUSE IT CONNECTS YOUR WORLD AND MINE.
THE WHOLE REASON WE CAN TALK LIKE THIS IS...
...BECAUSE OF THAT SHINJYU-KYOU.
SHE'S NOT A GHOST?
ぺたん…

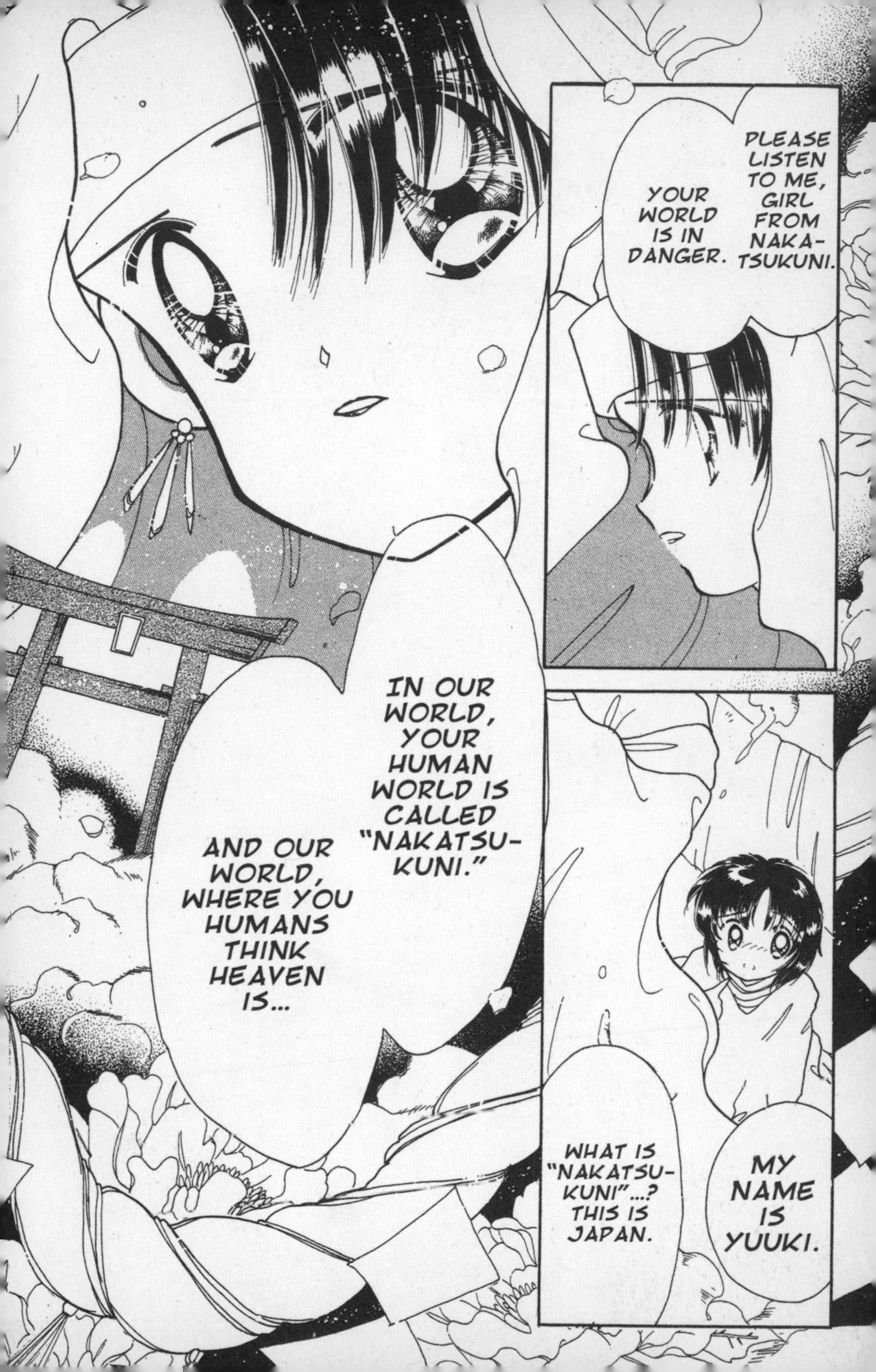
PLEASE LISTEN TO ME, GIRL FROM NAKA-TSUKUNI.
YOUR WORLD IS IN DANGER.
MY NAME IS YUUKI.
WHAT IS "NAKATSU-KUNI"...? THIS IS JAPAN.
IN OUR WORLD, YOUR HUMAN WORLD IS CALLED "NAKATSU-KUNI."
AND OUR WORLD, WHERE YOU HUMANS THINK HEAVEN IS...

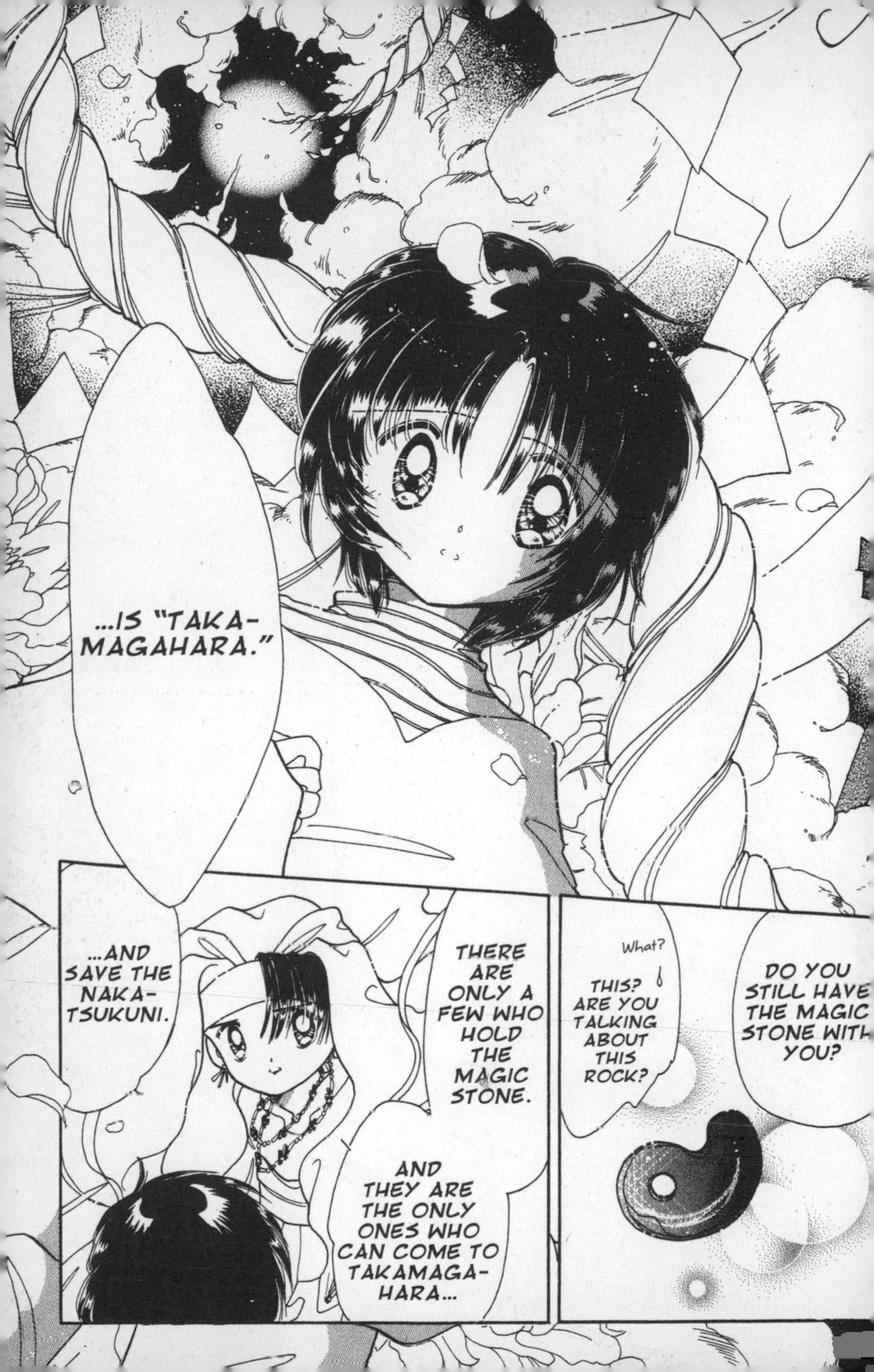
...IS "TAKA-MAGAHARA."
DO YOU STILL HAVE THE MAGIC STONE WITH YOU?
What?
THIS? ARE YOU TALKING ABOUT THIS ROCK?
THERE ARE ONLY A FEW WHO HOLD THE MAGIC STONE.
AND THEY ARE THE ONLY ONES WHO CAN COME TO TAKAMAGA-HARA...
...AND SAVE THE NAKA-TSUKUNI.

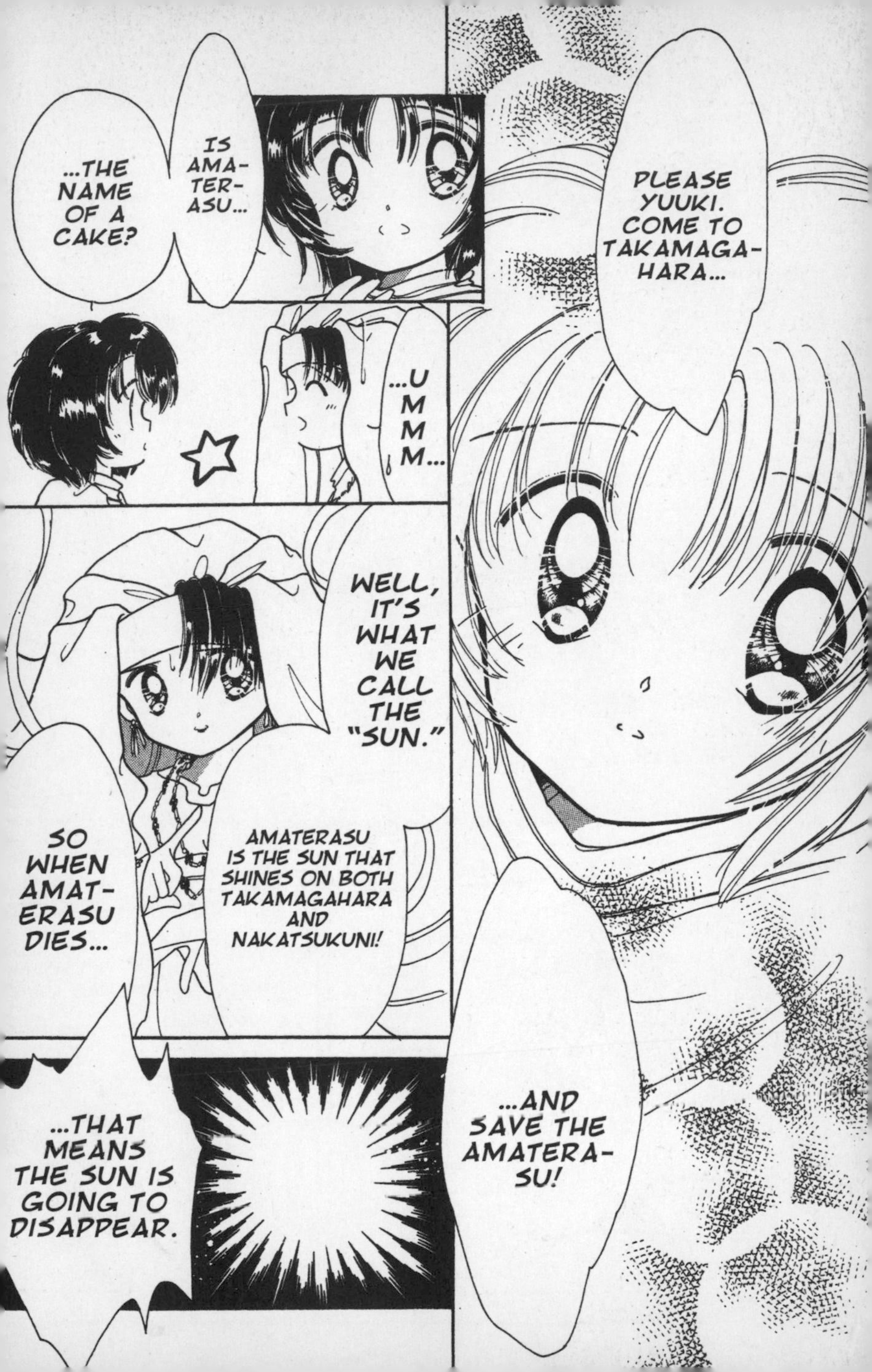
PLEASE YUUKI. COME TO TAKAMAGA-HARA...
...AND SAVE THE AMATERA-SU!
IS AMA-TER-ASU...
...THE NAME OF A CAKE?
...UMMM...
WELL, IT'S WHAT WE CALL THE "SUN."
AMATERASU IS THE SUN THAT SHINES ON BOTH TAKAMAGAHARA AND NAKATSUKUNI!
SO WHEN AMAT-ERASU DIES...
...THAT MEANS THE SUN IS GOING TO DISAPPEAR.

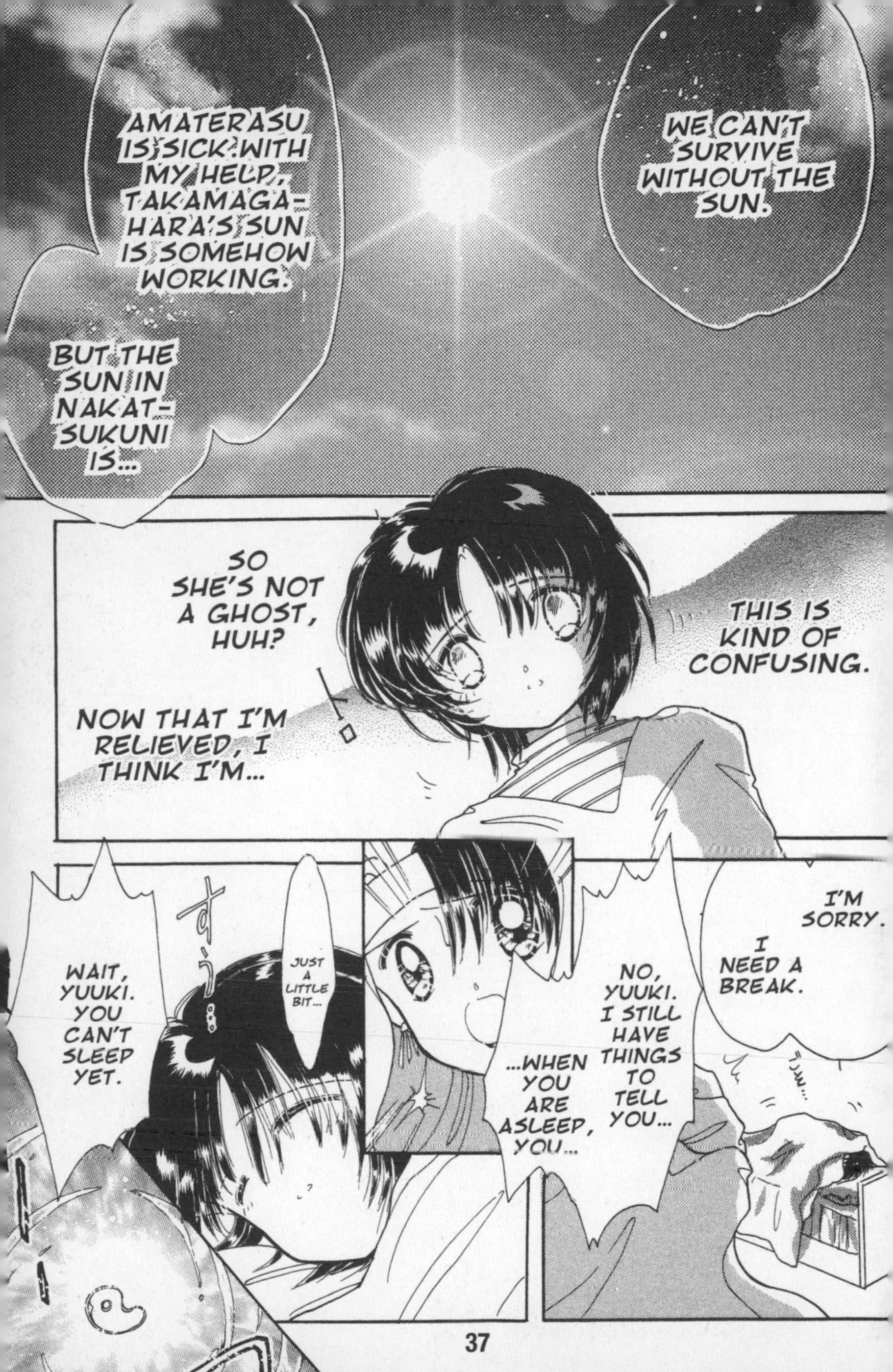
WE CAN'T SURVIVE WITHOUT THE SUN.
AMATERASU IS SICK. WITH MY HELP, TAKAMAGA-HARA'S SUN IS SOMEHOW WORKING.
BUT THE SUN IN NAKAT-SUKUNI IS...
THIS IS KIND OF CONFUSING.
SO SHE'S NOT A GHOST, HUH?
NOW THAT I'M RELIEVED, I THINK I'M...
I'M SORRY.
I NEED A BREAK.
NO, YUUKI. I STILL HAVE THINGS TO TELL YOU...
...WHEN YOU ARE ASLEEP, YOU...
JUST A LITTLE BIT...
WAIT, YUUKI. YOU CAN'T SLEEP YET.

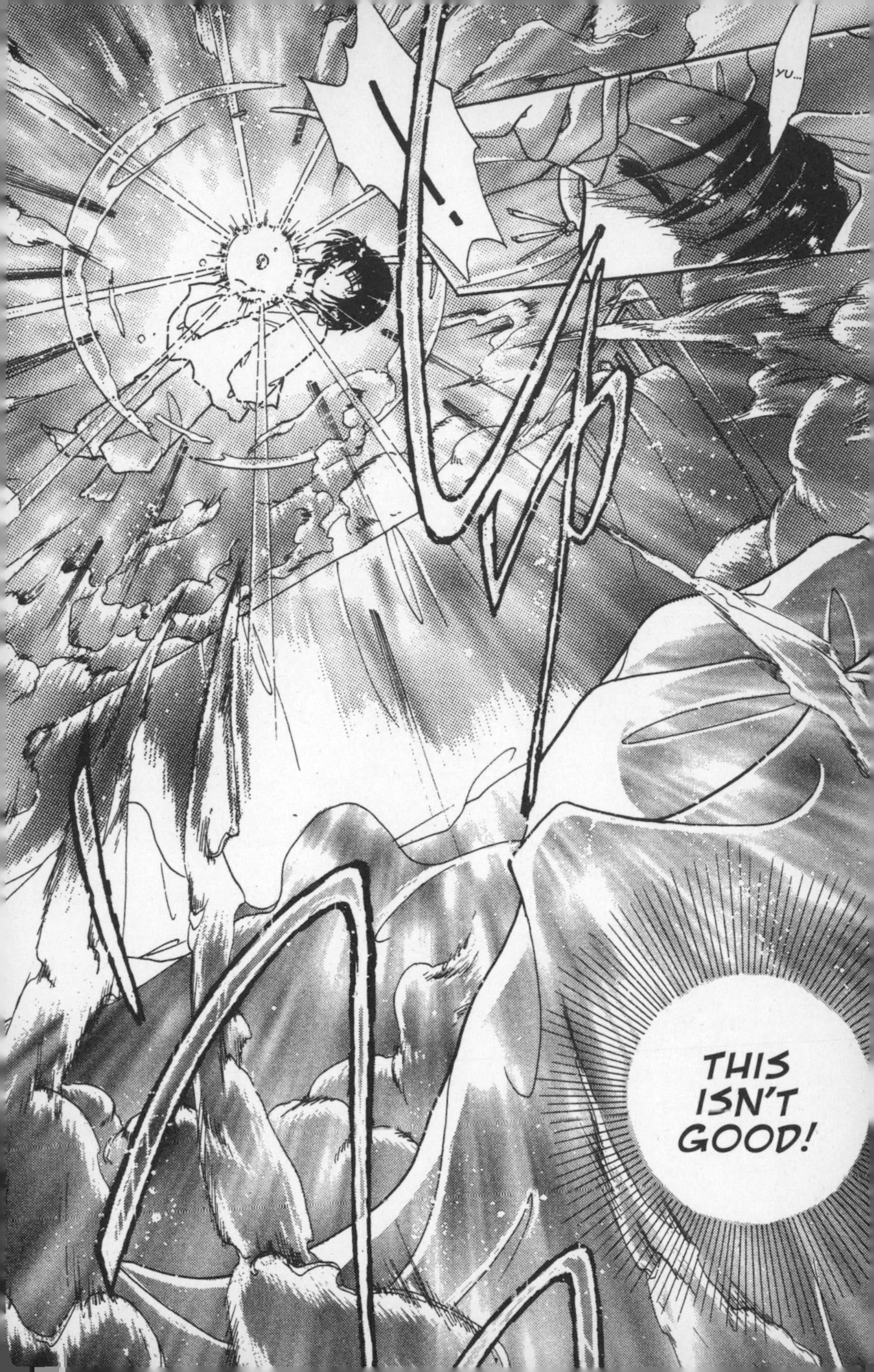
YU...
THIS ISN'T GOOD!

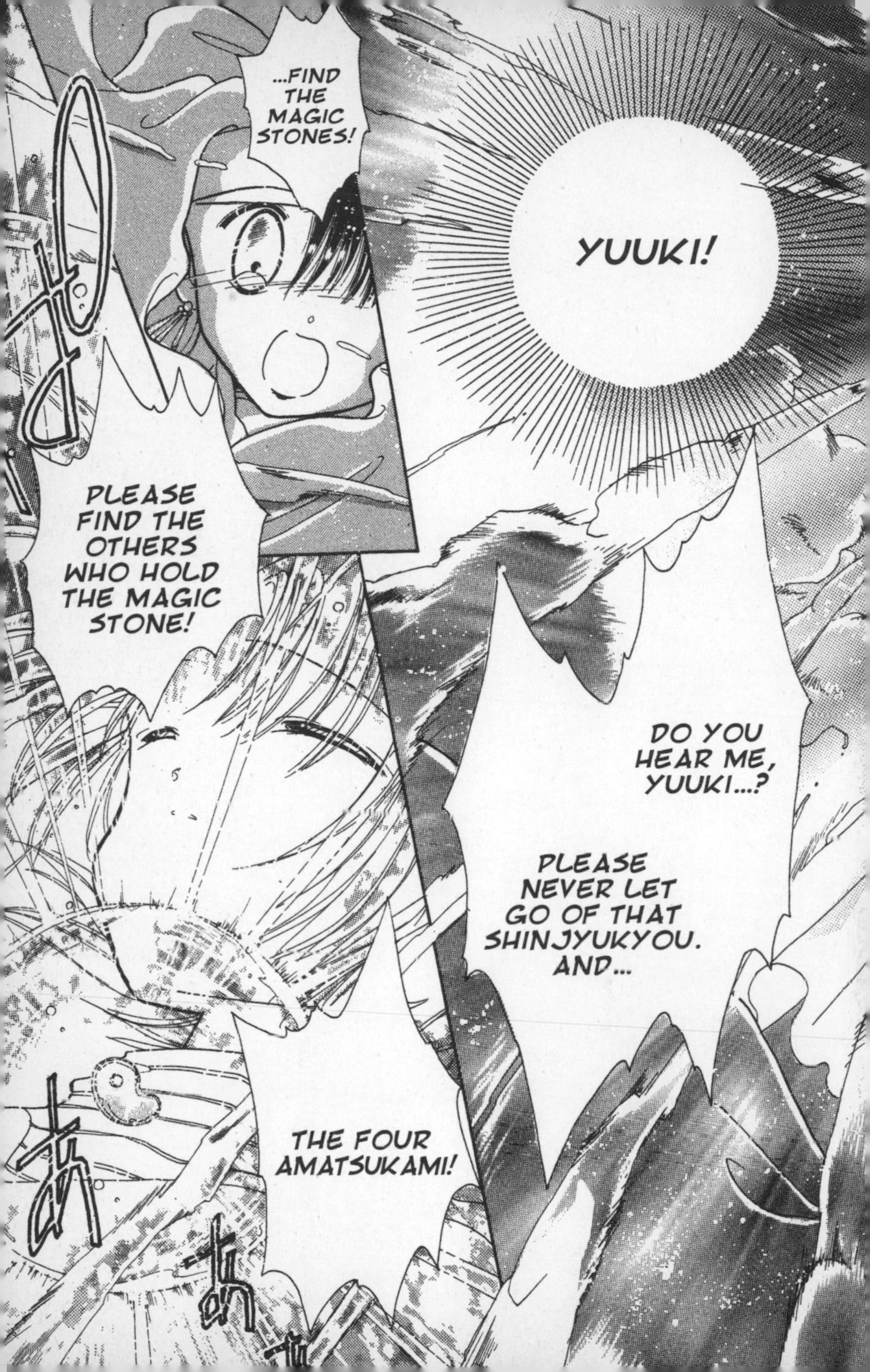
YUUKI!
DO YOU HEAR ME, YUUKI...?
PLEASE NEVER LET GO OF THAT SHINJYUKYOU. AND...
...FIND THE MAGIC STONES!
PLEASE FIND THE OTHERS WHO HOLD THE MAGIC STONE!
THE FOUR AMATSUKAMI!

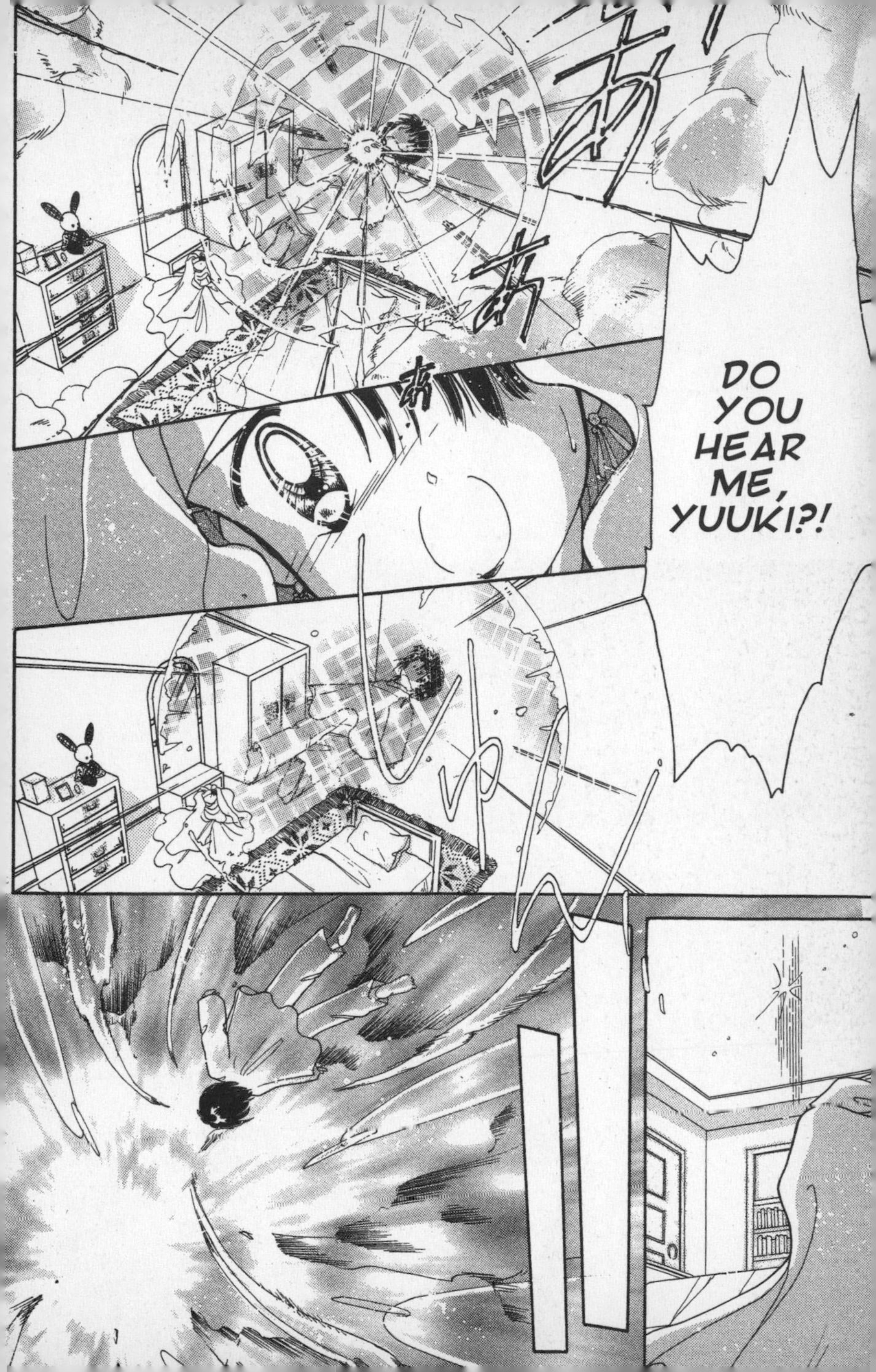
DO YOU HEAR ME, YUUKI?!

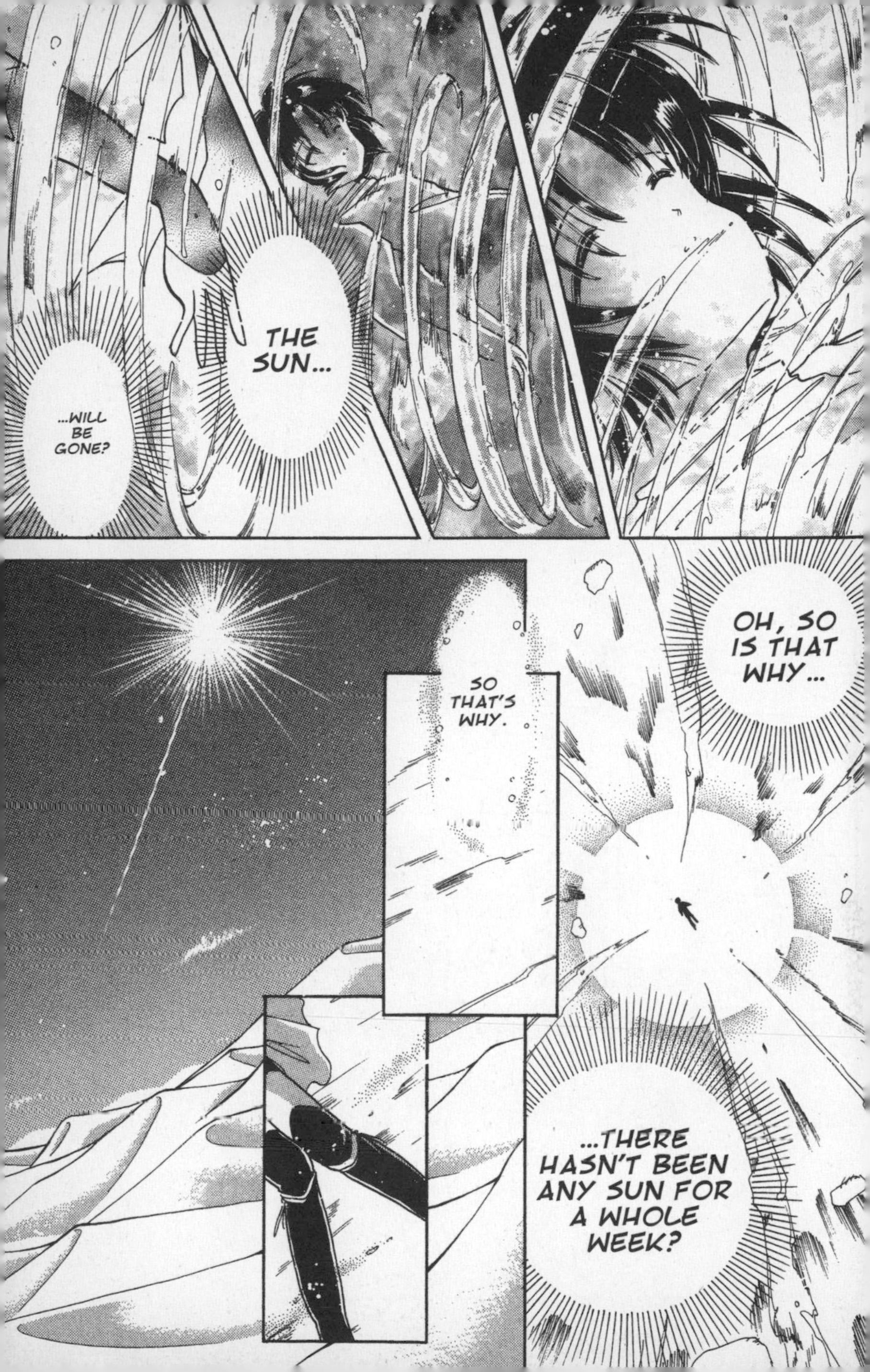
THE SUN...
...WILL BE GONE?
OH, SO IS THAT WHY...
SO THAT'S WHY.
...THERE HASN'T BEEN ANY SUN FOR A WHOLE WEEK?

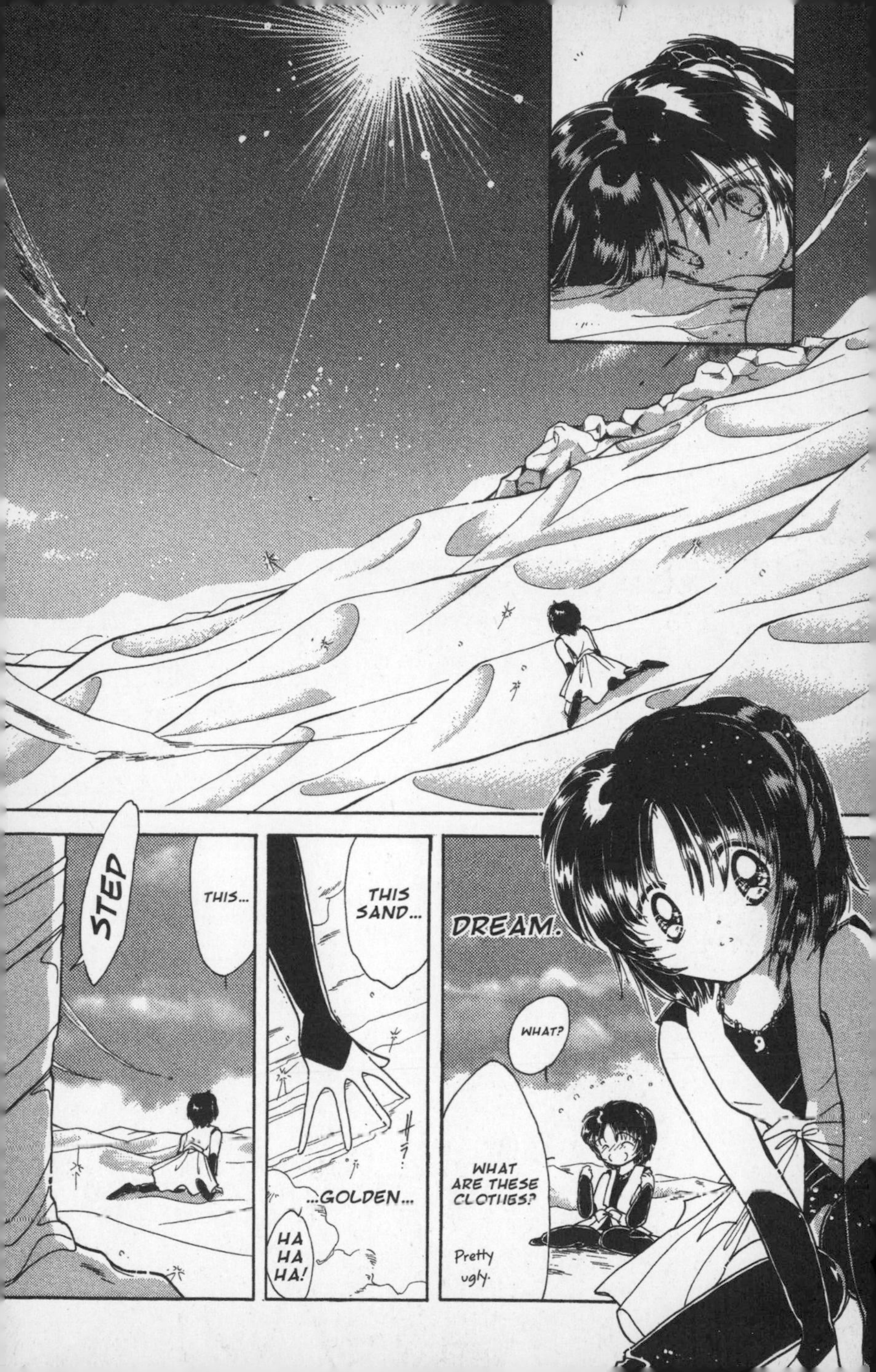
DREAM.
WHAT?
WHAT ARE THESE CLOTHES?
Pretty ugly.
THIS SAND...
...GOLDEN...
HA HA HA!
STEP
THIS...

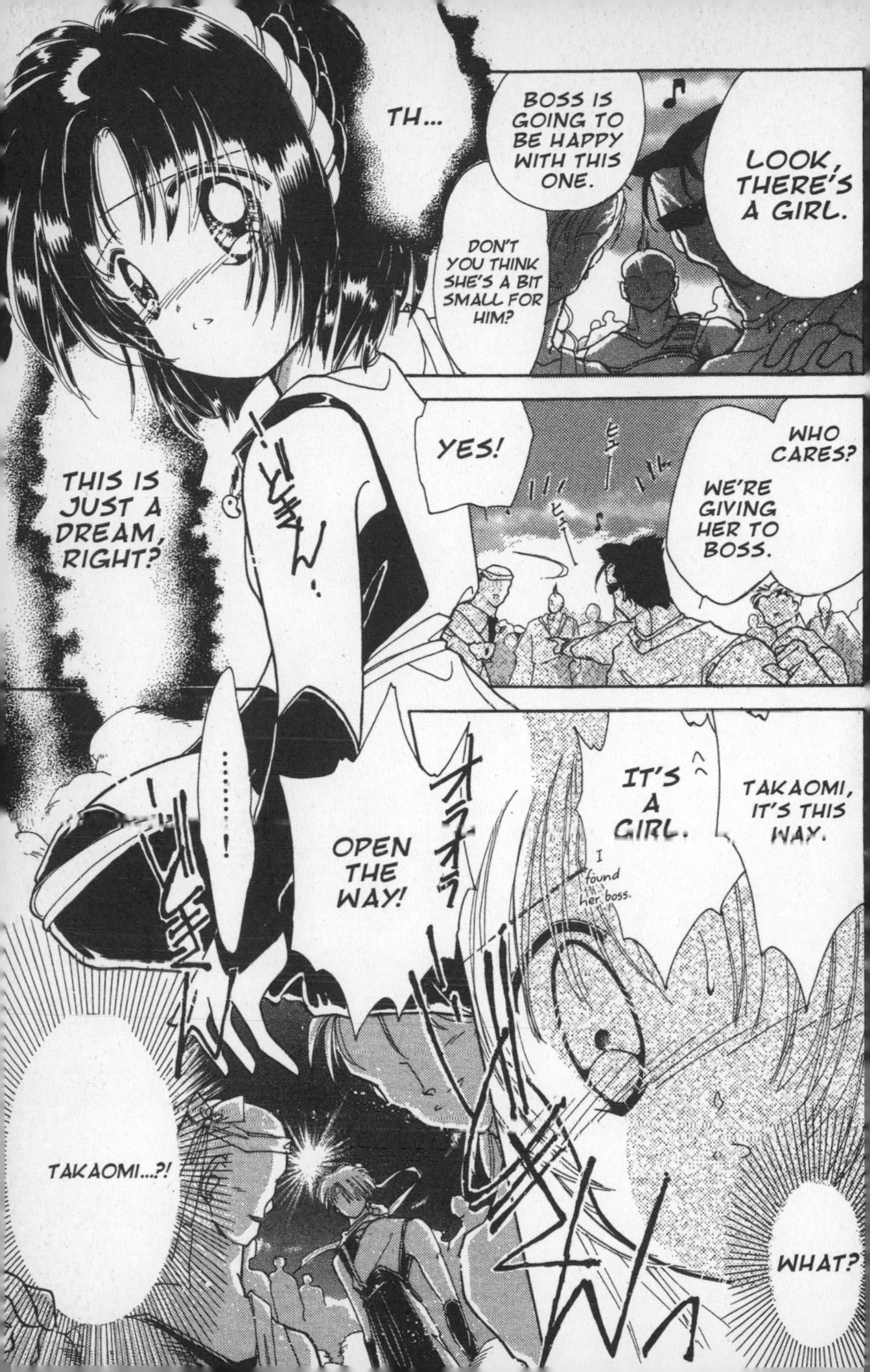
LOOK, THERE'S A GIRL.
BOSS IS GOING TO BE HAPPY WITH THIS ONE.
DON'T YOU THINK SHE'S A BIT SMALL FOR HIM?
WHO CARES?
WE'RE GIVING HER TO BOSS.
YES!
TH...
THIS IS JUST A DREAM, RIGHT?
......!
TAKAOMI, IT'S THIS WAY.
IT'S A GIRL.
I found her boss.
OPEN THE WAY!
WHAT?
TAKAOMI...?!

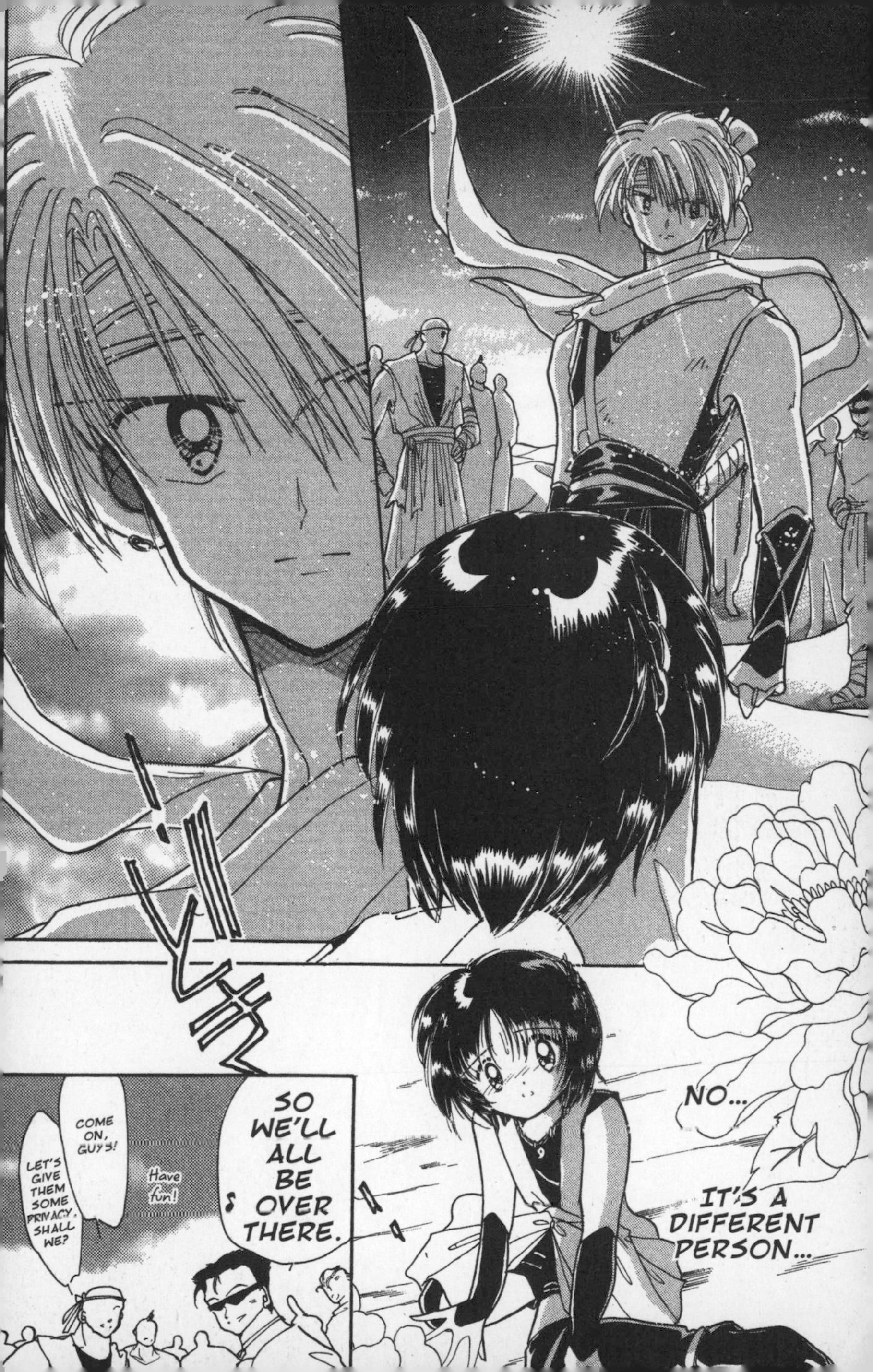
NO...
IT'S A DIFFERENT PERSON...
SO WE'LL ALL BE OVER THERE.
COME ON, GUYS!
Have fun!
LET'S GIVE THEM SOME PRIVACY, SHALL WE?

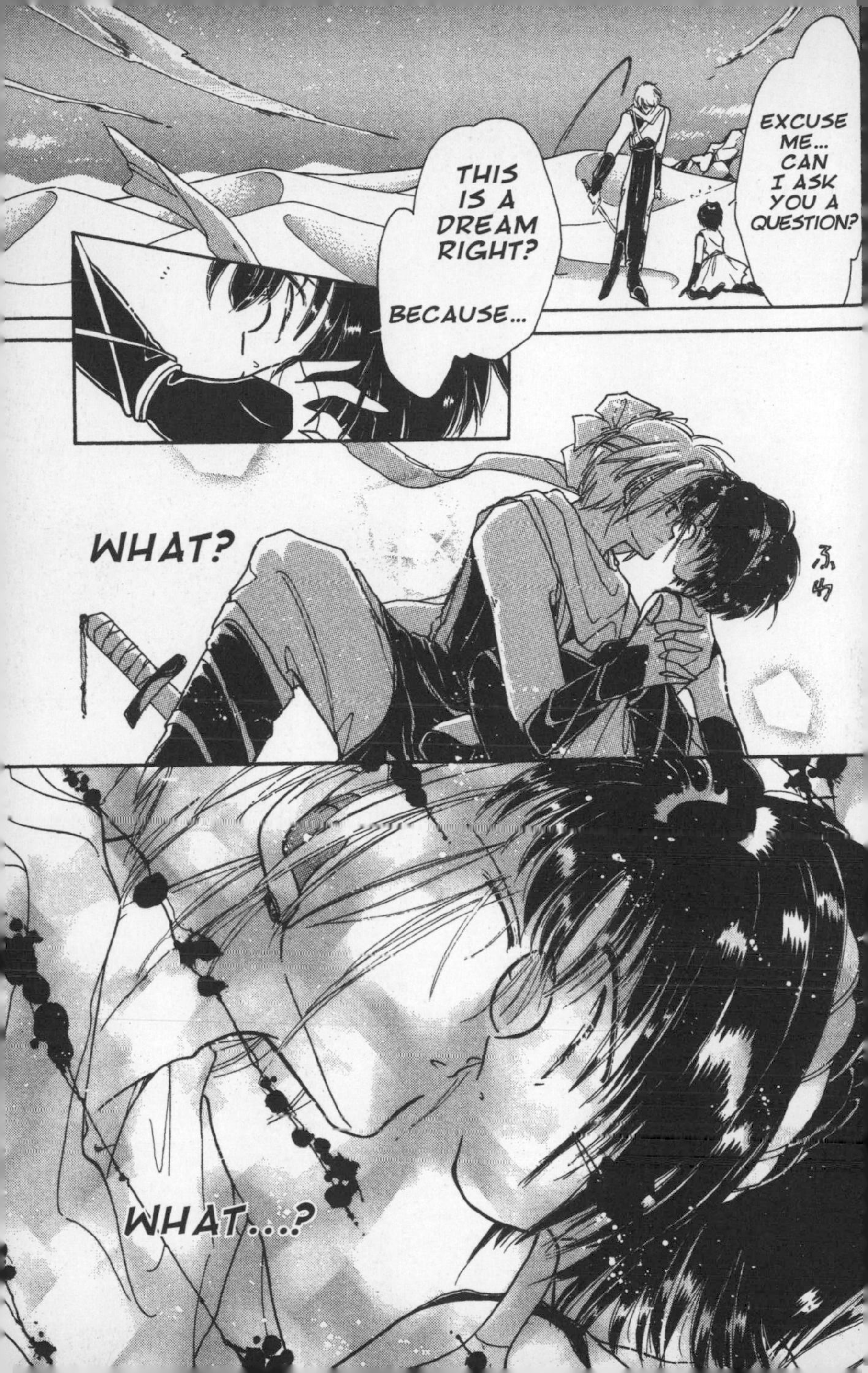
EXCUSE ME... CAN I ASK YOU A QUESTION?
THIS IS A DREAM RIGHT?
BECAUSE...
ふわ
WHAT?
WHAT...?

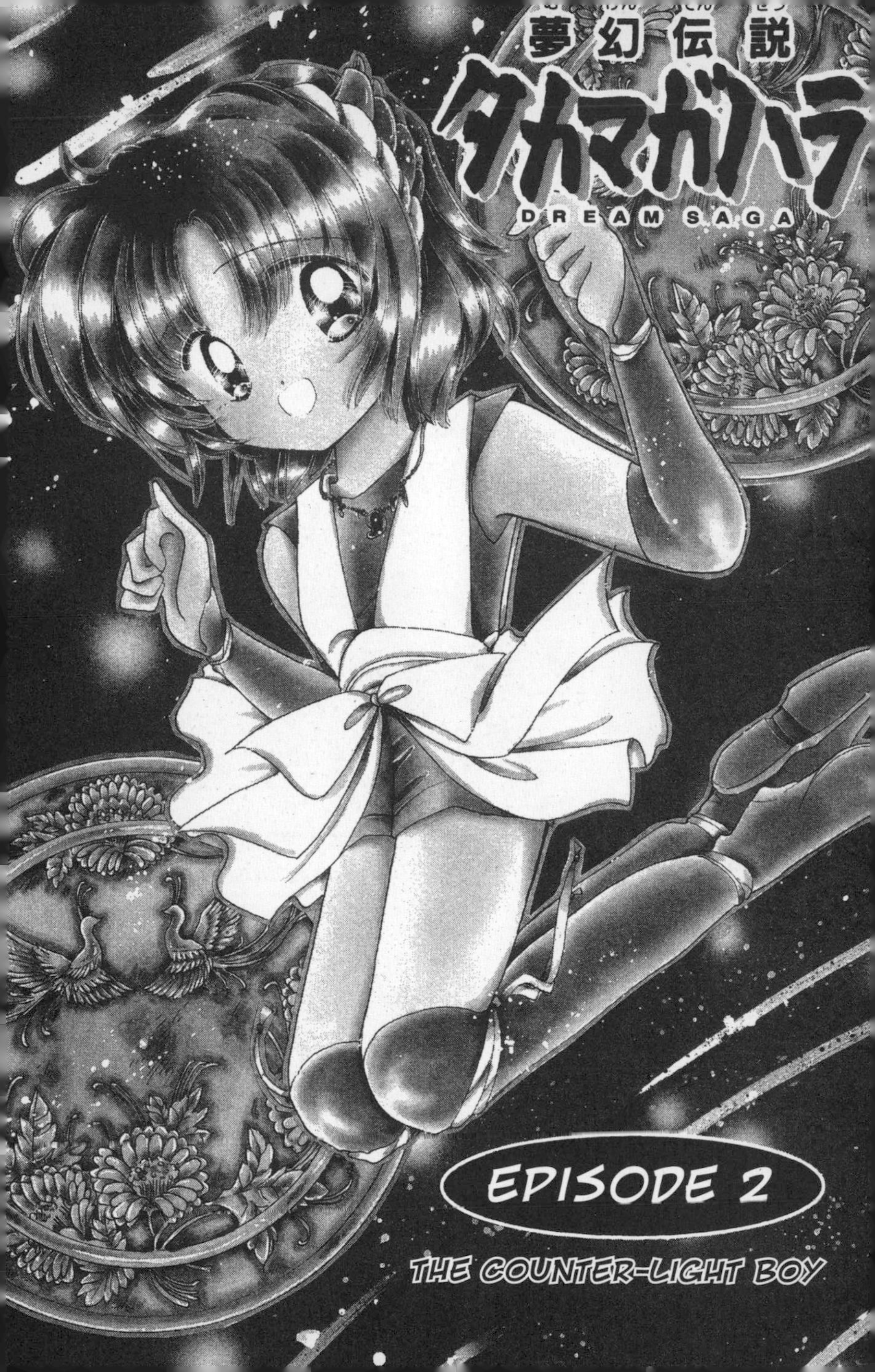

夢幻伝説
タカマガハラ
DREAM SAGA
EPISODE 2
THE COUNTER-LIGHT BOY

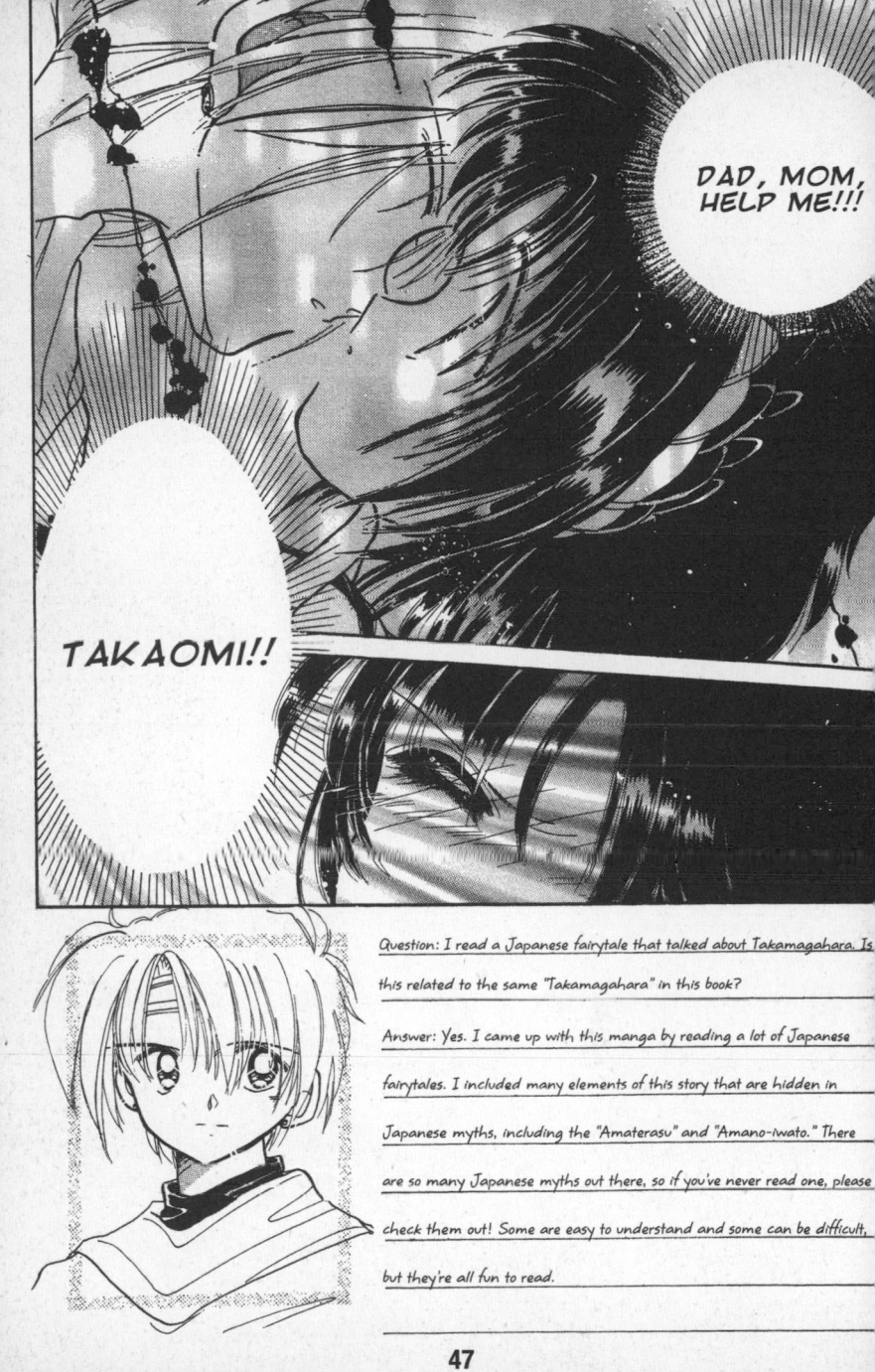

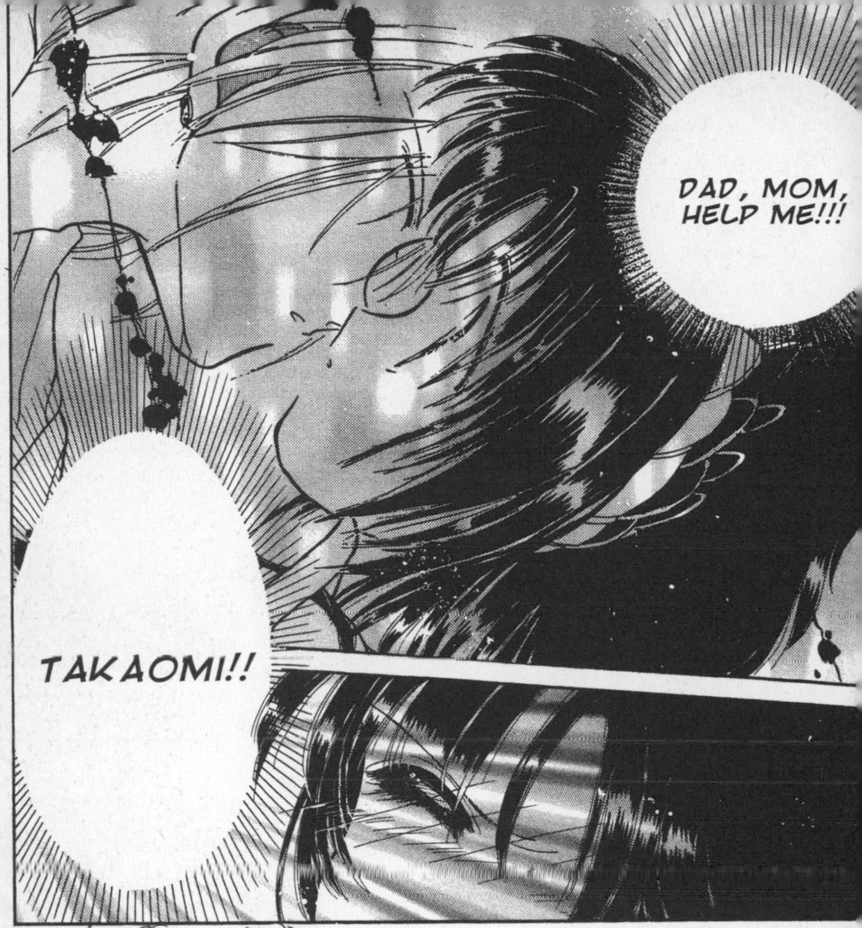
DAD, MOM, HELP ME!!!
TAKAOMI!!

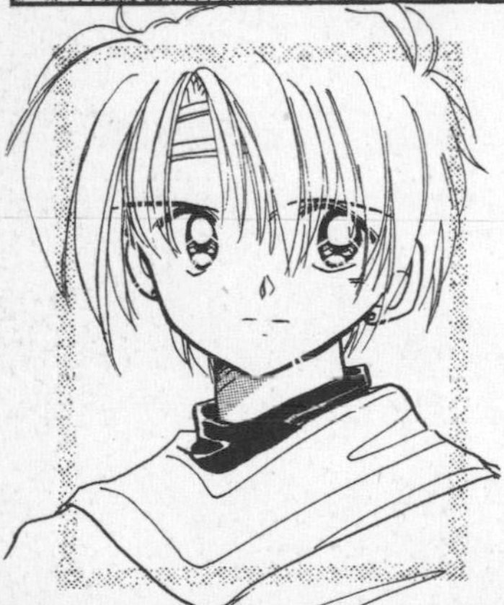

Question: I read a Japanese fairytale that talked about Takamagahara. Is this related to the same "Takamagahara" in this book?

Answer: Yes. I came up with this manga by reading a lot of Japanese fairytales. I included many elements of this story that are hidden in Japanese myths, including the "Amaterasu" and "Amano-iwato." There are so many Japanese myths out there, so if you've never read one, please check them out! Some are easy to understand and some can be difficult, but they're all fun to read.

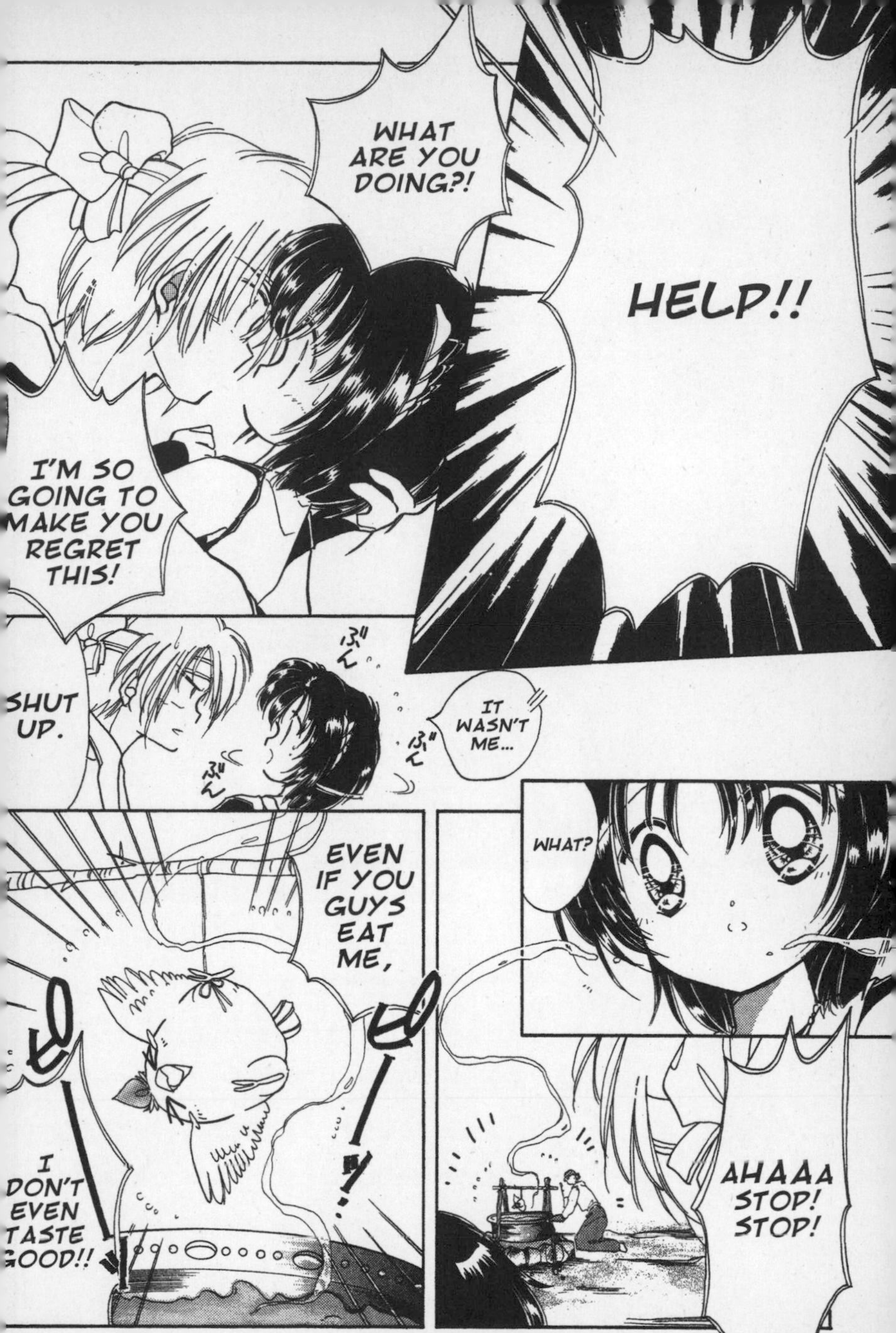
HELP!!
WHAT ARE YOU DOING?!
I'M SO GOING TO MAKE YOU REGRET THIS!
ぶん
ぶん
IT WASN'T ME...
ぶん
SHUT UP.
WHAT?
AHAAA STOP! STOP!
EVEN IF YOU GUYS EAT ME,
I DON'T EVEN TASTE GOOD!!

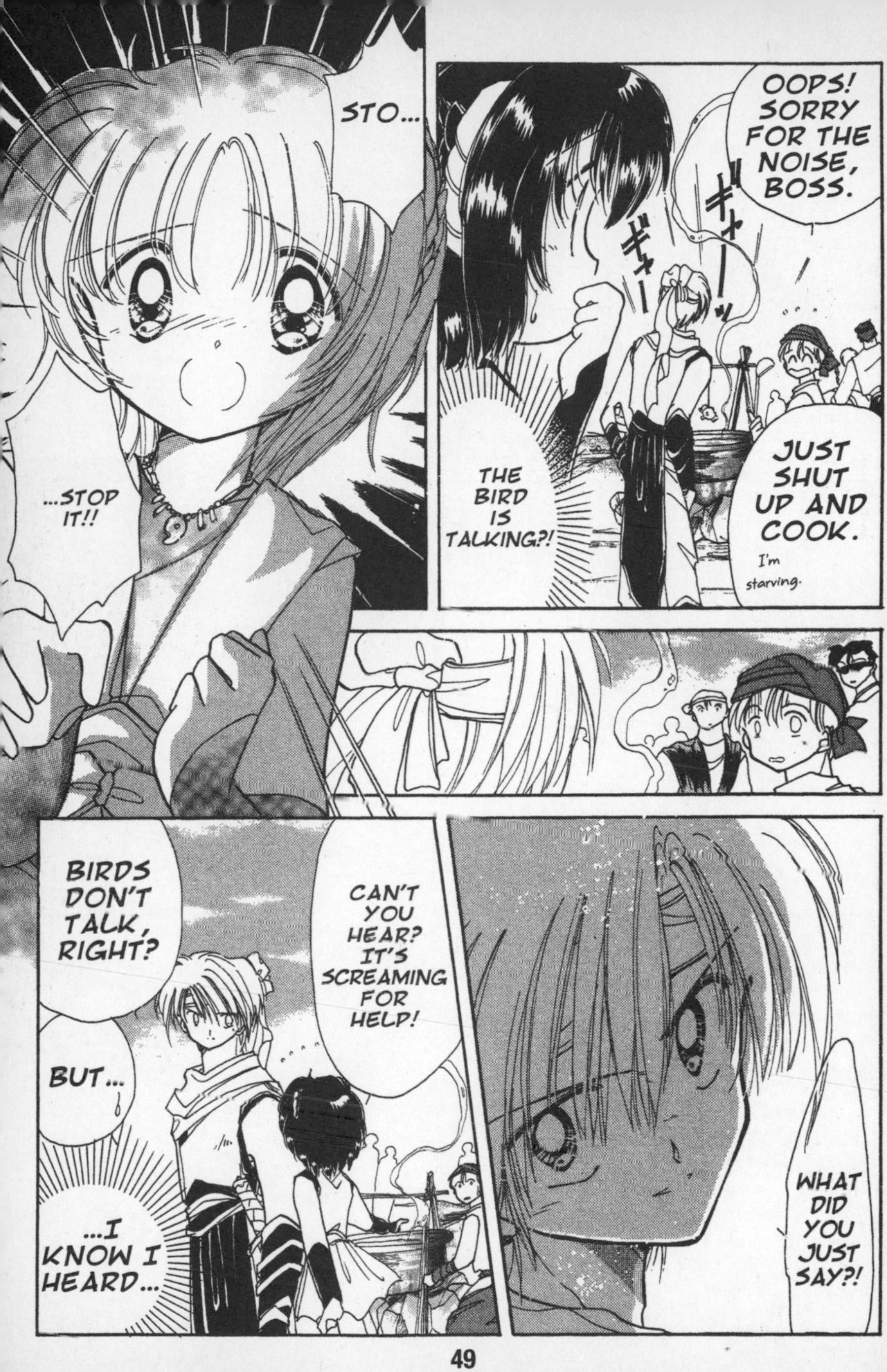

OOPS! SORRY FOR THE NOISE, BOSS.
ギャーッ
ギャー
JUST SHUT UP AND COOK.
I'm starving.
THE BIRD IS TALKING?!
STO...
...STOP IT!!
WHAT DID YOU JUST SAY?!
CAN'T YOU HEAR? IT'S SCREAMING FOR HELP!
BIRDS DON'T TALK, RIGHT?
BUT...
...I KNOW I HEARD...

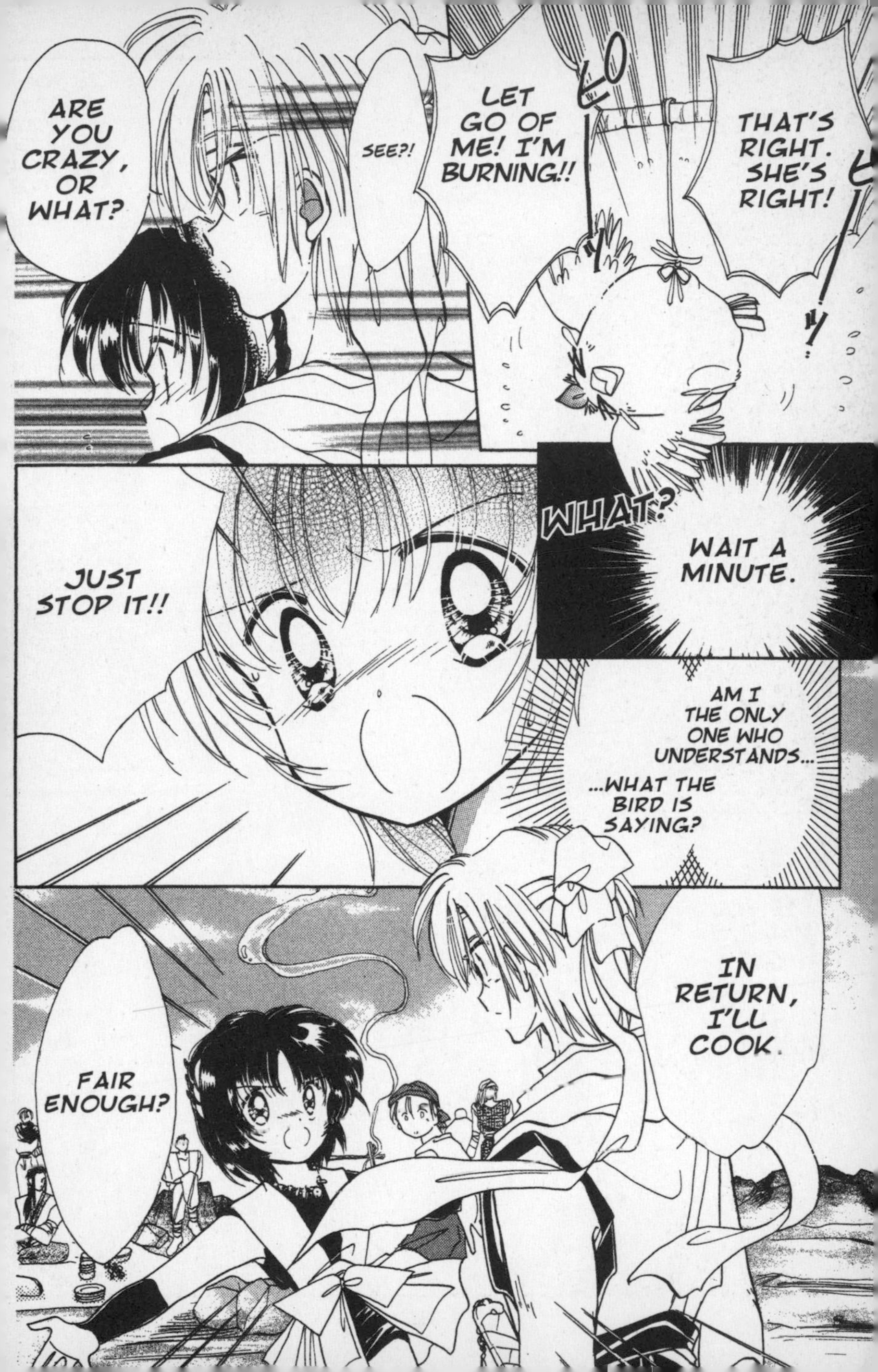
THAT'S RIGHT. SHE'S RIGHT!
LET GO OF ME! I'M BURNING!!
SEE?!
ARE YOU CRAZY, OR WHAT?
WHAT?
WAIT A MINUTE.
AM I THE ONLY ONE WHO UNDERSTANDS...
...WHAT THE BIRD IS SAYING?
JUST STOP IT!!
IN RETURN, I'LL COOK.
FAIR ENOUGH?

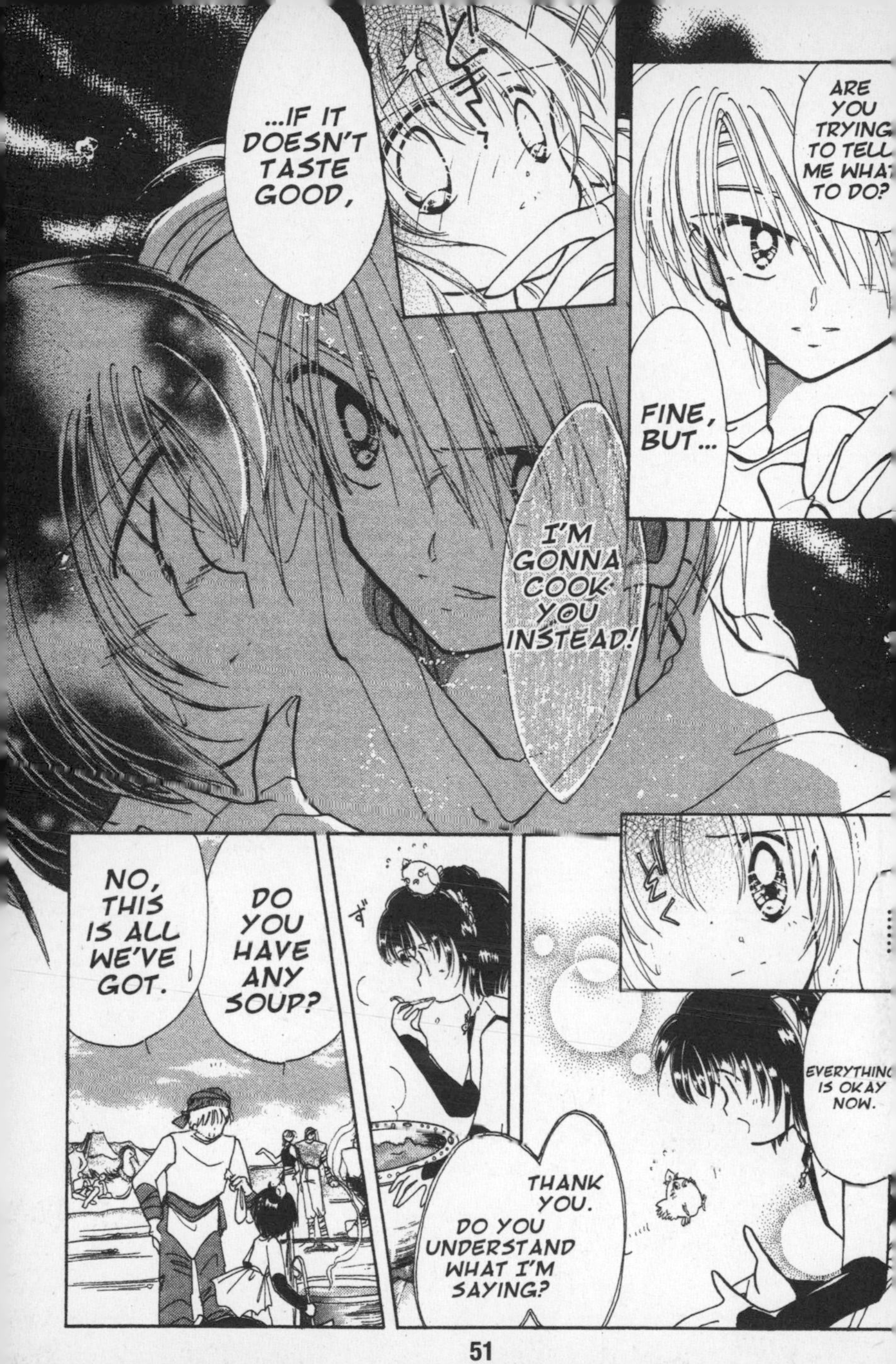
ARE YOU TRYING TO TELL ME WHAT TO DO?
FINE, BUT...
...IF IT DOESN'T TASTE GOOD,
I'M GONNA COOK YOU INSTEAD!
EVERYTHING IS OKAY NOW.
THANK YOU. DO YOU UNDERSTAND WHAT I'M SAYING?
ず
DO YOU HAVE ANY SOUP?
NO, THIS IS ALL WE'VE GOT.

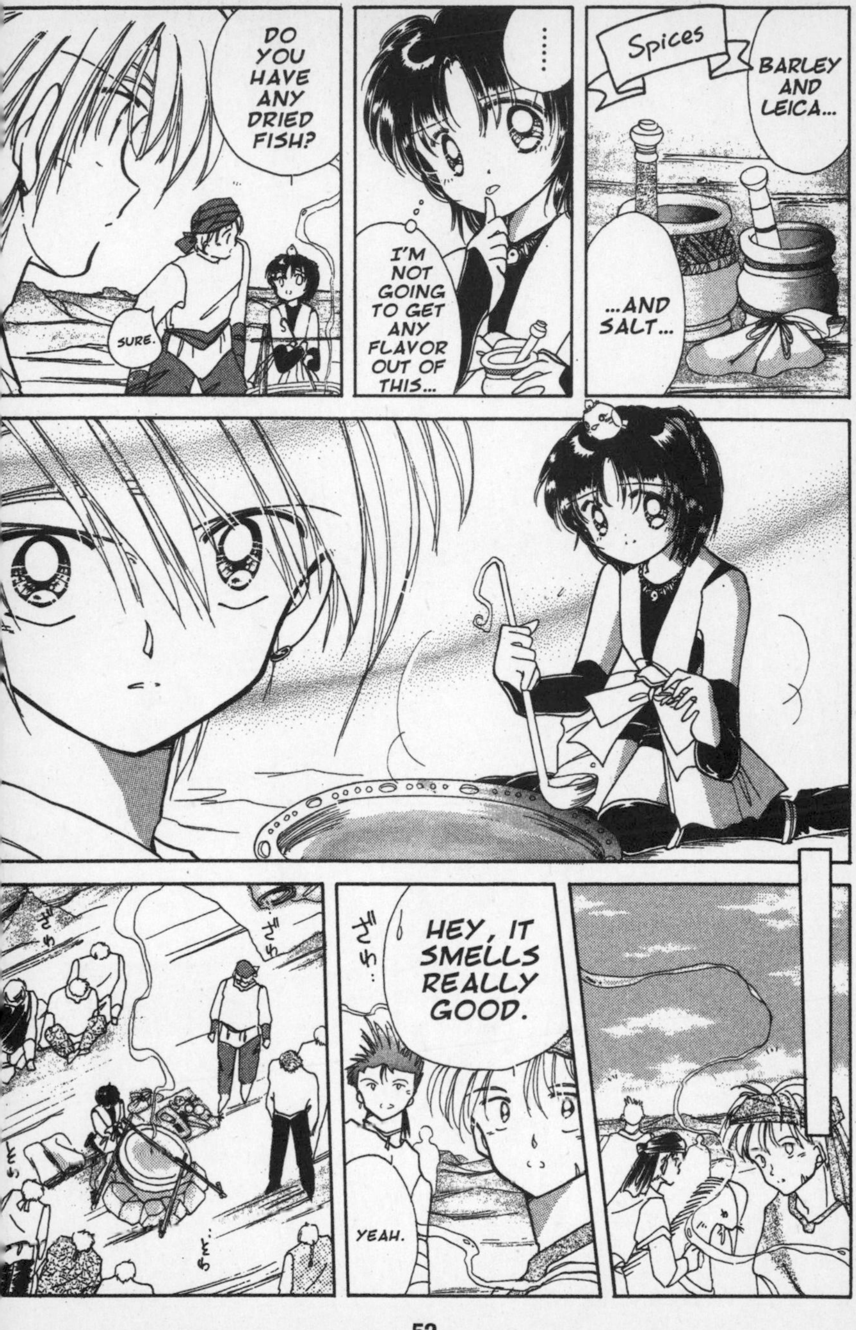
Spices
BARLEY AND LEICA...
...AND SALT...
......
I'M NOT GOING TO GET ANY FLAVOR OUT OF THIS...
DO YOU HAVE ANY DRIED FISH?
SURE.
ざわ..
HEY, IT SMELLS REALLY GOOD.
YEAH.

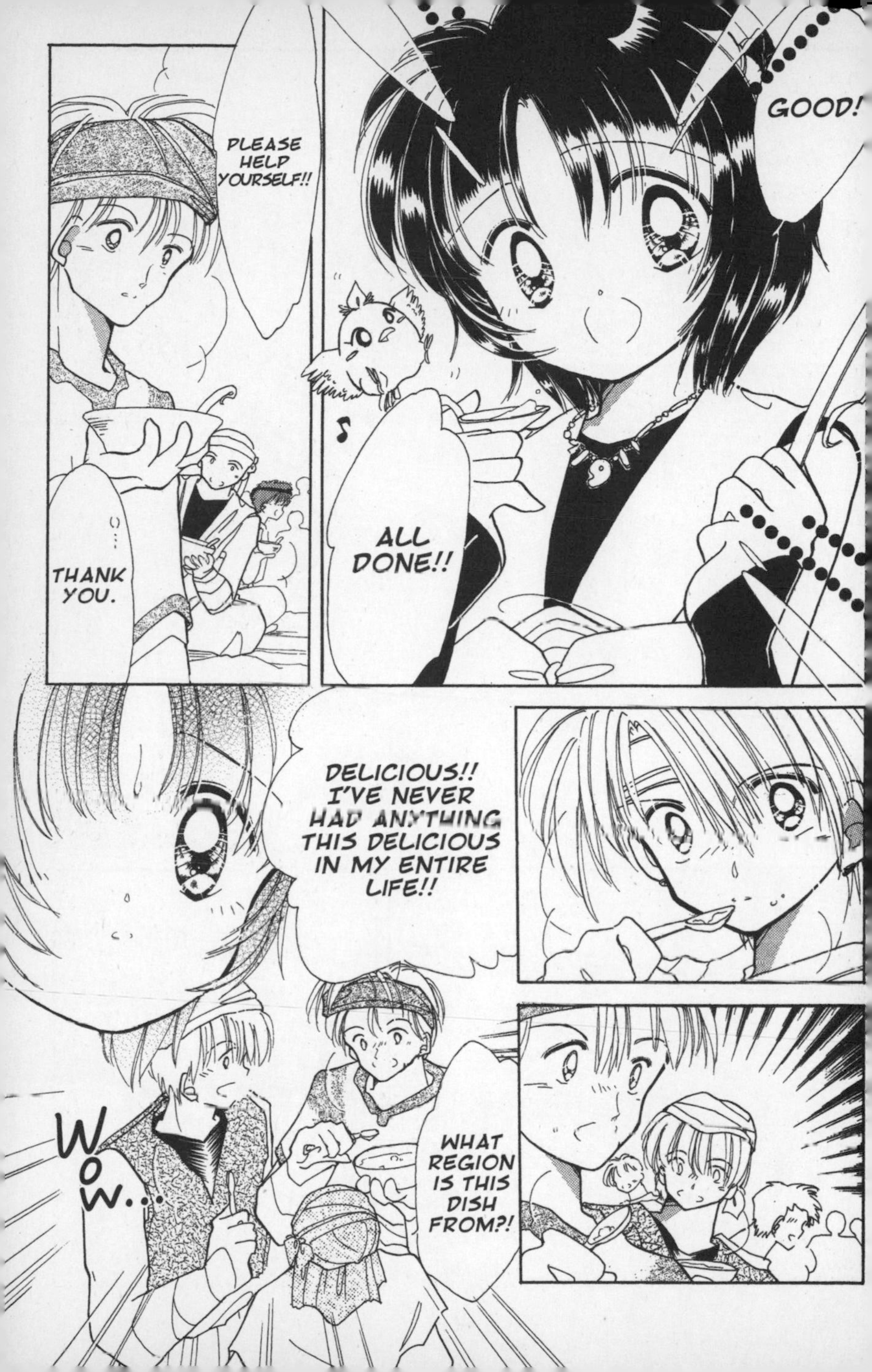
GOOD!
ALL DONE!!
PLEASE HELP YOURSELF!!
...THANK YOU.
WHAT REGION IS THIS DISH FROM?!
DELICIOUS!! I'VE NEVER HAD ANYTHING THIS DELICIOUS IN MY ENTIRE LIFE!!
WOW...

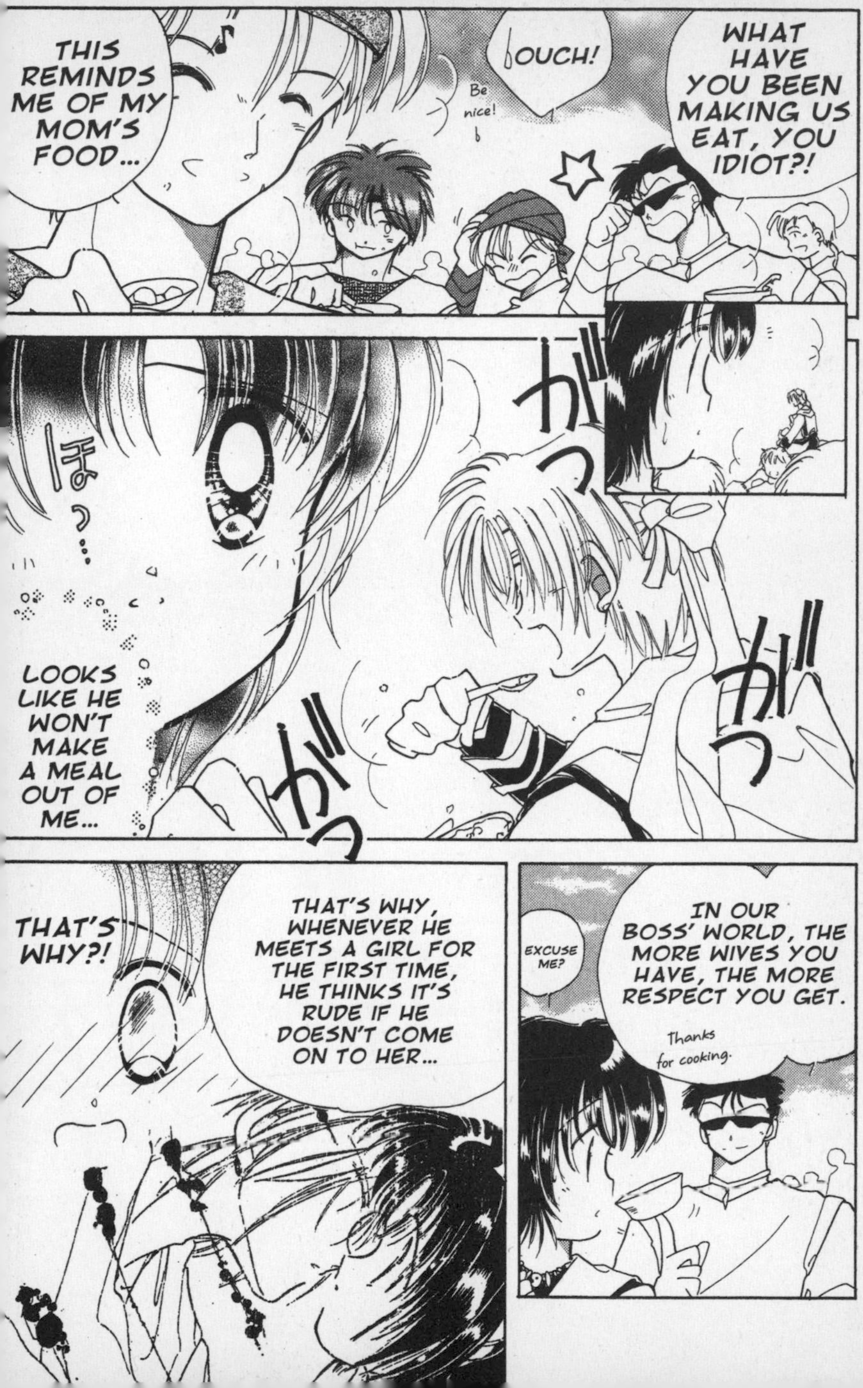
WHAT HAVE YOU BEEN MAKING US EAT, YOU IDIOT?!
OUCH!
Be nice!
THIS REMINDS ME OF MY MOM'S FOOD...
がつ
がつ
ほっ…
がつ
LOOKS LIKE HE WON'T MAKE A MEAL OUT OF ME...
IN OUR BOSS' WORLD, THE MORE WIVES YOU HAVE, THE MORE RESPECT YOU GET.
EXCUSE ME?
Thanks for cooking.
THAT'S WHY, WHENEVER HE MEETS A GIRL FOR THE FIRST TIME, HE THINKS IT'S RUDE IF HE DOESN'T COME ON TO HER...
THAT'S WHY?!

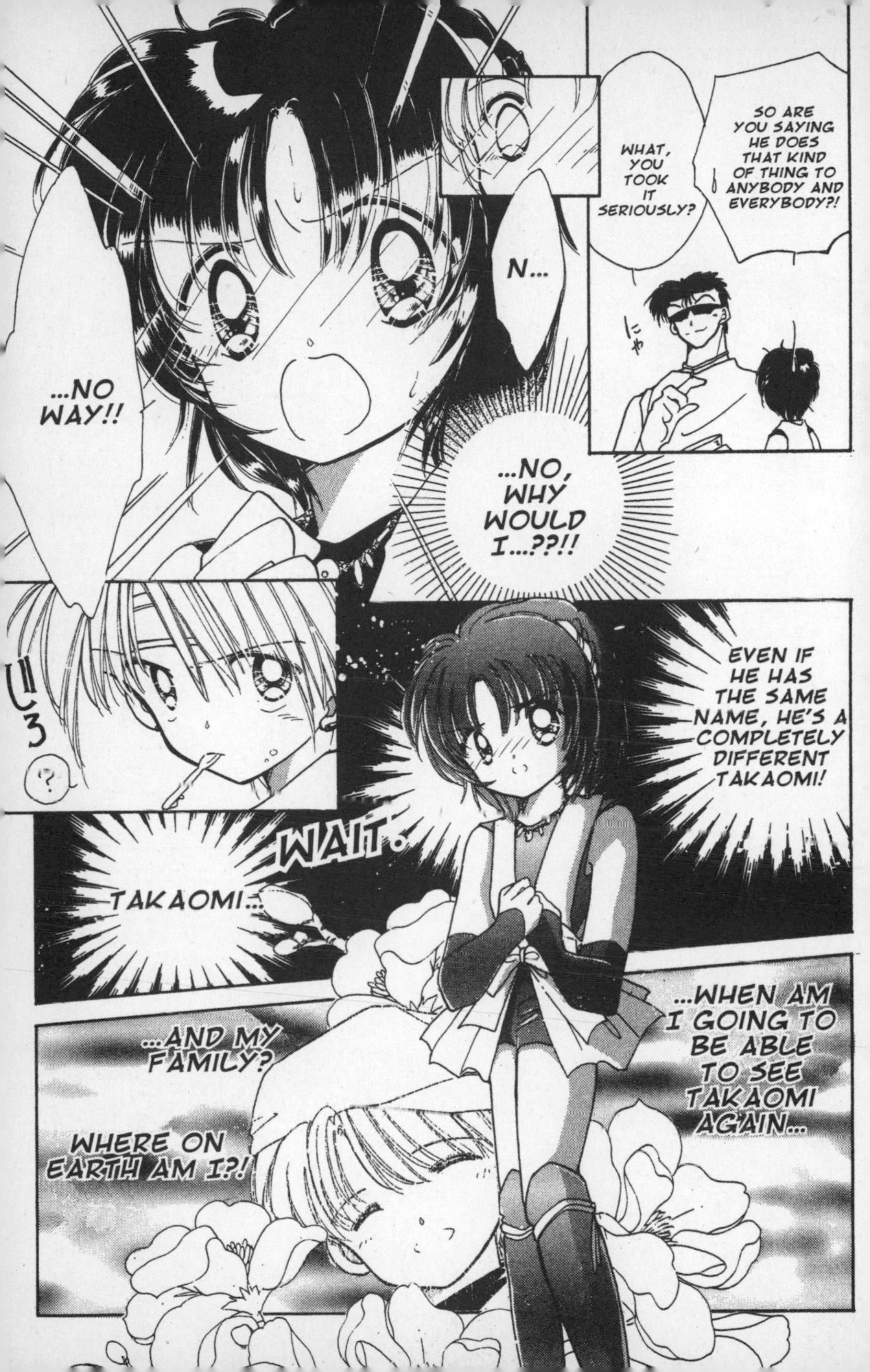
SO ARE YOU SAYING HE DOES THAT KIND OF THING TO ANYBODY AND EVERYBODY?!
WHAT, YOU TOOK IT SERIOUSLY?
にや
N...
...NO WAY!!
...NO, WHY WOULD I...??!!
EVEN IF HE HAS THE SAME NAME, HE'S A COMPLETELY DIFFERENT TAKAOMI!
?
WAIT.
TAKAOMI...
...WHEN AM I GOING TO BE ABLE TO SEE TAKAOMI AGAIN...
...AND MY FAMILY?
WHERE ON EARTH AM I?!

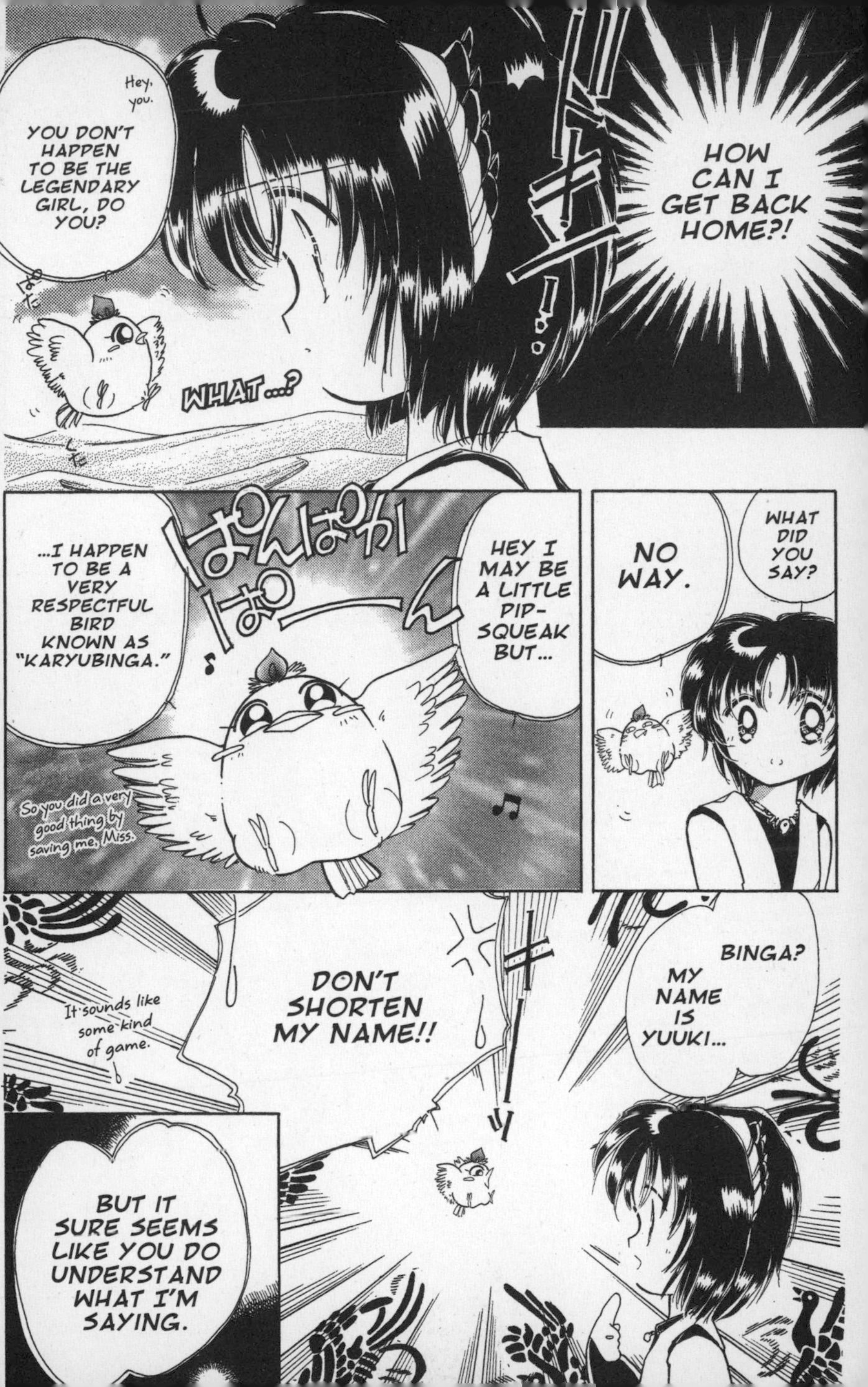
HOW CAN I GET BACK HOME?!
Hey, you.
YOU DON'T HAPPEN TO BE THE LEGENDARY GIRL, DO YOU?
WHAT...?
WHAT DID YOU SAY?
NO WAY.
HEY I MAY BE A LITTLE PIP-SQUEAK BUT...
...I HAPPEN TO BE A VERY RESPECTFUL BIRD KNOWN AS "KARYUBINGA."
So you did a very good thing by saving me, Miss.
BINGA?
MY NAME IS YUUKI...
DON'T SHORTEN MY NAME!!
It sounds like some kind of game.
BUT IT SURE SEEMS LIKE YOU DO UNDERSTAND WHAT I'M SAYING.

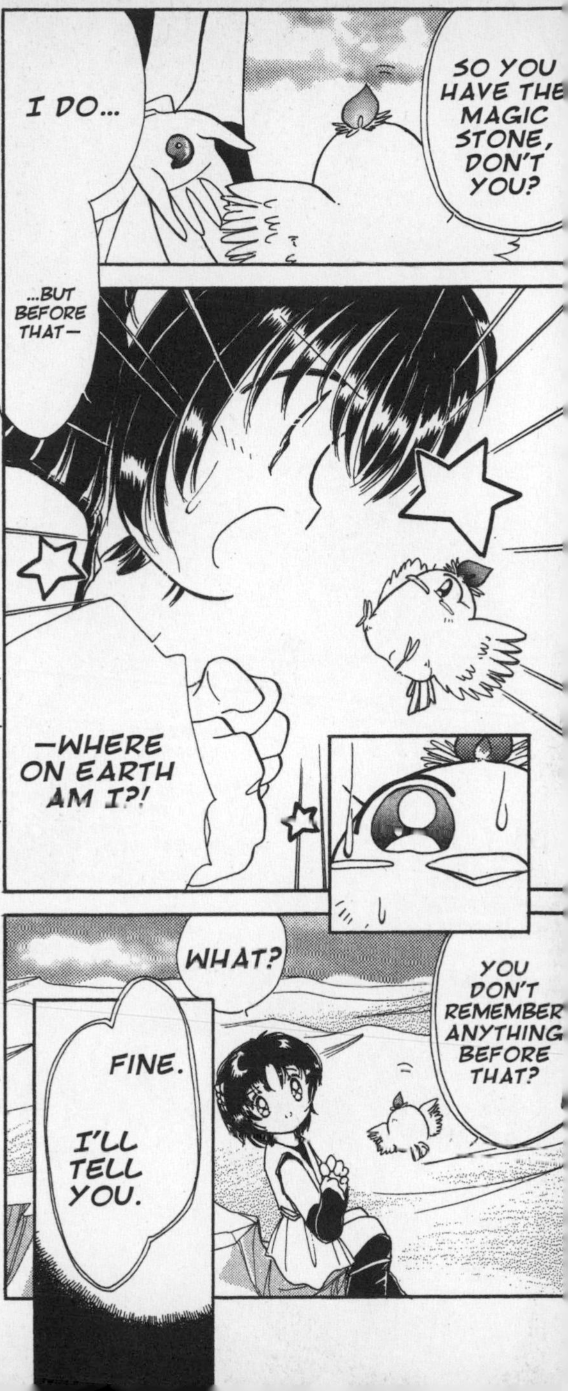
SO YOU HAVE THE MAGIC STONE, DON'T YOU?
I DO...
...BUT BEFORE THAT—
—WHERE ON EARTH AM I?!
YOU DON'T REMEMBER ANYTHING BEFORE THAT?
WHAT?
FINE.
I'LL TELL YOU.

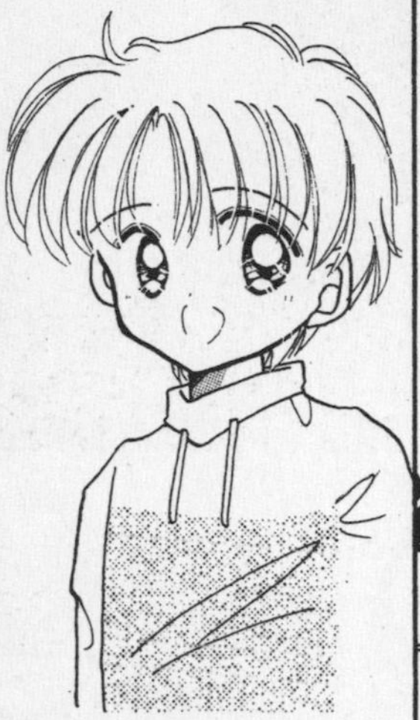

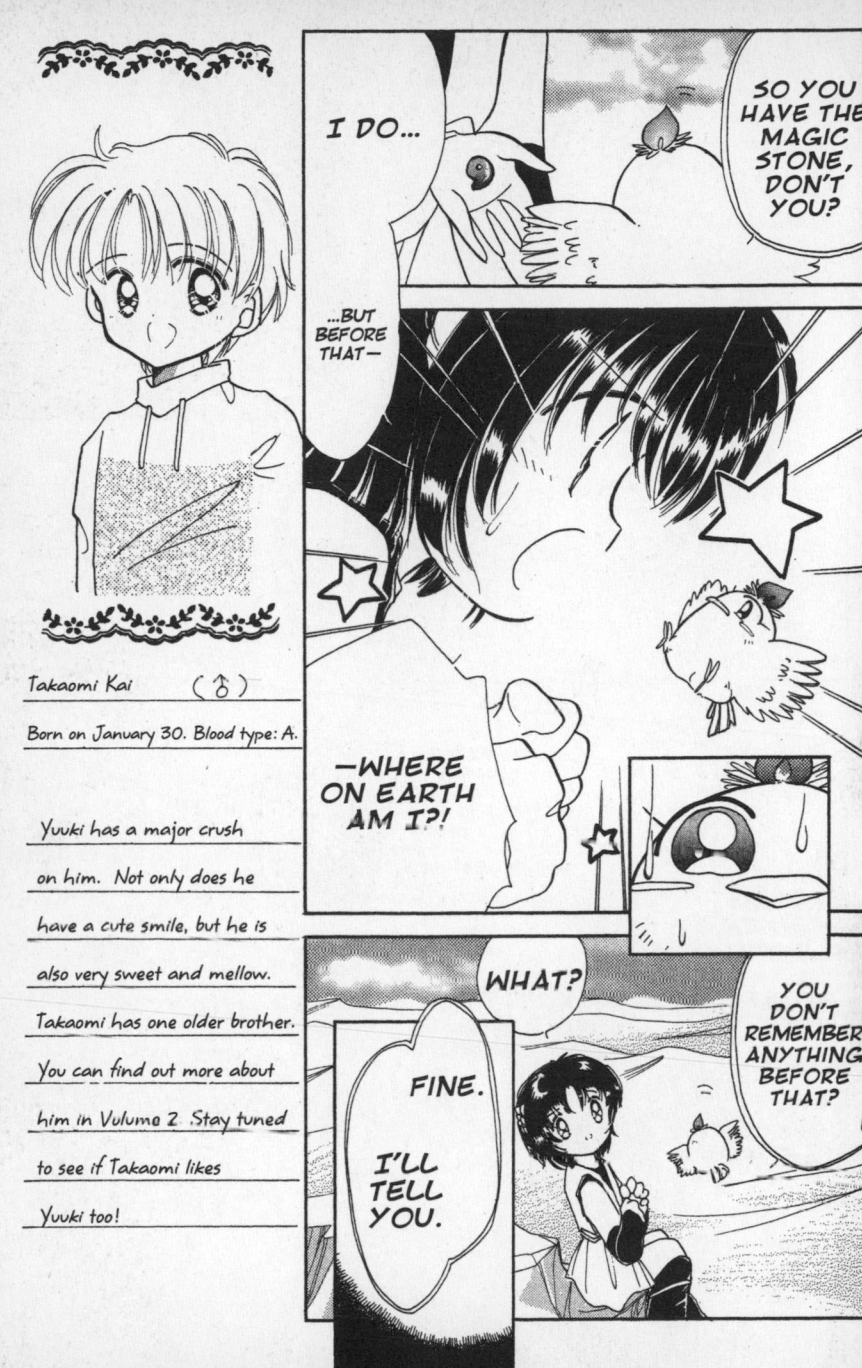

Takaomi Kai (♂)

Born on January 30. Blood type: A.

Yuuki has a major crush on him. Not only does he have a cute smile, but he is also very sweet and mellow. Takaomi has one older brother. You can find out more about him in Volume 2. Stay tuned to see if Takaomi likes Yuuki too!

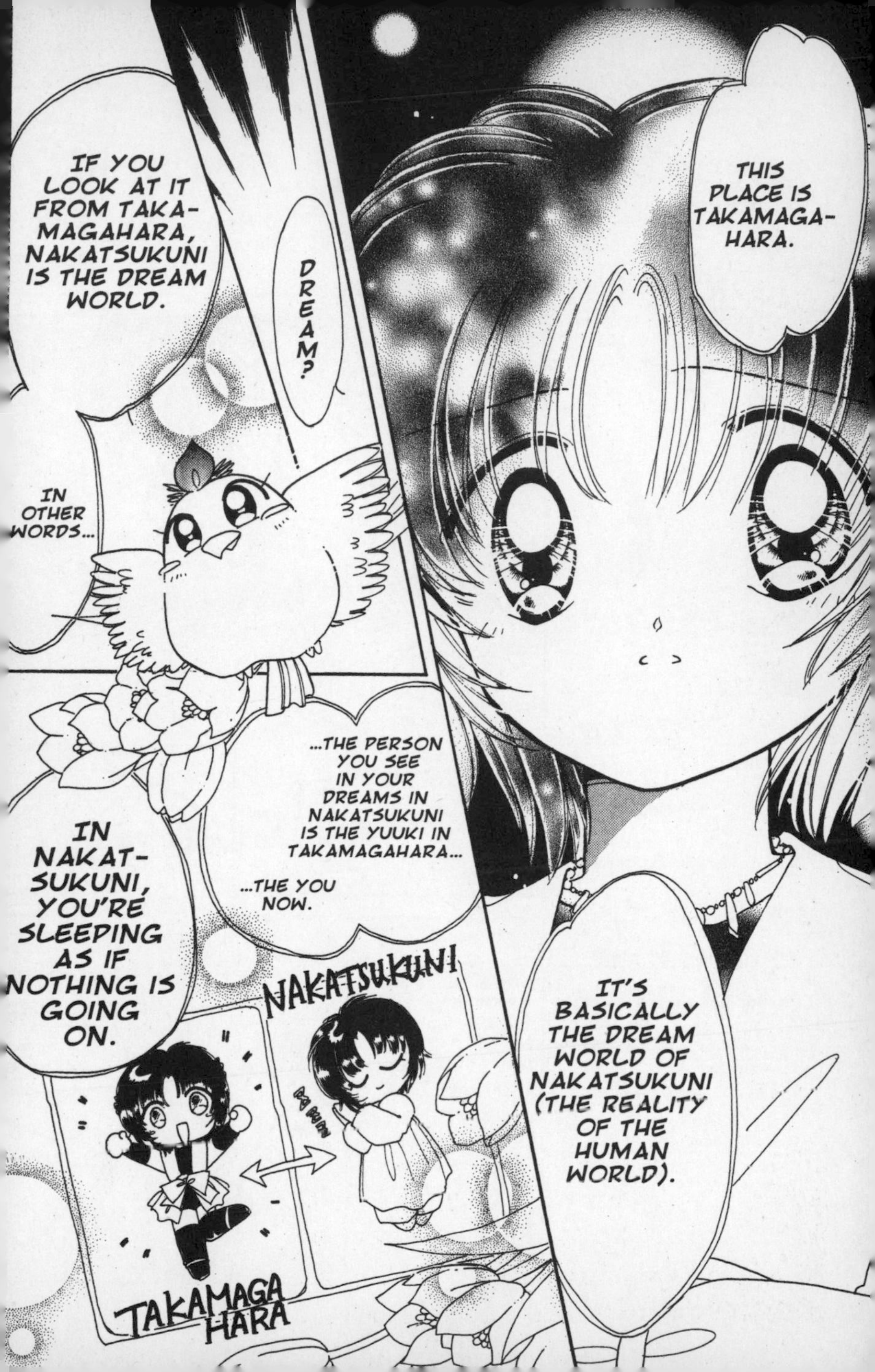
THIS PLACE IS TAKAMAGA-HARA.
IT'S BASICALLY THE DREAM WORLD OF NAKATSUKUNI (THE REALITY OF THE HUMAN WORLD).
DREAM?
IF YOU LOOK AT IT FROM TAKA-MAGAHARA, NAKATSUKUNI IS THE DREAM WORLD.
IN OTHER WORDS...
...THE PERSON YOU SEE IN YOUR DREAMS IN NAKATSUKUNI IS THE YUUKI IN TAKAMAGAHARA...
...THE YOU NOW.
IN NAKAT-SUKUNI, YOU'RE SLEEPING AS IF NOTHING IS GOING ON.
NAKATSUKUNI
TAKAMAGA HARA

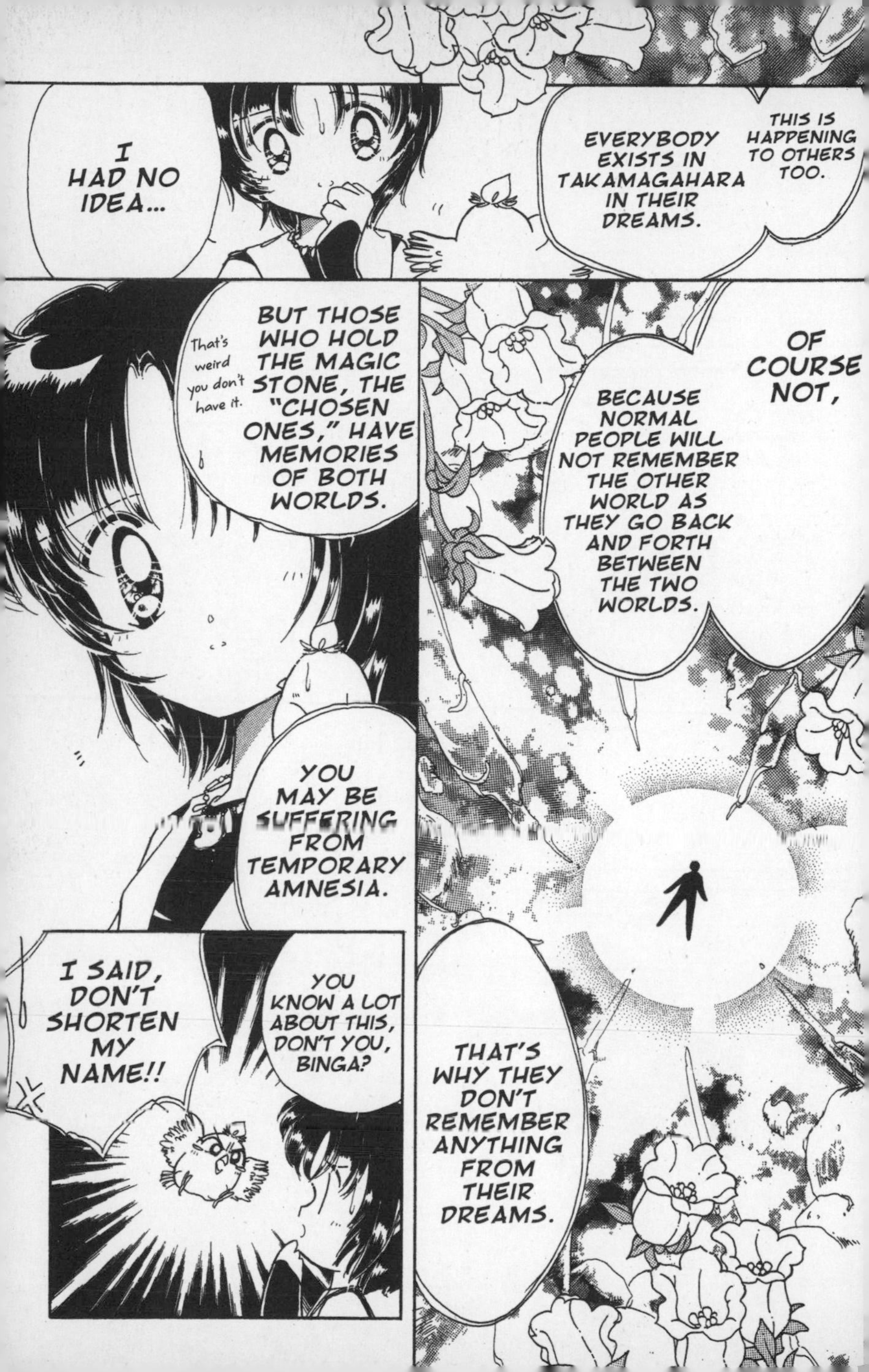
THIS IS HAPPENING TO OTHERS TOO.
EVERYBODY EXISTS IN TAKAMAGAHARA IN THEIR DREAMS.
I HAD NO IDEA...
OF COURSE NOT,
BECAUSE NORMAL PEOPLE WILL NOT REMEMBER THE OTHER WORLD AS THEY GO BACK AND FORTH BETWEEN THE TWO WORLDS.
THAT'S WHY THEY DON'T REMEMBER ANYTHING FROM THEIR DREAMS.
BUT THOSE WHO HOLD THE MAGIC STONE, THE "CHOSEN ONES," HAVE MEMORIES OF BOTH WORLDS.
That's weird you don't have it.
YOU MAY BE SUFFERING FROM TEMPORARY AMNESIA.
YOU KNOW A LOT ABOUT THIS, DON'T YOU, BINGA?
I SAID, DON'T SHORTEN MY NAME!!

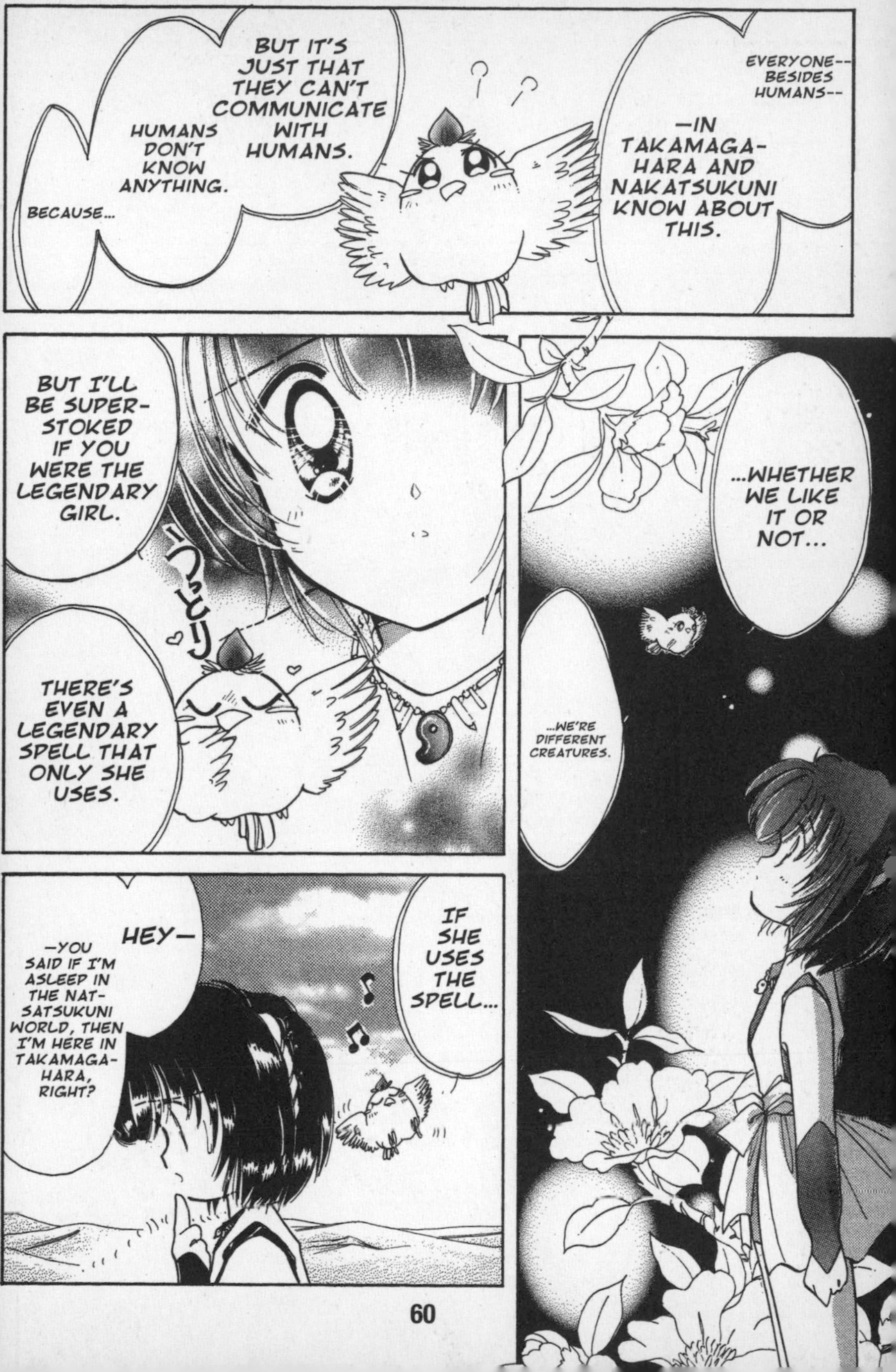
EVERYONE-- BESIDES HUMANS--
—IN TAKAMAGA-HARA AND NAKATSUKUNI KNOW ABOUT THIS.
BUT IT'S JUST THAT THEY CAN'T COMMUNICATE WITH HUMANS.
HUMANS DON'T KNOW ANYTHING.
BECAUSE...
...WHETHER WE LIKE IT OR NOT...
...WE'RE DIFFERENT CREATURES.
BUT I'LL BE SUPER-STOKED IF YOU WERE THE LEGENDARY GIRL.
うっとり
THERE'S EVEN A LEGENDARY SPELL THAT ONLY SHE USES.
IF SHE USES THE SPELL...
HEY—
—YOU SAID IF I'M ASLEEP IN THE NAT-SATSUKUNI WORLD, THEN I'M HERE IN TAKAMAGA-HARA, RIGHT?

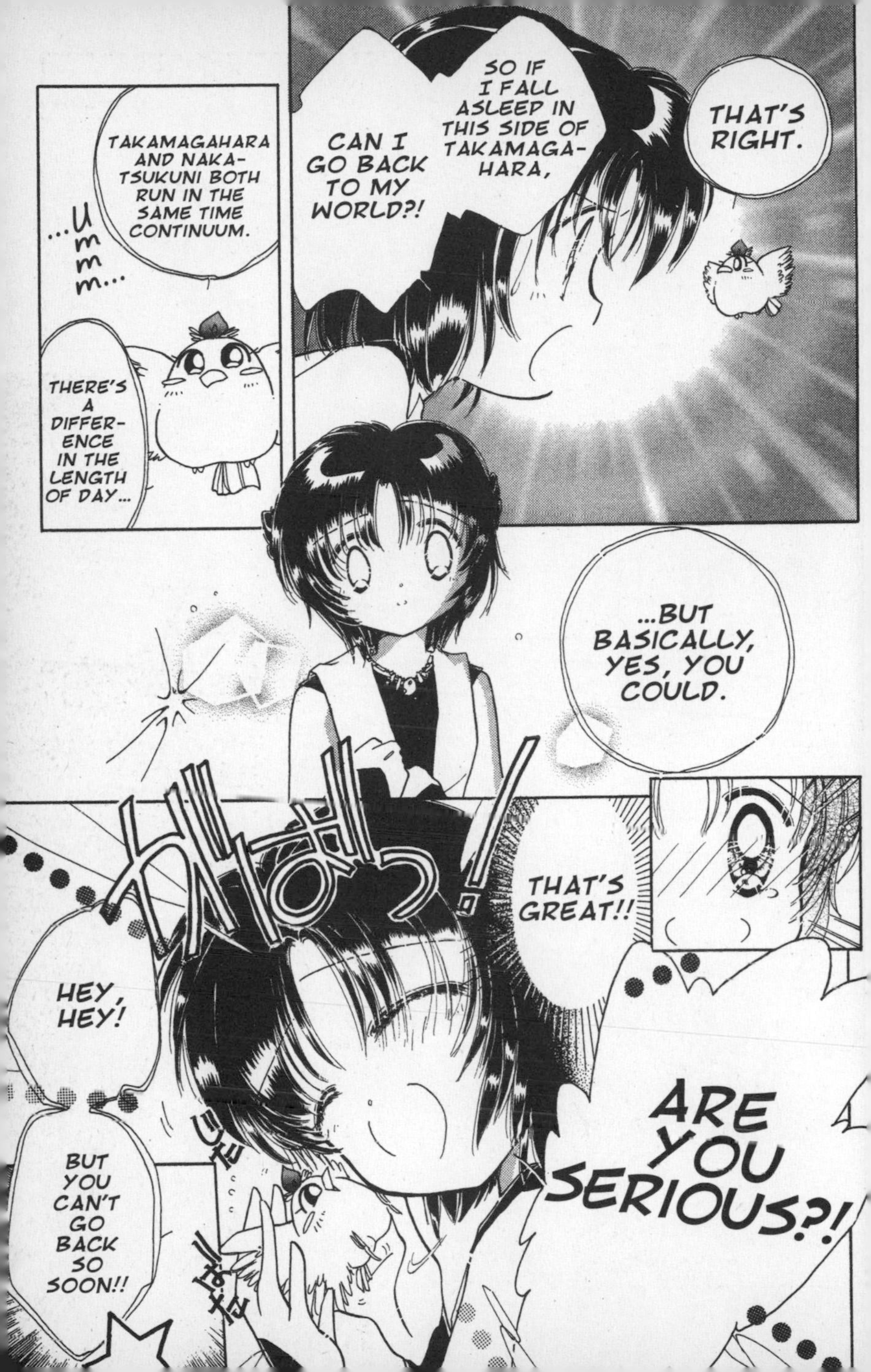
SO IF I FALL ASLEEP IN THIS SIDE OF TAKAMAGA-HARA,
CAN I GO BACK TO MY WORLD?!
THAT'S RIGHT.
TAKAMAGAHARA AND NAKA-TSUKUNI BOTH RUN IN THE SAME TIME CONTINUUM.
...Ummm...
THERE'S A DIFFER-ENCE IN THE LENGTH OF DAY...
...BUT BASICALLY, YES, YOU COULD.
THAT'S GREAT!!
ARE YOU SERIOUS?!
HEY, HEY!
BUT YOU CAN'T GO BACK SO SOON!!

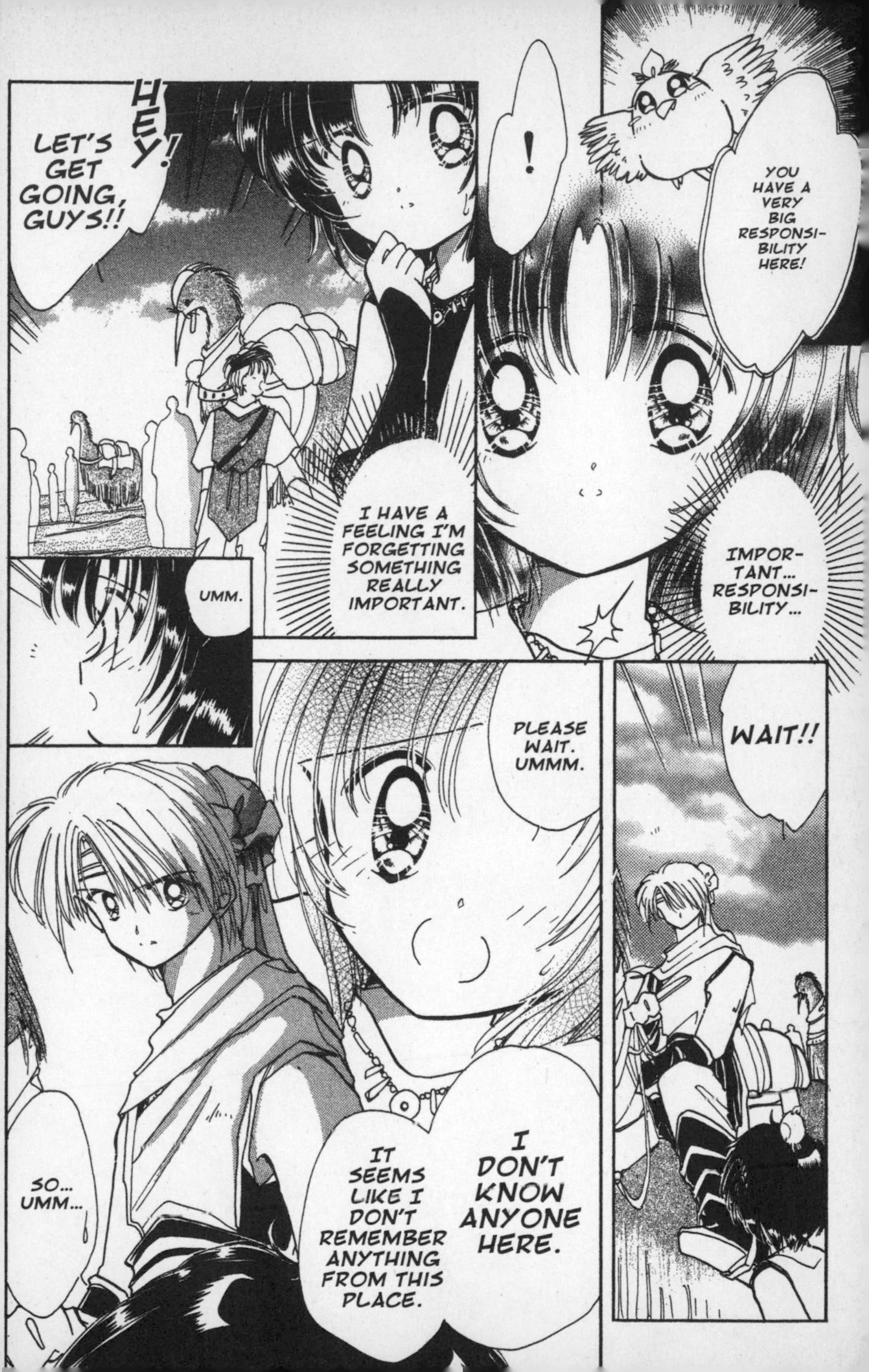
YOU HAVE A VERY BIG RESPONSIBILITY HERE!
!
IMPORTANT... RESPONSIBILITY...
HEY!
LET'S GET GOING, GUYS!!
I HAVE A FEELING I'M FORGETTING SOMETHING REALLY IMPORTANT.
UMM.
WAIT!!
PLEASE WAIT. UMMM.
I DON'T KNOW ANYONE HERE.
IT SEEMS LIKE I DON'T REMEMBER ANYTHING FROM THIS PLACE.
SO... UMM...

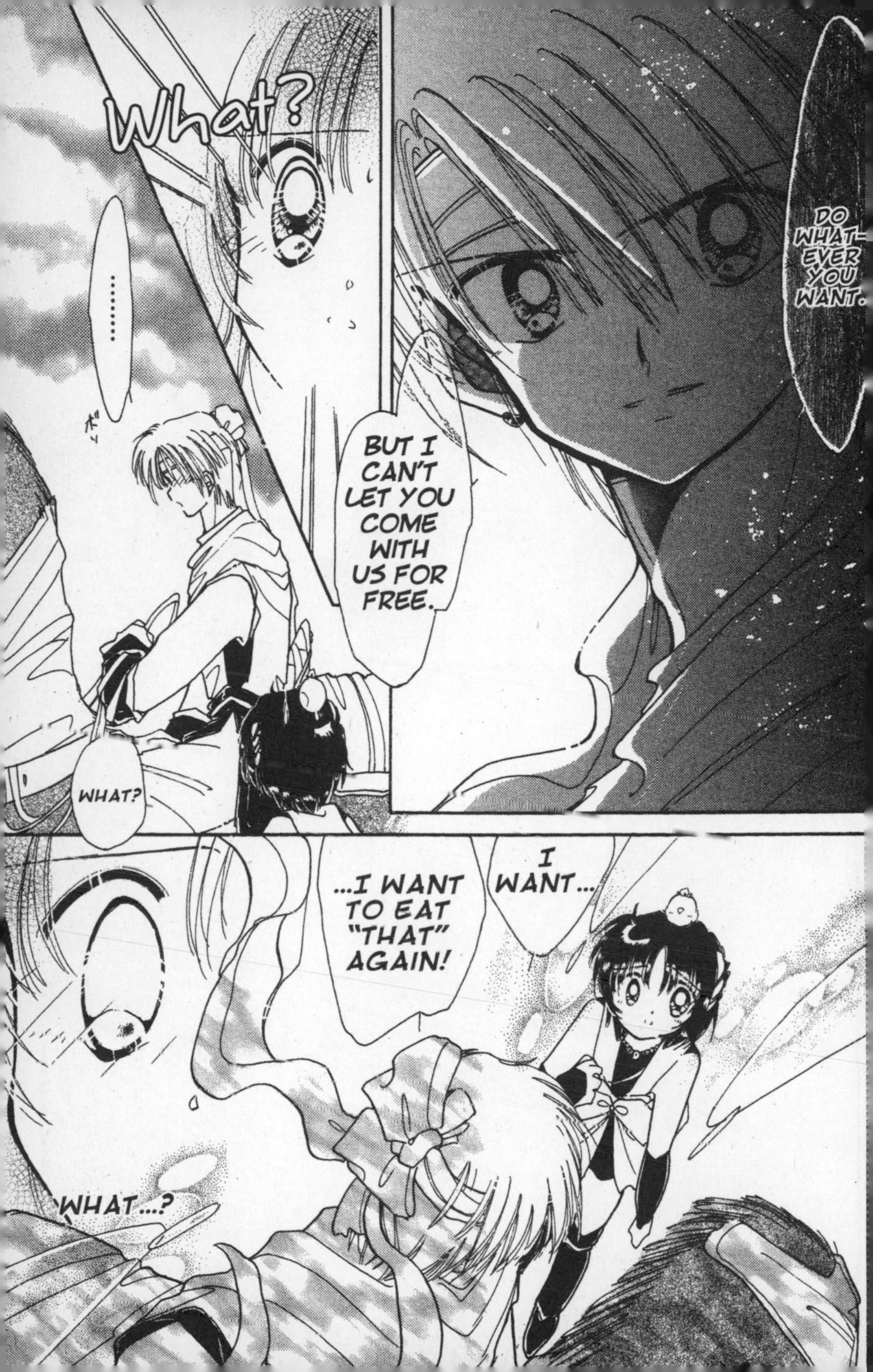
DO WHAT-EVER YOU WANT.
BUT I CAN'T LET YOU COME WITH US FOR FREE.
What?
......
WHAT?
I WANT...
...I WANT TO EAT "THAT" AGAIN!
WHAT...?

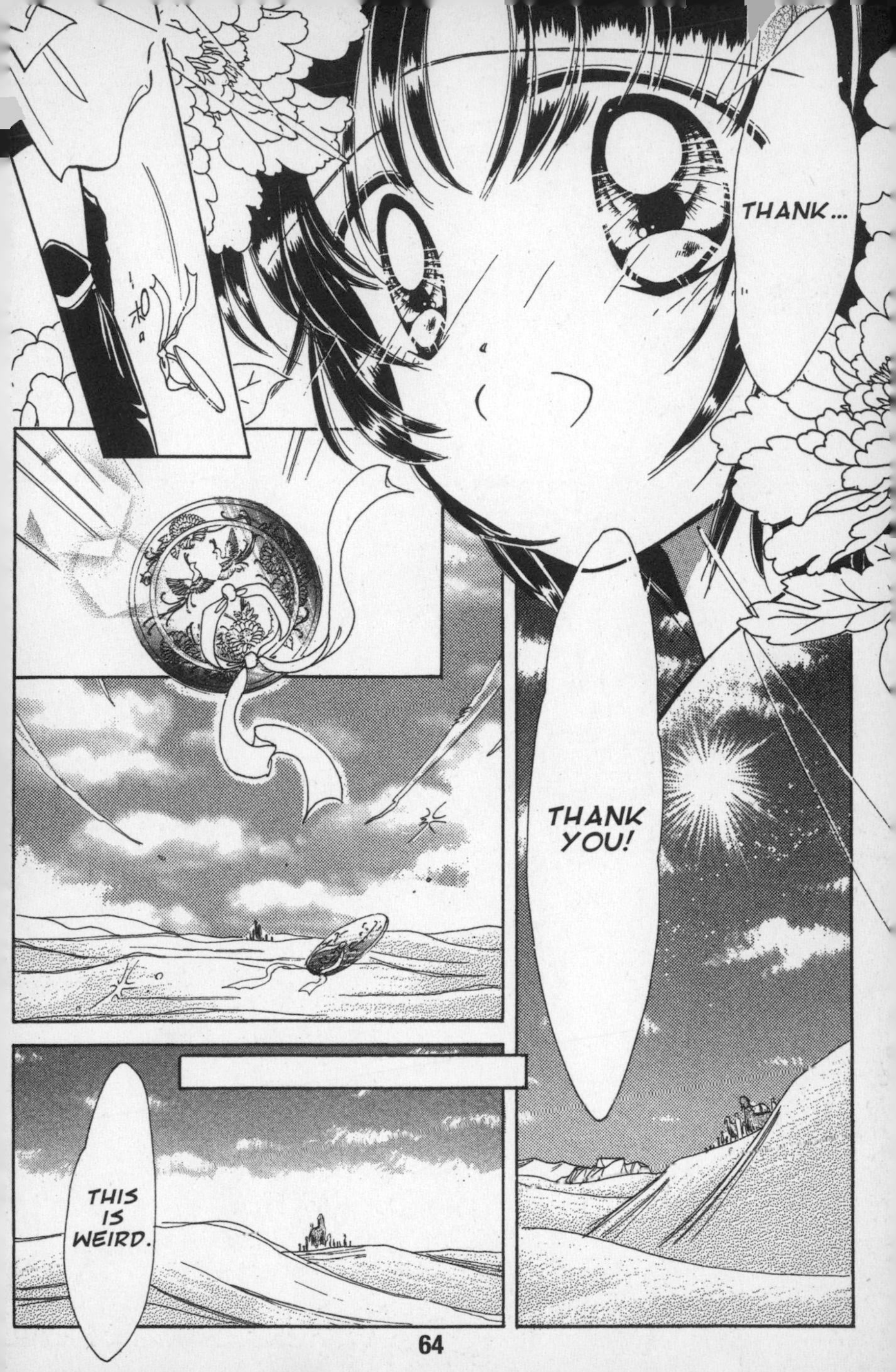
THANK...
THANK YOU!
THIS IS WEIRD.

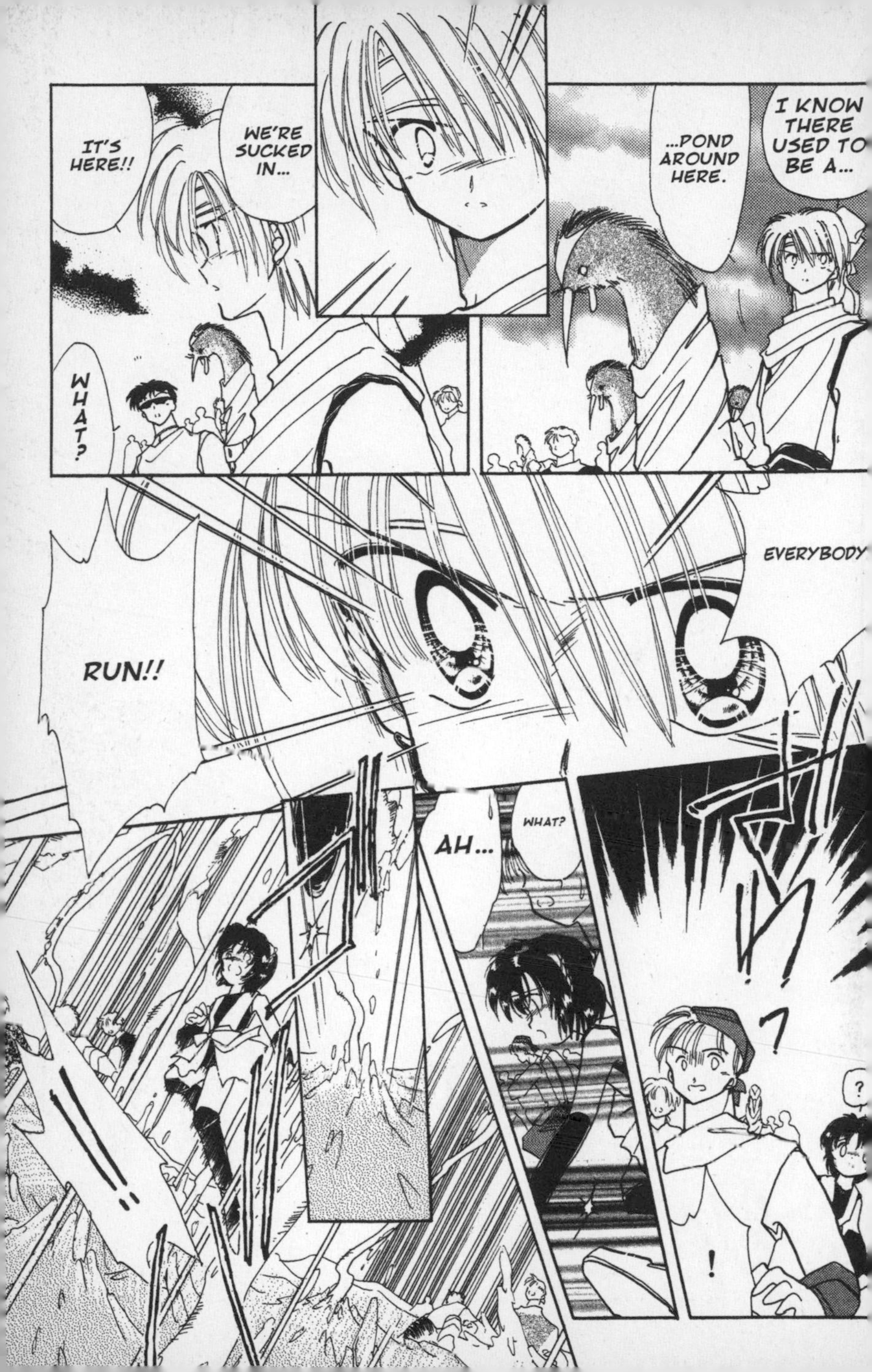
I KNOW THERE USED TO BE A...
...POND AROUND HERE.
WE'RE SUCKED IN...
IT'S HERE!!
WHAT?
EVERYBODY
RUN!!
?
?
!
WHAT?
AH...
!!

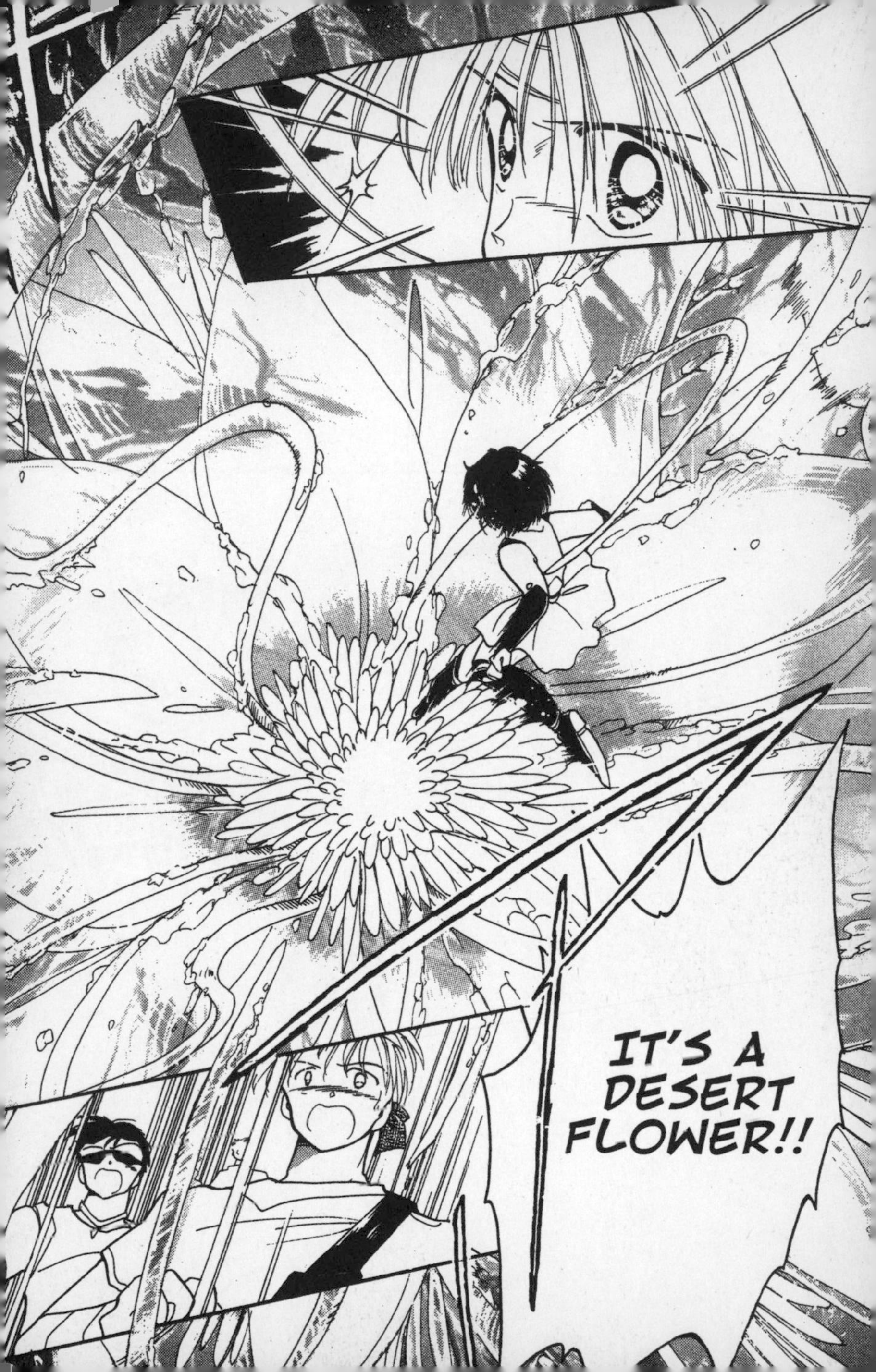
IT'S A DESERT FLOWER!!

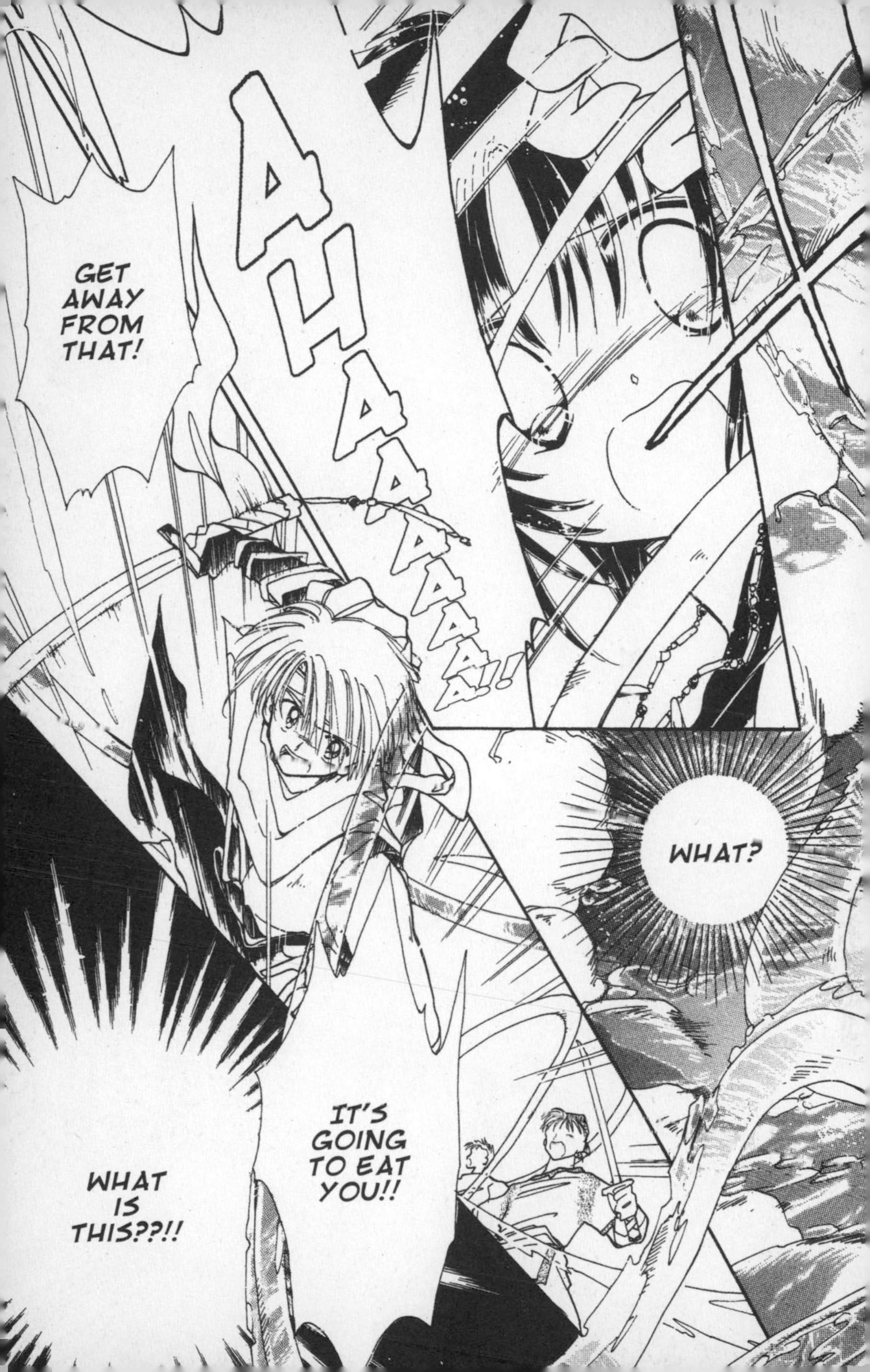
AHAAAAAAA!!
GET AWAY FROM THAT!
WHAT?
IT'S GOING TO EAT YOU!!
WHAT IS THIS??!!

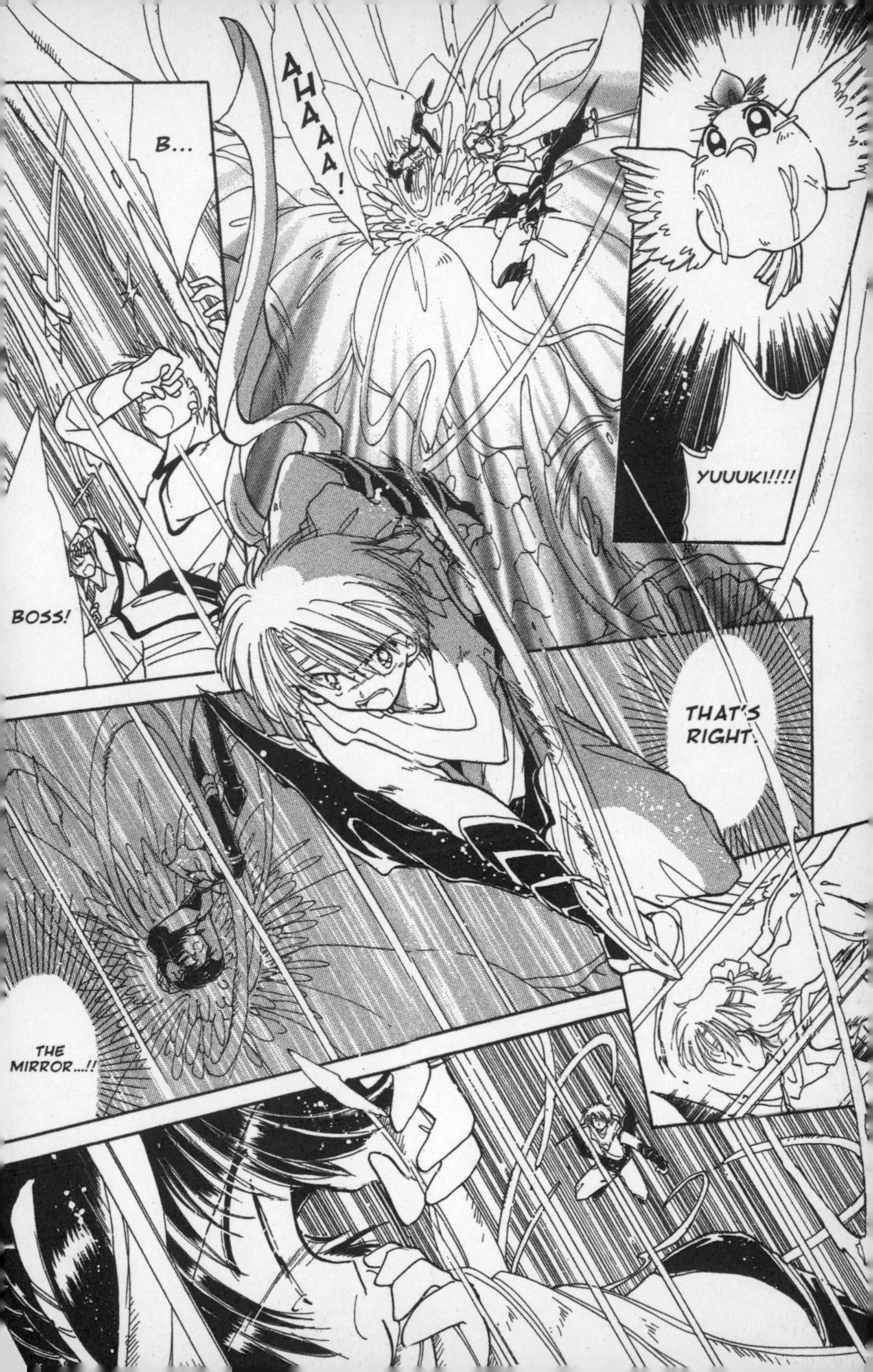
YUUUKI!!!!
AHAAAA!
B...
BOSS!
THAT'S RIGHT.
THE MIRROR...!!

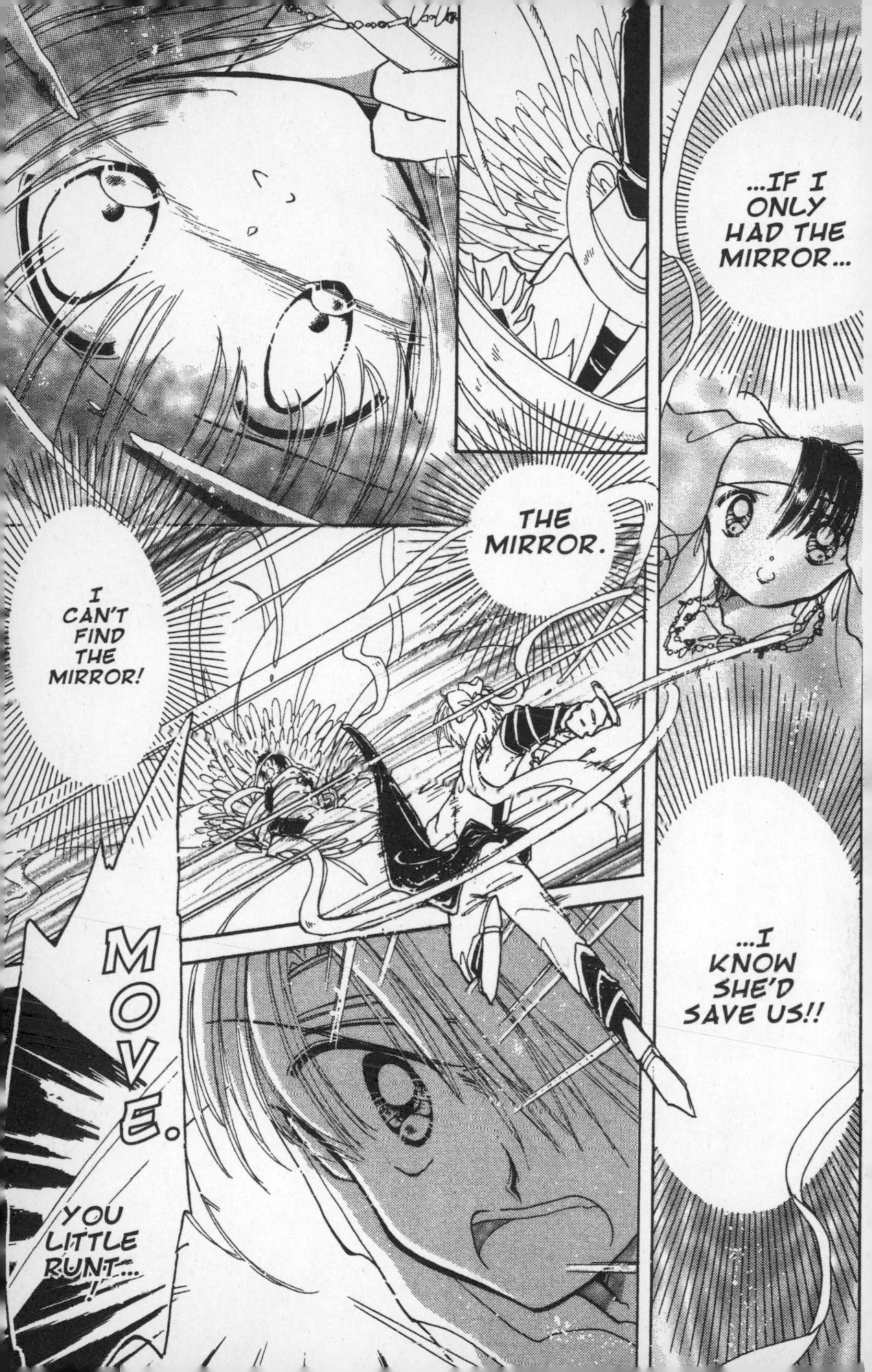
...IF I ONLY HAD THE MIRROR...
...I KNOW SHE'D SAVE US!!
THE MIRROR.
I CAN'T FIND THE MIRROR!
MOVE.
YOU LITTLE RUNT...!!

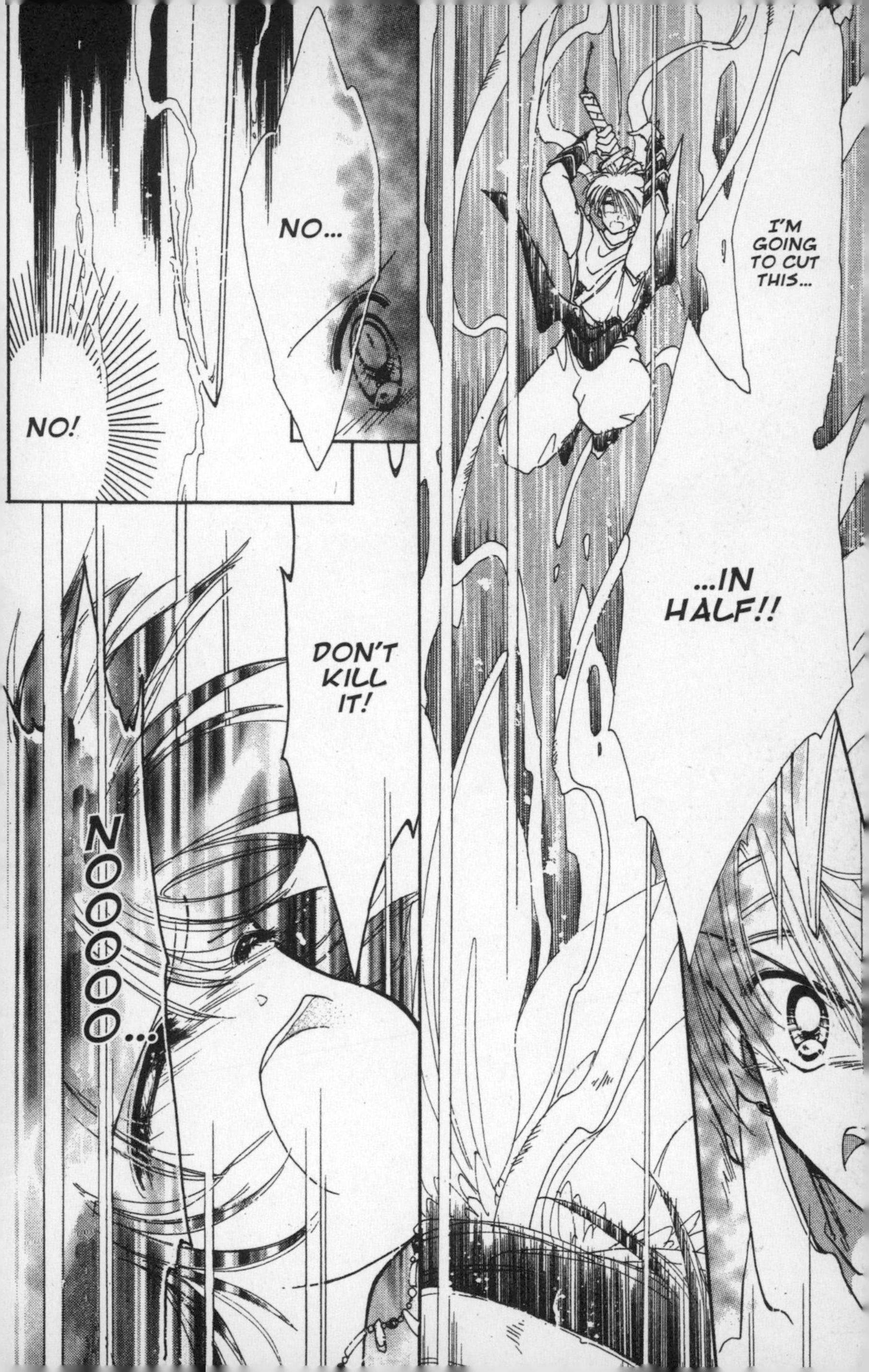
I'M GOING TO CUT THIS...
...IN HALF!!
NO...
NO!
DON'T KILL IT!
NOOOOOO...

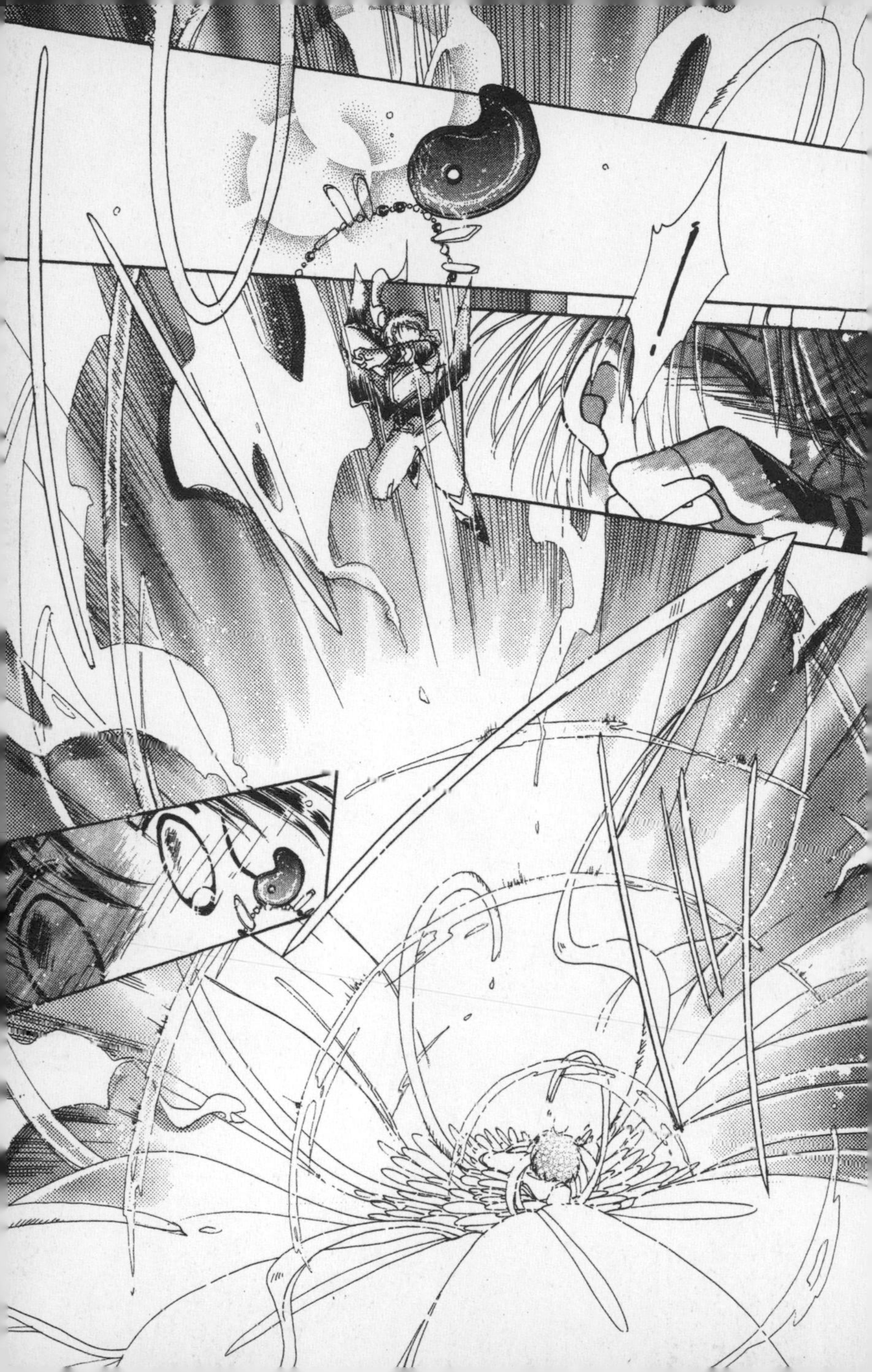
!

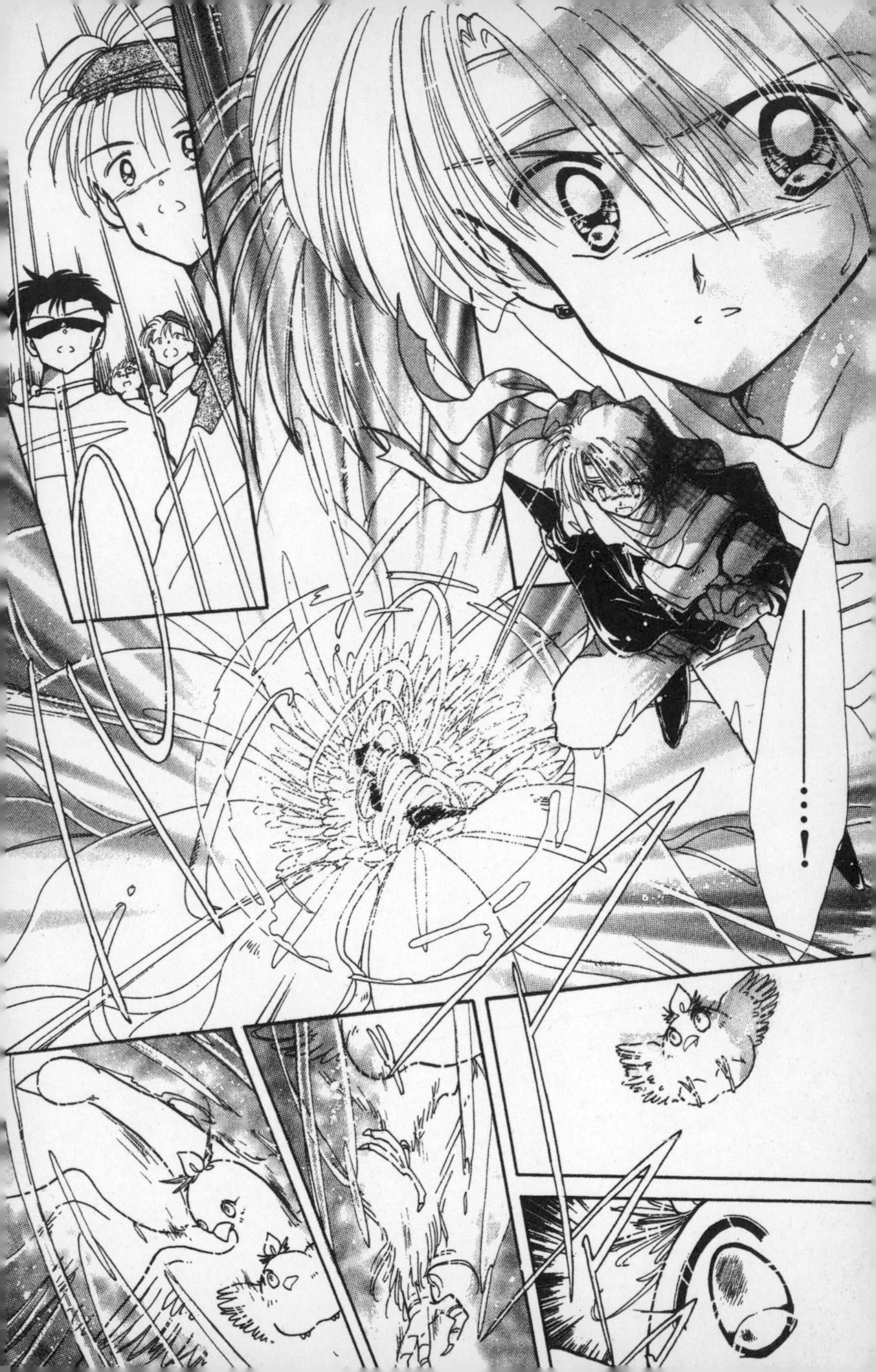
...!

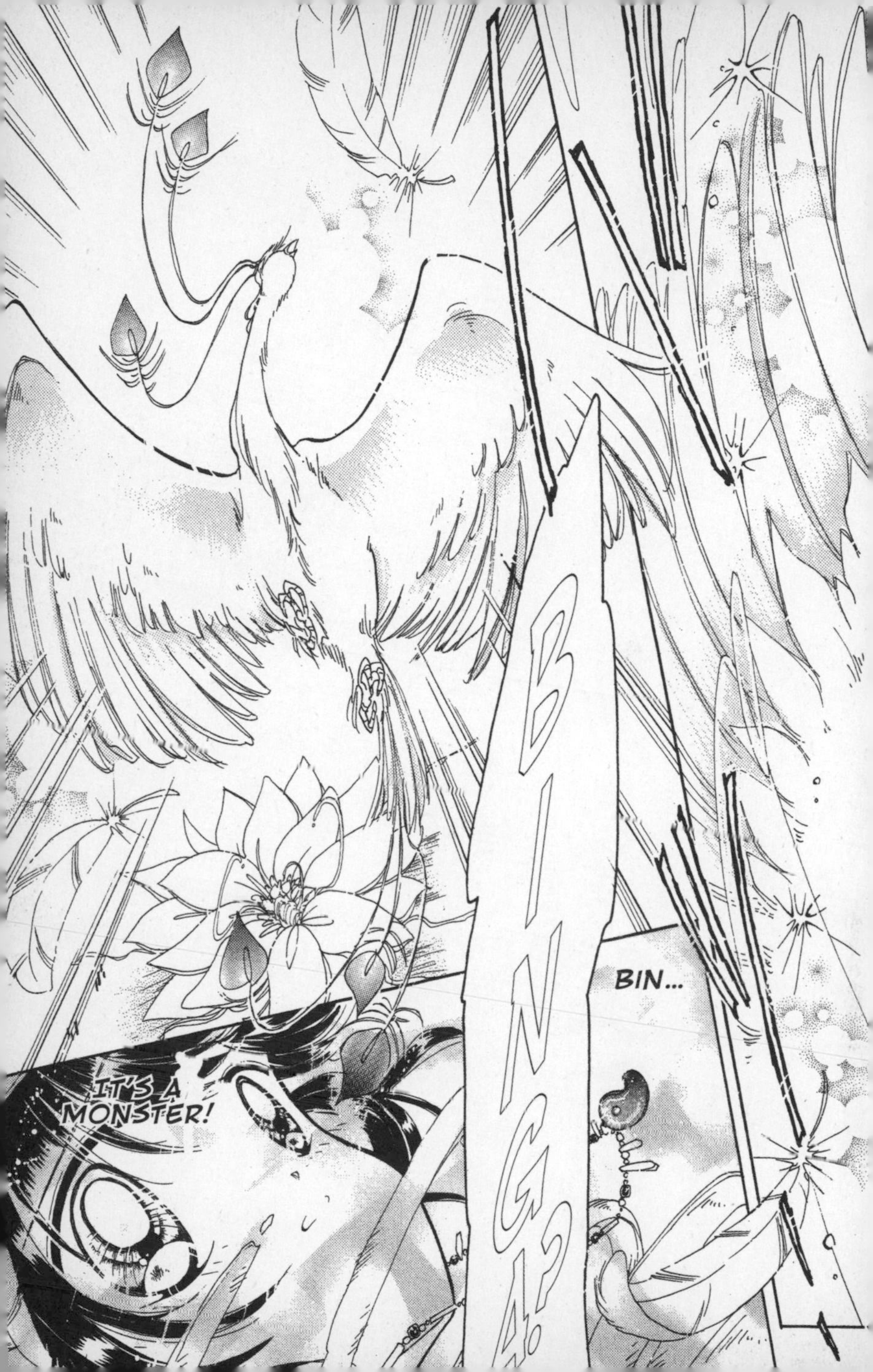
BIN...
BINGA!?
IT'S A MONSTER!

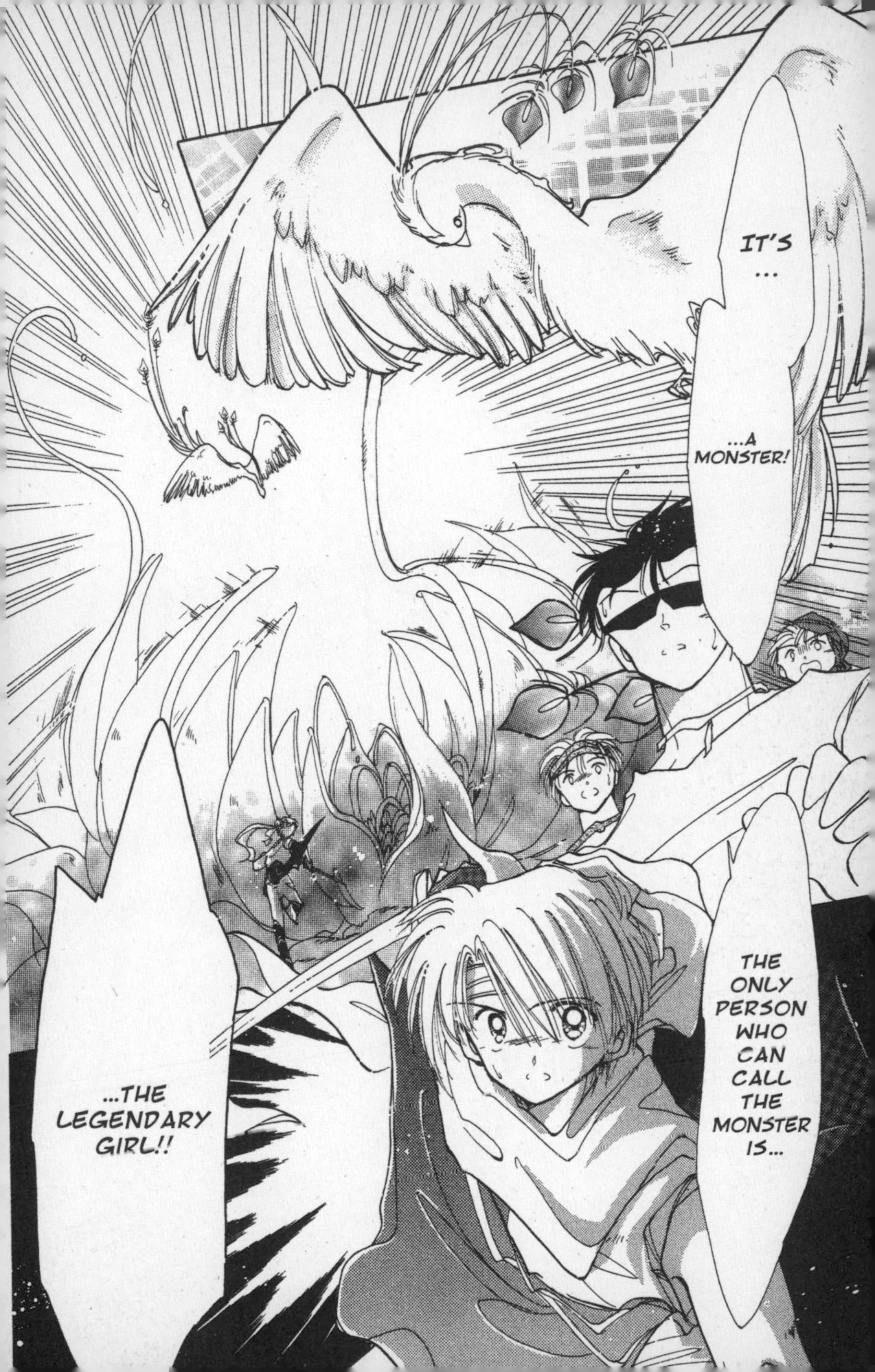
IT'S ...
...A MONSTER!
THE ONLY PERSON WHO CAN CALL THE MONSTER IS...
...THE LEGENDARY GIRL!!

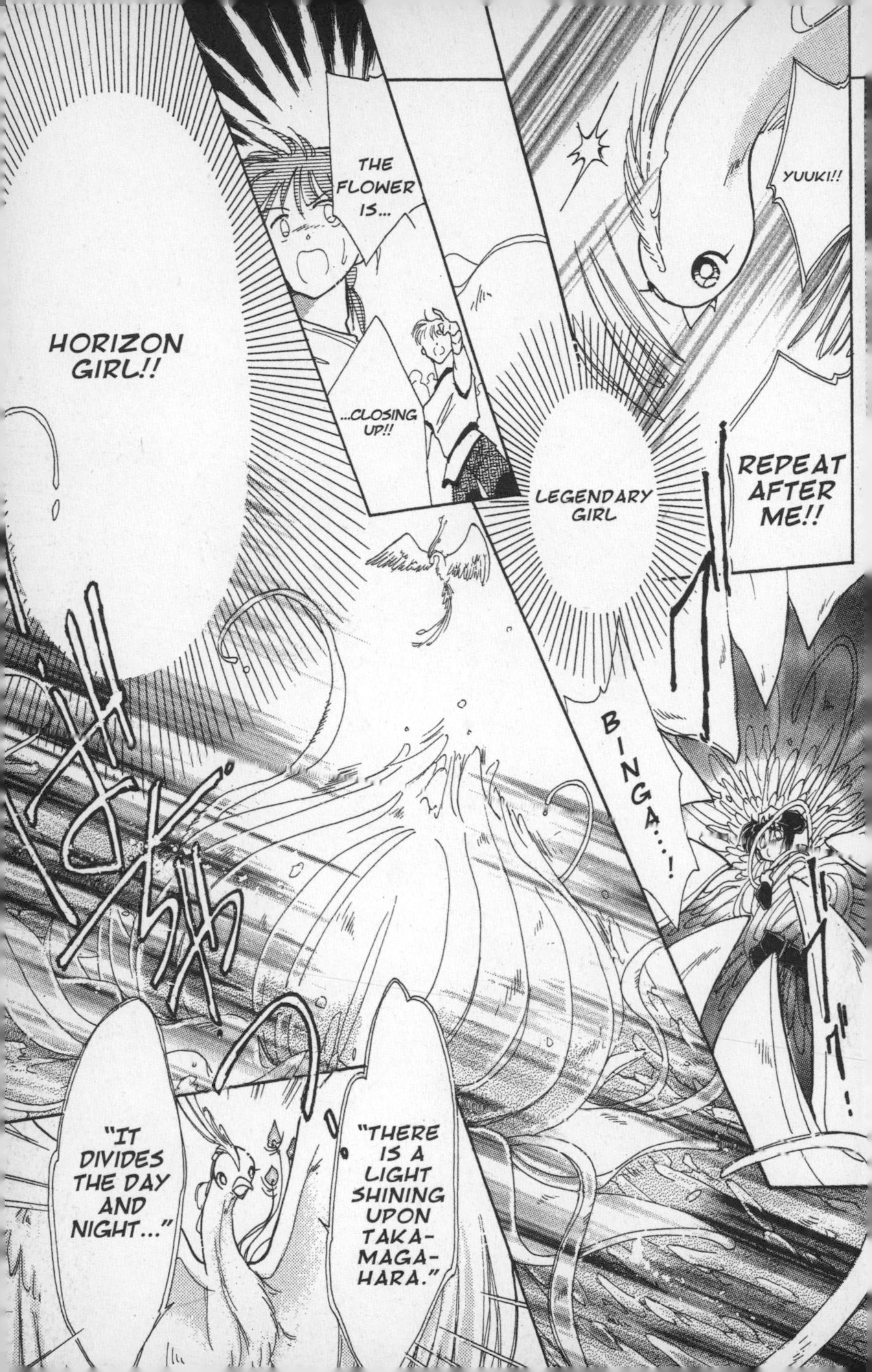
YUUKI!!
THE FLOWER IS...
...CLOSING UP!!
REPEAT AFTER ME!!
LEGENDARY GIRL
BINGA...!
HORIZON GIRL!!
"THERE IS A LIGHT SHINING UPON TAKA-MAGA-HARA."
"IT DIVIDES THE DAY AND NIGHT..."

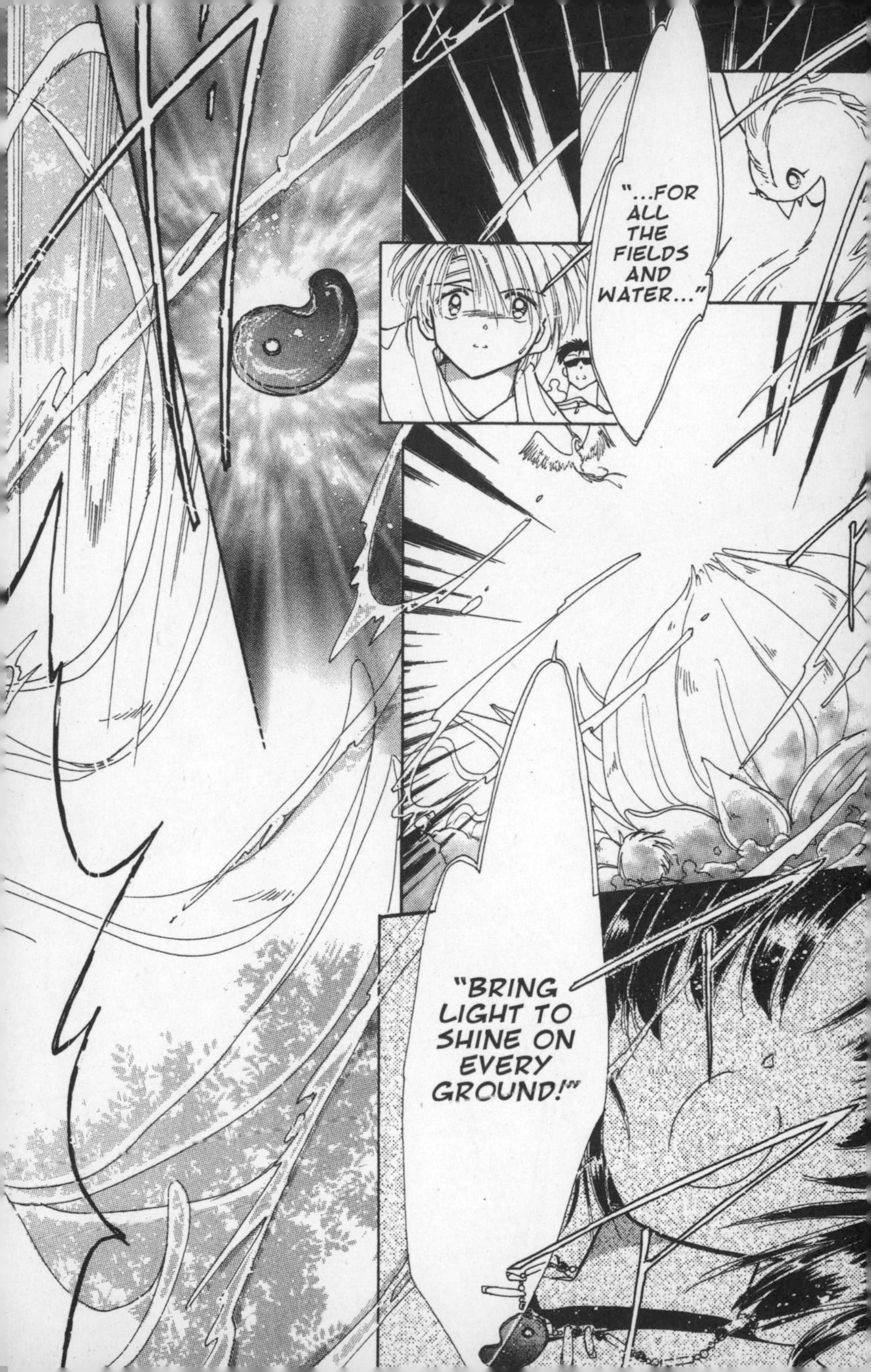
"...FOR ALL THE FIELDS AND WATER..."
"BRING LIGHT TO SHINE ON EVERY GROUND!"

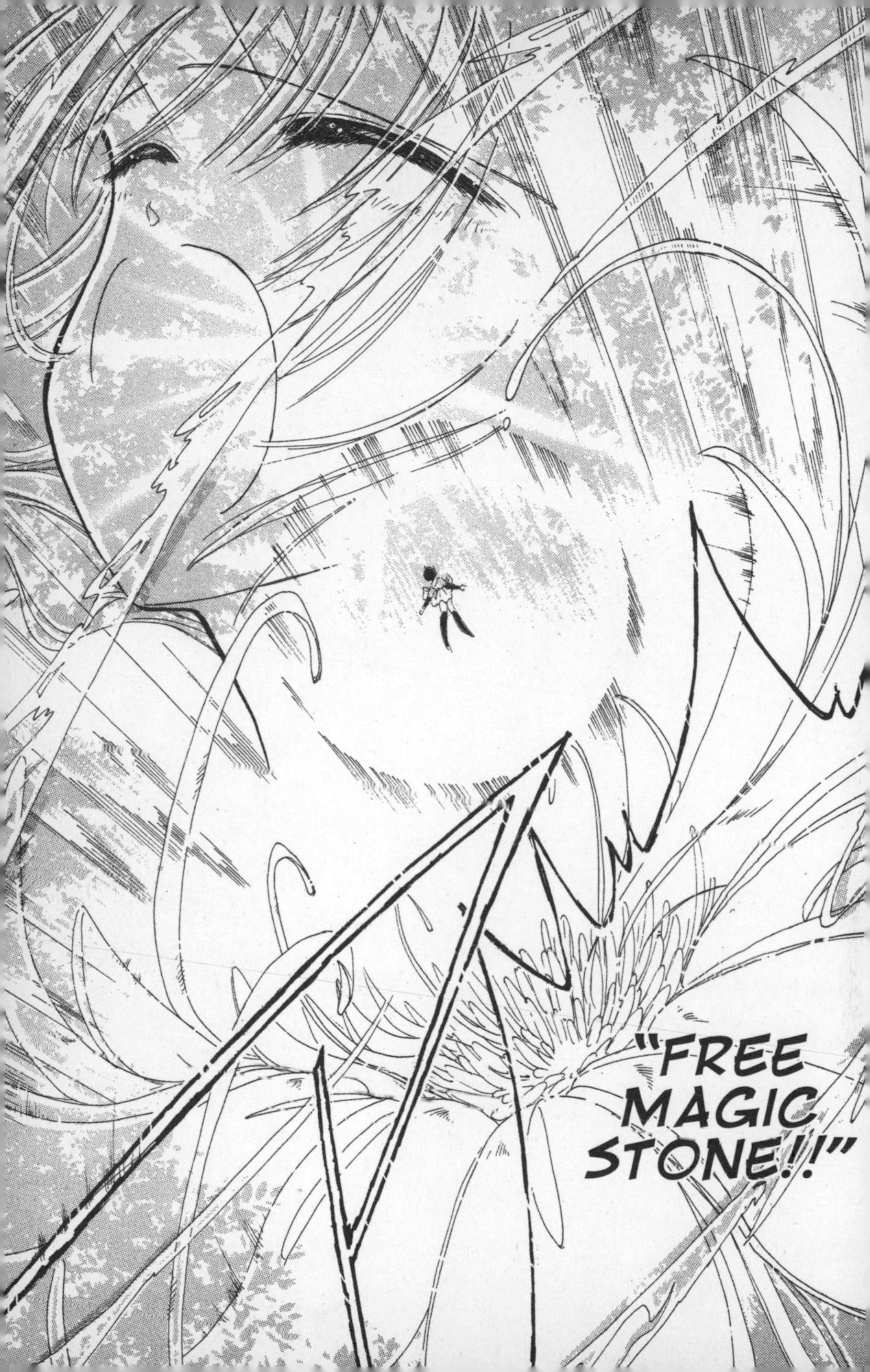
"FREE MAGIC STONE!!"

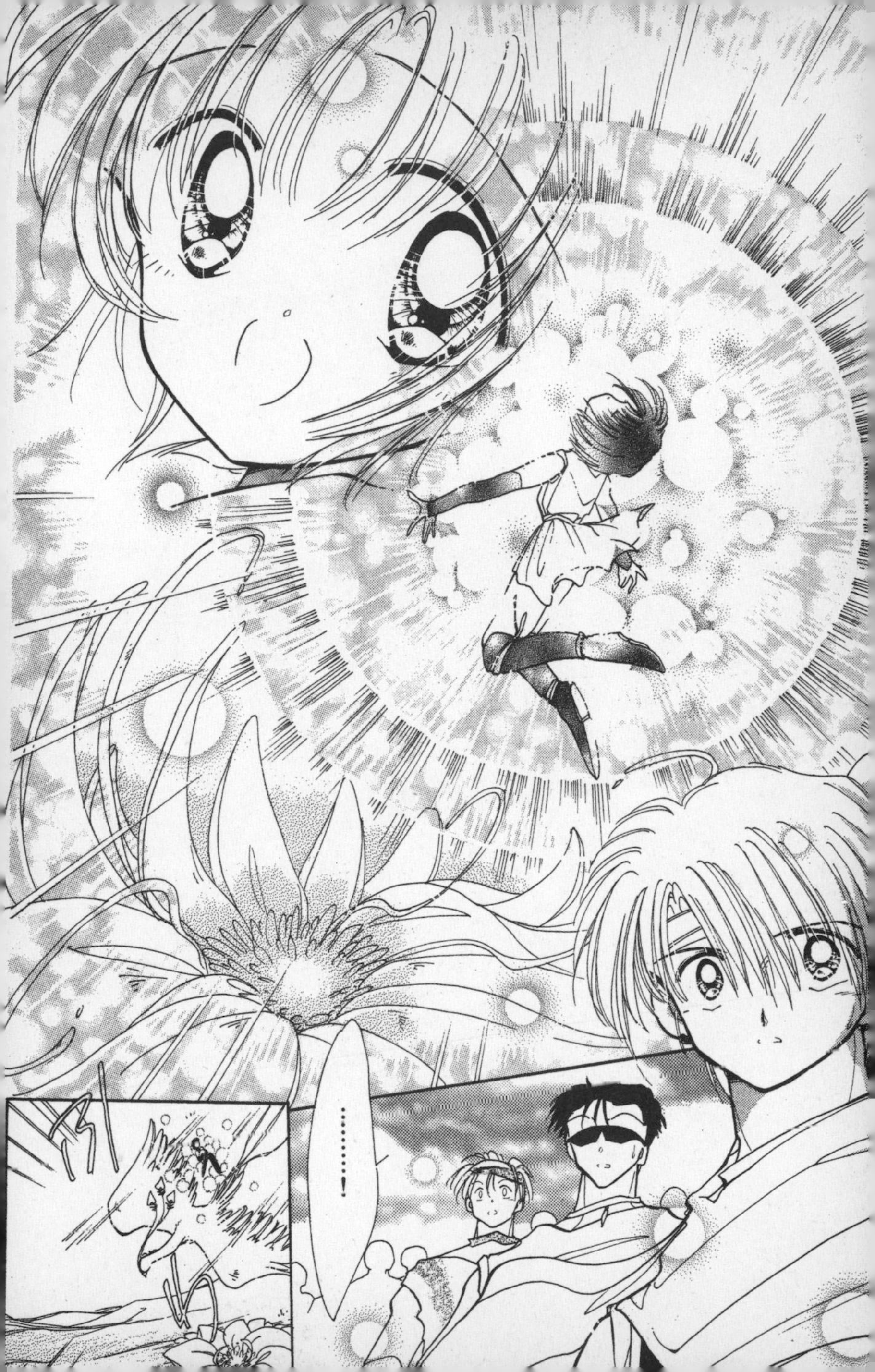
........!

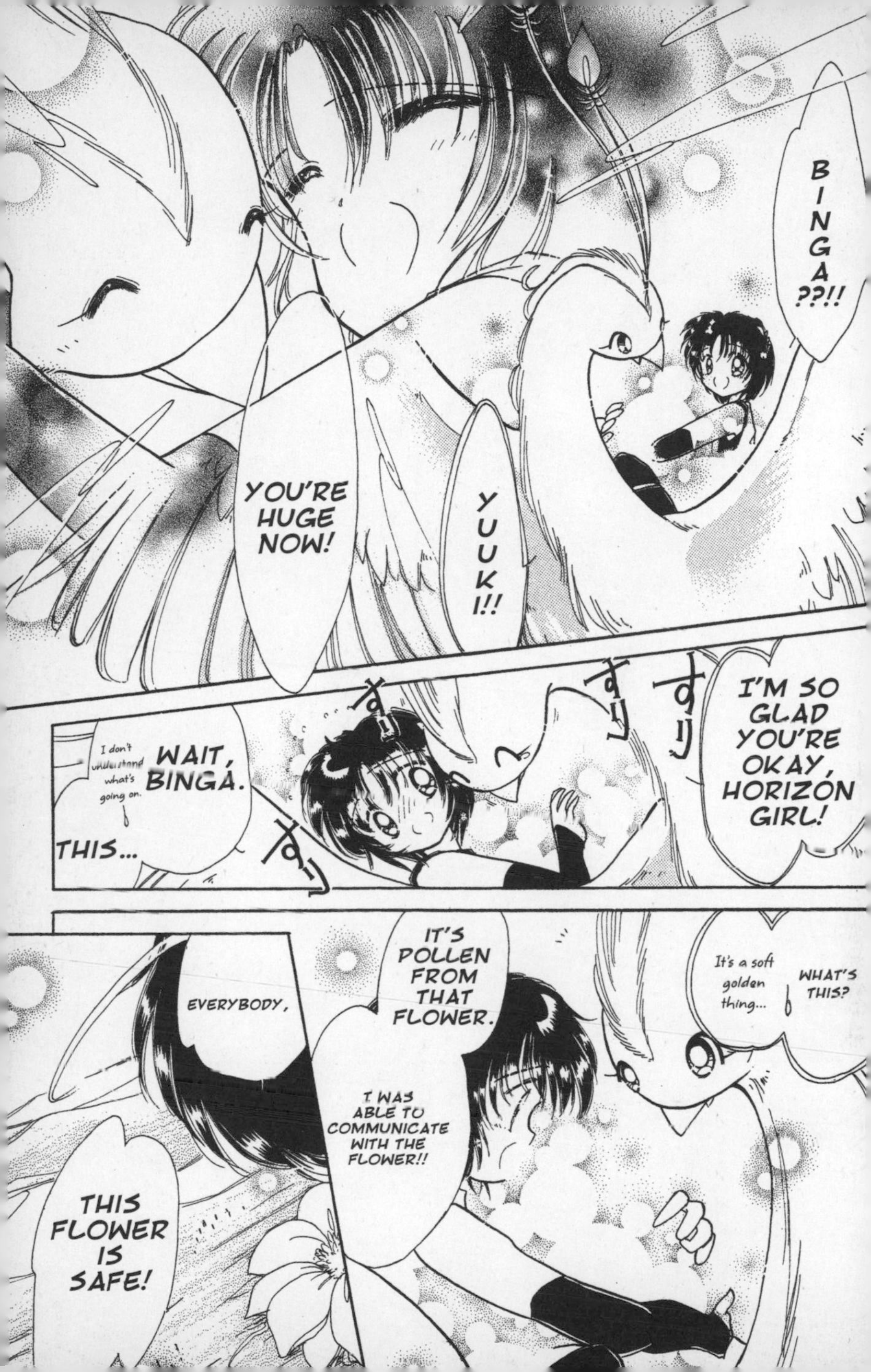

BINGA??!!
YUUKI!!
YOU'RE HUGE NOW!
I'M SO GLAD YOU'RE OKAY, HORIZON GIRL!
すり すり
WAIT, BINGA.
I don't understand what's going on.
THIS...
WHAT'S THIS?
It's a soft golden thing...
IT'S POLLEN FROM THAT FLOWER.
EVERYBODY,
I WAS ABLE TO COMMUNICATE WITH THE FLOWER!!
THIS FLOWER IS SAFE!

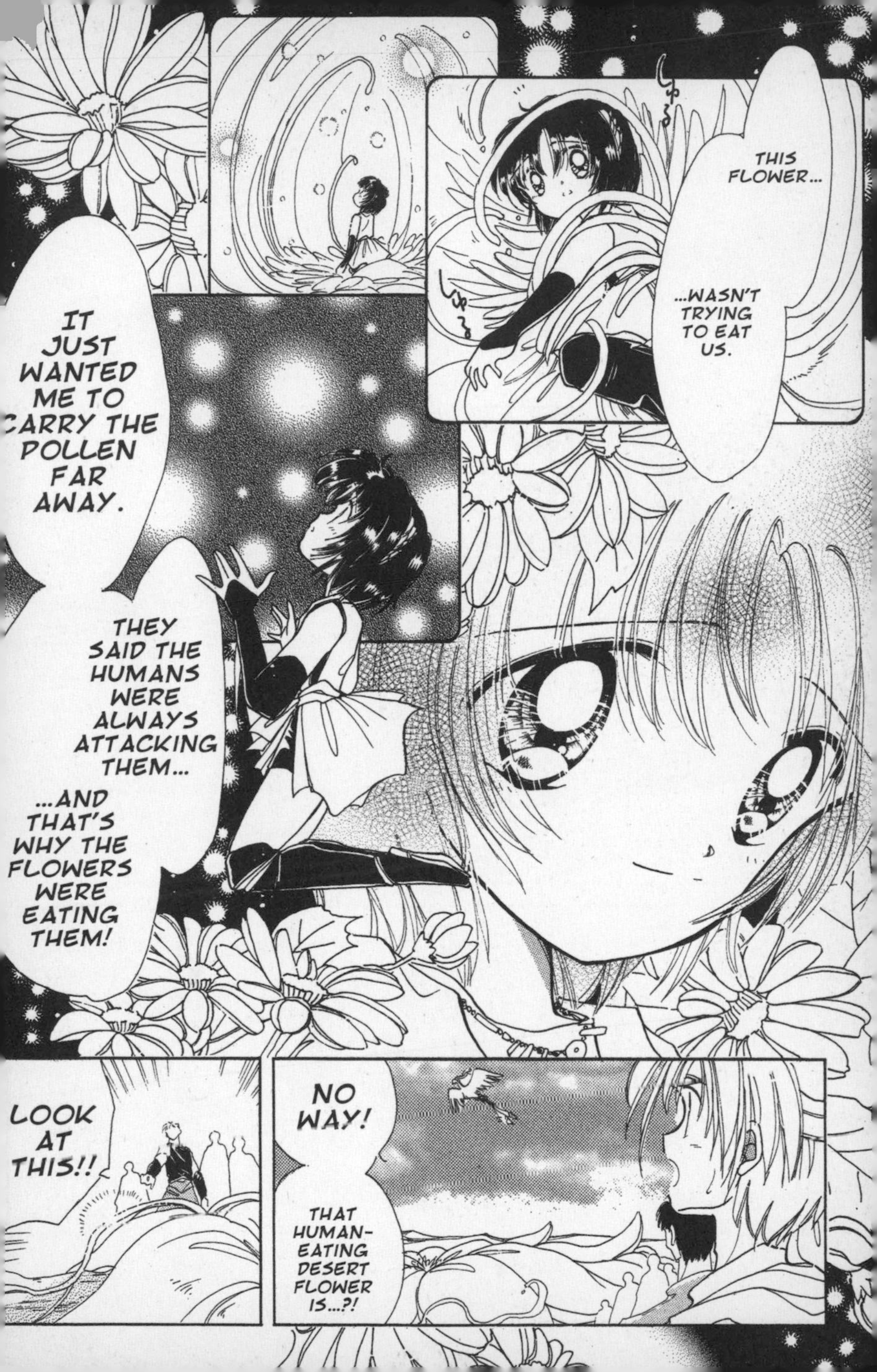

THIS FLOWER...
...WASN'T TRYING TO EAT US.
IT JUST WANTED ME TO CARRY THE POLLEN FAR AWAY.
THEY SAID THE HUMANS WERE ALWAYS ATTACKING THEM...
...AND THAT'S WHY THE FLOWERS WERE EATING THEM!
NO WAY!
THAT HUMAN-EATING DESERT FLOWER IS...?!
LOOK AT THIS!!

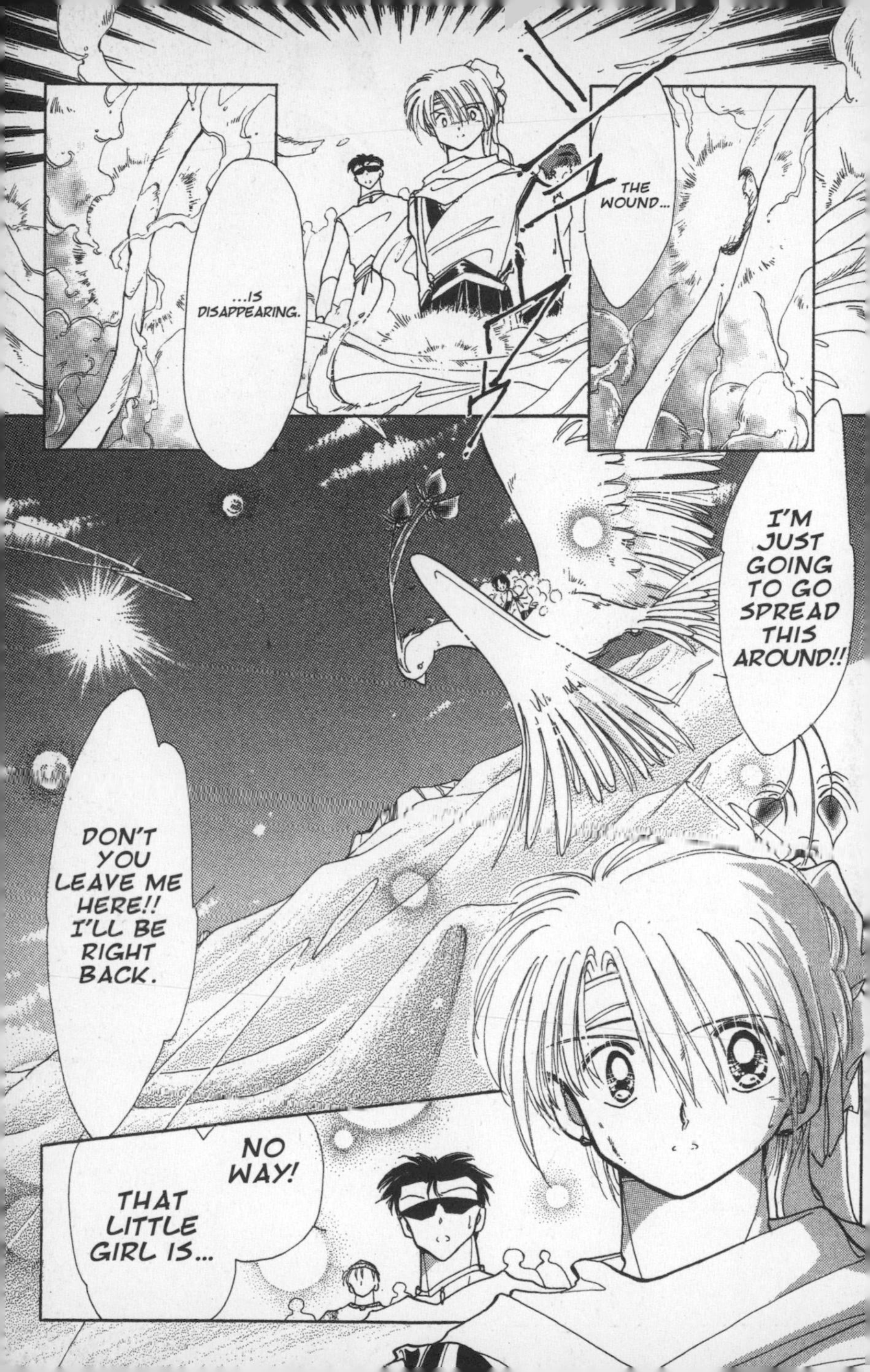
THE WOUND...
...IS DISAPPEARING.
I'M JUST GOING TO GO SPREAD THIS AROUND!!
DON'T YOU LEAVE ME HERE!! I'LL BE RIGHT BACK.
NO WAY!
THAT LITTLE GIRL IS...

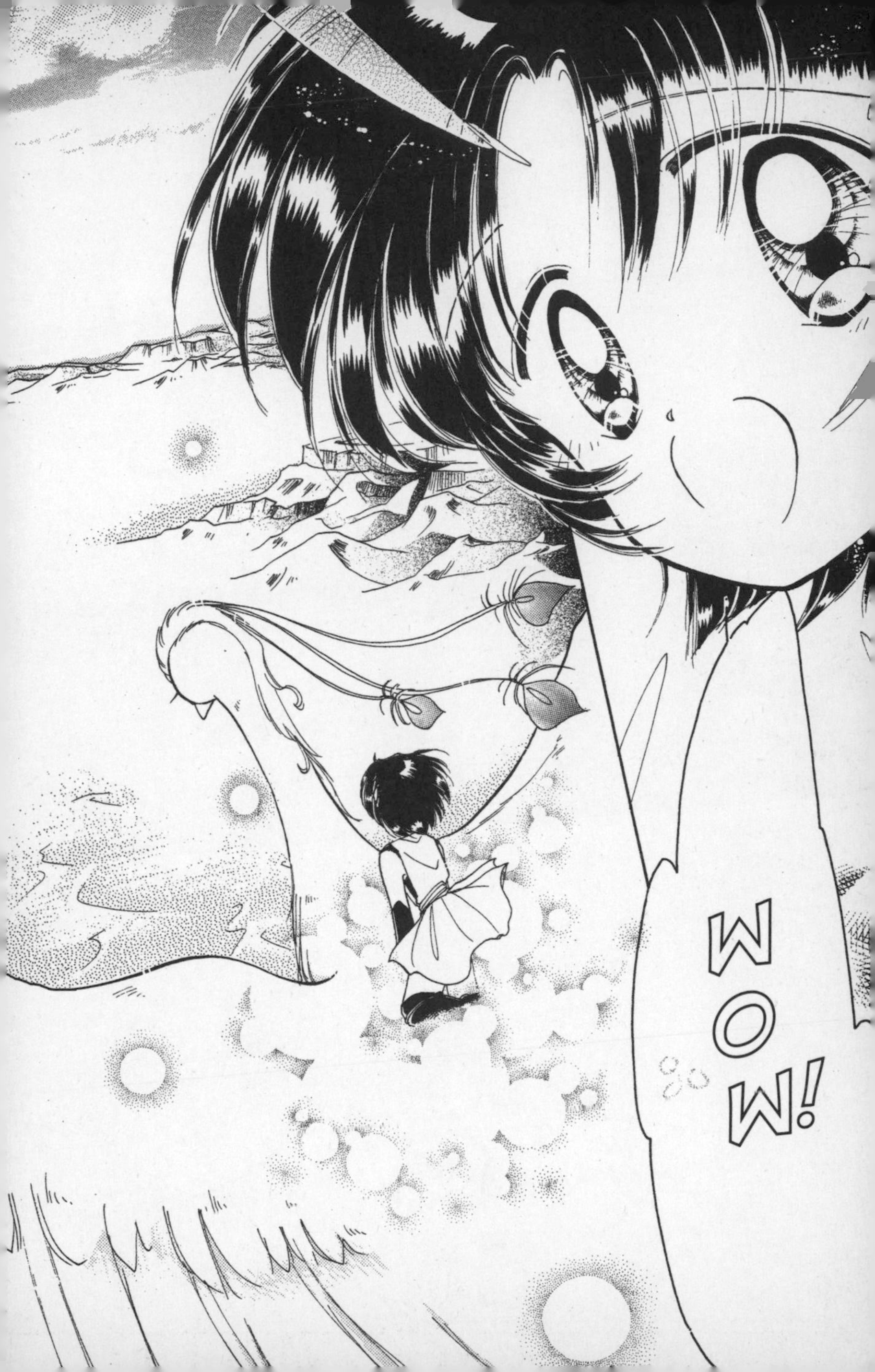
WOW!

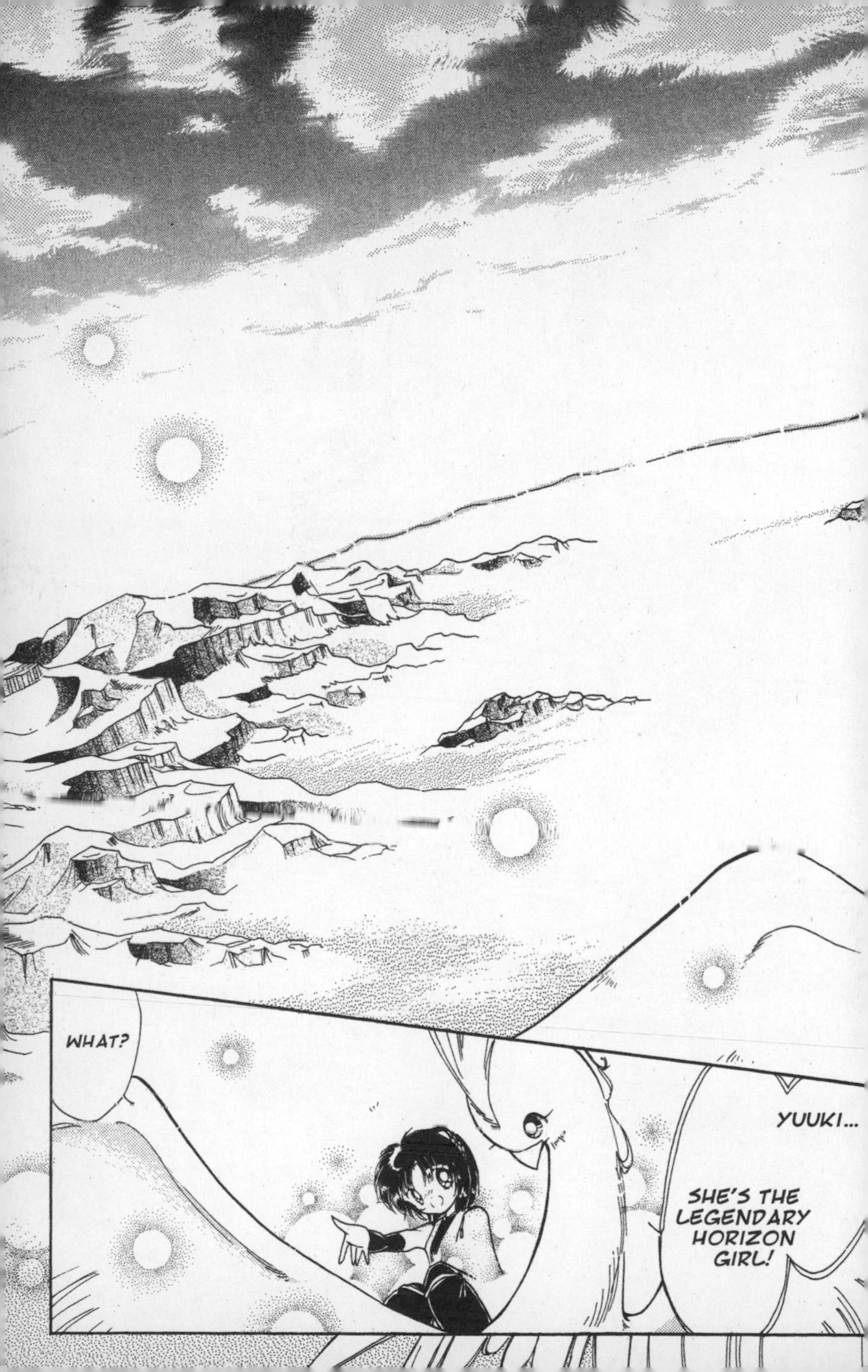
YUUKI...
SHE'S THE LEGENDARY HORIZON GIRL!
WHAT?

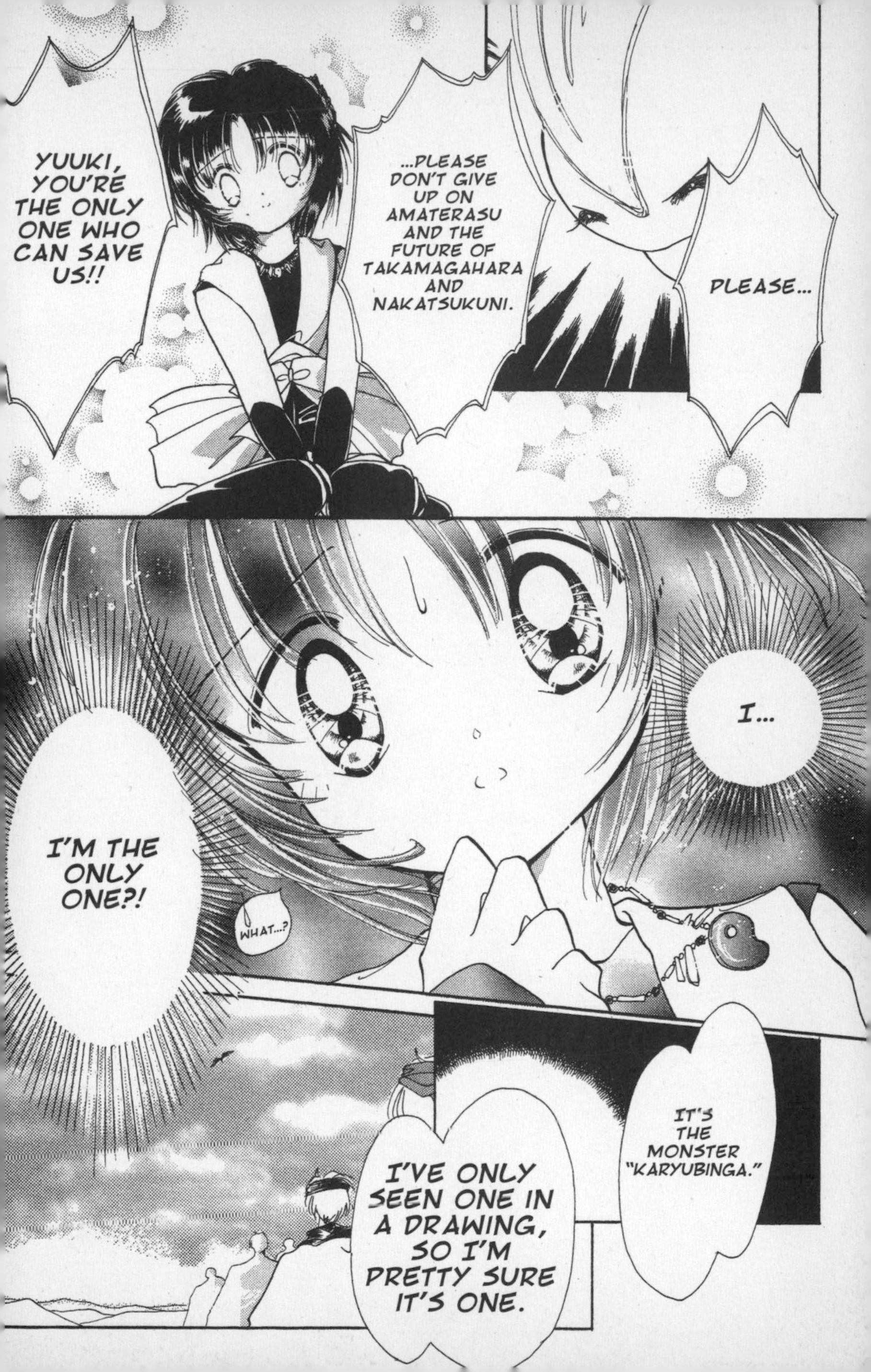
PLEASE...
...PLEASE DON'T GIVE UP ON AMATERASU AND THE FUTURE OF TAKAMAGAHARA AND NAKATSUKUNI.
YUUKI, YOU'RE THE ONLY ONE WHO CAN SAVE US!!
I...
I'M THE ONLY ONE?!
WHAT...?
IT'S THE MONSTER "KARYUBINGA."
I'VE ONLY SEEN ONE IN A DRAWING, SO I'M PRETTY SURE IT'S ONE.

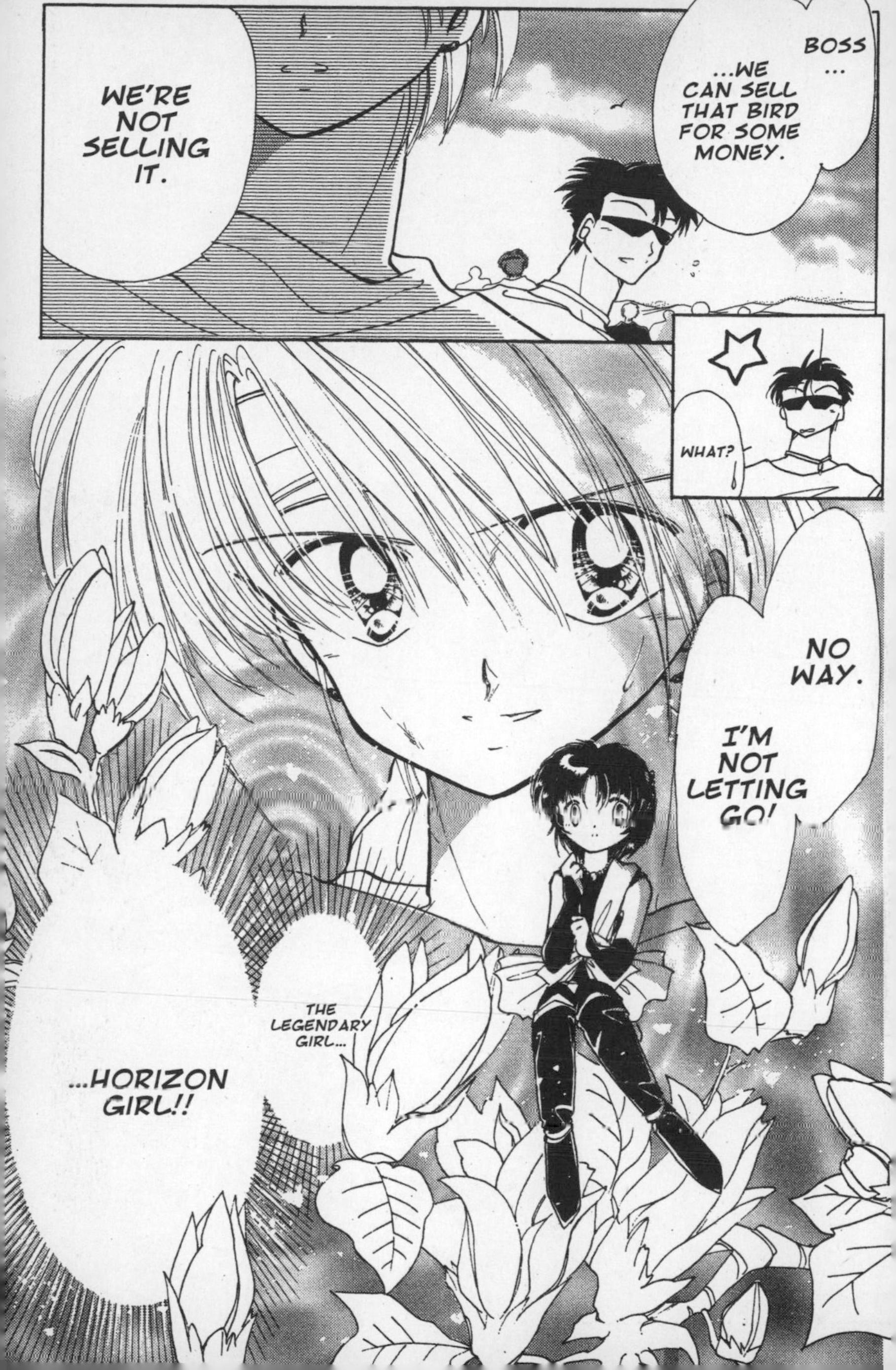
BOSS ...
...WE CAN SELL THAT BIRD FOR SOME MONEY.
WE'RE NOT SELLING IT.
WHAT?
NO WAY.
I'M NOT LETTING GO!
THE LEGENDARY GIRL...
...HORIZON GIRL!!

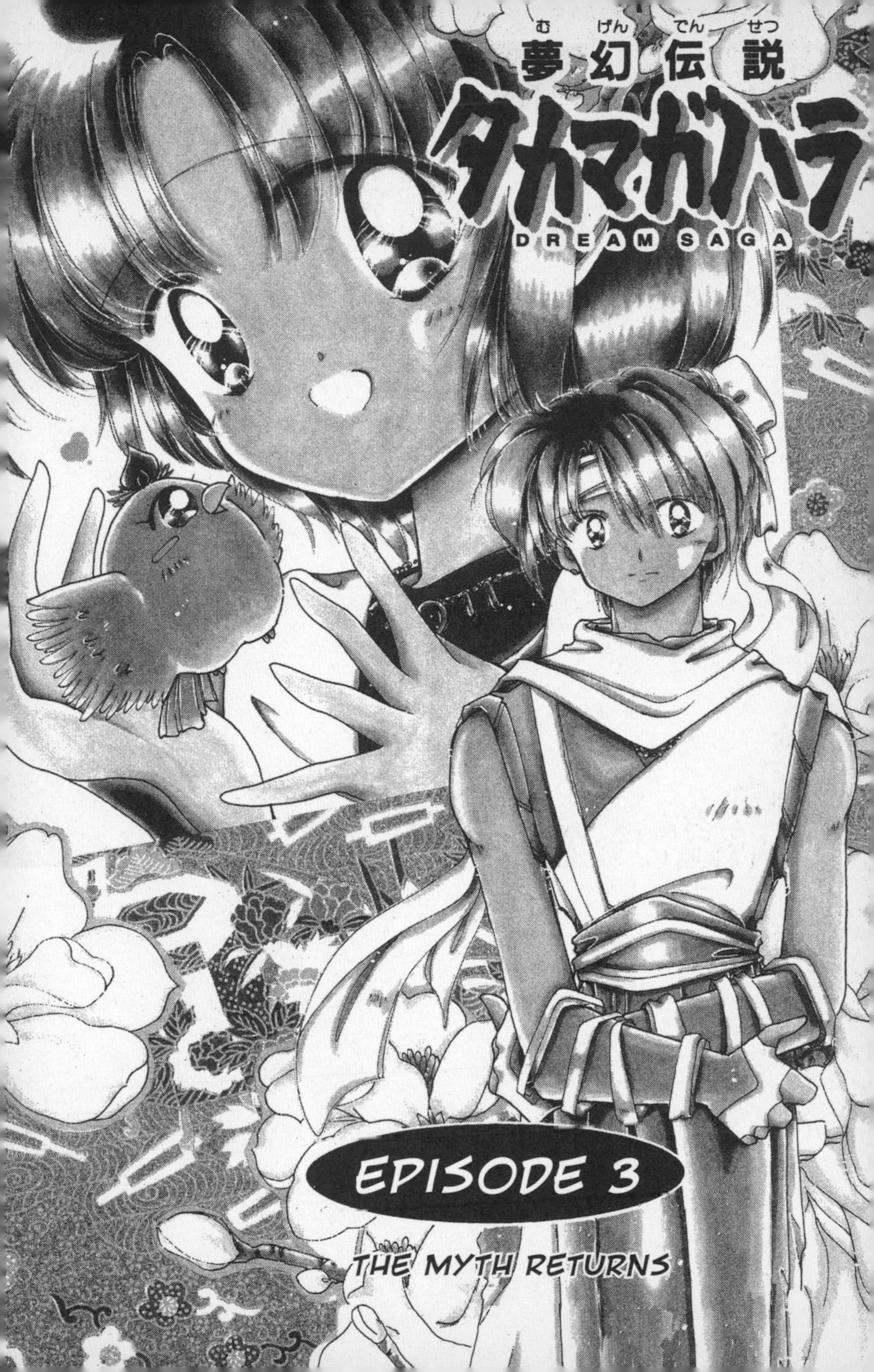

夢幻伝説
むげんでんせつ
タカマガハラ
DREAM SAGA
EPISODE 3
THE MYTH RETURNS

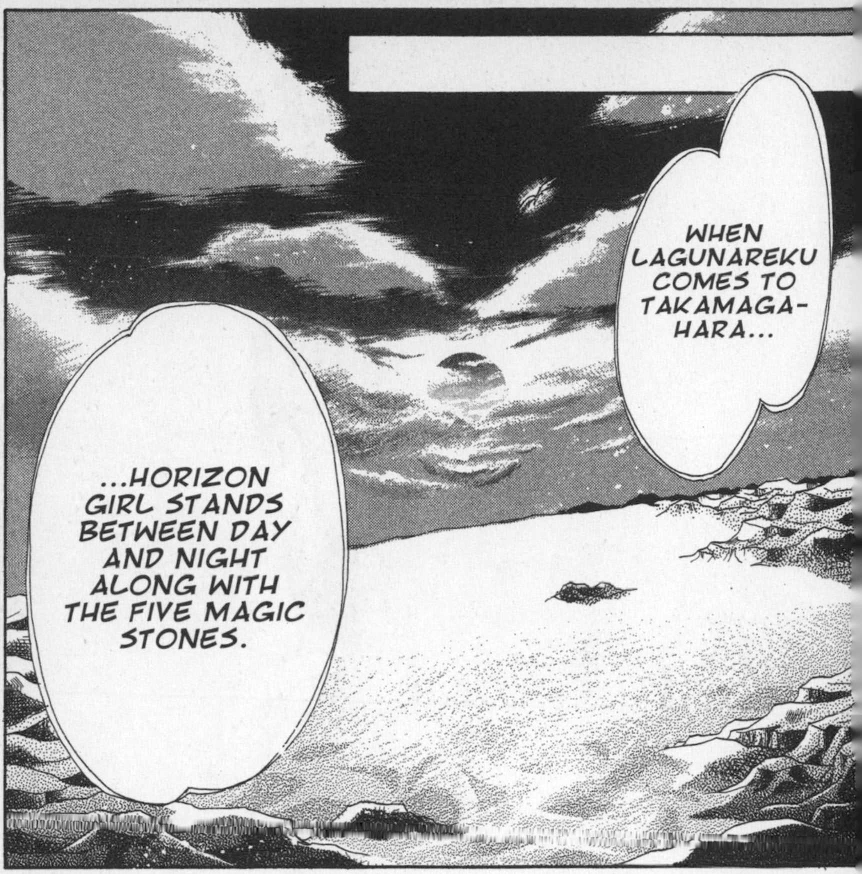
WHEN LAGUNAREKU COMES TO TAKAMAGA-HARA...
...HORIZON GIRL STANDS BETWEEN DAY AND NIGHT ALONG WITH THE FIVE MAGIC STONES.

Question: Is there a "Karyubinga" bird in real life?

Answer: It is a legendary, imaginary bird in India. So, no, it doesn't exist in real life. I heard that the Chinese Phoenix came from Karyubinga. I wish they existed in real life too.

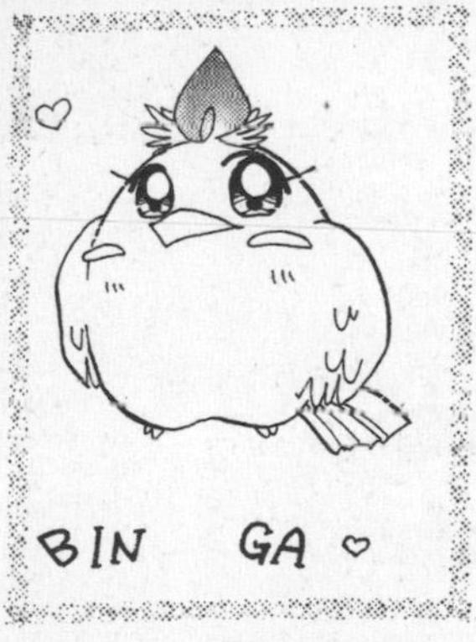
BIN GA

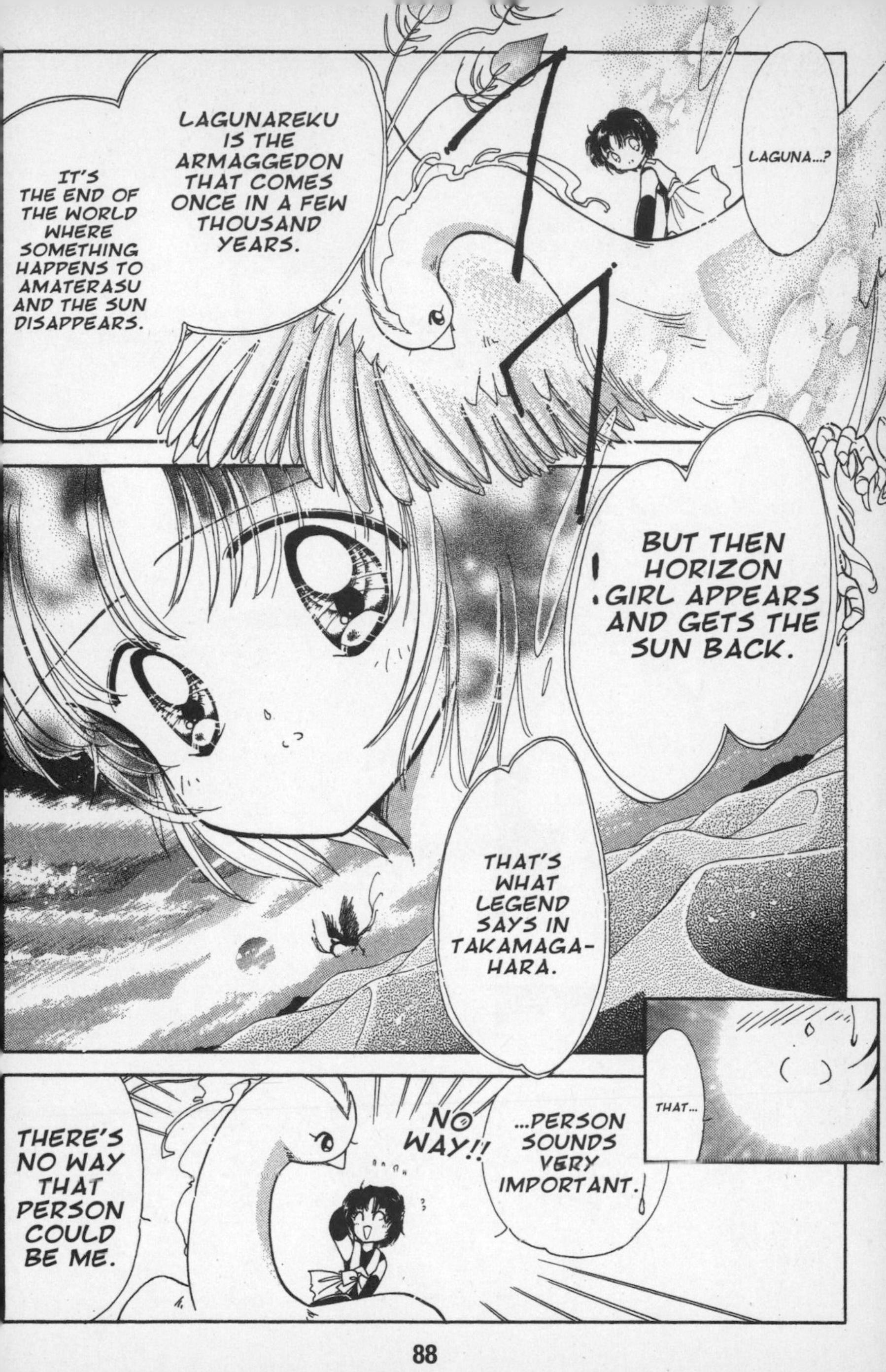
LAGUNA...?
LAGUNAREKU IS THE ARMAGGEDON THAT COMES ONCE IN A FEW THOUSAND YEARS.
IT'S THE END OF THE WORLD WHERE SOMETHING HAPPENS TO AMATERASU AND THE SUN DISAPPEARS.
BUT THEN HORIZON GIRL APPEARS AND GETS THE SUN BACK.
THAT'S WHAT LEGEND SAYS IN TAKAMAGA-HARA.
THAT...
...PERSON SOUNDS VERY IMPORTANT.
NO WAY!!
THERE'S NO WAY THAT PERSON COULD BE ME.

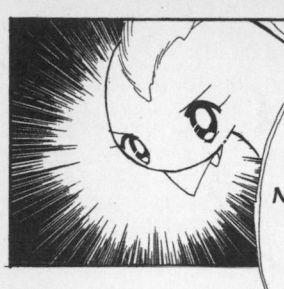

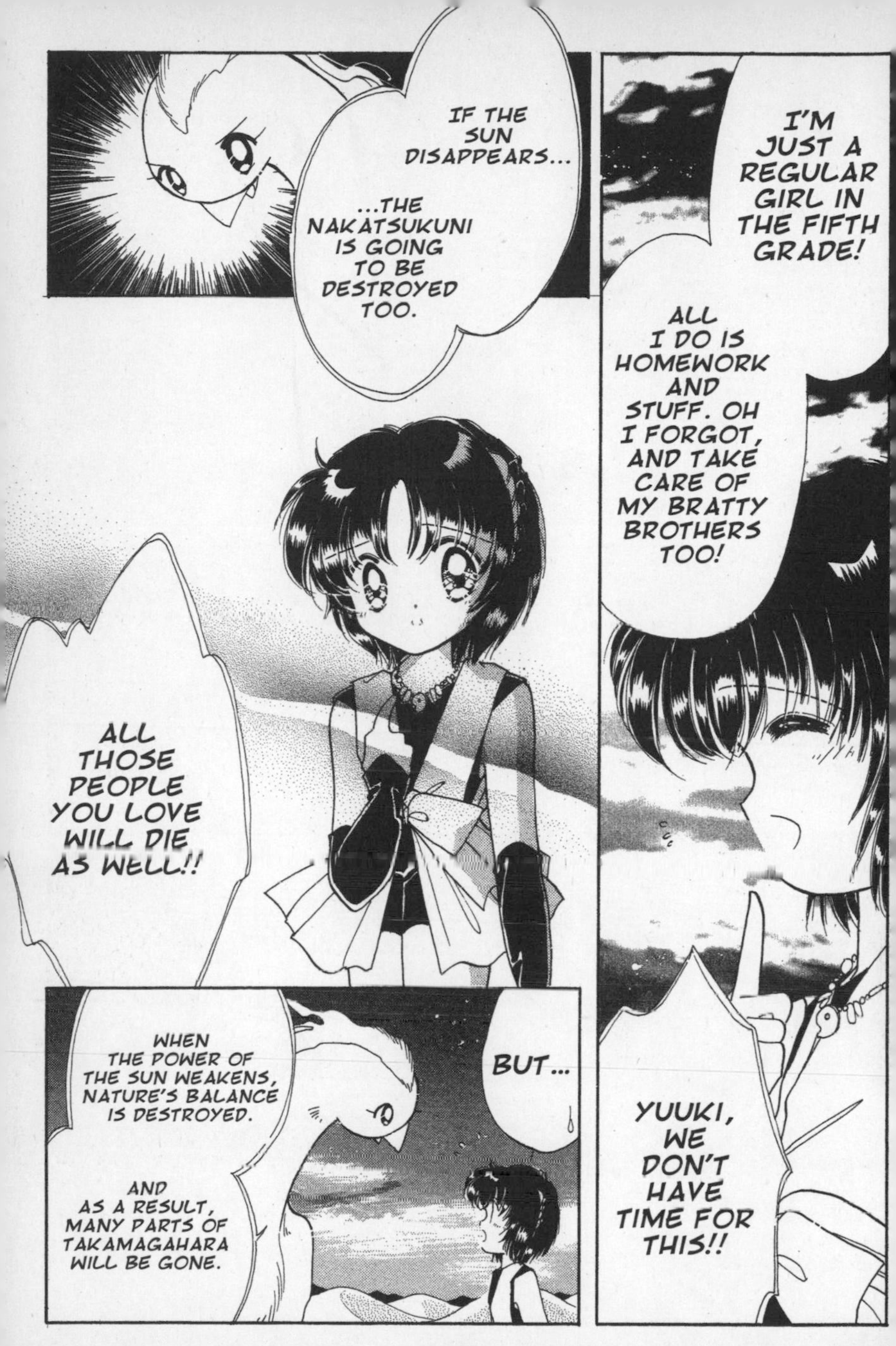

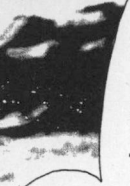

I'M JUST A REGULAR GIRL IN THE FIFTH GRADE!
ALL I DO IS HOMEWORK AND STUFF. OH I FORGOT, AND TAKE CARE OF MY BRATTY BROTHERS TOO!
IF THE SUN DISAPPEARS...
...THE NAKATSUKUNI IS GOING TO BE DESTROYED TOO.
ALL THOSE PEOPLE YOU LOVE WILL DIE AS WELL!!
YUUKI, WE DON'T HAVE TIME FOR THIS!!
BUT...
WHEN THE POWER OF THE SUN WEAKENS, NATURE'S BALANCE IS DESTROYED.
AND AS A RESULT, MANY PARTS OF TAKAMAGAHARA WILL BE GONE.

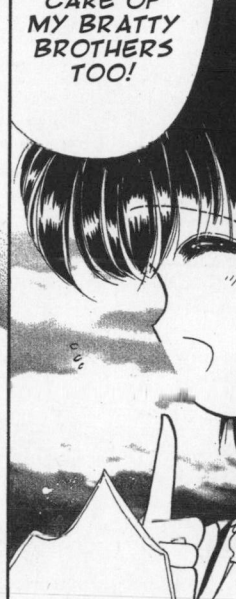

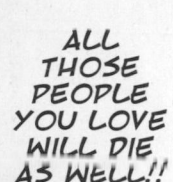

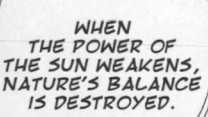

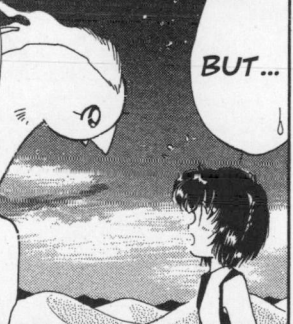

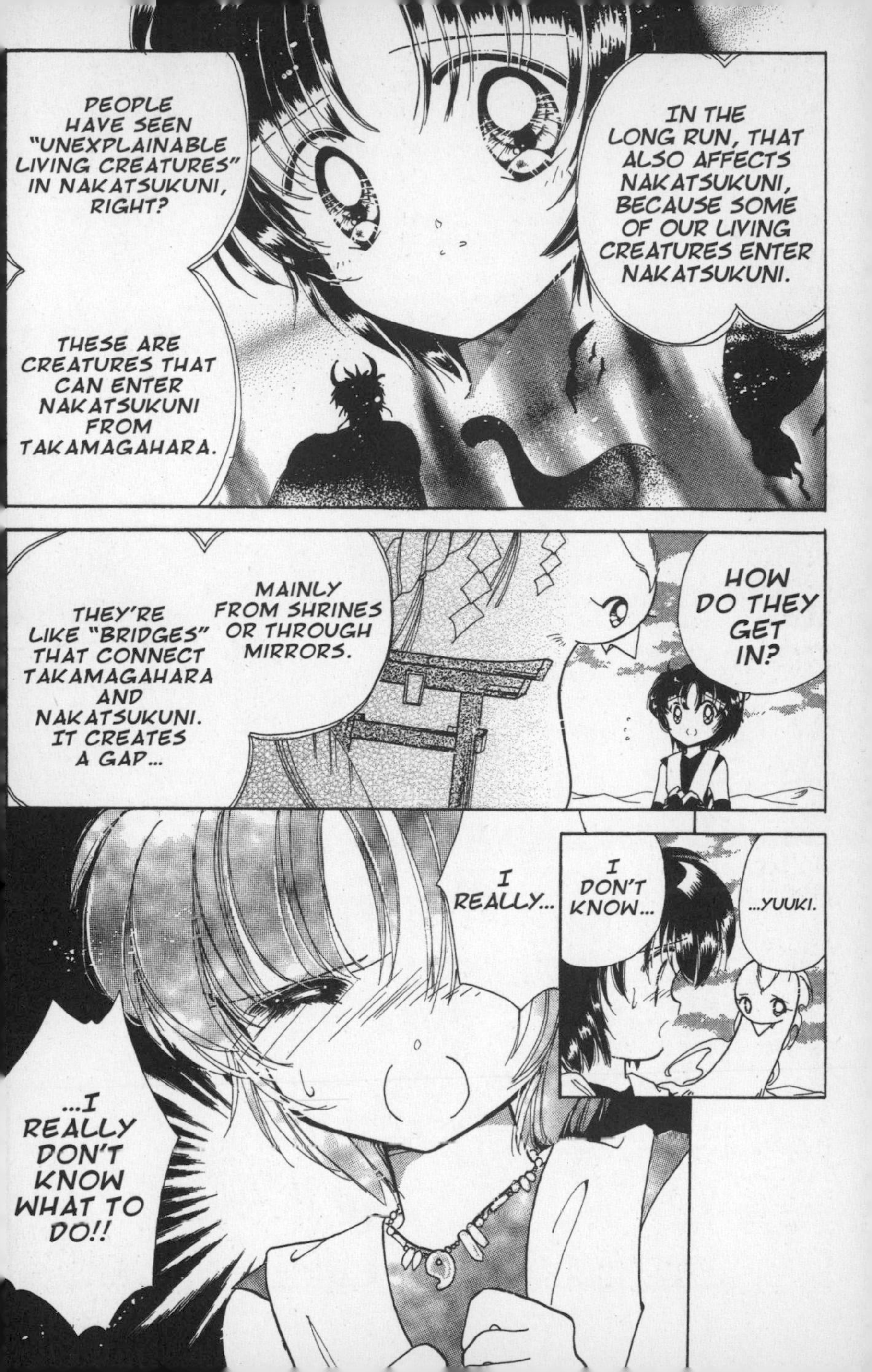
IN THE LONG RUN, THAT ALSO AFFECTS NAKATSUKUNI, BECAUSE SOME OF OUR LIVING CREATURES ENTER NAKATSUKUNI.
PEOPLE HAVE SEEN "UNEXPLAINABLE LIVING CREATURES" IN NAKATSUKUNI, RIGHT?
THESE ARE CREATURES THAT CAN ENTER NAKATSUKUNI FROM TAKAMAGAHARA.
HOW DO THEY GET IN?
MAINLY FROM SHRINES OR THROUGH MIRRORS.
THEY'RE LIKE "BRIDGES" THAT CONNECT TAKAMAGAHARA AND NAKATSUKUNI. IT CREATES A GAP...
...YUUKI.
I DON'T KNOW...
I REALLY...
...I REALLY DON'T KNOW WHAT TO DO!!

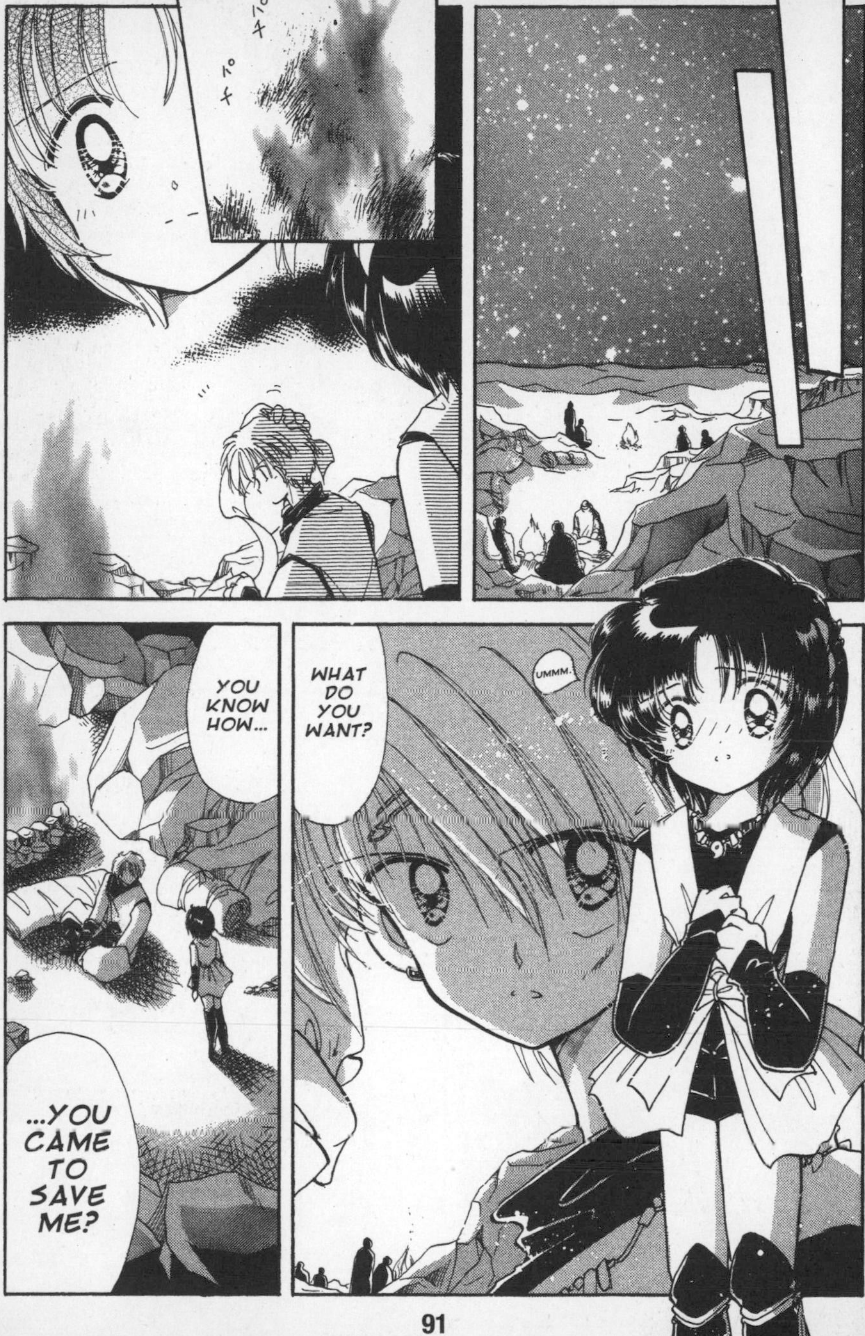
UMMM.
WHAT DO YOU WANT?
YOU KNOW HOW...
...YOU CAME TO SAVE ME?

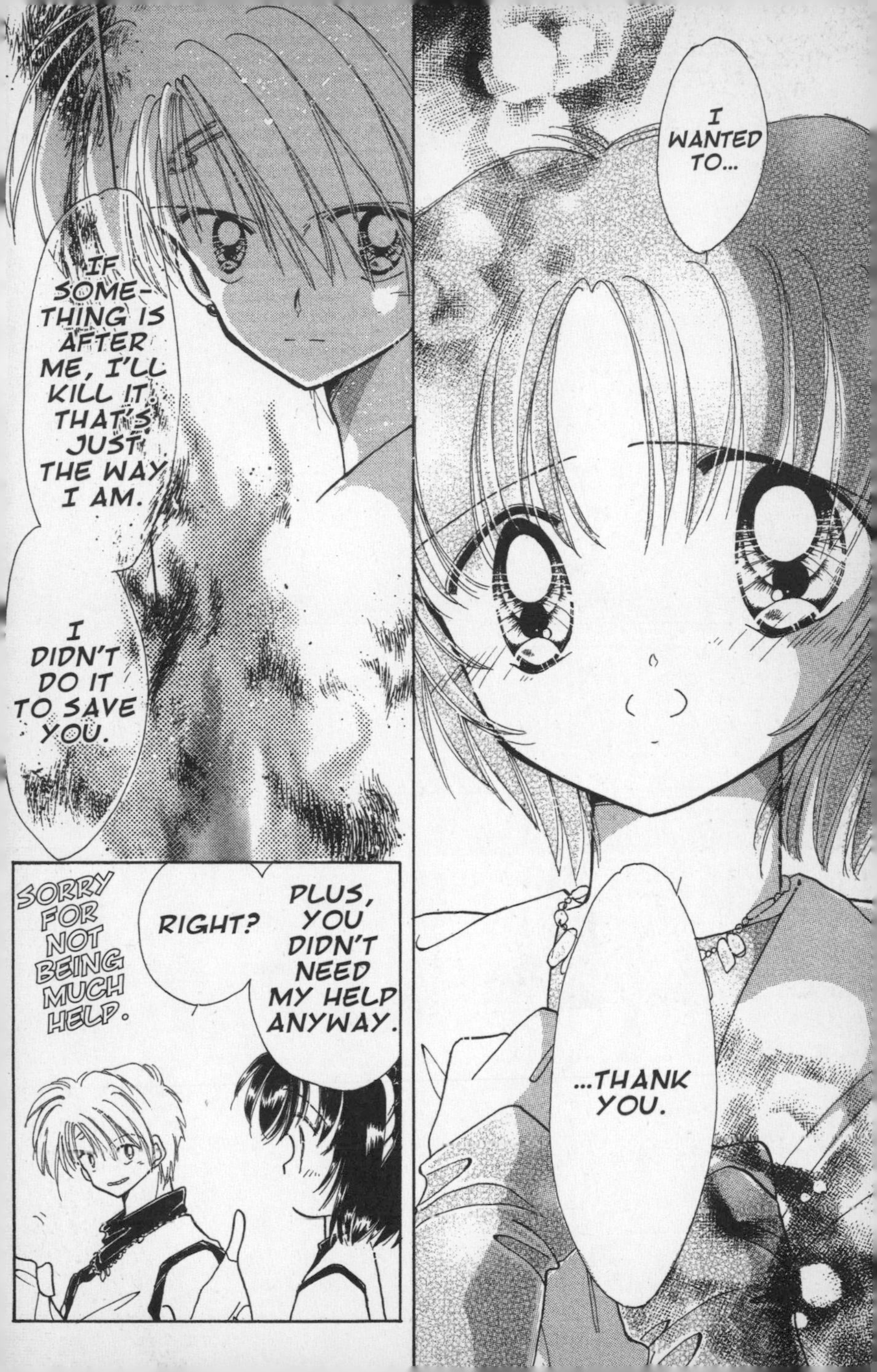
I WANTED TO...
...THANK YOU.
IF SOME-THING IS AFTER ME, I'LL KILL IT. THAT'S JUST THE WAY I AM.
I DIDN'T DO IT TO SAVE YOU.
PLUS, YOU DIDN'T NEED MY HELP ANYWAY.
RIGHT?
SORRY FOR NOT BEING MUCH HELP.

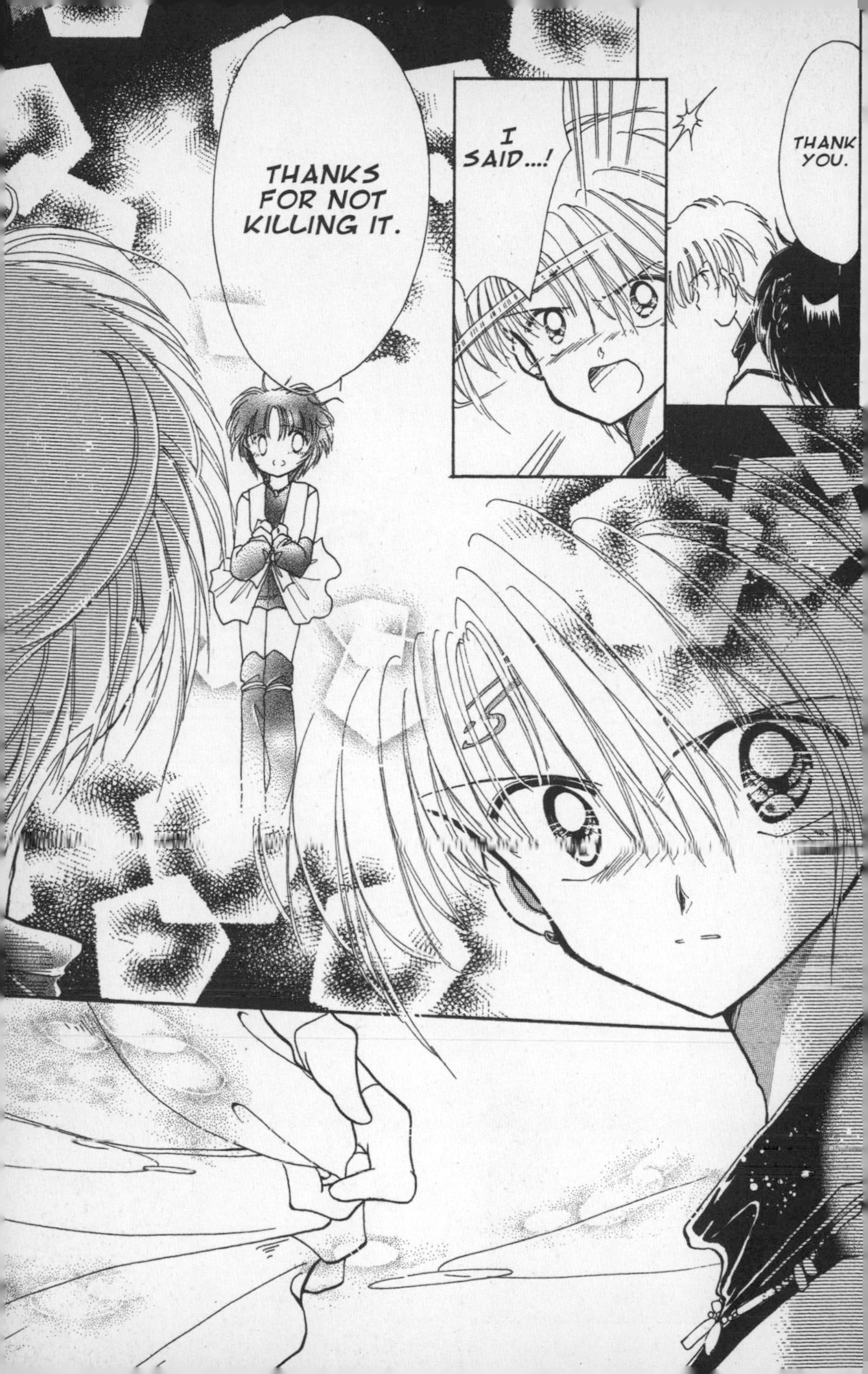
THANK YOU.
I SAID...!
THANKS FOR NOT KILLING IT.

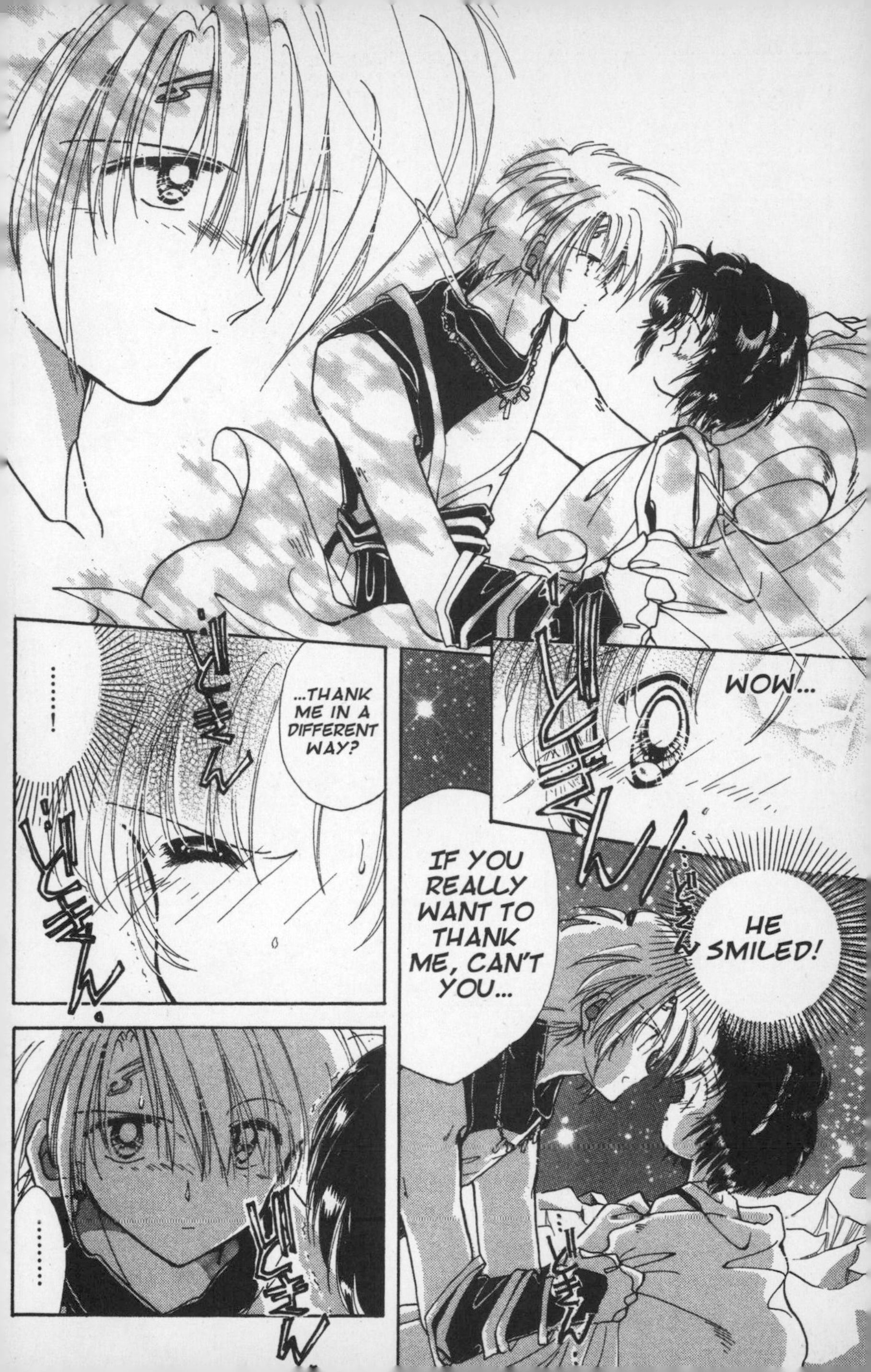
WOW...
HE SMILED!
IF YOU REALLY WANT TO THANK ME, CAN'T YOU...
...THANK ME IN A DIFFERENT WAY?
......!
......

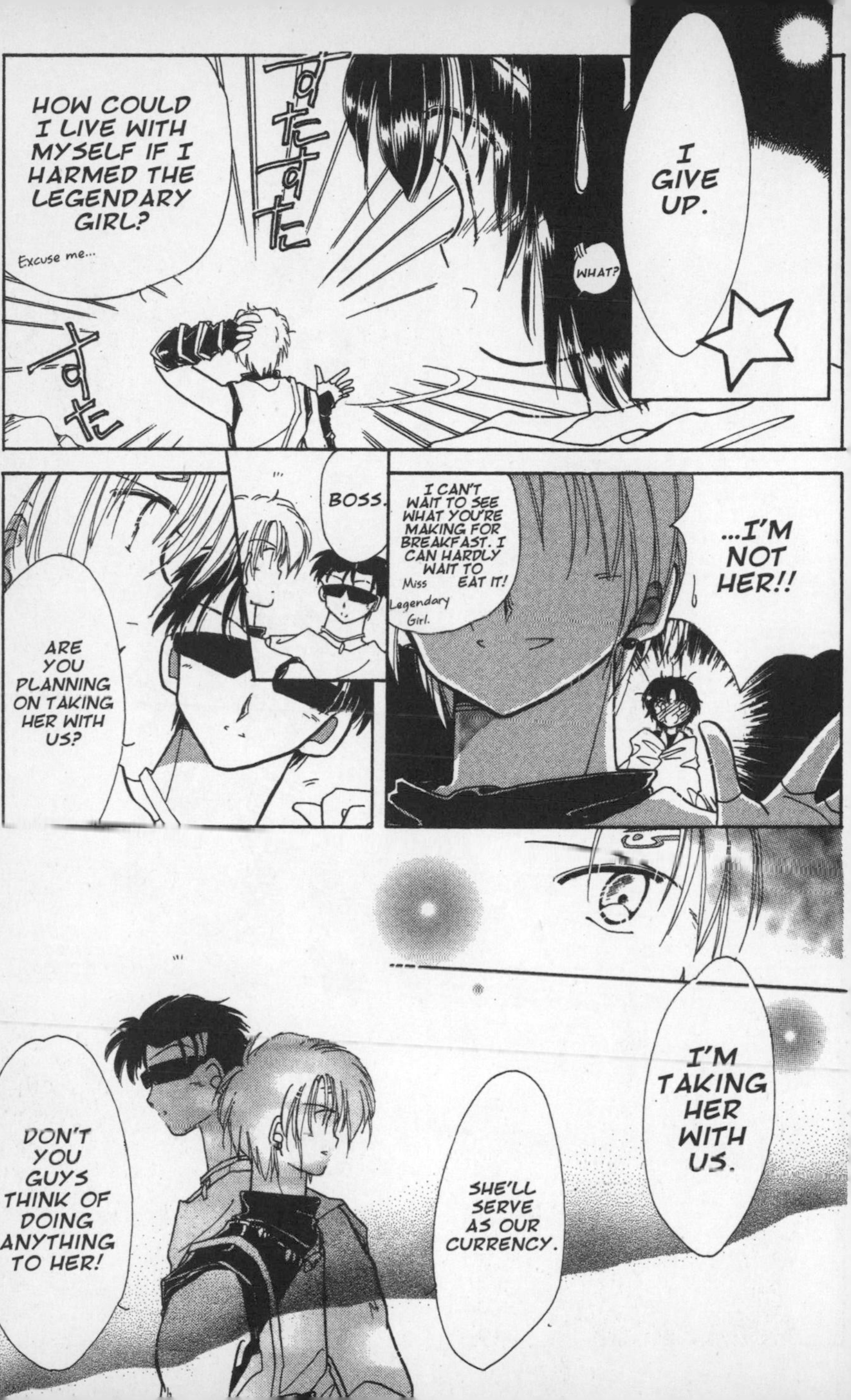
I GIVE UP.
WHAT?
HOW COULD I LIVE WITH MYSELF IF I HARMED THE LEGENDARY GIRL?
Excuse me...
すたすた
すた
...I'M NOT HER!!
I CAN'T WAIT TO SEE WHAT YOU'RE MAKING FOR BREAKFAST. I CAN HARDLY WAIT TO EAT IT!
Miss Legendary Girl.
BOSS.
ARE YOU PLANNING ON TAKING HER WITH US?
I'M TAKING HER WITH US.
SHE'LL SERVE AS OUR CURRENCY.
DON'T YOU GUYS THINK OF DOING ANYTHING TO HER!

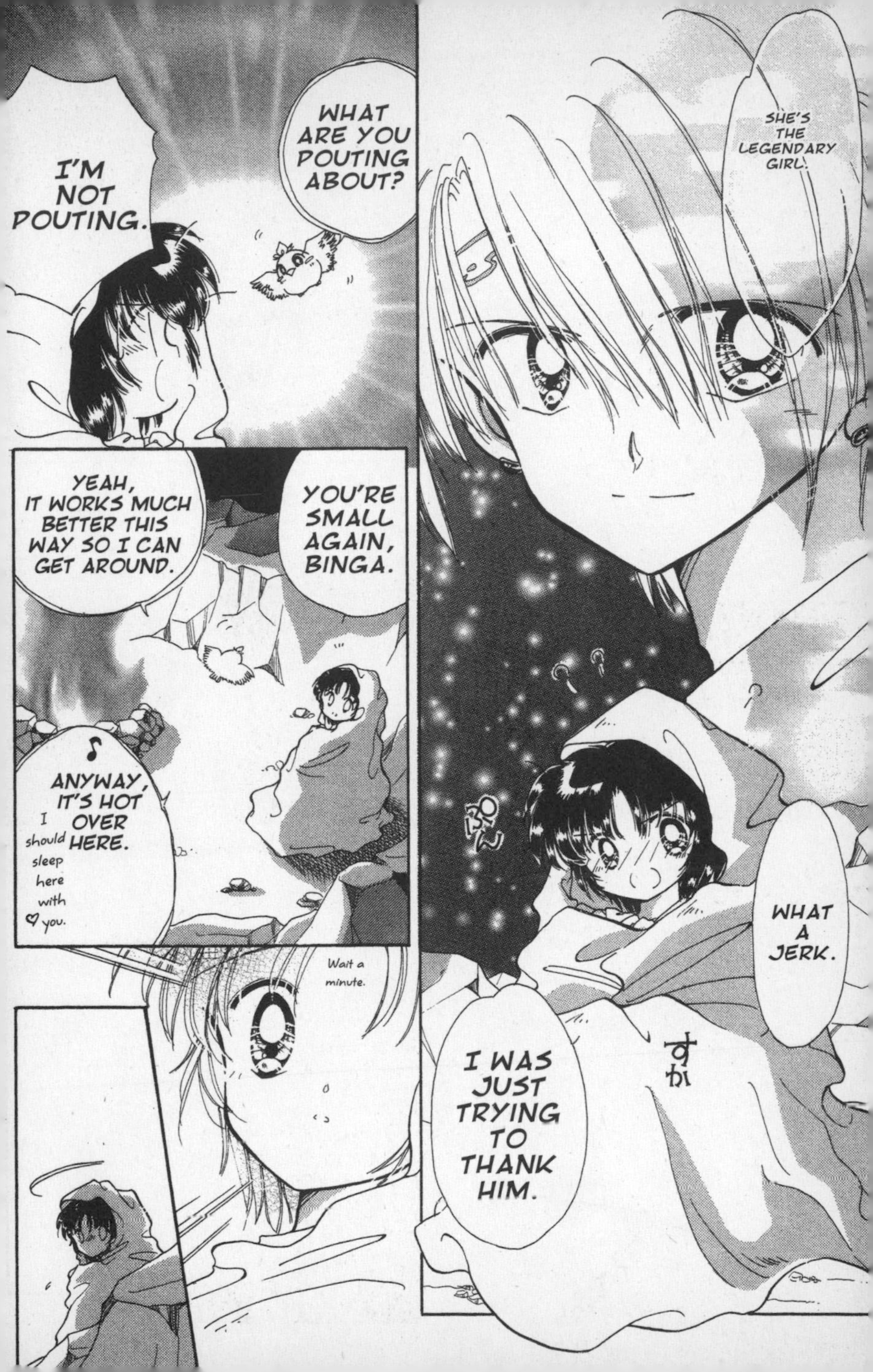
SHE'S THE LEGENDARY GIRL.
ぷん
WHAT A JERK.
すか
I WAS JUST TRYING TO THANK HIM.
WHAT ARE YOU POUTING ABOUT?
I'M NOT POUTING.
YOU'RE SMALL AGAIN, BINGA.
YEAH, IT WORKS MUCH BETTER THIS WAY SO I CAN GET AROUND.
♪ ANYWAY, IT'S HOT OVER HERE.
I should sleep here with ♡ you.
Wait a minute.

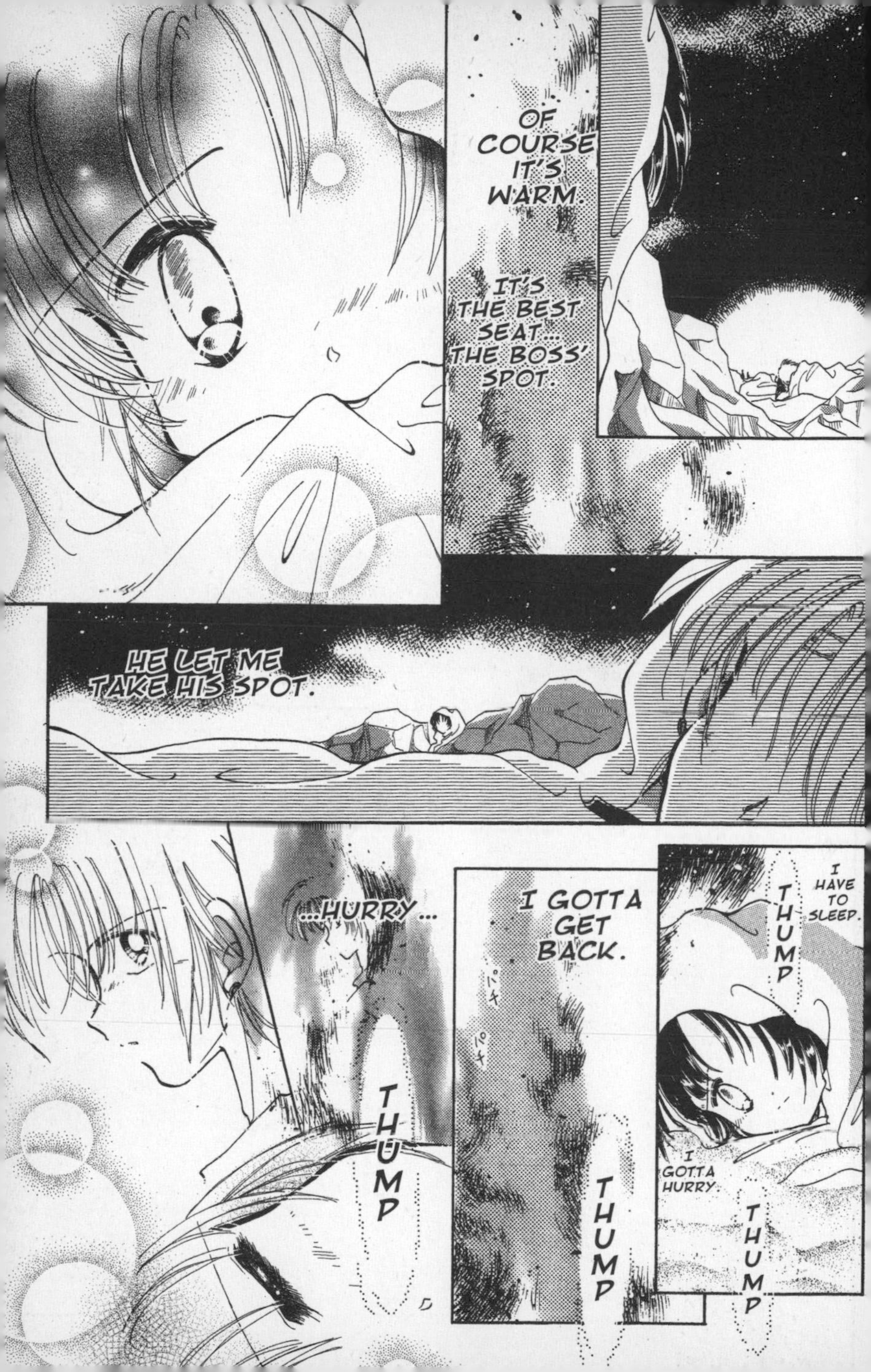
OF COURSE IT'S WARM.
IT'S THE BEST SEAT... THE BOSS' SPOT.
HE LET ME TAKE HIS SPOT.
I HAVE TO SLEEP.
THUMP
I GOTTA HURRY.
THUMP
I GOTTA GET BACK.
パキ
パチ
THUMP
...HURRY...
THUMP

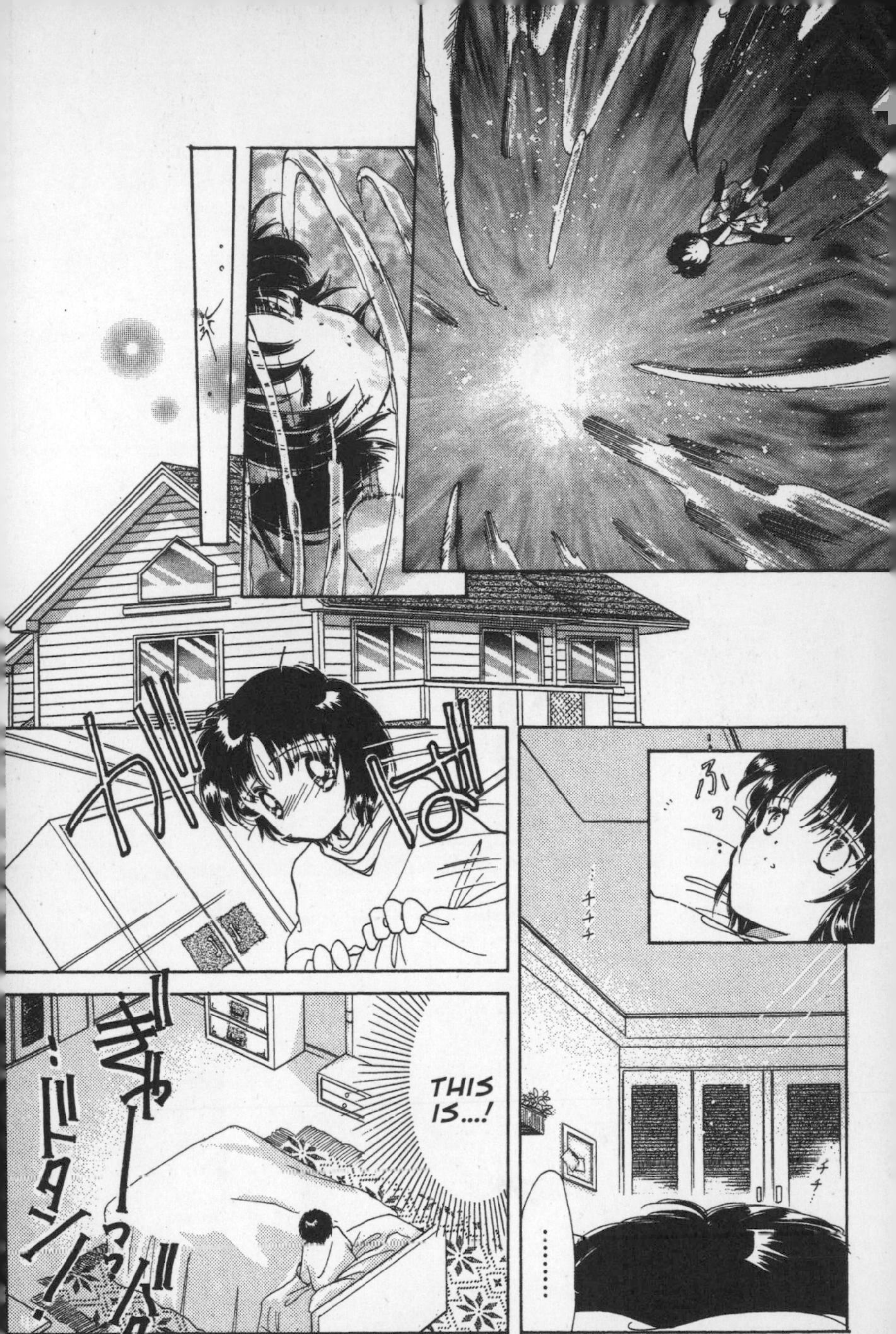
ふっ
THIS IS...!

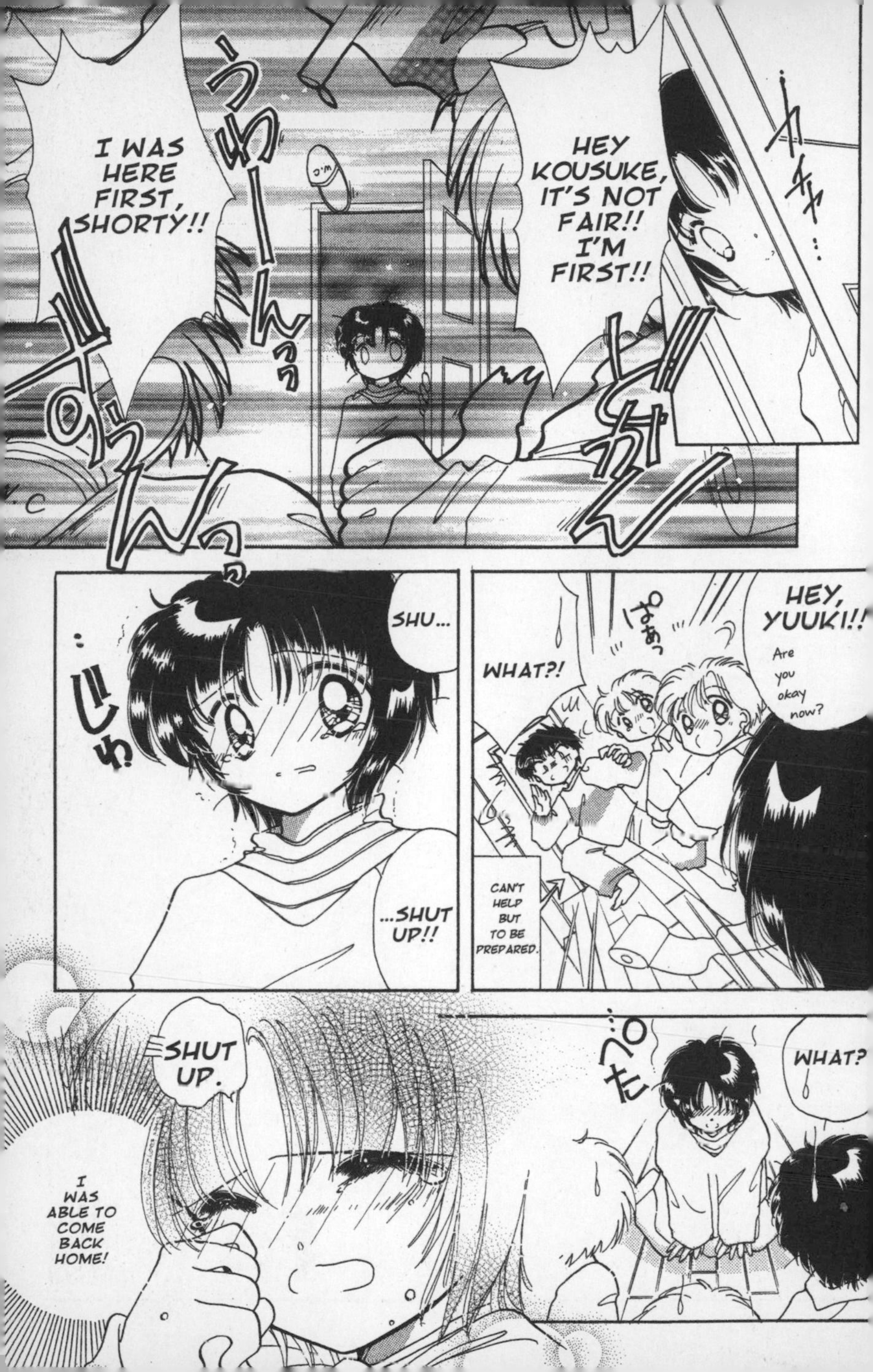
HEY KOUSUKE, IT'S NOT FAIR!! I'M FIRST!!
I WAS HERE FIRST, SHORTY!!
HEY, YUUKI!!
Are you okay now?
WHAT?!
CAN'T HELP BUT TO BE PREPARED.
SHU...
...SHUT UP!!
WHAT?
SHUT UP.
I WAS ABLE TO COME BACK HOME!

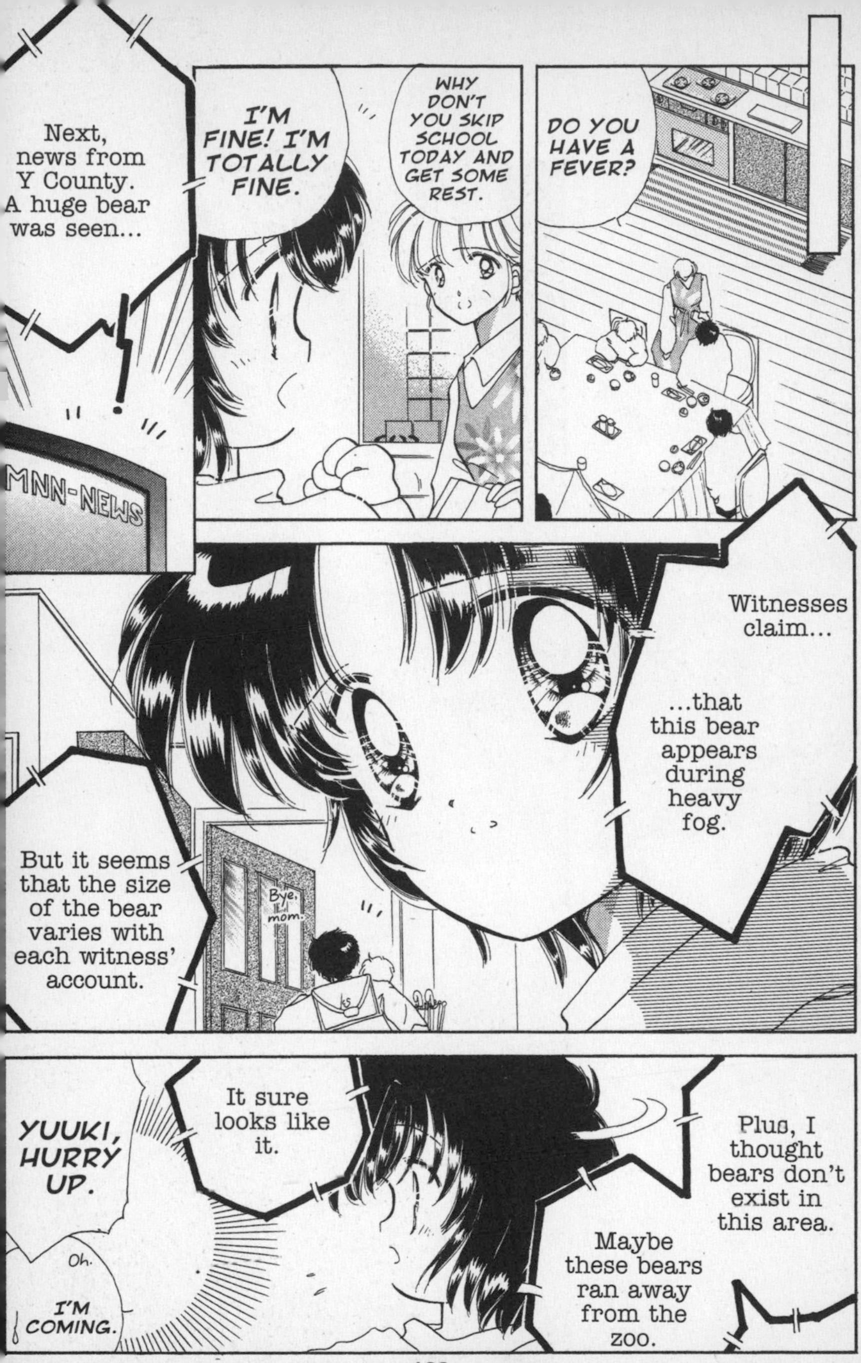
DO YOU HAVE A FEVER?
WHY DON'T YOU SKIP SCHOOL TODAY AND GET SOME REST.
I'M FINE! I'M TOTALLY FINE.
Next, news from Y County. A huge bear was seen...
MNN-NEWS
Witnesses claim...
...that this bear appears during heavy fog.
But it seems that the size of the bear varies with each witness' account.
Bye, mom.
Plus, I thought bears don't exist in this area.
Maybe these bears ran away from the zoo.
It sure looks like it.
YUUKI, HURRY UP.
Oh.
I'M COMING.

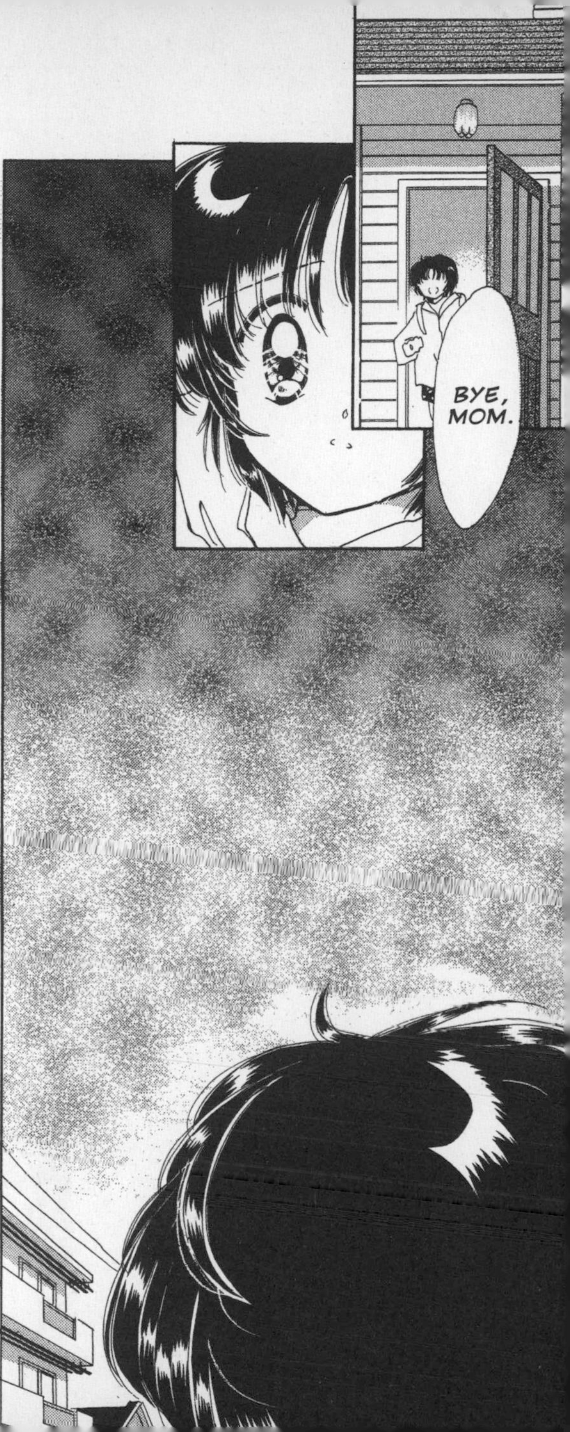
BYE, MOM.

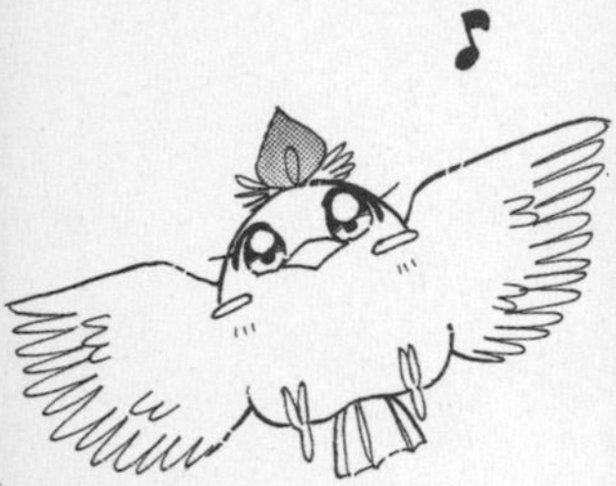

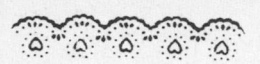

Binga (♀)

Birthdate: unknown.

Blood type: unknown.

The bird is called Karyubinga. She's a female bird. "Binga" is what Yuuki calls her. With Yuuki's mysterious powers, she can make Binga bigger in size anytime she wants. Only those who hold the magic stone can communicate with Binga. Binga has a bit of a temper.

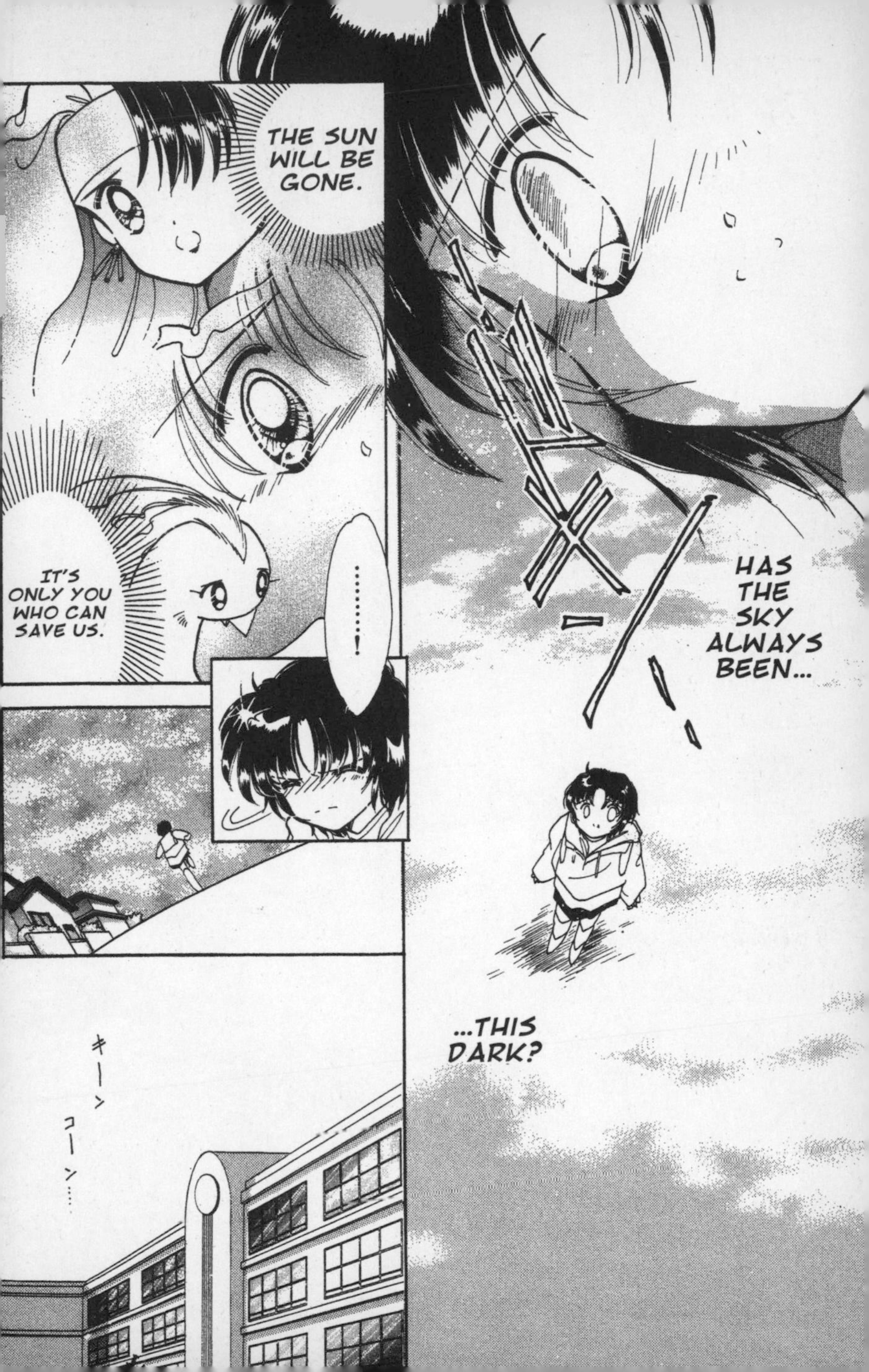
HAS THE SKY ALWAYS BEEN...
...THIS DARK?
THE SUN WILL BE GONE.
IT'S ONLY YOU WHO CAN SAVE US.
......!
キーン
コーン……

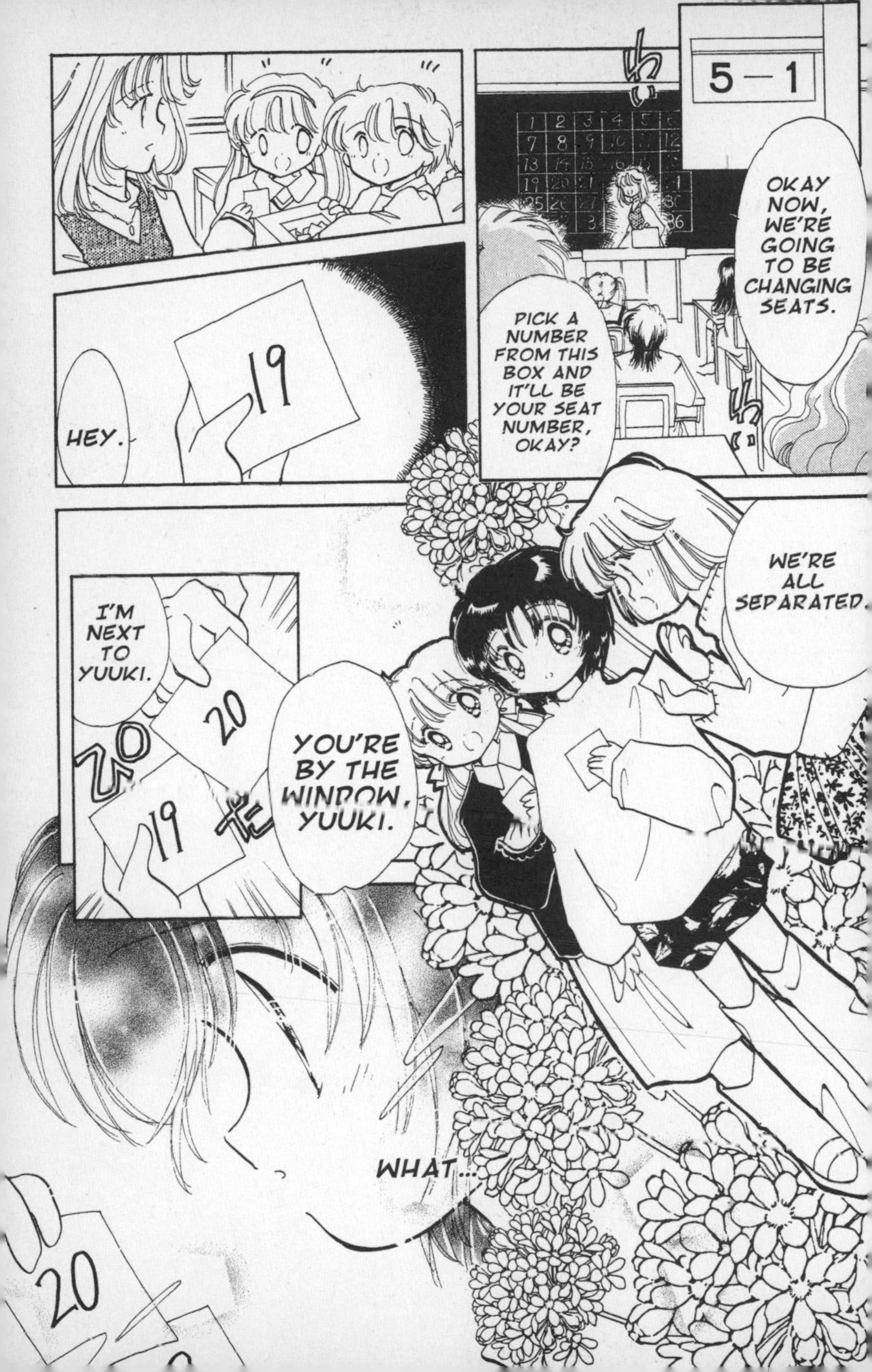
5 — 1
OKAY NOW, WE'RE GOING TO BE CHANGING SEATS.
PICK A NUMBER FROM THIS BOX AND IT'LL BE YOUR SEAT NUMBER, OKAY?
HEY.
19
WE'RE ALL SEPARATED.
YOU'RE BY THE WINDOW, YUUKI.
I'M NEXT TO YUUKI.
20
19
WHAT...
20

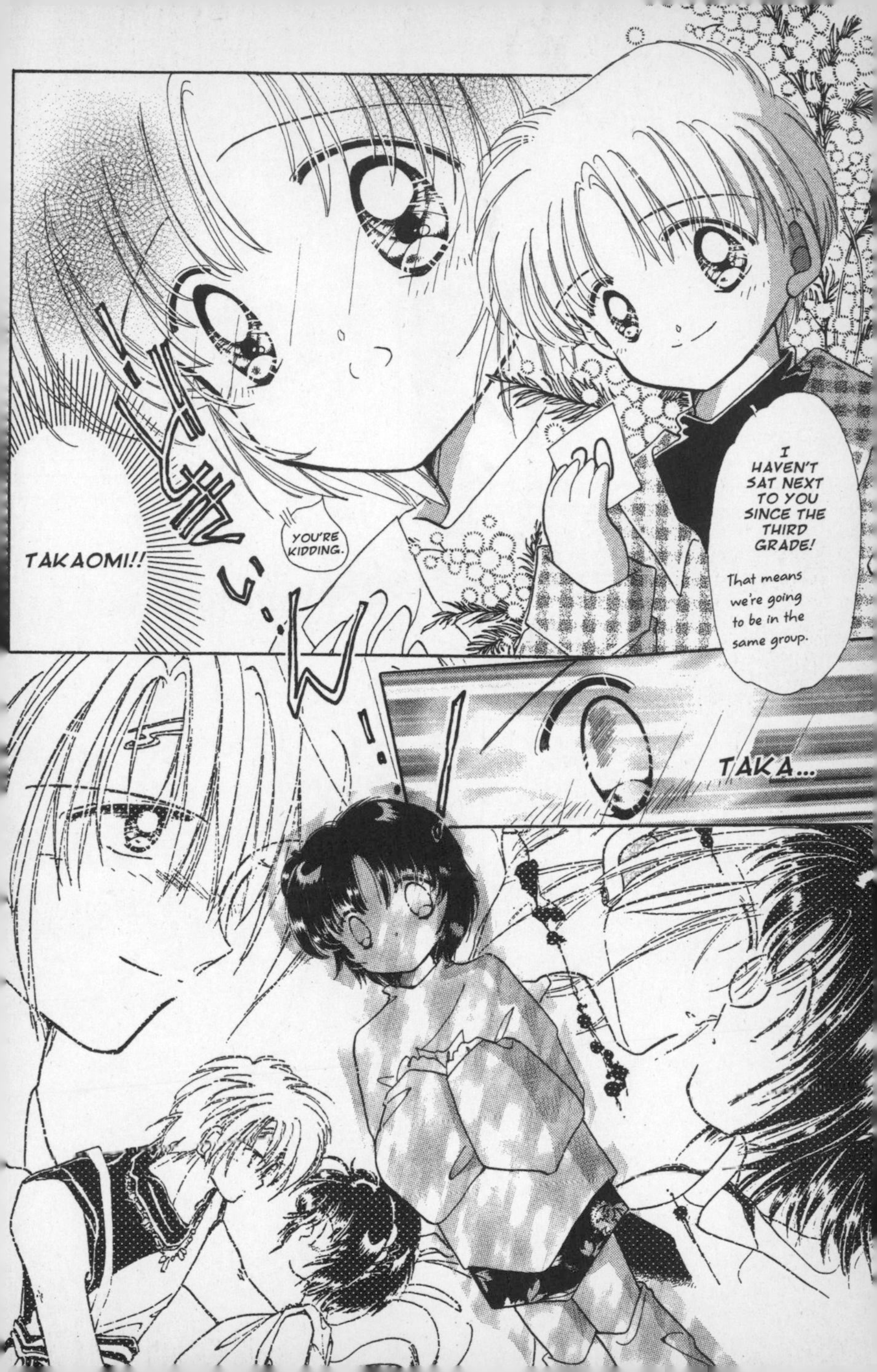
I HAVEN'T SAT NEXT TO YOU SINCE THE THIRD GRADE!
That means we're going to be in the same group.
YOU'RE KIDDING.
TAKAOMI!!
TAKA...

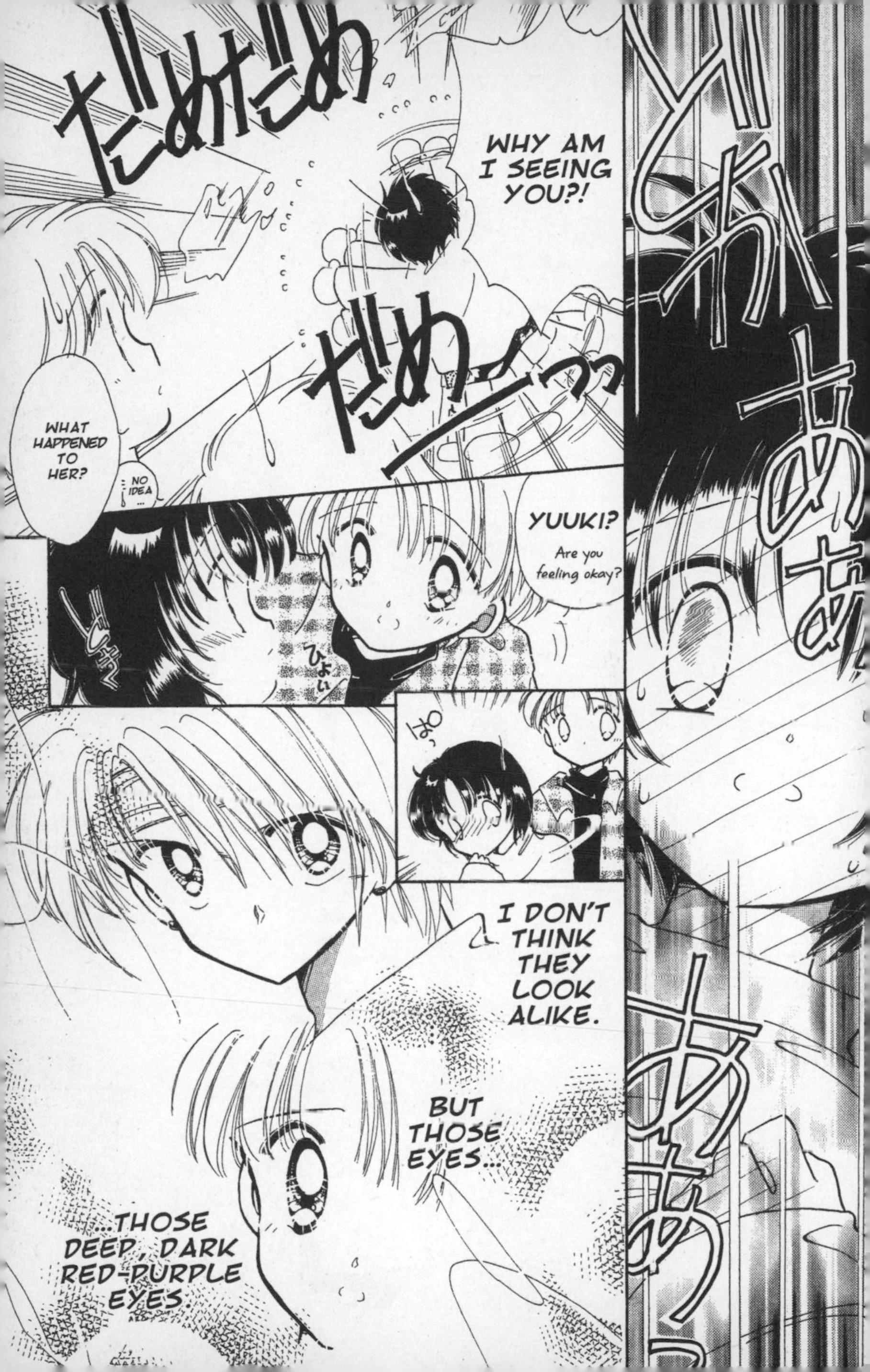
いやあああ
だめだめ
WHY AM I SEEING YOU?!
だめーっ
WHAT HAPPENED TO HER?
NO IDEA...
YUUKI?
Are you feeling okay?
ひょい
ぽっ
I DON'T THINK THEY LOOK ALIKE.
BUT THOSE EYES...
...THOSE DEEP, DARK RED-PURPLE EYES.

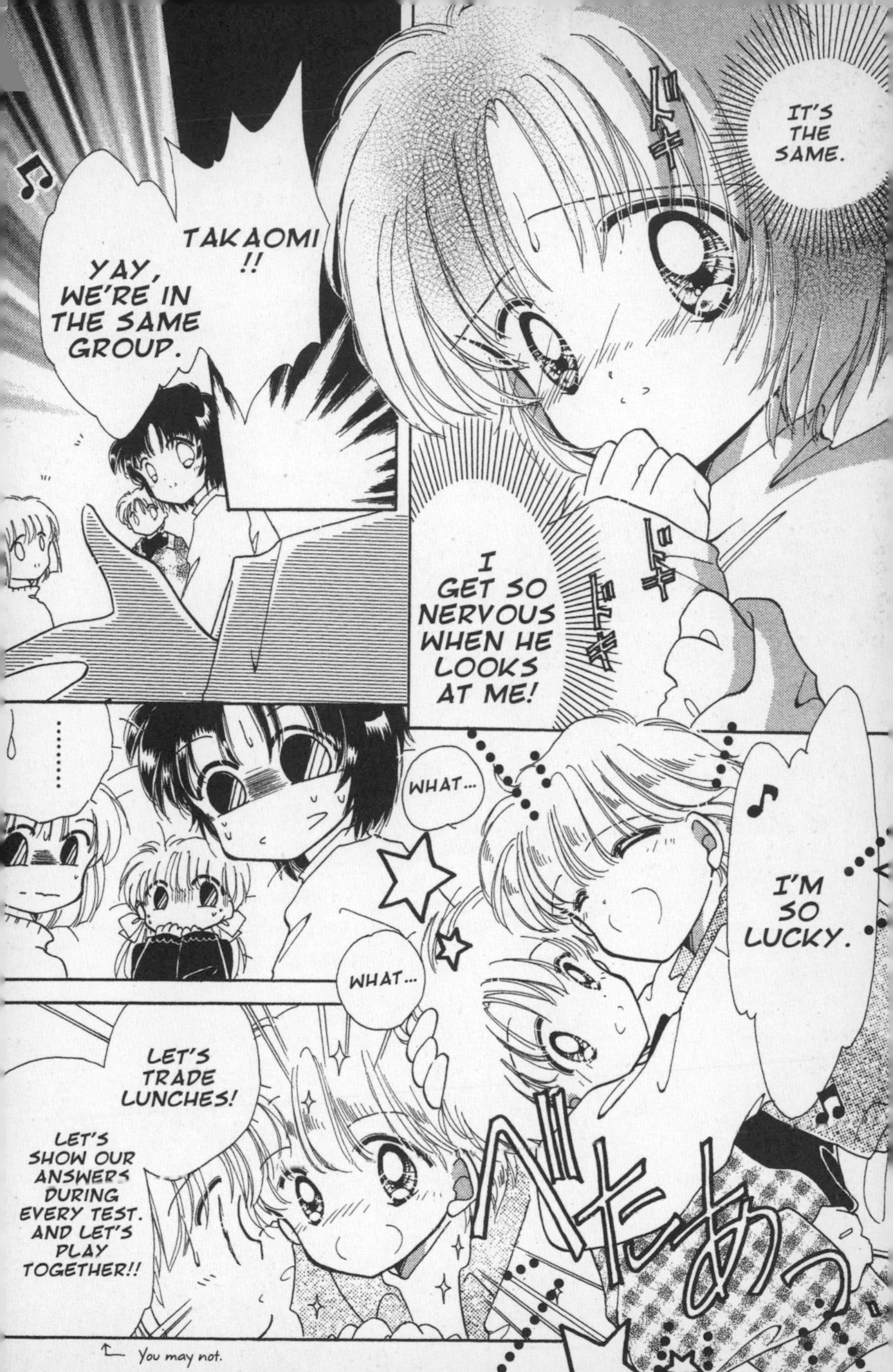
IT'S THE SAME.
I GET SO NERVOUS WHEN HE LOOKS AT ME!
TAKAOMI!!
YAY, WE'RE IN THE SAME GROUP.
I'M SO LUCKY.
WHAT...
WHAT...
......
LET'S TRADE LUNCHES!
LET'S SHOW OUR ANSWERS DURING EVERY TEST. AND LET'S PLAY TOGETHER!!

↖ You may not.

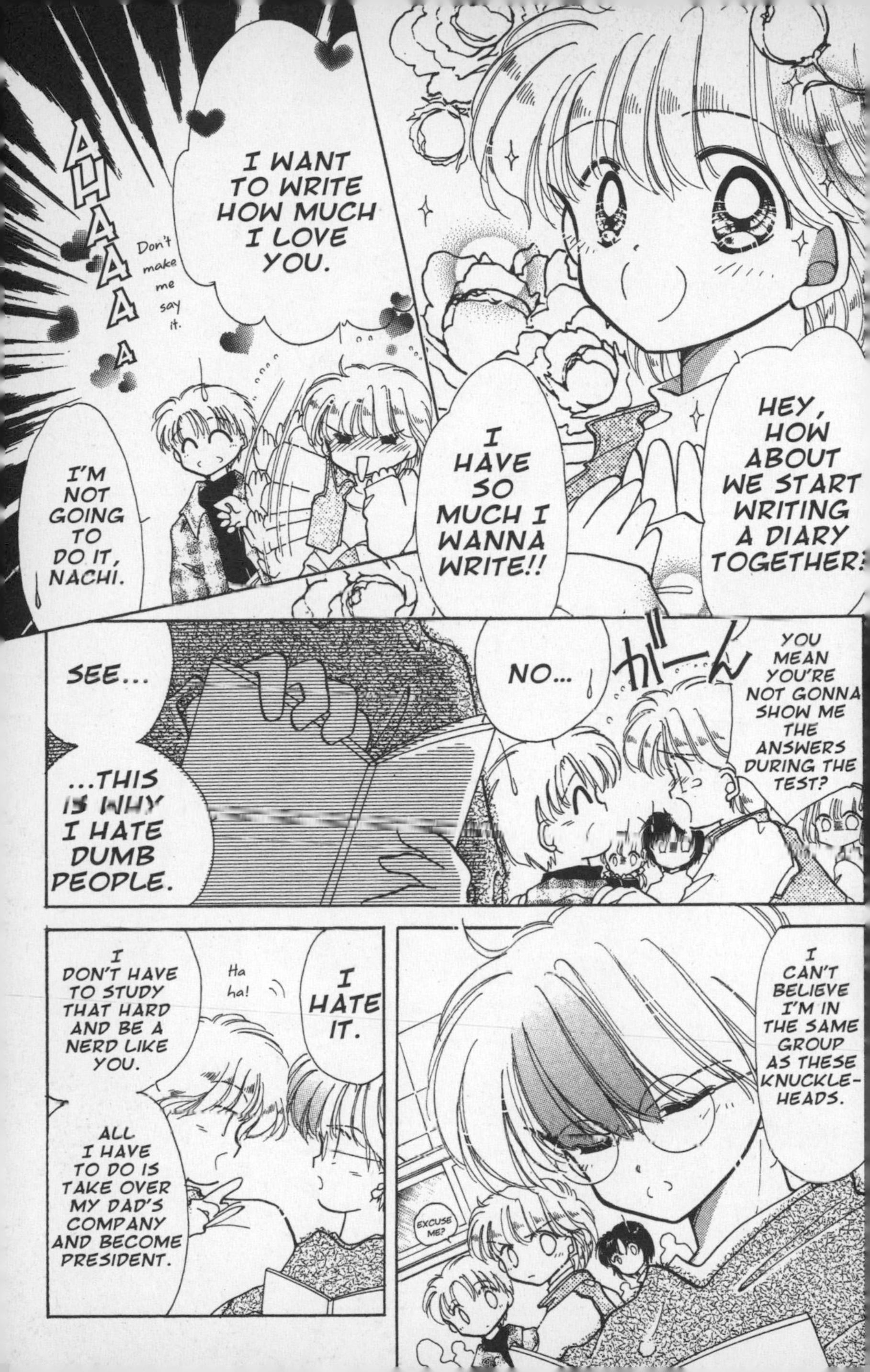
HEY, HOW ABOUT WE START WRITING A DIARY TOGETHER!?
I HAVE SO MUCH I WANNA WRITE!!
I WANT TO WRITE HOW MUCH I LOVE YOU.
AHAAAAA
Don't make me say it.
I'M NOT GOING TO DO IT, NACHI.
YOU MEAN YOU'RE NOT GONNA SHOW ME THE ANSWERS DURING THE TEST?
がーん
NO...
SEE...
...THIS IS WHY I HATE DUMB PEOPLE.
I CAN'T BELIEVE I'M IN THE SAME GROUP AS THESE KNUCKLE-HEADS.
EXCUSE ME?
I HATE IT.
Ha ha!
I DON'T HAVE TO STUDY THAT HARD AND BE A NERD LIKE YOU.
ALL I HAVE TO DO IS TAKE OVER MY DAD'S COMPANY AND BECOME PRESIDENT.

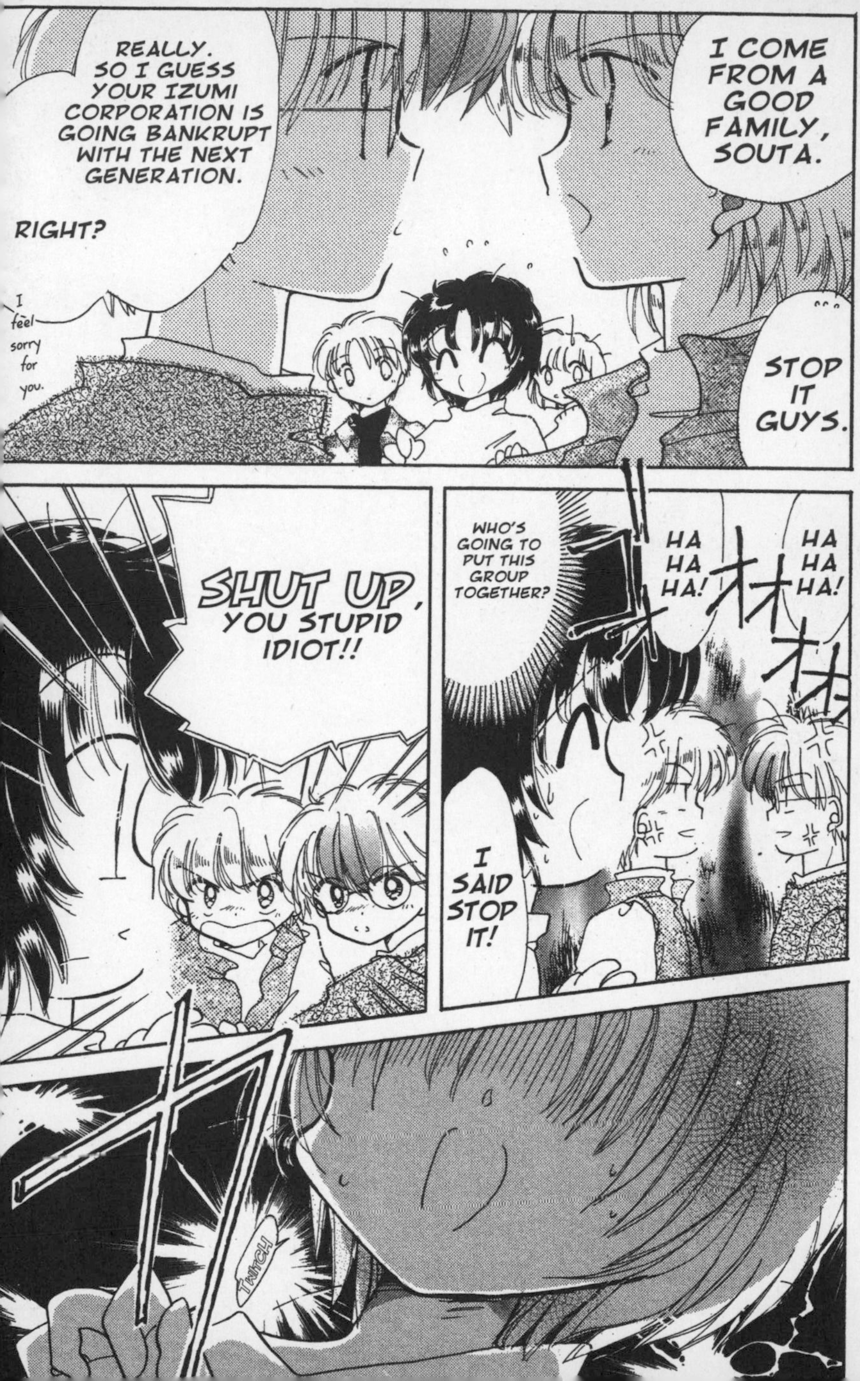
I COME FROM A GOOD FAMILY, SOUTA.
REALLY. SO I GUESS YOUR IZUMI CORPORATION IS GOING BANKRUPT WITH THE NEXT GENERATION.
RIGHT?
...
STOP IT GUYS.
I feel sorry for you.
HA HA HA!
HA HA HA!
WHO'S GOING TO PUT THIS GROUP TOGETHER?
I SAID STOP IT!
SHUT UP, YOU STUPID IDIOT!!
TWITCH

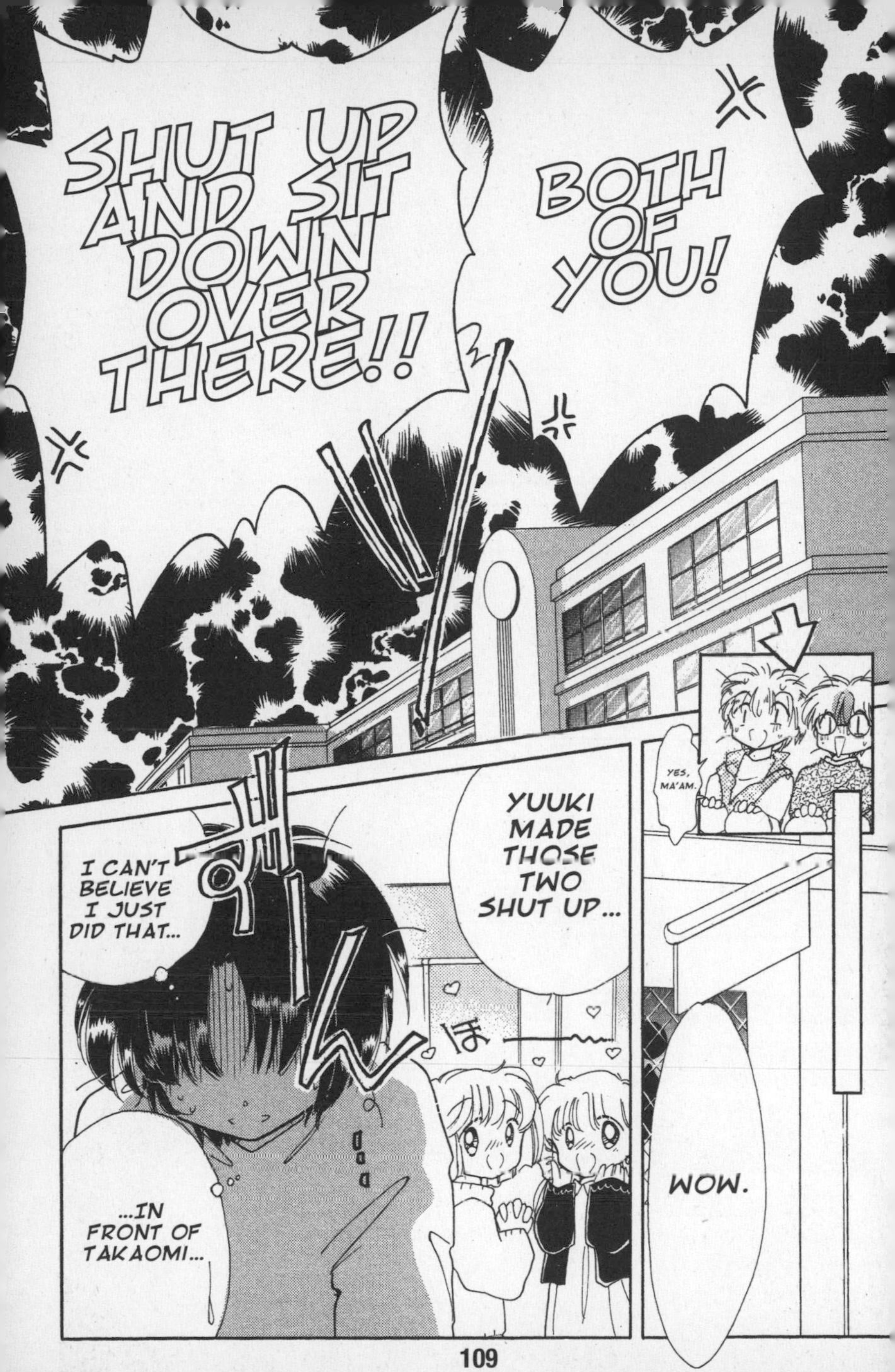
SHUT UP AND SIT DOWN OVER THERE!!
BOTH OF YOU!
YES, MA'AM.
WOW.
YUUKI MADE THOSE TWO SHUT UP...
ほ
I CAN'T BELIEVE I JUST DID THAT...
...IN FRONT OF TAKAOMI...

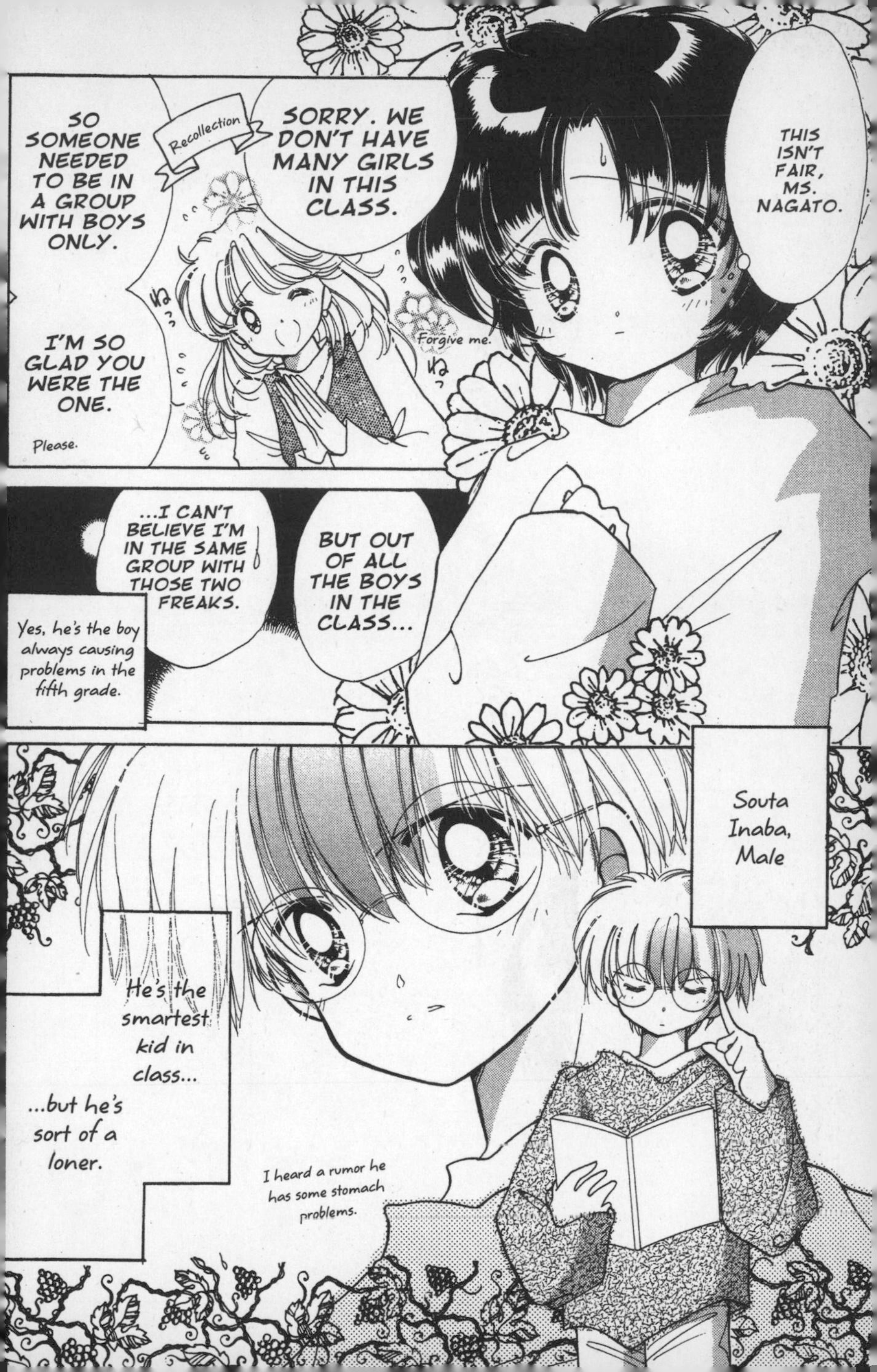
THIS ISN'T FAIR, MS. NAGATO.
Recollection
SORRY. WE DON'T HAVE MANY GIRLS IN THIS CLASS.
Forgive me.
SO SOMEONE NEEDED TO BE IN A GROUP WITH BOYS ONLY.
I'M SO GLAD YOU WERE THE ONE.
Please.
BUT OUT OF ALL THE BOYS IN THE CLASS...
...I CAN'T BELIEVE I'M IN THE SAME GROUP WITH THOSE TWO FREAKS.
Yes, he's the boy always causing problems in the fifth grade.
Souta Inaba, Male
He's the smartest kid in class...
...but he's sort of a loner.
I heard a rumor he has some stomach problems.

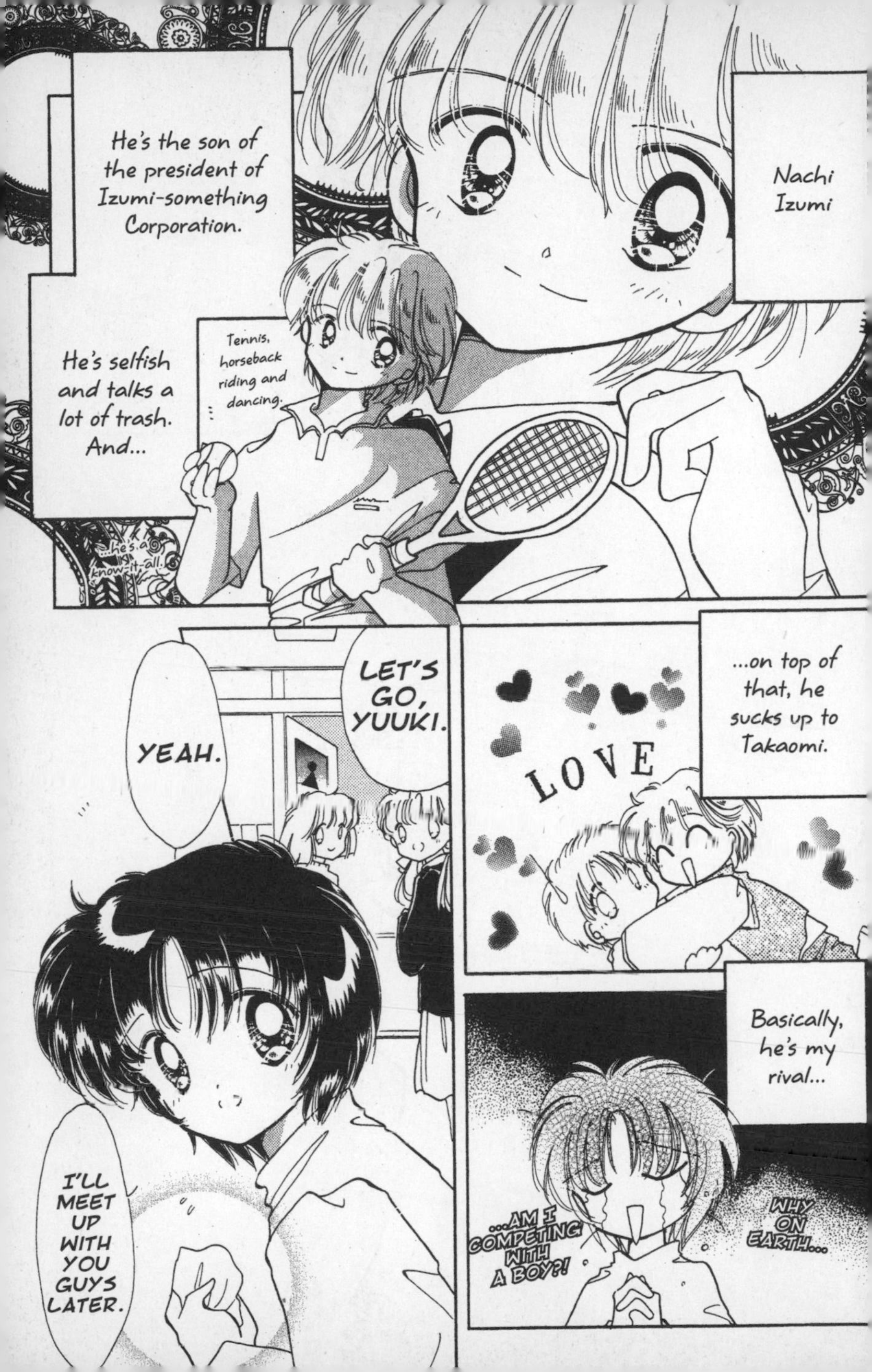
Nachi Izumi
He's the son of the president of Izumi-something Corporation.
Tennis, horseback riding and dancing.
He's selfish and talks a lot of trash. And...
...he's a know-it-all.
...on top of that, he sucks up to Takaomi.
LOVE
Basically, he's my rival...
WHY ON EARTH...
...AM I COMPETING WITH A BOY?!
LET'S GO, YUUKI.
YEAH.
I'LL MEET UP WITH YOU GUYS LATER.

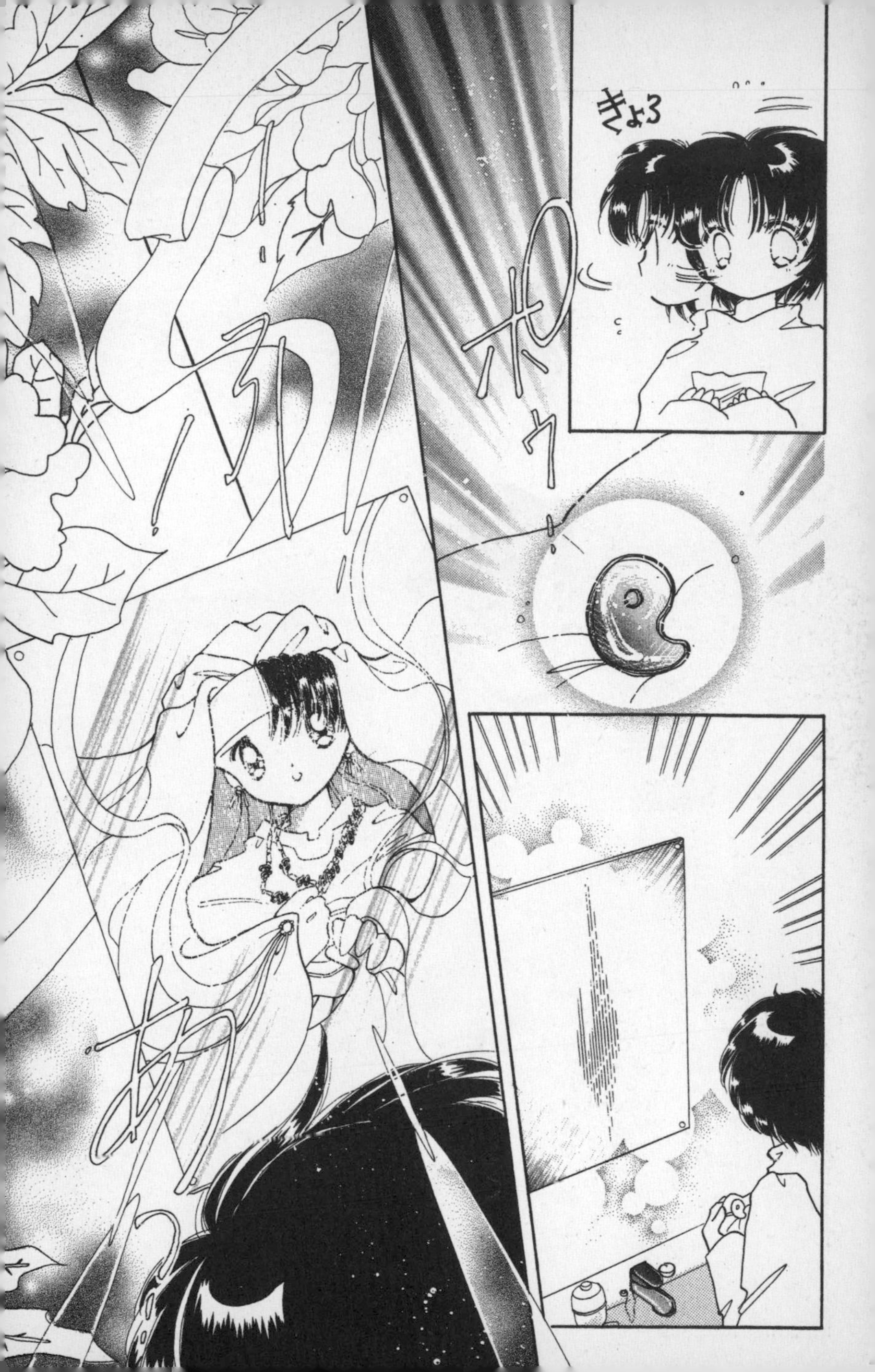
きょろ
ポゥ
あっ

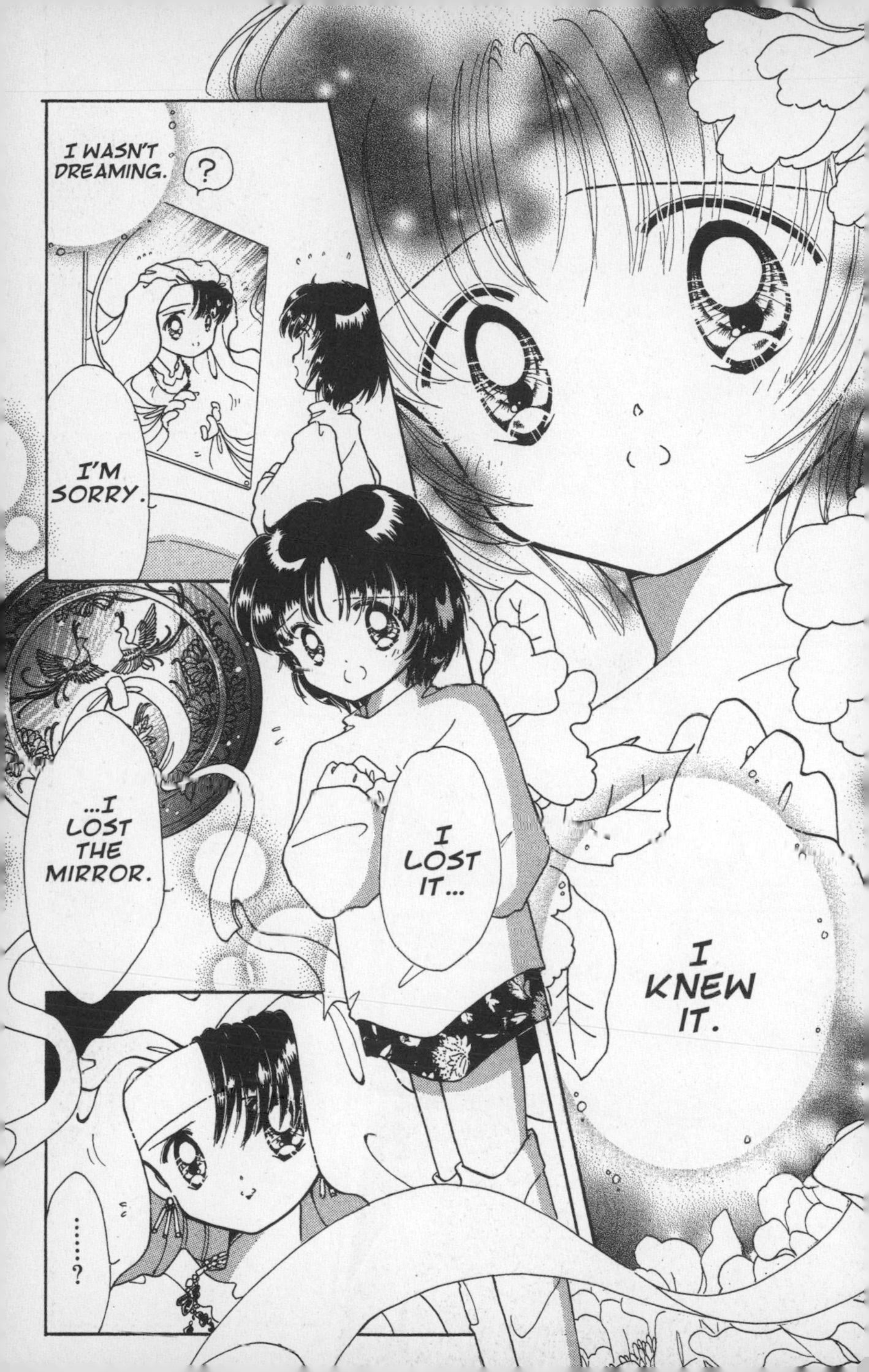
I KNEW IT.
I LOST IT...
...I LOST THE MIRROR.
?
I WASN'T DREAMING.
I'M SORRY.
......?

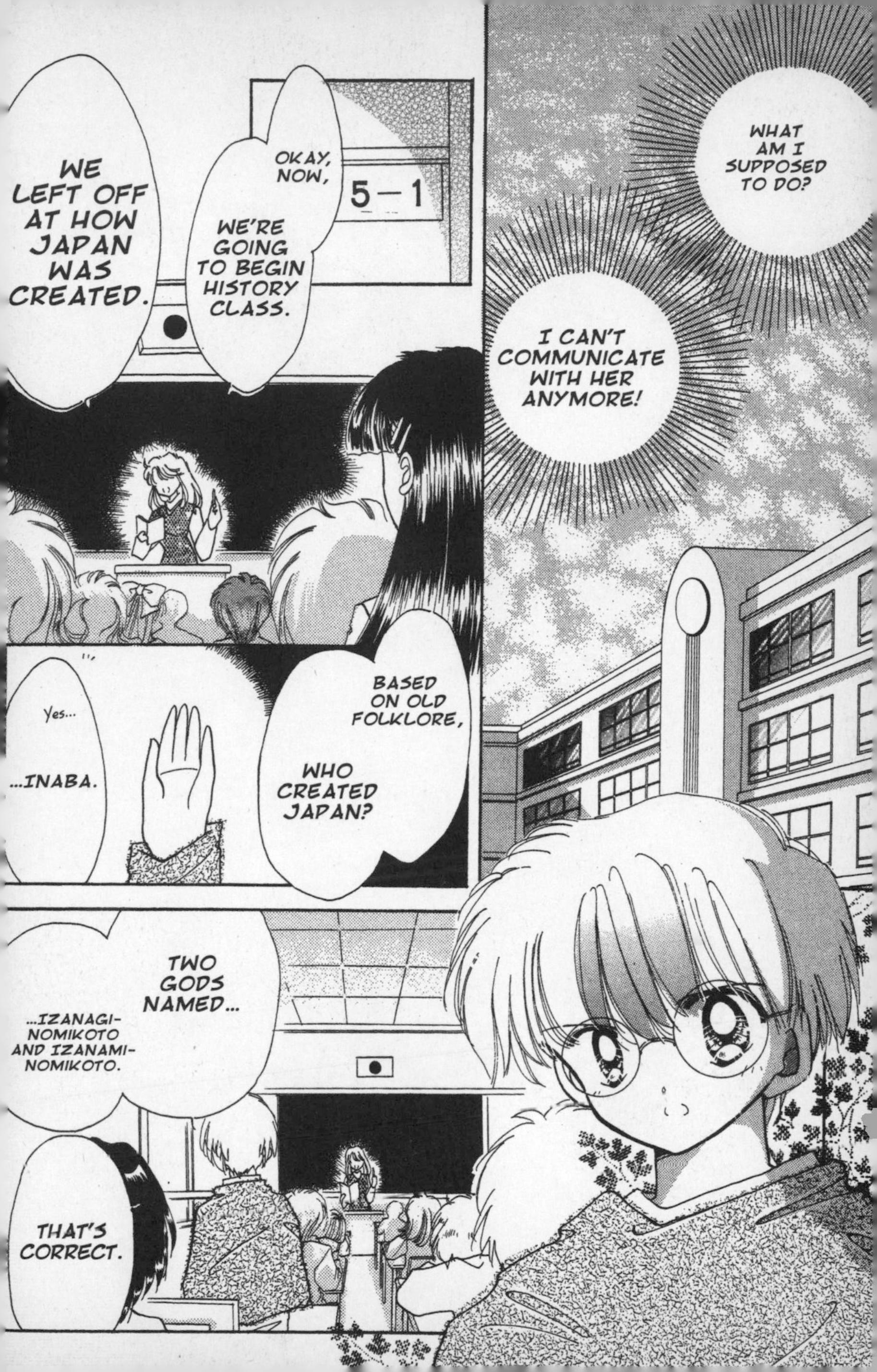
WHAT AM I SUPPOSED TO DO?
I CAN'T COMMUNICATE WITH HER ANYMORE!
OKAY, NOW,
WE'RE GOING TO BEGIN HISTORY CLASS.
5-1
WE LEFT OFF AT HOW JAPAN WAS CREATED.
BASED ON OLD FOLKLORE,
WHO CREATED JAPAN?
Yes...
...INABA.
TWO GODS NAMED...
...IZANAGI-NOMIKOTO AND IZANAMI-NOMIKOTO.
THAT'S CORRECT.

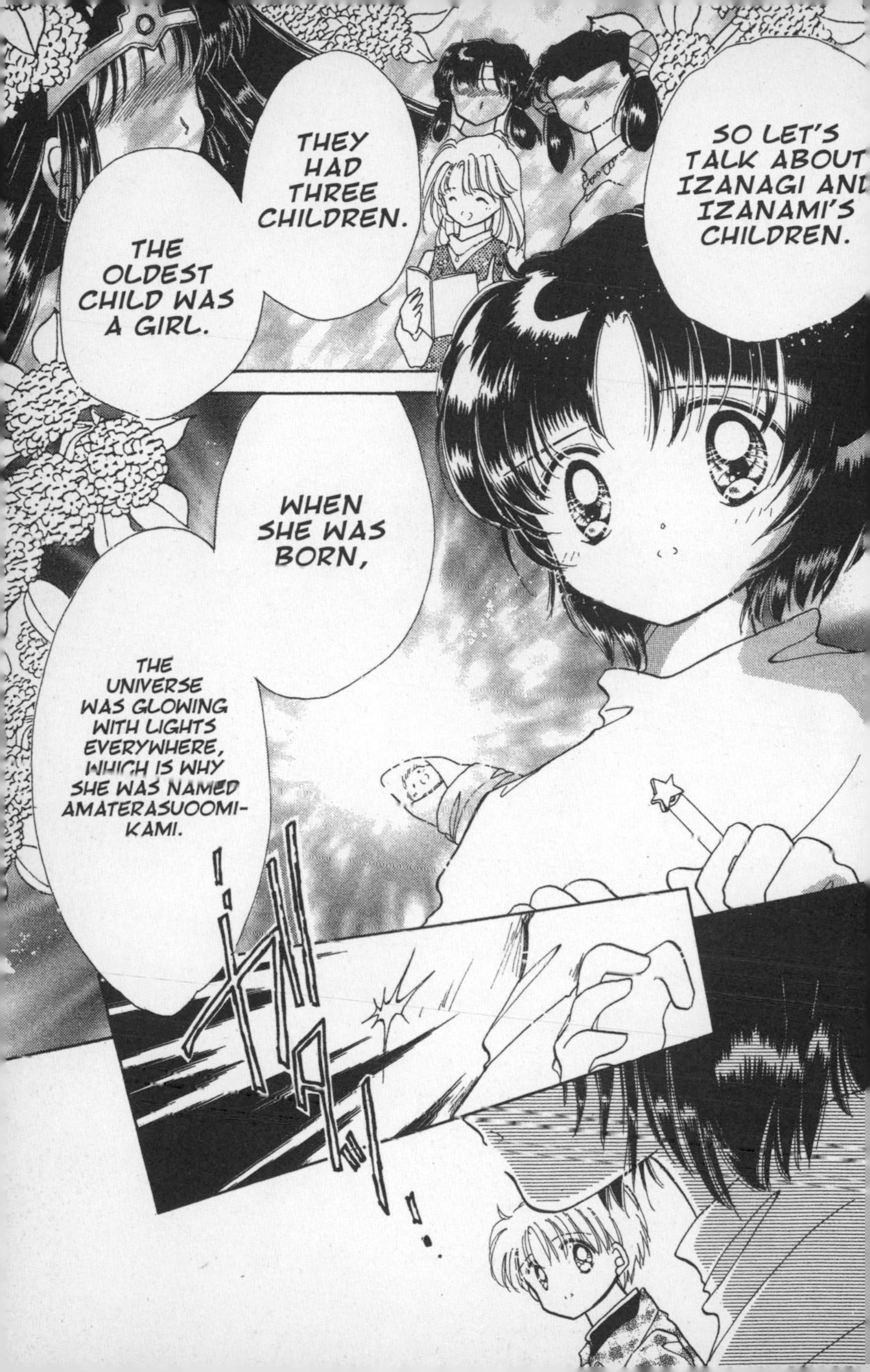
SO LET'S TALK ABOUT IZANAGI AND IZANAMI'S CHILDREN.
THEY HAD THREE CHILDREN.
THE OLDEST CHILD WAS A GIRL.
WHEN SHE WAS BORN,
THE UNIVERSE WAS GLOWING WITH LIGHTS EVERYWHERE, WHICH IS WHY SHE WAS NAMED AMATERASUOOMI-KAMI.

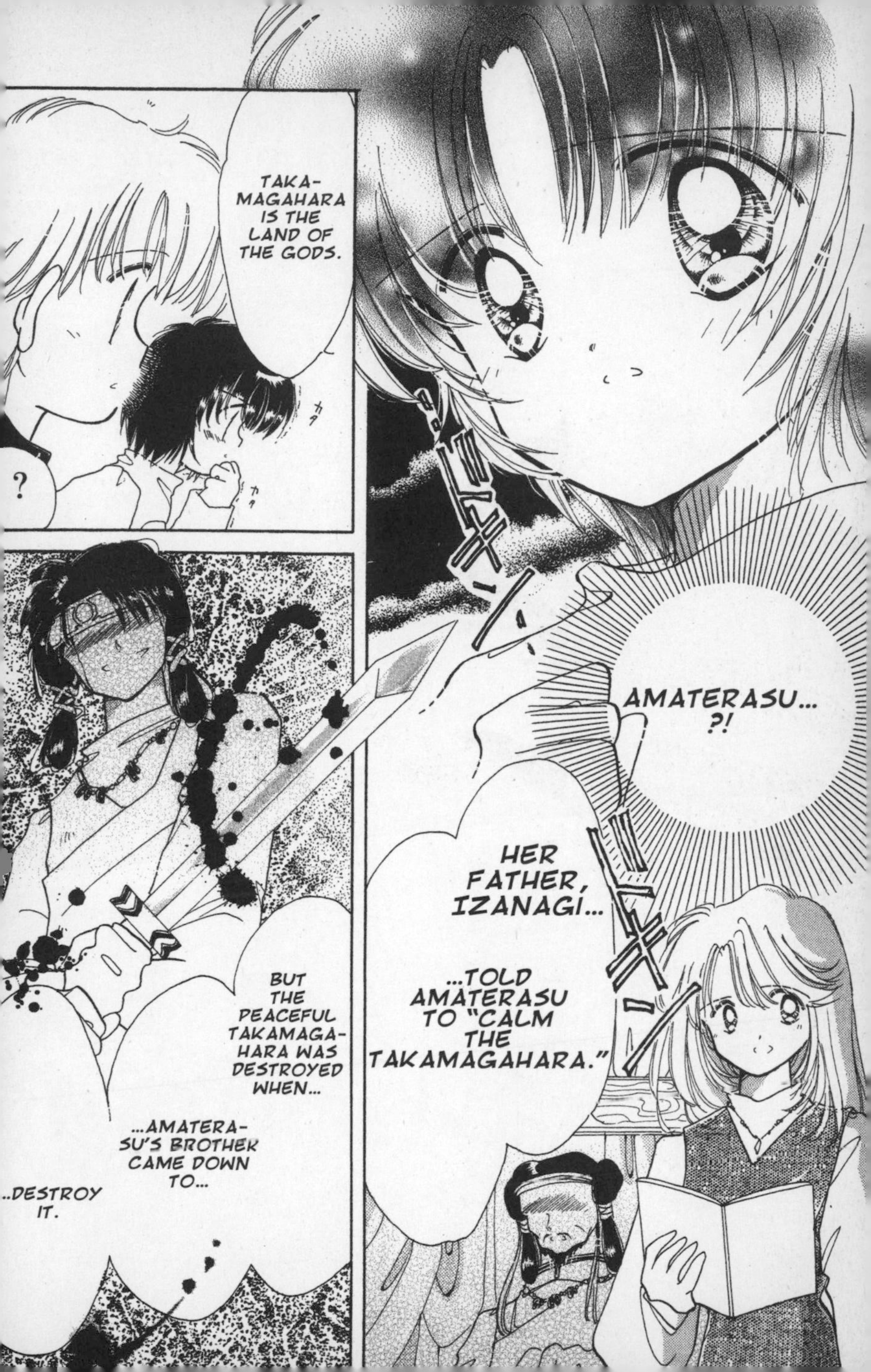
AMATERASU... ?!
HER FATHER, IZANAGI...
...TOLD AMATERASU TO "CALM THE TAKAMAGAHARA."
TAKA-MAGAHARA IS THE LAND OF THE GODS.
?
BUT THE PEACEFUL TAKAMAGA-HARA WAS DESTROYED WHEN...
...AMATERA-SU'S BROTHER CAME DOWN TO...
..DESTROY IT.

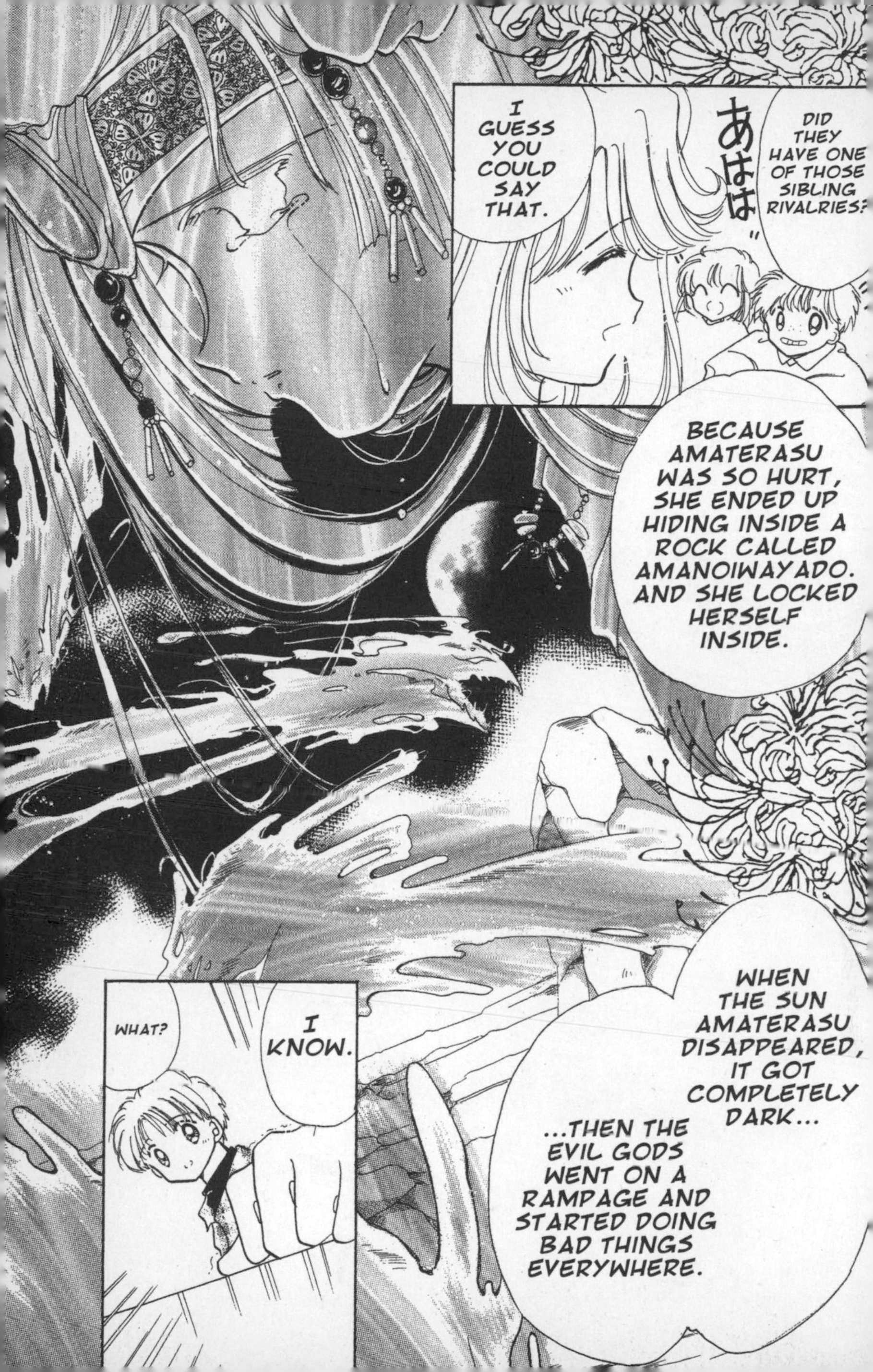
DID THEY HAVE ONE OF THOSE SIBLING RIVALRIES?
あはは
I GUESS YOU COULD SAY THAT.
BECAUSE AMATERASU WAS SO HURT, SHE ENDED UP HIDING INSIDE A ROCK CALLED AMANOIWAYADO. AND SHE LOCKED HERSELF INSIDE.
WHEN THE SUN AMATERASU DISAPPEARED, IT GOT COMPLETELY DARK...
...THEN THE EVIL GODS WENT ON A RAMPAGE AND STARTED DOING BAD THINGS EVERYWHERE.
I KNOW.
WHAT?

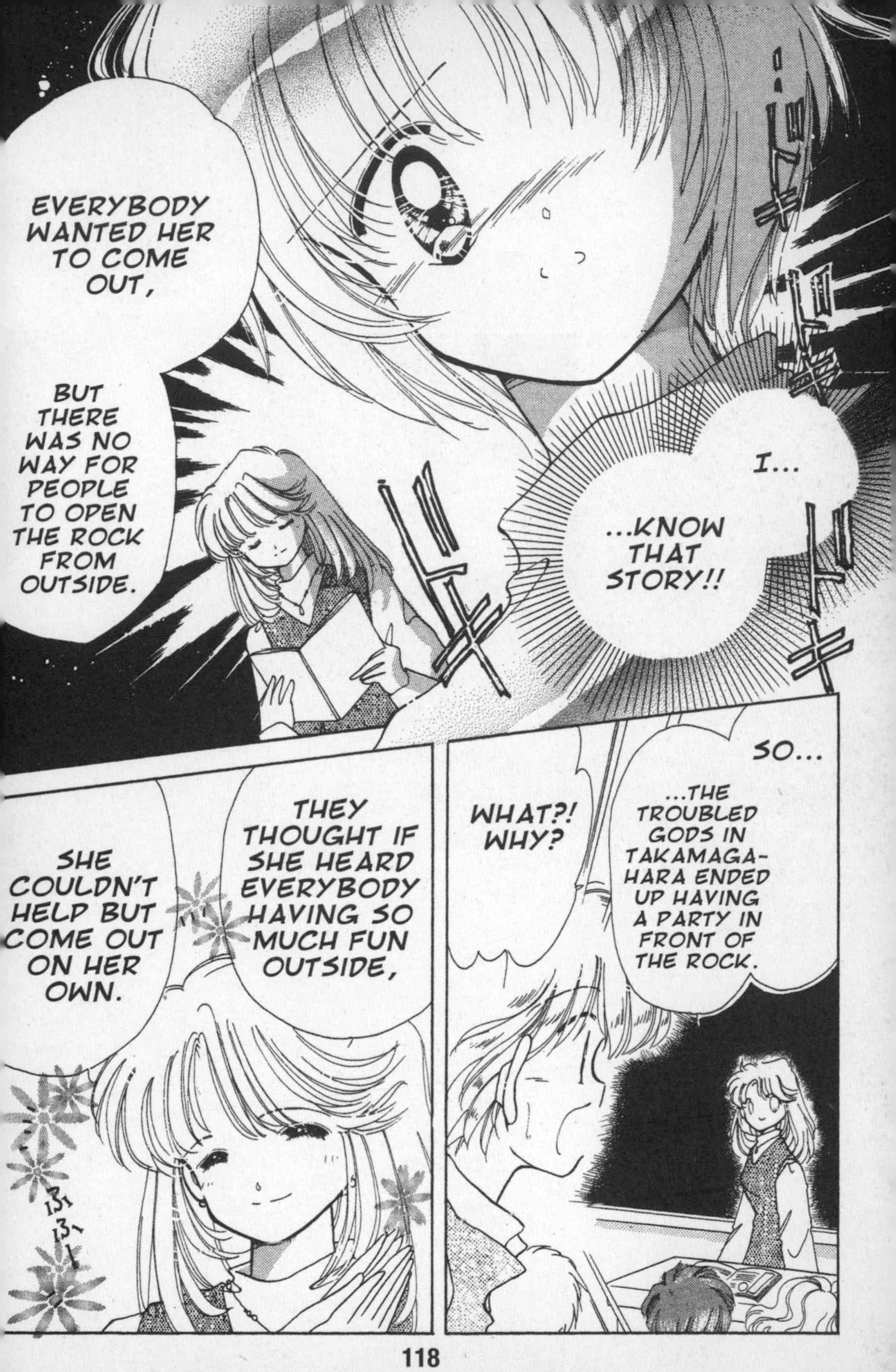
I...
...KNOW THAT STORY!!
EVERYBODY WANTED HER TO COME OUT,
BUT THERE WAS NO WAY FOR PEOPLE TO OPEN THE ROCK FROM OUTSIDE.
SO...
...THE TROUBLED GODS IN TAKAMAGA-HARA ENDED UP HAVING A PARTY IN FRONT OF THE ROCK.
WHAT?! WHY?
THEY THOUGHT IF SHE HEARD EVERYBODY HAVING SO MUCH FUN OUTSIDE,
SHE COULDN'T HELP BUT COME OUT ON HER OWN.

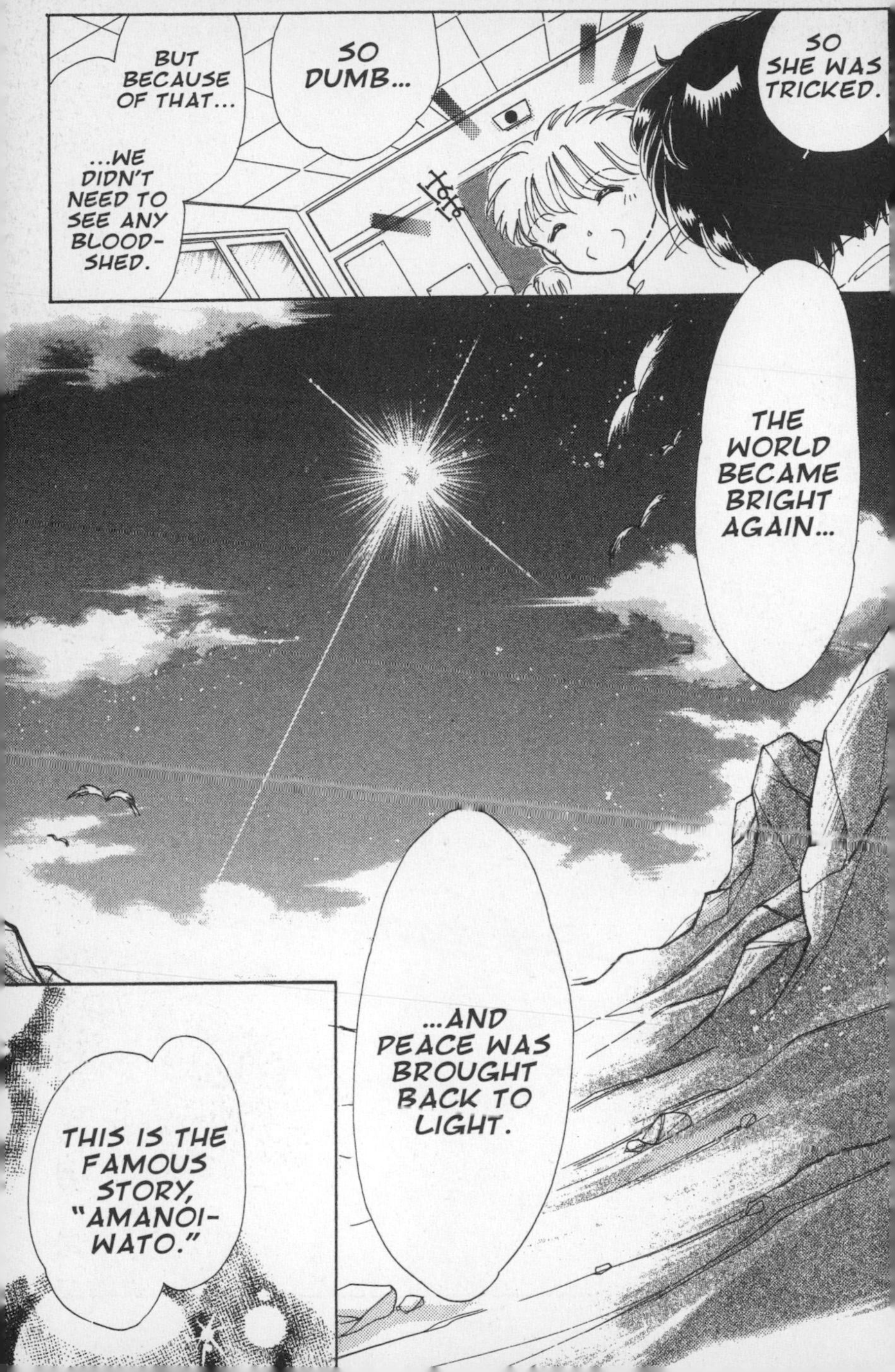
SO SHE WAS TRICKED.
SO DUMB...
BUT BECAUSE OF THAT...
...WE DIDN'T NEED TO SEE ANY BLOOD-SHED.
THE WORLD BECAME BRIGHT AGAIN...
...AND PEACE WAS BROUGHT BACK TO LIGHT.
THIS IS THE FAMOUS STORY, "AMANOI-WATO."

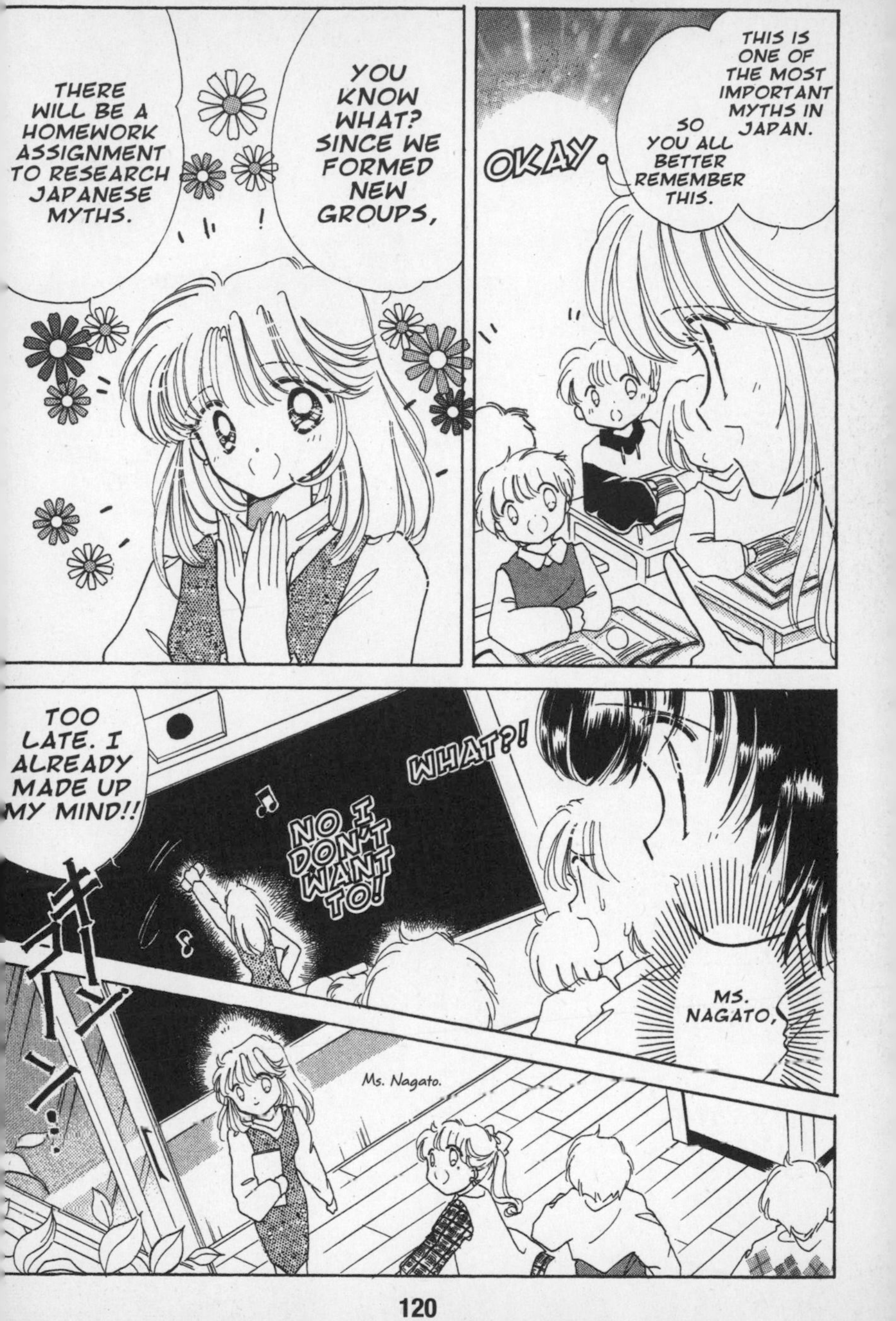
THIS IS ONE OF THE MOST IMPORTANT MYTHS IN JAPAN.
SO YOU ALL BETTER REMEMBER THIS.
OKAY.
YOU KNOW WHAT? SINCE WE FORMED NEW GROUPS,
THERE WILL BE A HOMEWORK ASSIGNMENT TO RESEARCH JAPANESE MYTHS.
MS. NAGATO,
WHAT?!
NO I DON'T WANT TO!
TOO LATE. I ALREADY MADE UP MY MIND!!
Ms. Nagato.

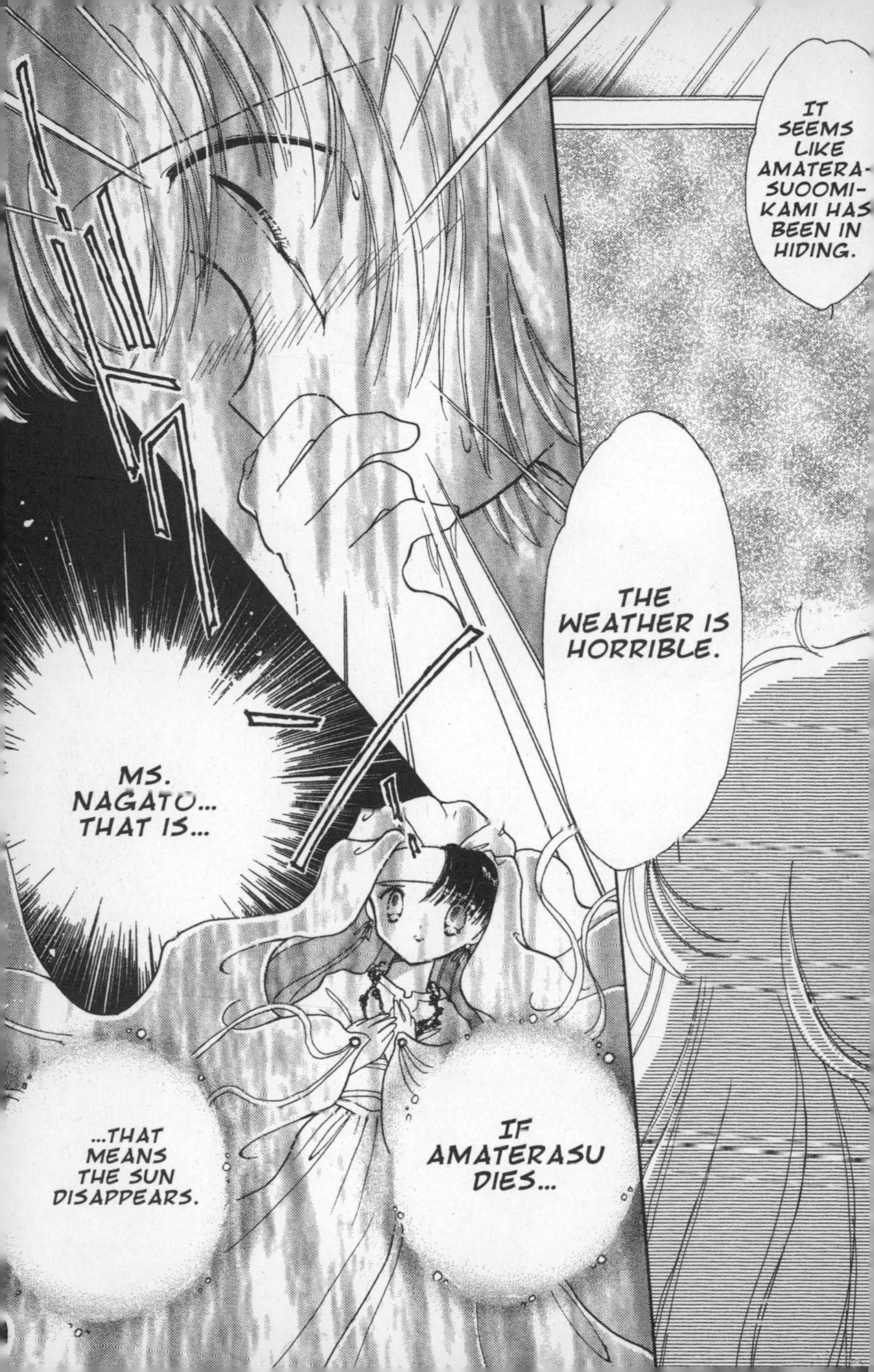
IT SEEMS LIKE AMATERA-SUOOMI-KAMI HAS BEEN IN HIDING.
THE WEATHER IS HORRIBLE.
MS. NAGATO... THAT IS...
IF AMATERASU DIES...
...THAT MEANS THE SUN DISAPPEARS.

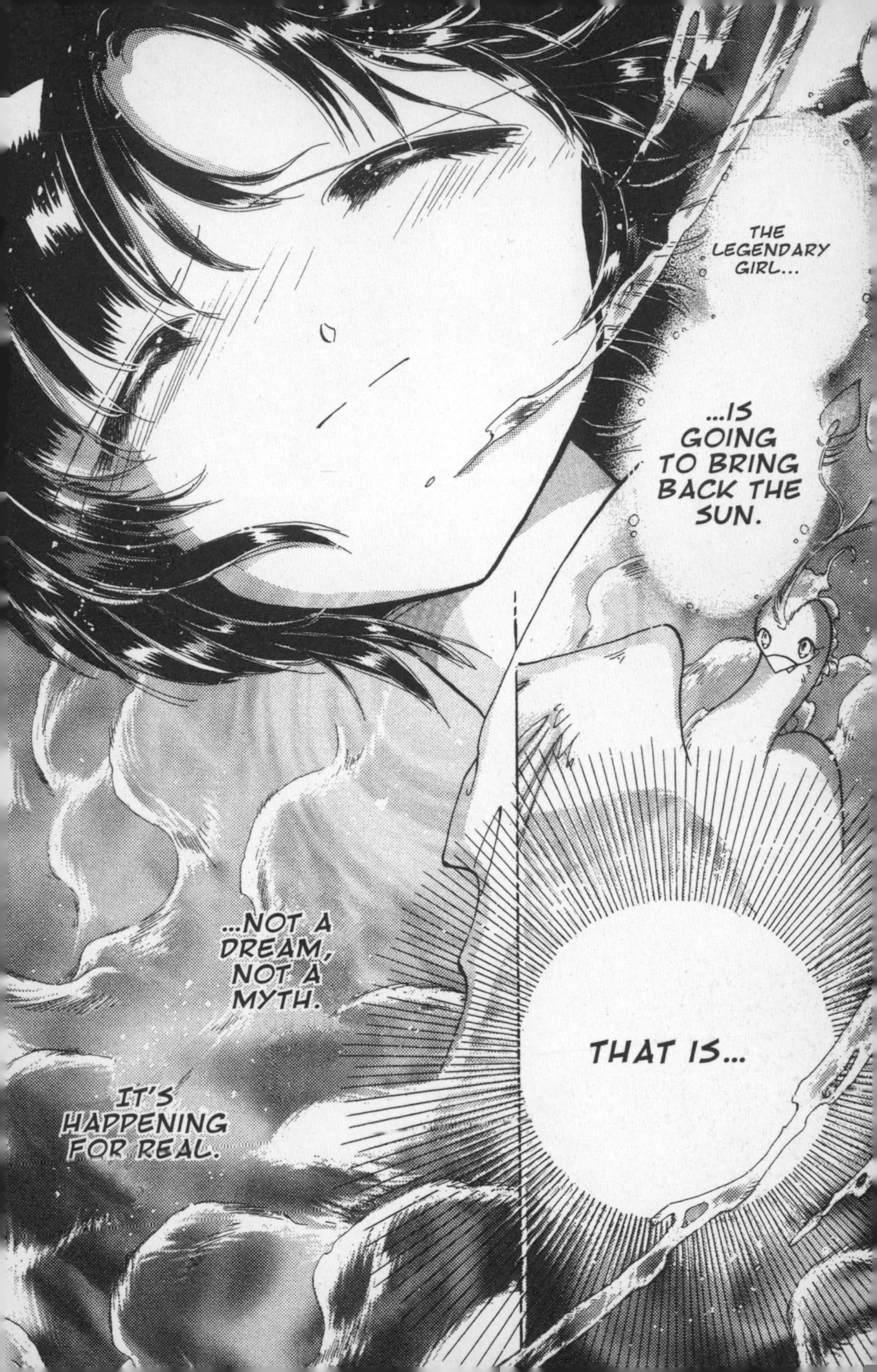
THE LEGENDARY GIRL...
...IS GOING TO BRING BACK THE SUN.
THAT IS...
...NOT A DREAM, NOT A MYTH.
IT'S HAPPENING FOR REAL.

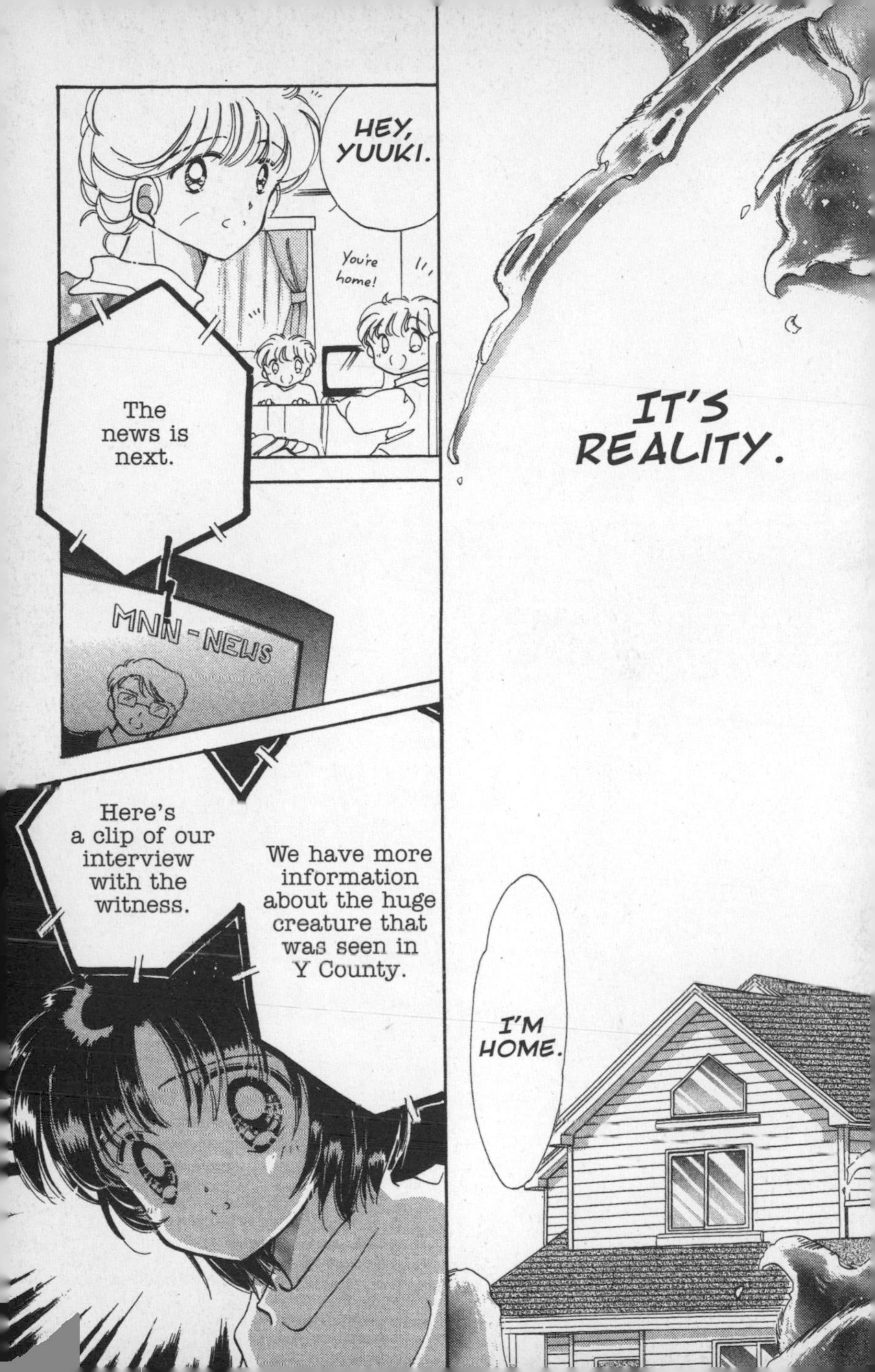
IT'S REALITY.
I'M HOME.
HEY, YUUKI.
You're home!
The news is next.
MNN-NEWS
We have more information about the huge creature that was seen in Y County.
Here's a clip of our interview with the witness.

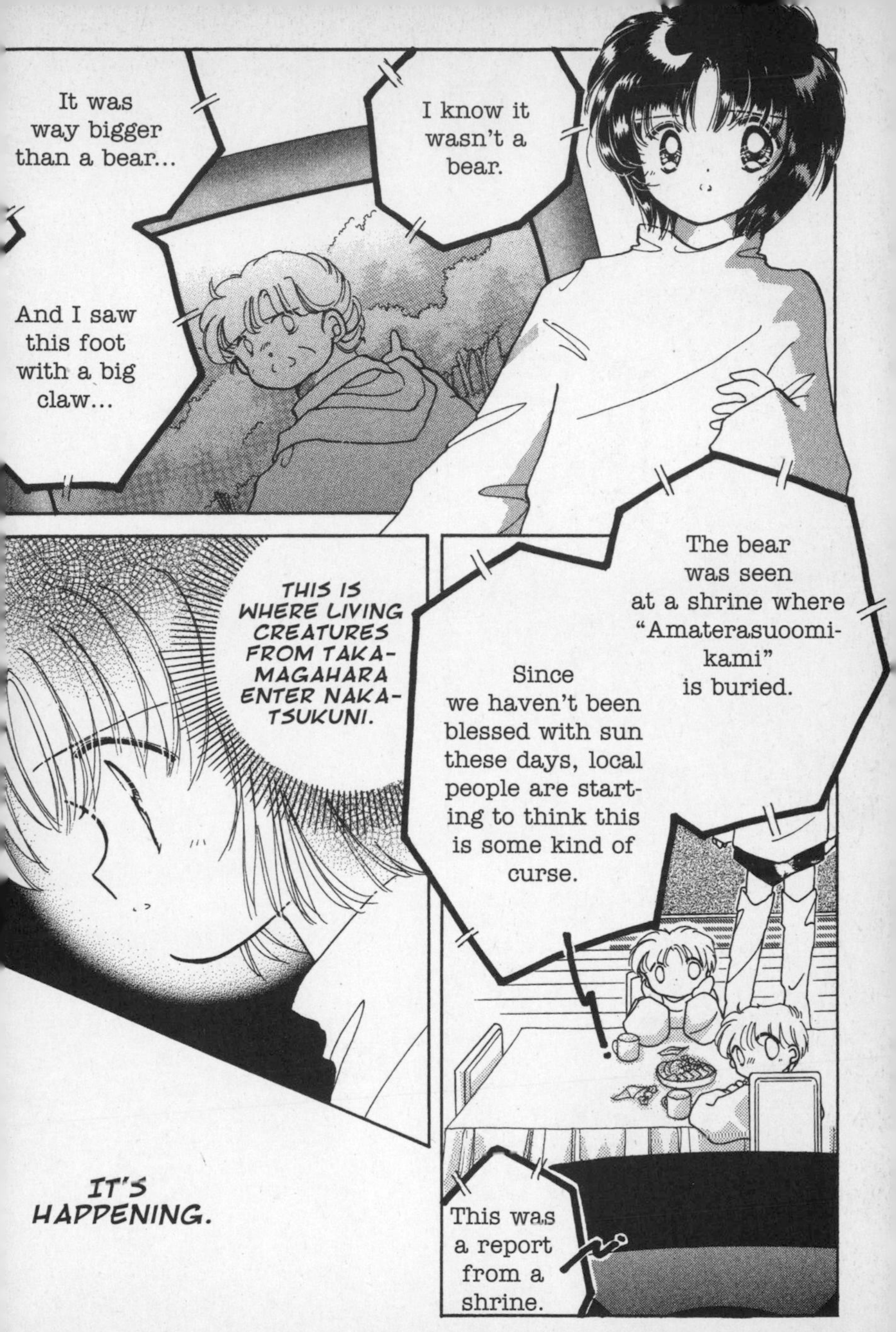
I know it wasn't a bear.
It was way bigger than a bear...
And I saw this foot with a big claw...
The bear was seen at a shrine where "Amaterasuoomi-kami" is buried.
Since we haven't been blessed with sun these days, local people are starting to think this is some kind of curse.
This was a report from a shrine.
THIS IS WHERE LIVING CREATURES FROM TAKAMAGAHARA ENTER NAKATSUKUNI.
IT'S HAPPENING.

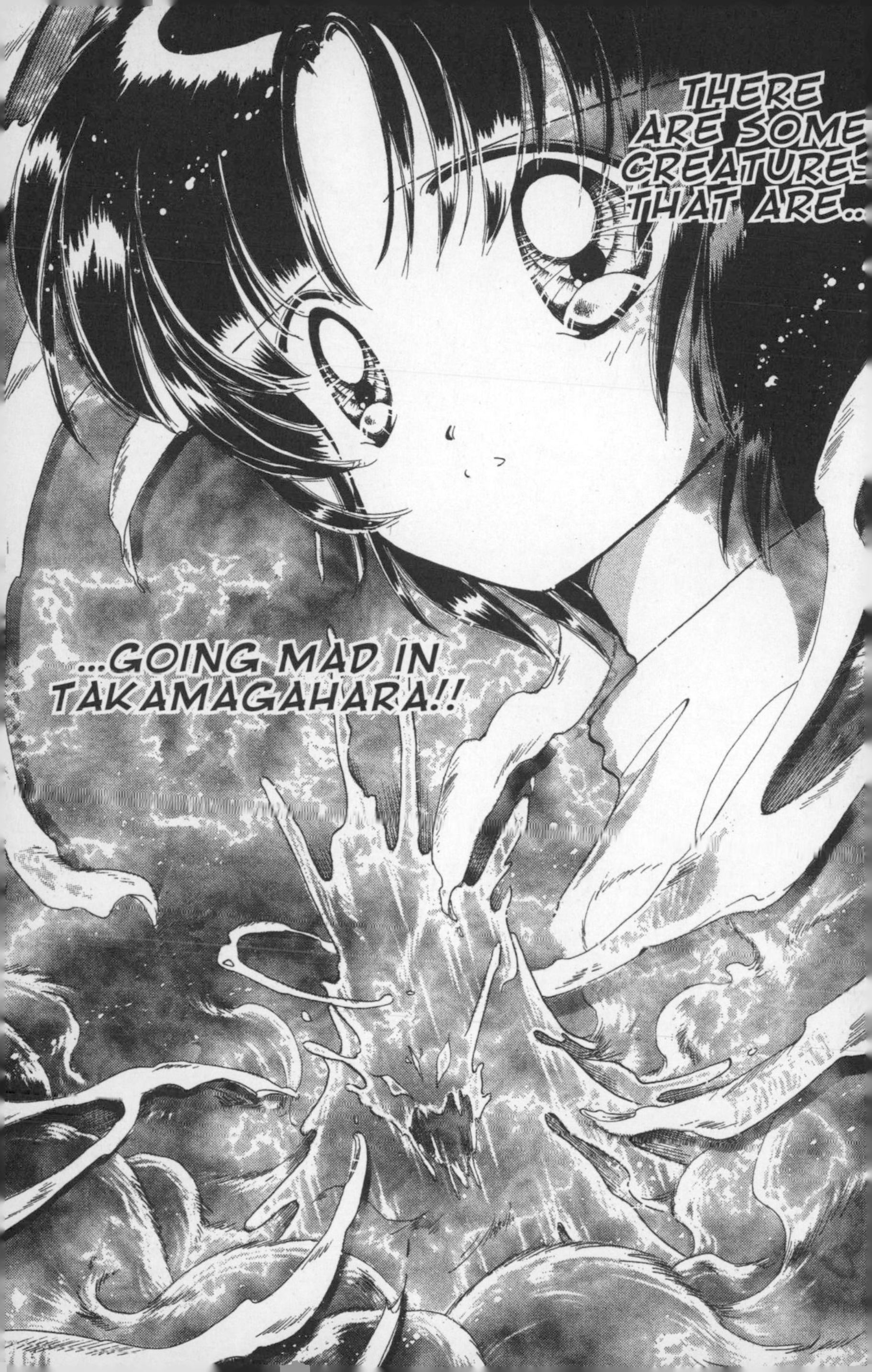
THERE ARE SOME CREATURES THAT ARE...
...GOING MAD IN TAKAMAGAHARA!!

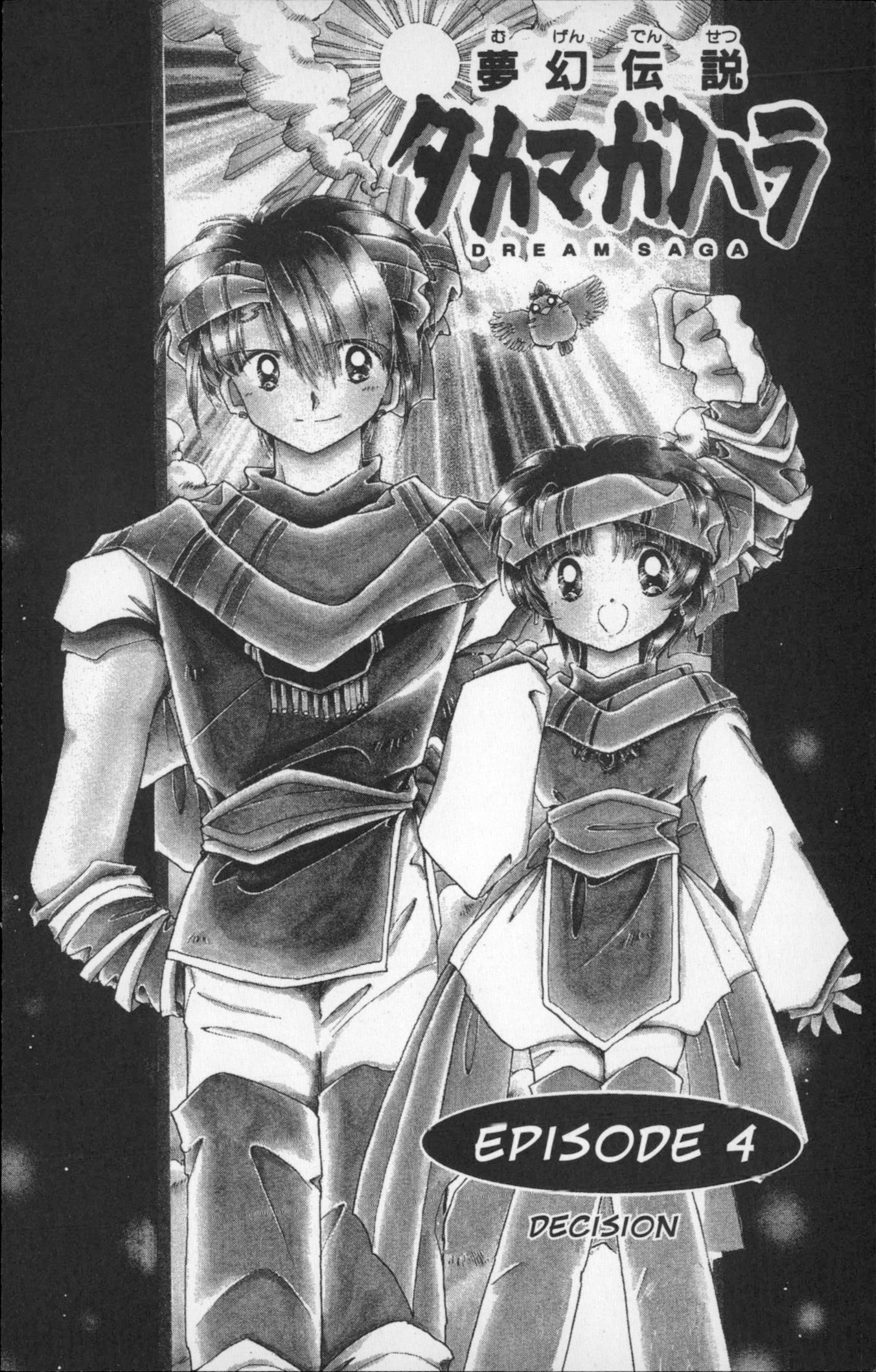
むげんでんせつ
夢幻伝説
タカマガハラ
DREAM SAGA
EPISODE 4
DECISION

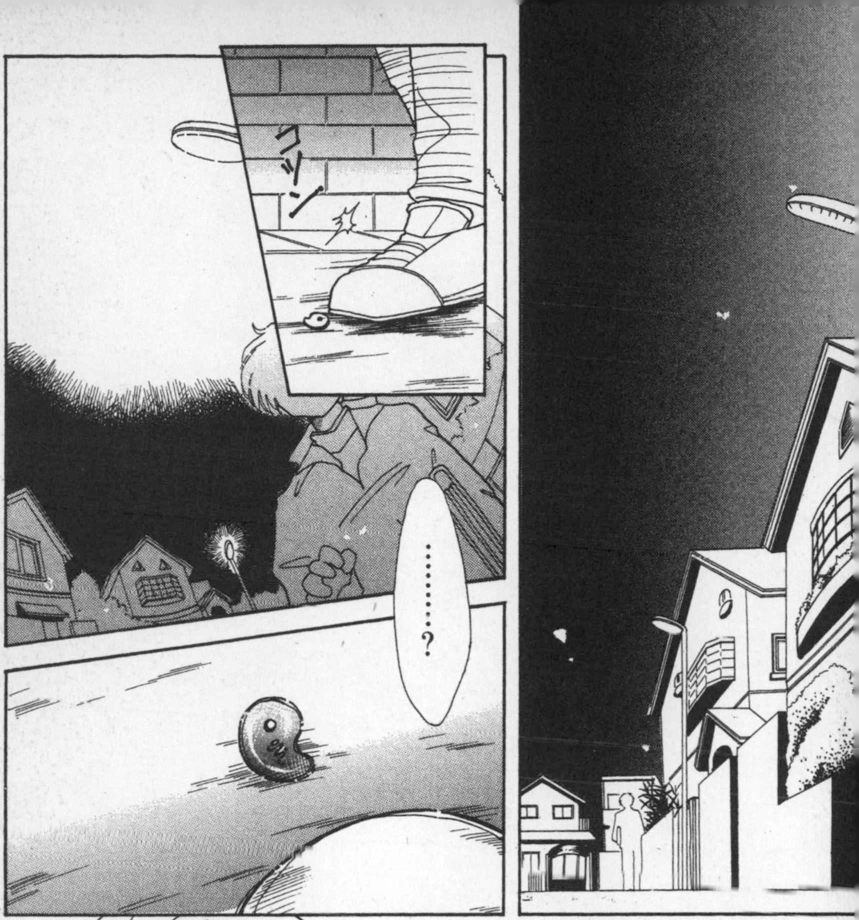
........?

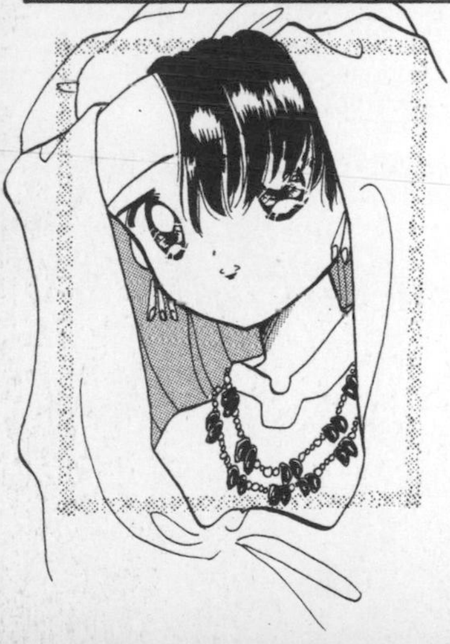

Question: Do you like playing video games?

Answer: I love video games but I haven't played for a while because I've been extremely busy. I normally play role-playing games such as Final Fantasy or Dragon Quest. I've also played Mother and Shining Force too, and liked it.

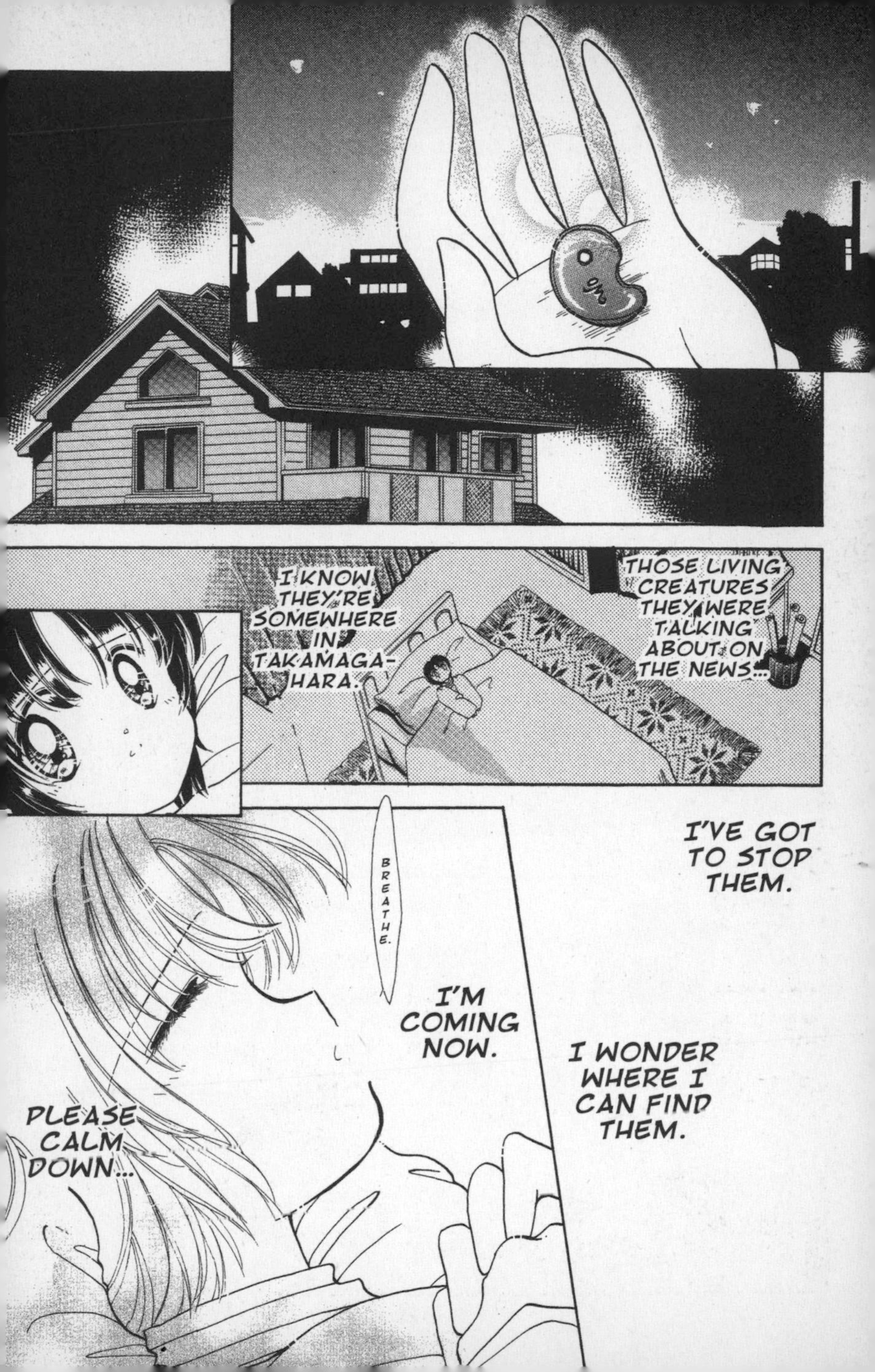
THOSE LIVING CREATURES THEY WERE TALKING ABOUT ON THE NEWS...
I KNOW THEY'RE SOMEWHERE IN TAKAMAGA-HARA.
I'VE GOT TO STOP THEM.
I WONDER WHERE I CAN FIND THEM.
BREATHE.
I'M COMING NOW.
PLEASE CALM DOWN...

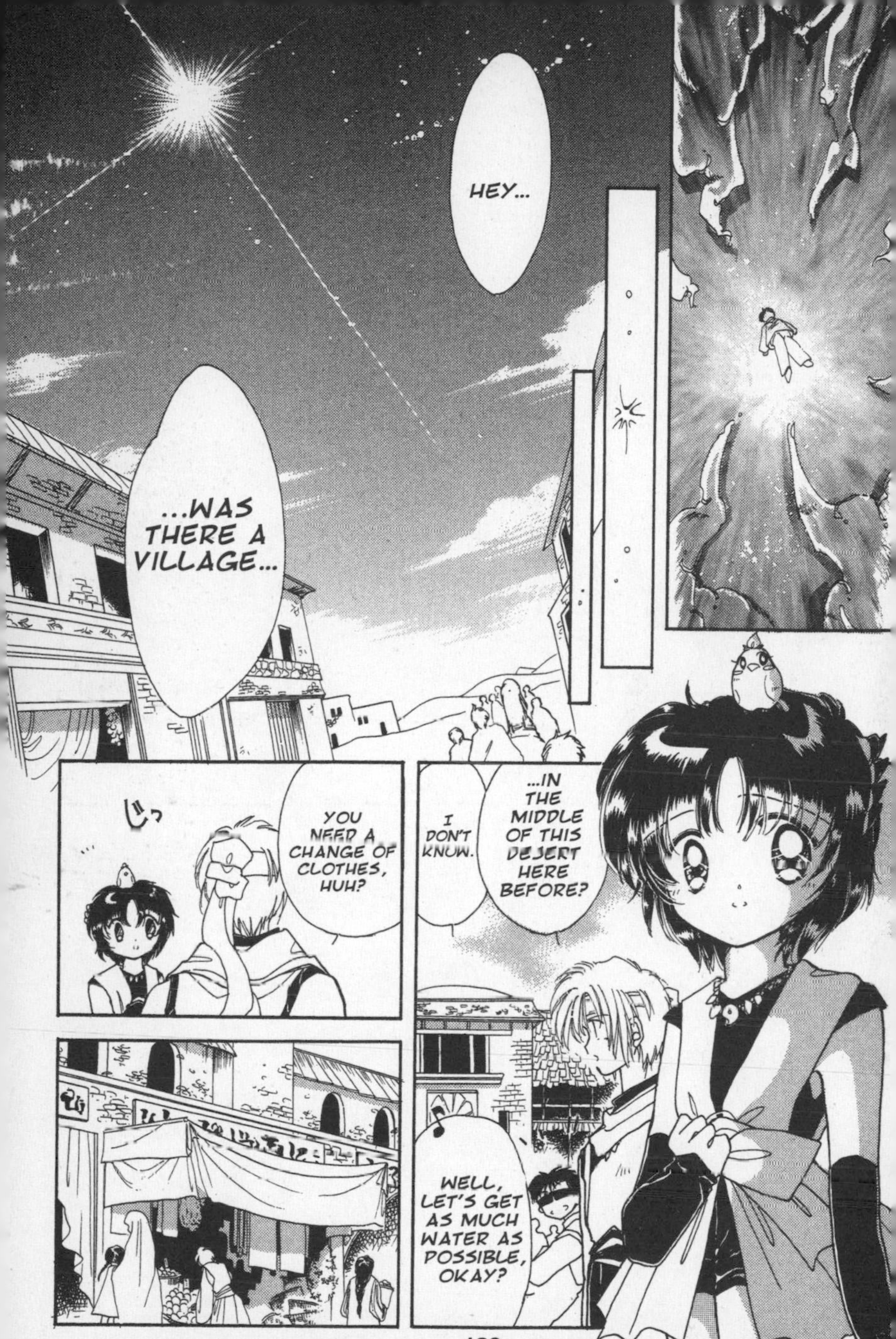
HEY...
...WAS THERE A VILLAGE...
...IN THE MIDDLE OF THIS DESERT HERE BEFORE?
I DON'T KNOW.
YOU NEED A CHANGE OF CLOTHES, HUH?
じっ
WELL, LET'S GET AS MUCH WATER AS POSSIBLE, OKAY?

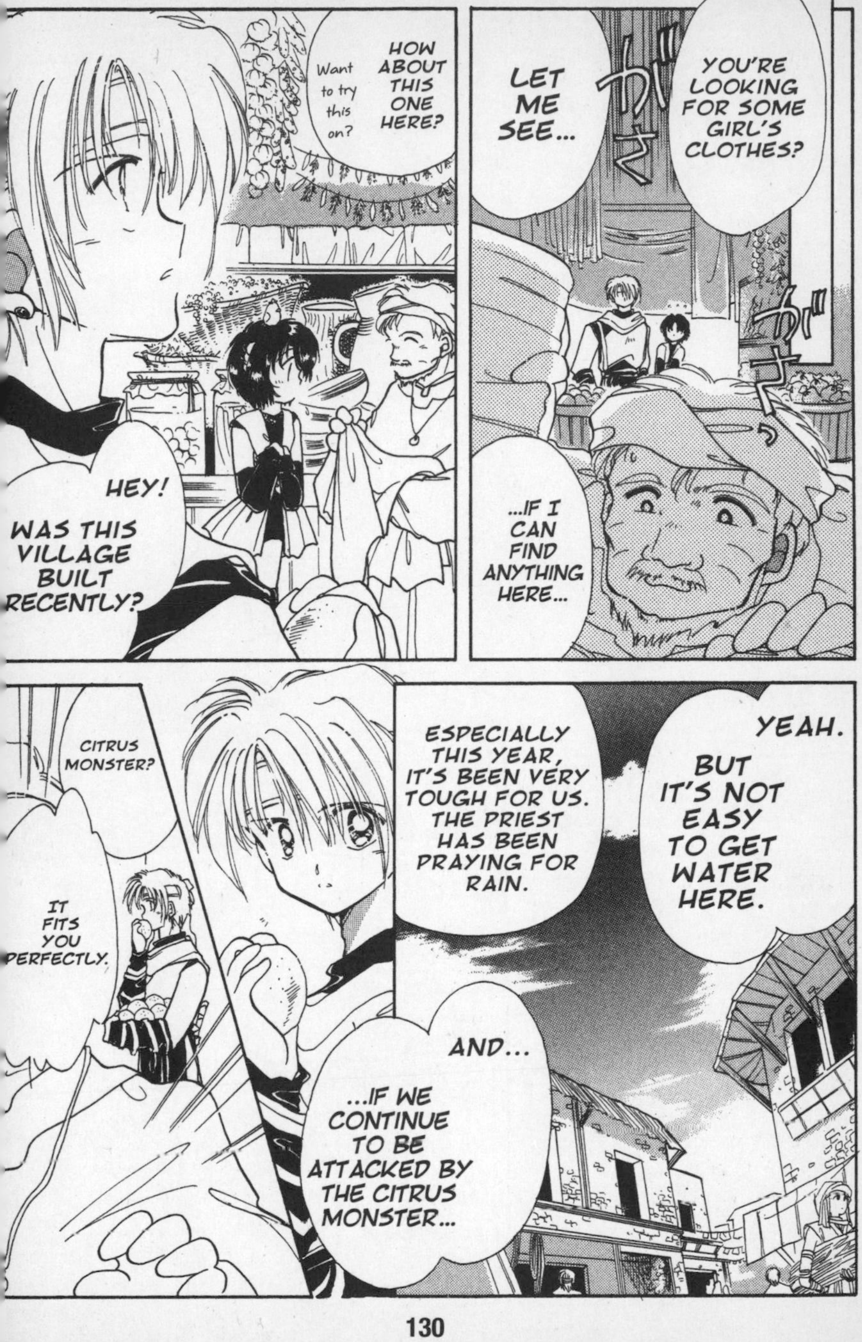
YOU'RE LOOKING FOR SOME GIRL'S CLOTHES?
LET ME SEE...
...IF I CAN FIND ANYTHING HERE...
HOW ABOUT THIS ONE HERE?
Want to try this on?
HEY! WAS THIS VILLAGE BUILT RECENTLY?
YEAH.
BUT IT'S NOT EASY TO GET WATER HERE.
ESPECIALLY THIS YEAR, IT'S BEEN VERY TOUGH FOR US. THE PRIEST HAS BEEN PRAYING FOR RAIN.
AND...
...IF WE CONTINUE TO BE ATTACKED BY THE CITRUS MONSTER...
CITRUS MONSTER?
IT FITS YOU PERFECTLY.

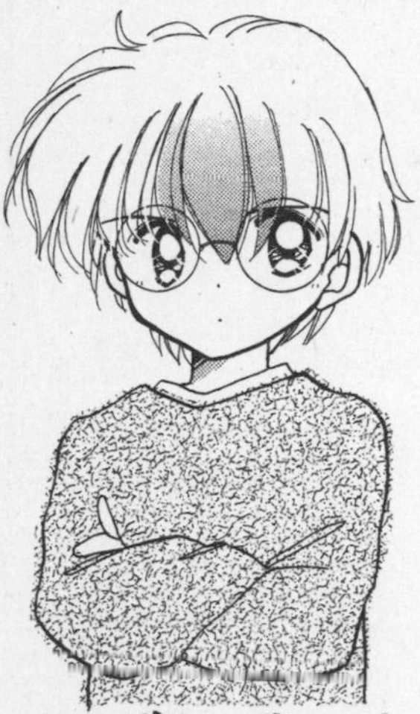

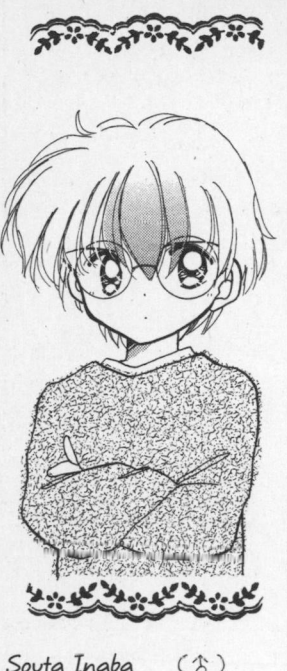

Souta Inaba (♂)

Born on April 10. Blood type: A.

Yuuki and Takaomi's classmate. He loves studying and is a very smart boy. He has no siblings. His eyesight is very bad so he wears glasses. The Souta you see in Takamagahara shares the same memory with the Souta in Nakatsukuni. But they have different personalities and bodies. You will find out more about Souta in Takamagahara in Volume 2.

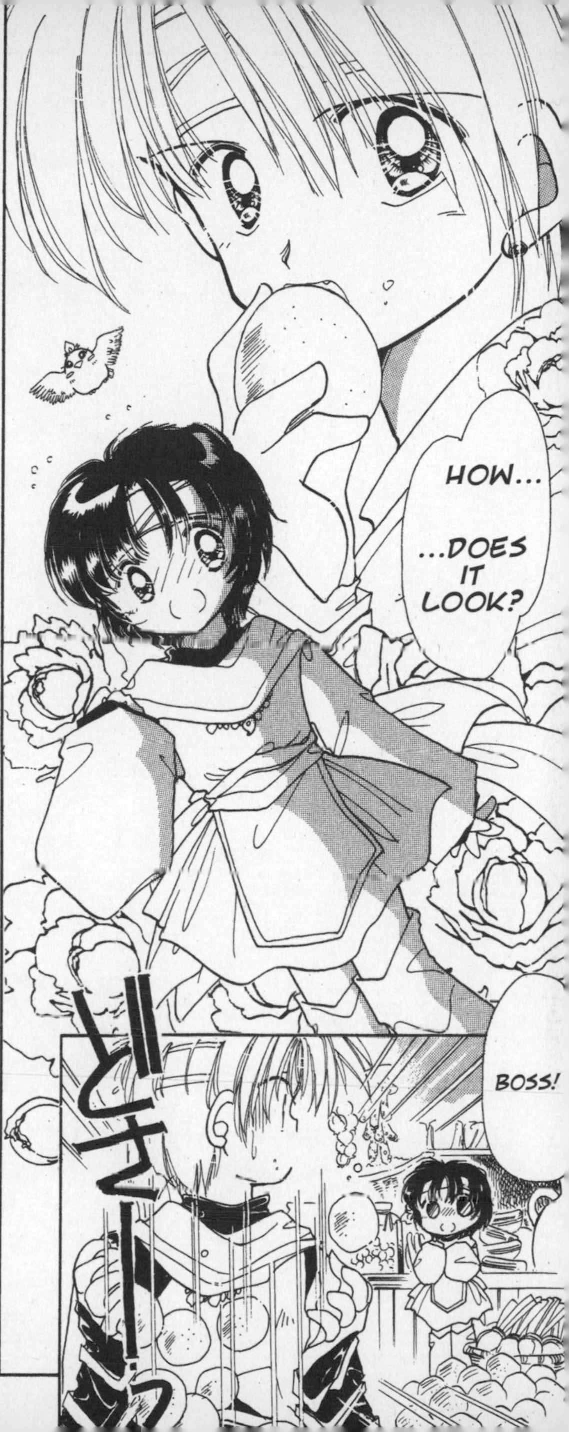
HOW...
...DOES IT LOOK?
BOSS!

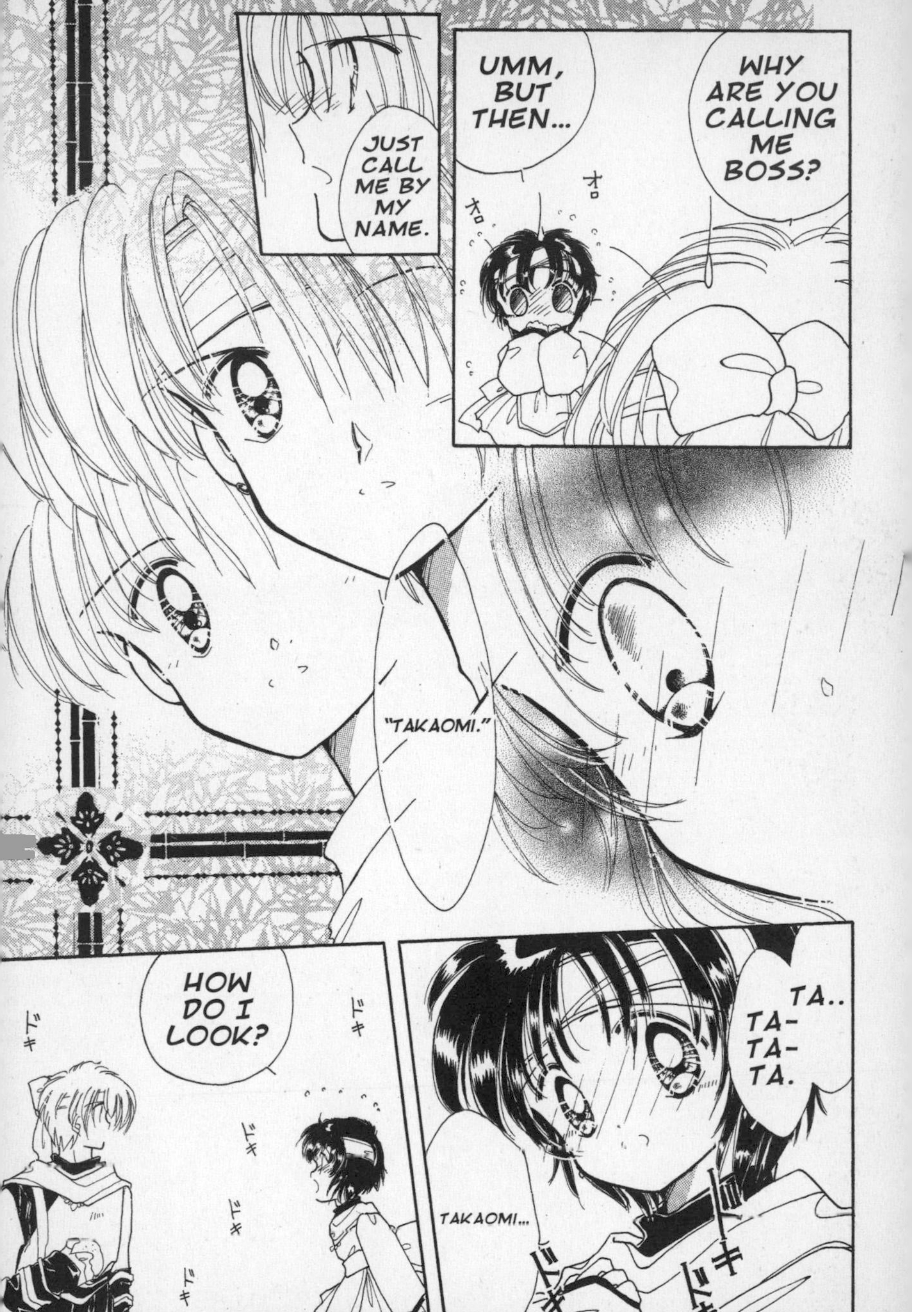
WHY ARE YOU CALLING ME BOSS?
UMM, BUT THEN...
オロ
オロ
JUST CALL ME BY MY NAME.
"TAKAOMI."
TA.. TA-TA-TA.
TAKAOMI...
ドキ ドキ
ドキ ドキ
HOW DO I LOOK?
ドキ
ドキ
ドキ
ドキ
ドキ

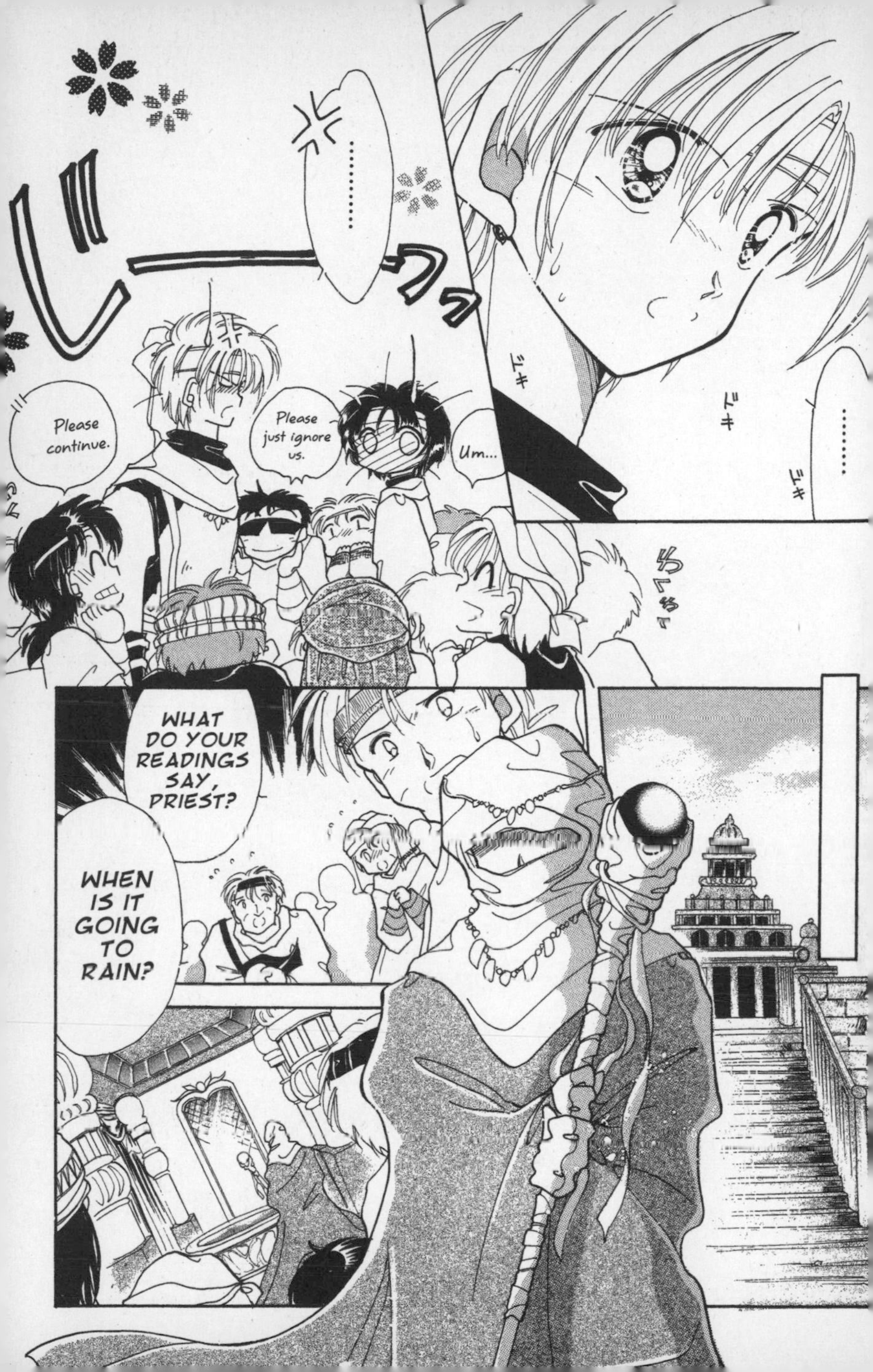
......
ドキ
ドキ
ドキ
......
Um...
Please just ignore us.
Please continue.
WHAT DO YOUR READINGS SAY, PRIEST?
WHEN IS IT GOING TO RAIN?

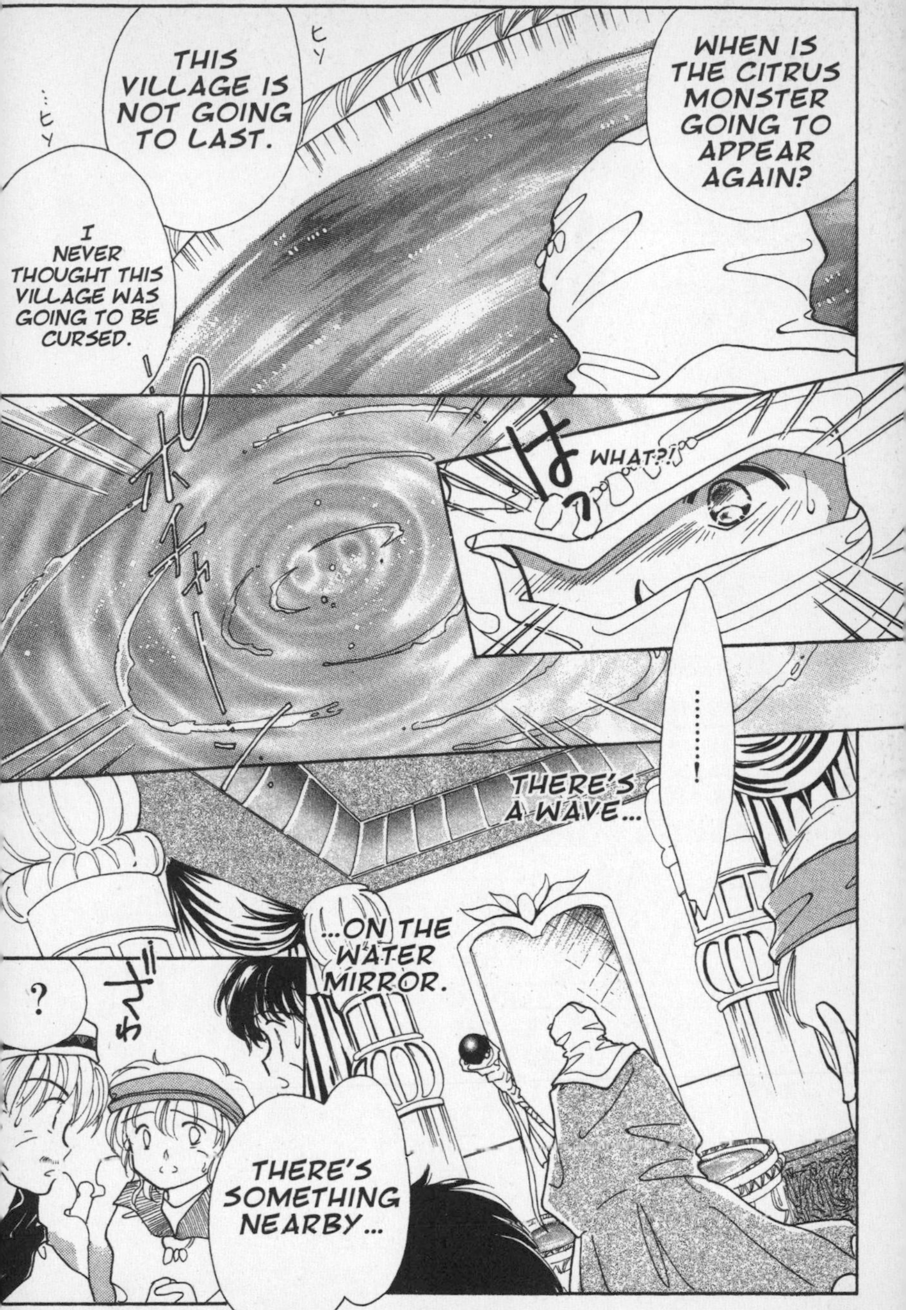
WHEN IS THE CITRUS MONSTER GOING TO APPEAR AGAIN?
ヒソ
THIS VILLAGE IS NOT GOING TO LAST.
…ヒソ
I NEVER THOUGHT THIS VILLAGE WAS GOING TO BE CURSED.
はっ
WHAT?!
........!
THERE'S A WAVE...
...ON THE WATER MIRROR.
?
THERE'S SOMETHING NEARBY...

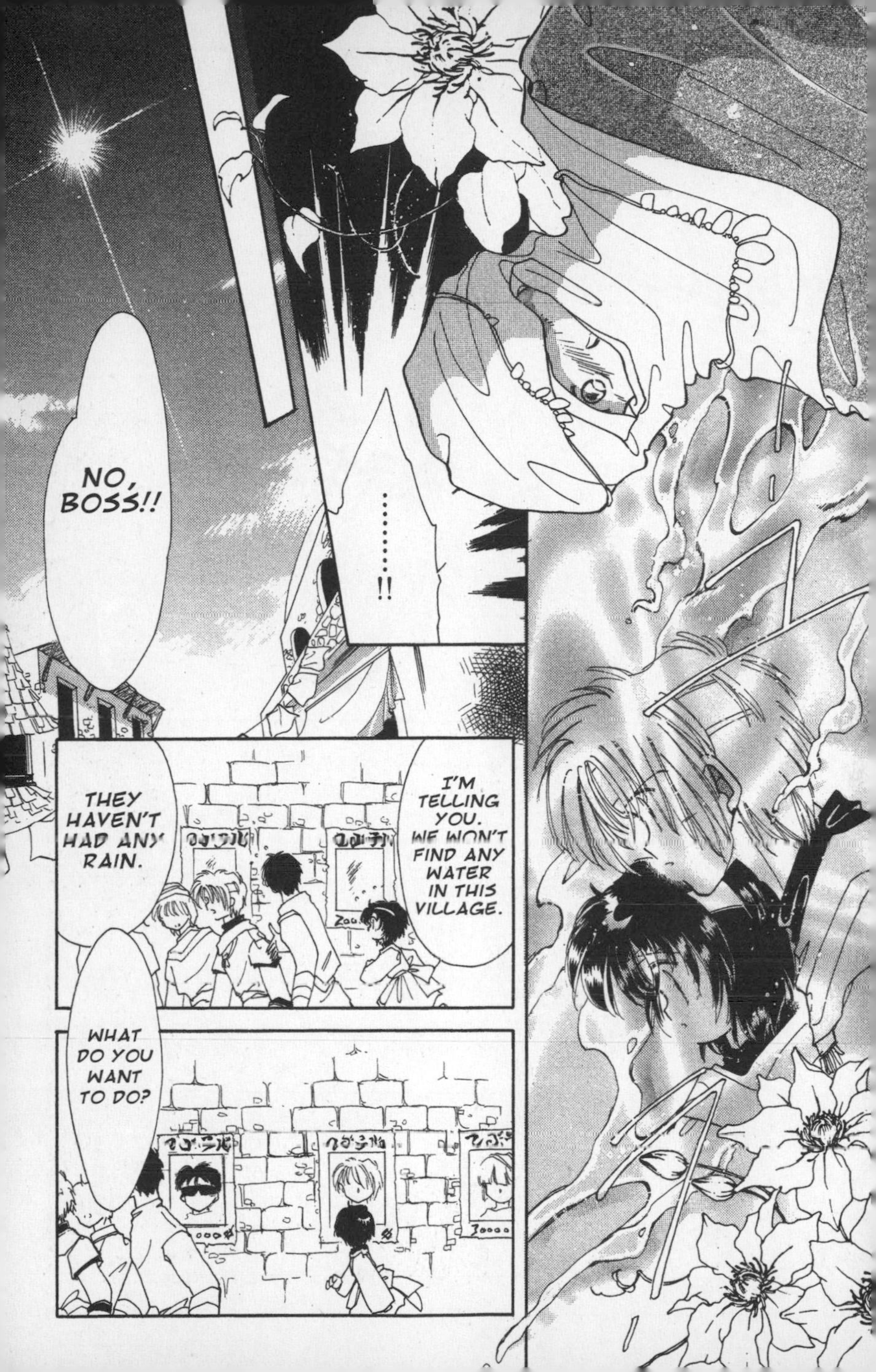
......!!
NO, BOSS!!
I'M TELLING YOU. WE WON'T FIND ANY WATER IN THIS VILLAGE.
THEY HAVEN'T HAD ANY RAIN.
WHAT DO YOU WANT TO DO?

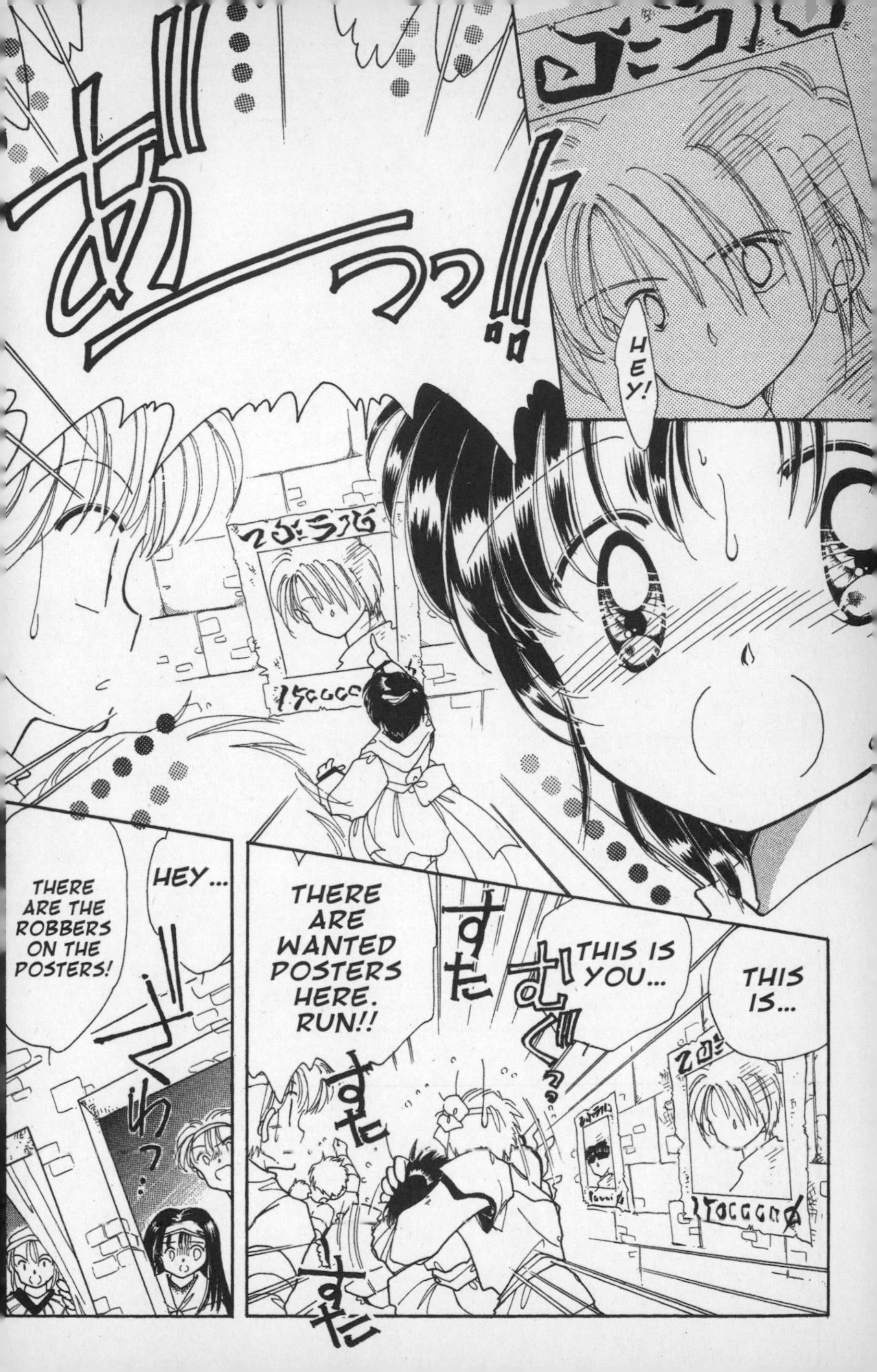
HEY!
あーっ!!
THIS IS...
THIS IS YOU...
THERE ARE WANTED POSTERS HERE. RUN!!
すたすた
HEY...
THERE ARE THE ROBBERS ON THE POSTERS!

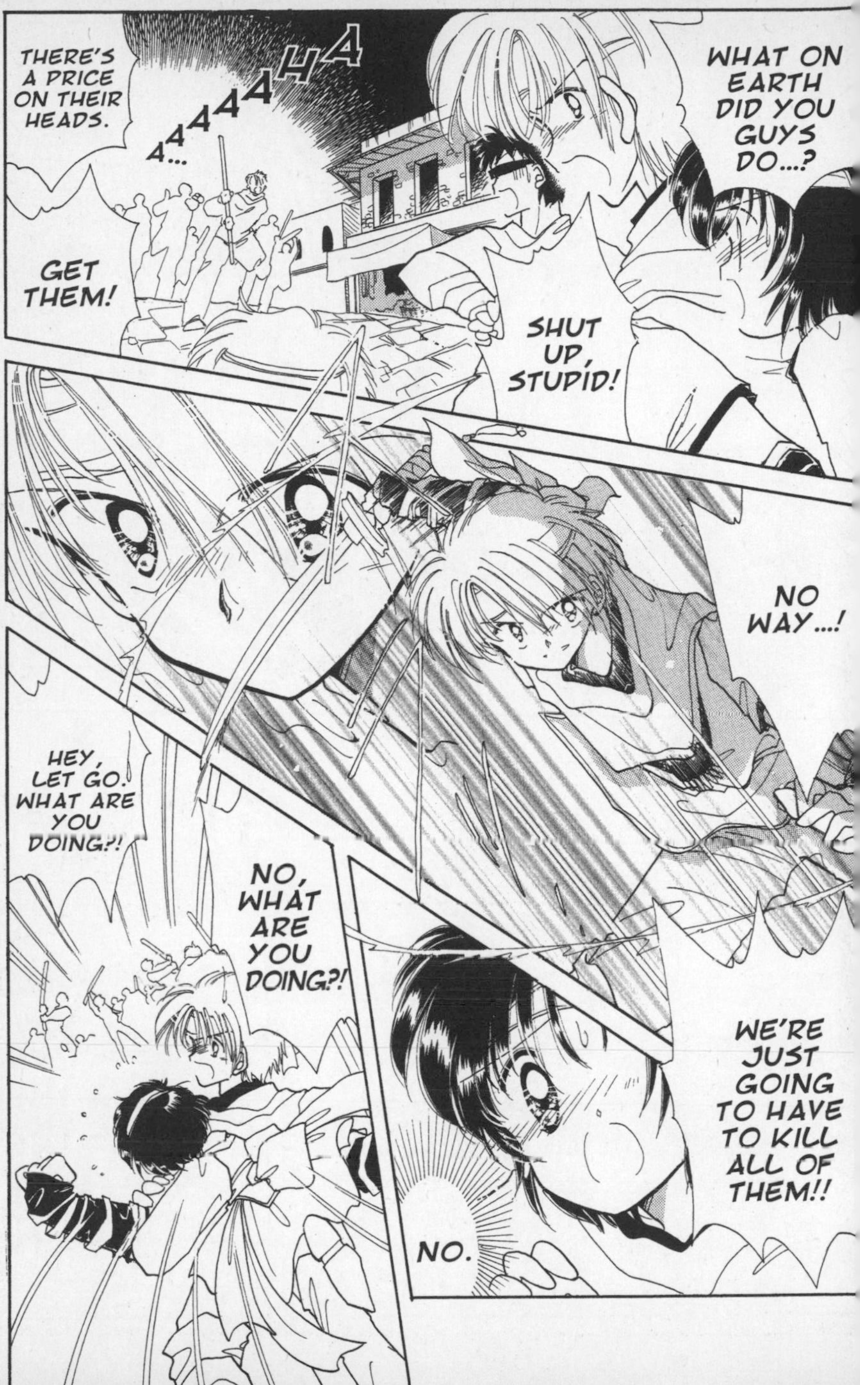
WHAT ON EARTH DID YOU GUYS DO...?
SHUT UP, STUPID!
A... AAAAHA
THERE'S A PRICE ON THEIR HEADS.
GET THEM!
NO WAY...!
WE'RE JUST GOING TO HAVE TO KILL ALL OF THEM!!
NO.
HEY, LET GO. WHAT ARE YOU DOING?!
NO, WHAT ARE YOU DOING?!

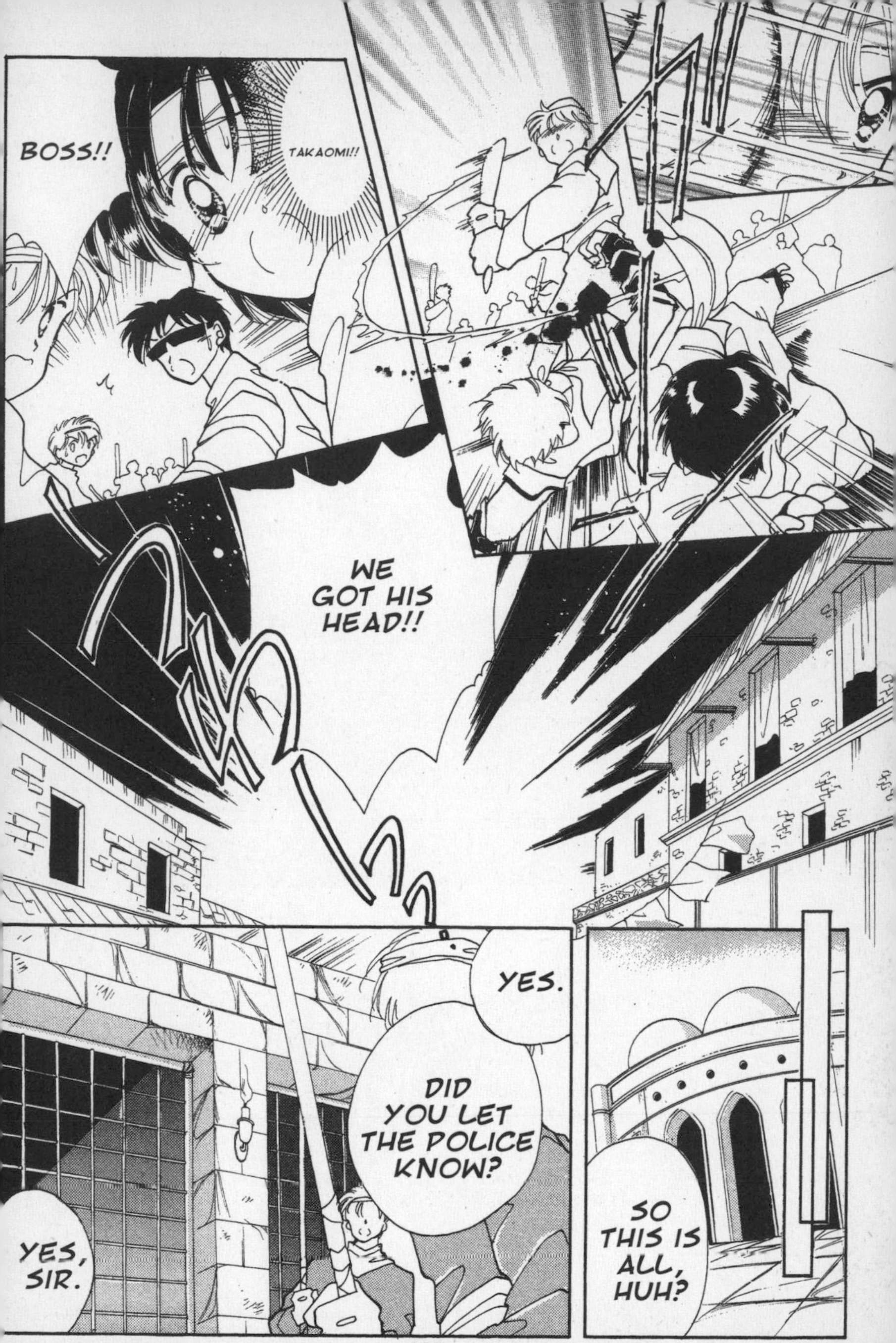
TAKAOMI!!
BOSS!!
WE GOT HIS HEAD!!
SO THIS IS ALL, HUH?
YES.
DID YOU LET THE POLICE KNOW?
YES, SIR.

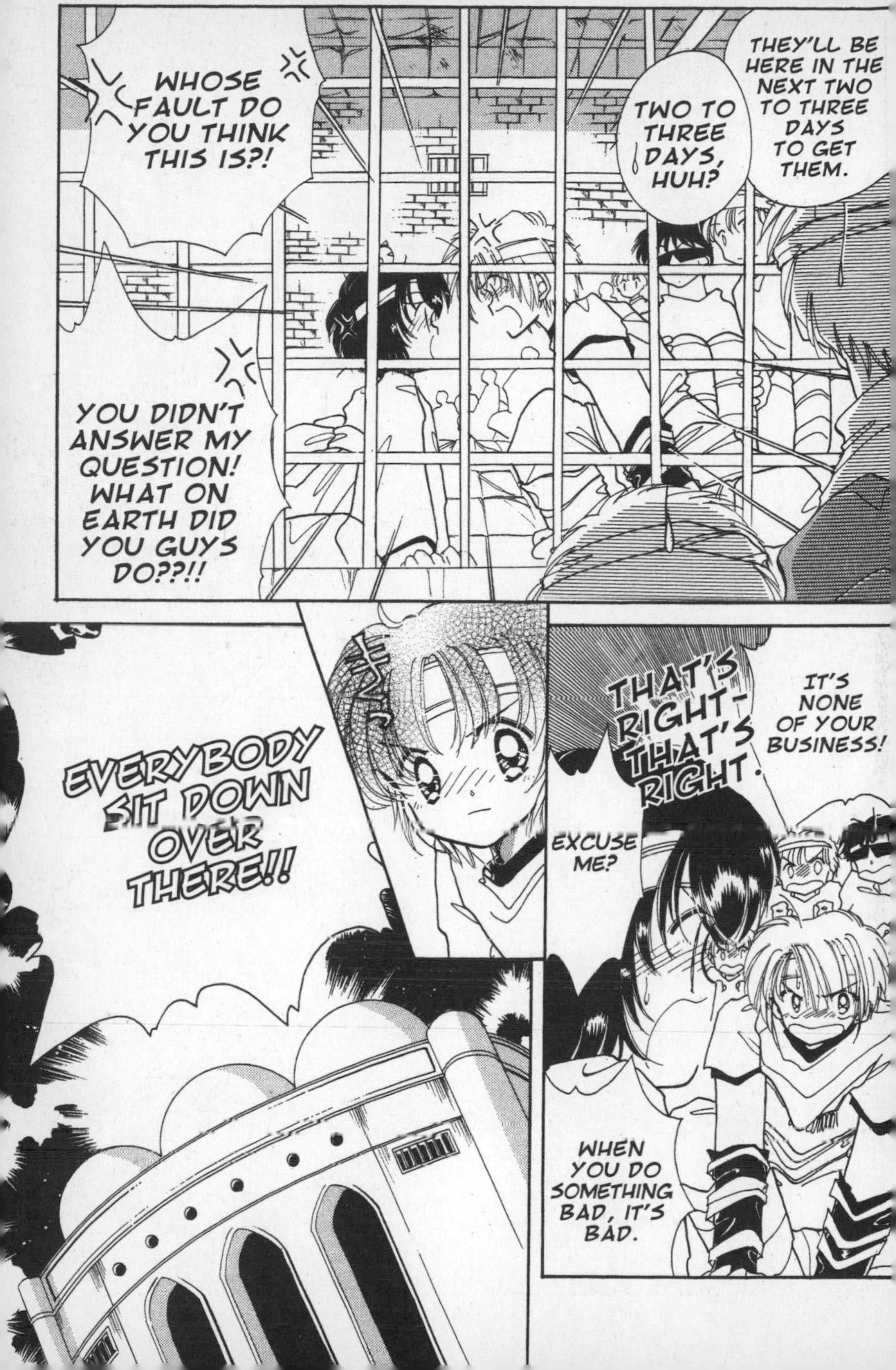
THEY'LL BE HERE IN THE NEXT TWO TO THREE DAYS TO GET THEM.
TWO TO THREE DAYS, HUH?
WHOSE FAULT DO YOU THINK THIS IS?!
YOU DIDN'T ANSWER MY QUESTION! WHAT ON EARTH DID YOU GUYS DO??!!
IT'S NONE OF YOUR BUSINESS!
THAT'S RIGHT- THAT'S RIGHT.
EXCUSE ME?
WHEN YOU DO SOMETHING BAD, IT'S BAD.
EVERYBODY SIT DOWN OVER THERE!!

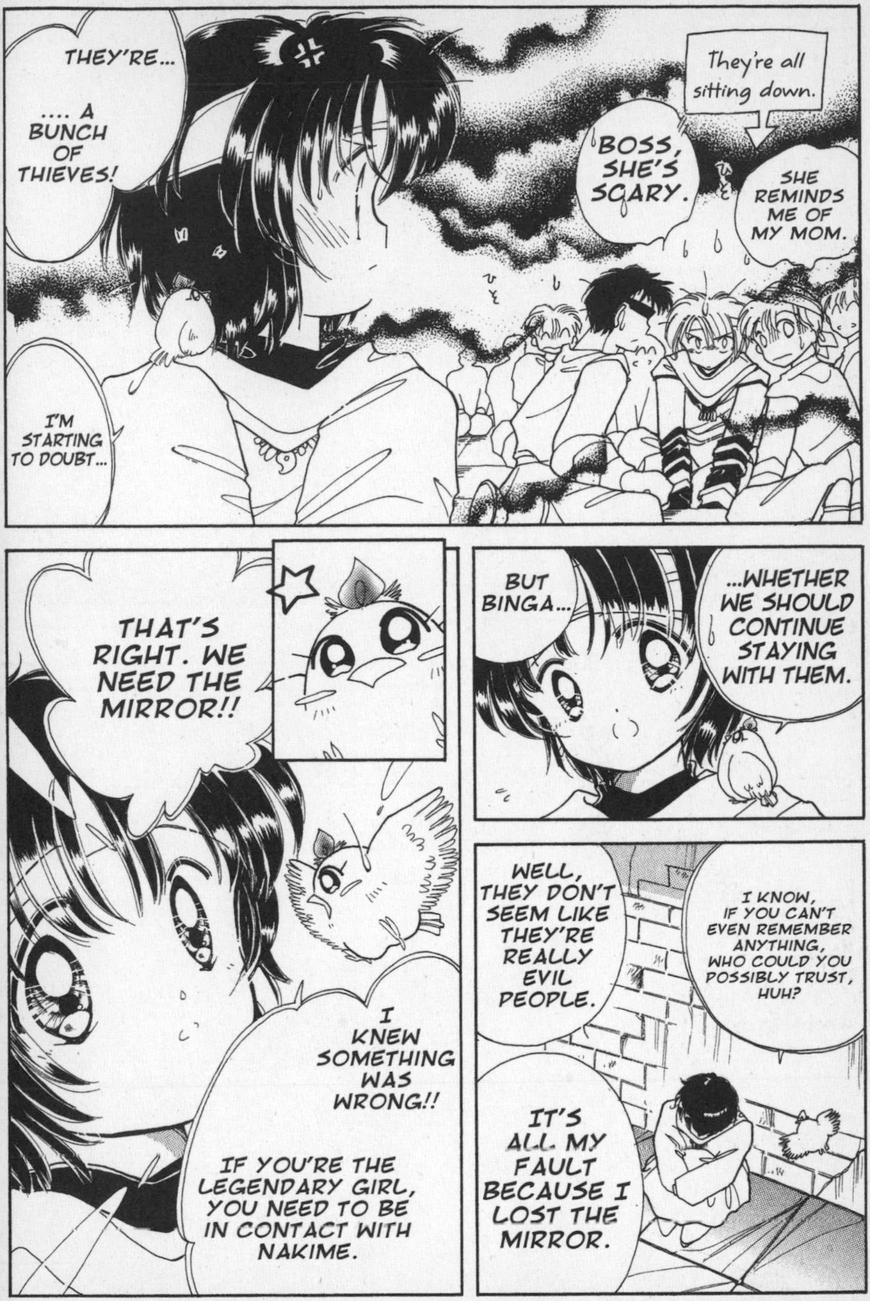
They're all sitting down.
SHE REMINDS ME OF MY MOM.
BOSS, SHE'S SCARY.
THEY'RE...
.... A BUNCH OF THIEVES!
I'M STARTING TO DOUBT...
...WHETHER WE SHOULD CONTINUE STAYING WITH THEM.
BUT BINGA...
I KNOW, IF YOU CAN'T EVEN REMEMBER ANYTHING, WHO COULD YOU POSSIBLY TRUST, HUH?
WELL, THEY DON'T SEEM LIKE THEY'RE REALLY EVIL PEOPLE.
IT'S ALL MY FAULT BECAUSE I LOST THE MIRROR.
THAT'S RIGHT. WE NEED THE MIRROR!!
I KNEW SOMETHING WAS WRONG!!
IF YOU'RE THE LEGENDARY GIRL, YOU NEED TO BE IN CONTACT WITH NAKIME.

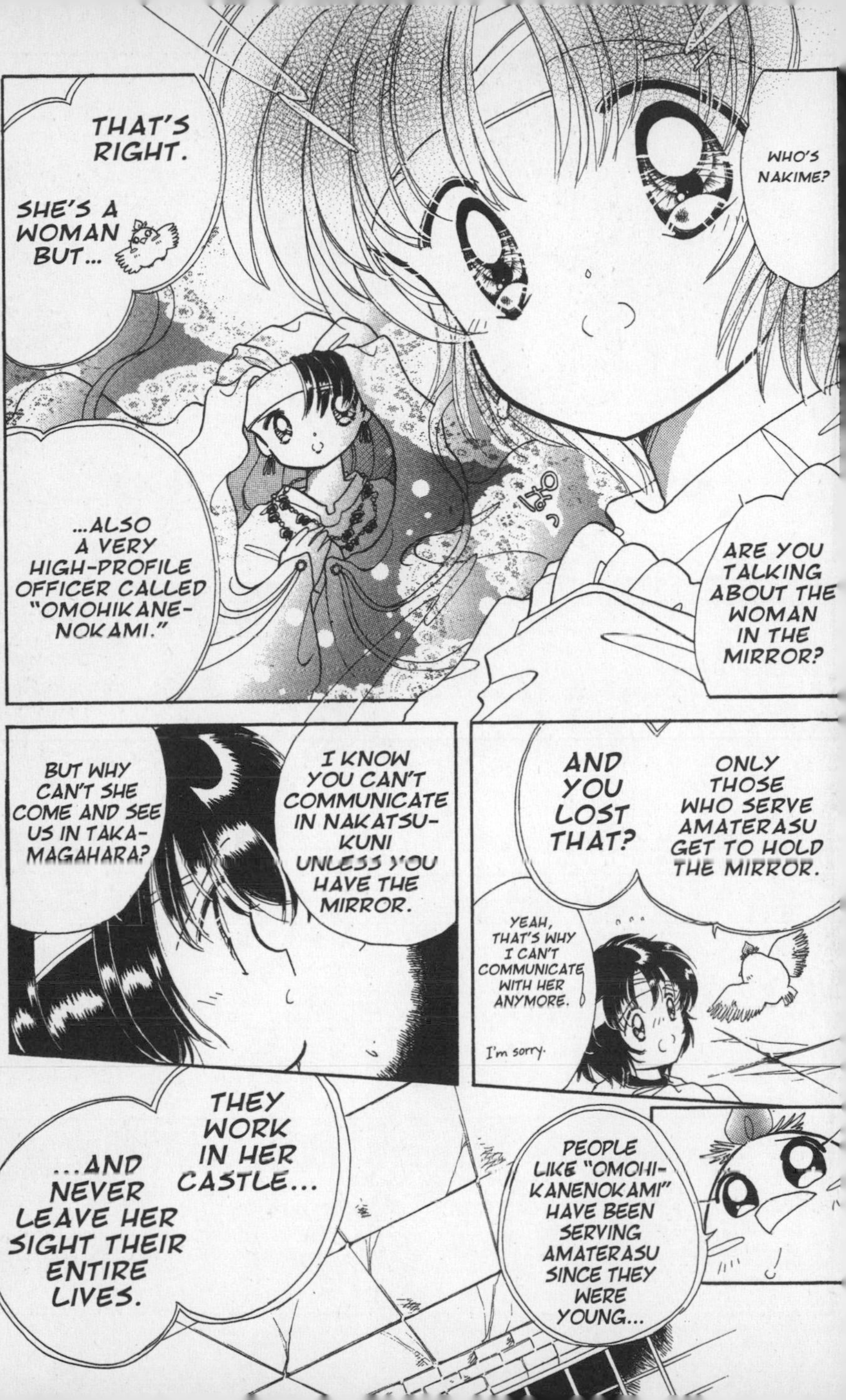
WHO'S NAKIME?
ARE YOU TALKING ABOUT THE WOMAN IN THE MIRROR?
THAT'S RIGHT.
SHE'S A WOMAN BUT...
...ALSO A VERY HIGH-PROFILE OFFICER CALLED "OMOHIKANE-NOKAMI."
ONLY THOSE WHO SERVE AMATERASU GET TO HOLD THE MIRROR.
AND YOU LOST THAT?
YEAH, THAT'S WHY I CAN'T COMMUNICATE WITH HER ANYMORE.
I'm sorry.
I KNOW YOU CAN'T COMMUNICATE IN NAKATSU-KUNI UNLESS YOU HAVE THE MIRROR.
BUT WHY CAN'T SHE COME AND SEE US IN TAKA-MAGAHARA?
PEOPLE LIKE "OMOHI-KANENOKAMI" HAVE BEEN SERVING AMATERASU SINCE THEY WERE YOUNG...
THEY WORK IN HER CASTLE...
...AND NEVER LEAVE HER SIGHT THEIR ENTIRE LIVES.

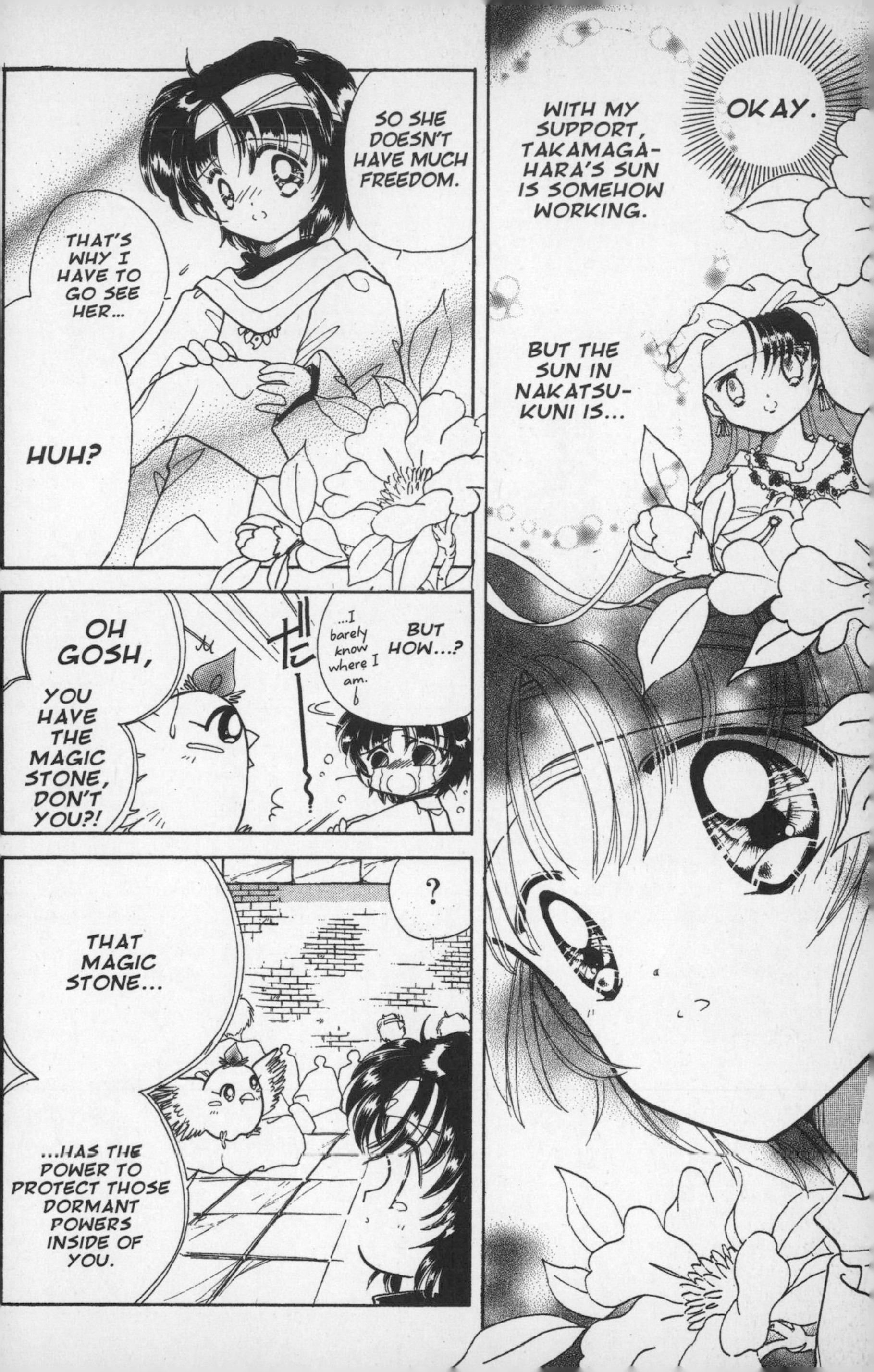
OKAY.
WITH MY SUPPORT, TAKAMAGA-HARA'S SUN IS SOMEHOW WORKING.
BUT THE SUN IN NAKATSU-KUNI IS...
SO SHE DOESN'T HAVE MUCH FREEDOM.
THAT'S WHY I HAVE TO GO SEE HER...
HUH?
BUT HOW...?
...I barely know where I am.
OH GOSH, YOU HAVE THE MAGIC STONE, DON'T YOU?!
?
THAT MAGIC STONE...
...HAS THE POWER TO PROTECT THOSE DORMANT POWERS INSIDE OF YOU.

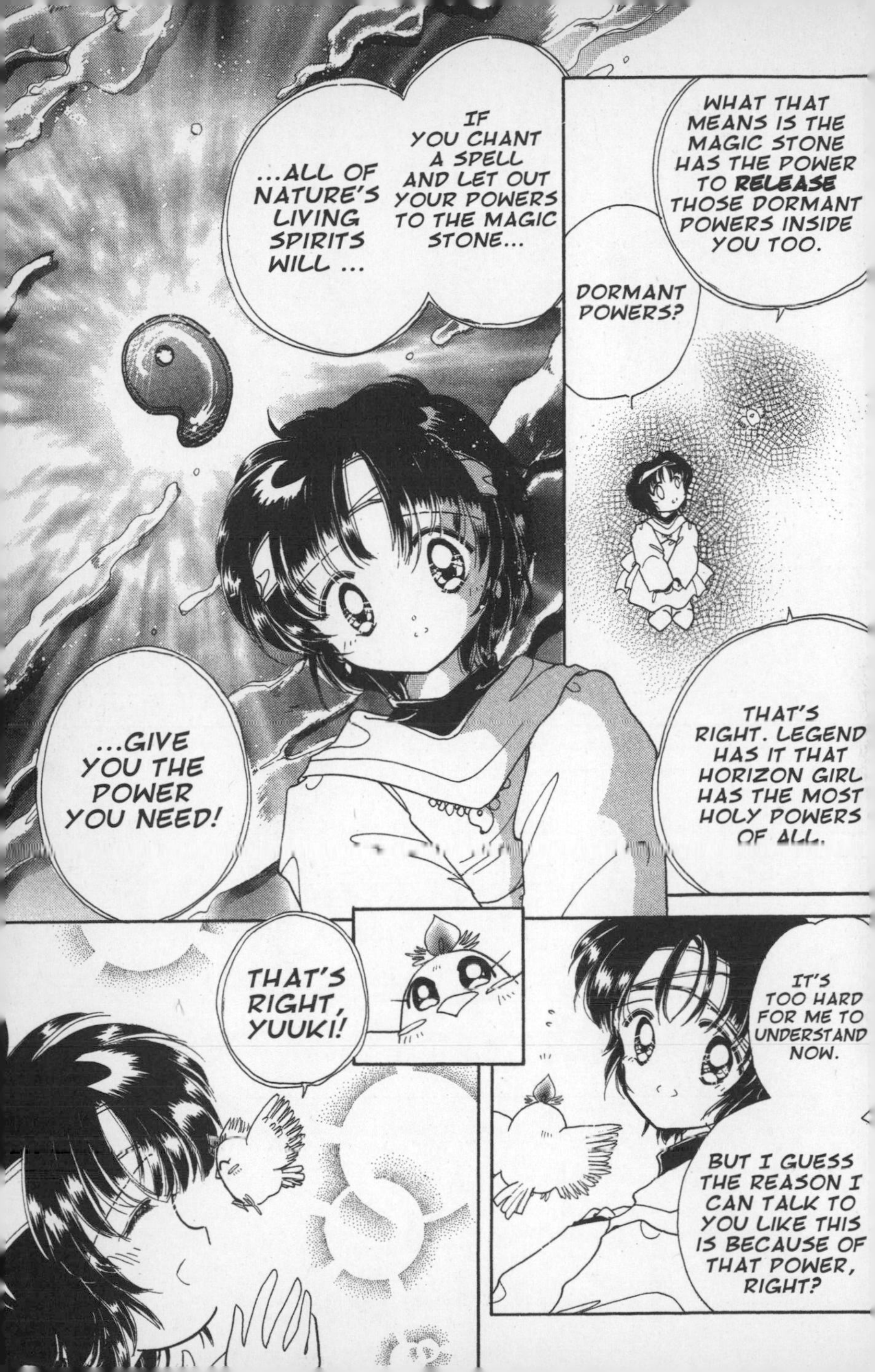
WHAT THAT MEANS IS THE MAGIC STONE HAS THE POWER TO **RELEASE** THOSE DORMANT POWERS INSIDE YOU TOO.
DORMANT POWERS?
THAT'S RIGHT. LEGEND HAS IT THAT HORIZON GIRL HAS THE MOST HOLY POWERS OF ALL.
IF YOU CHANT A SPELL AND LET OUT YOUR POWERS TO THE MAGIC STONE...
...ALL OF NATURE'S LIVING SPIRITS WILL ...
...GIVE YOU THE POWER YOU NEED!
IT'S TOO HARD FOR ME TO UNDERSTAND NOW.
BUT I GUESS THE REASON I CAN TALK TO YOU LIKE THIS IS BECAUSE OF THAT POWER, RIGHT?
THAT'S RIGHT, YUUKI!

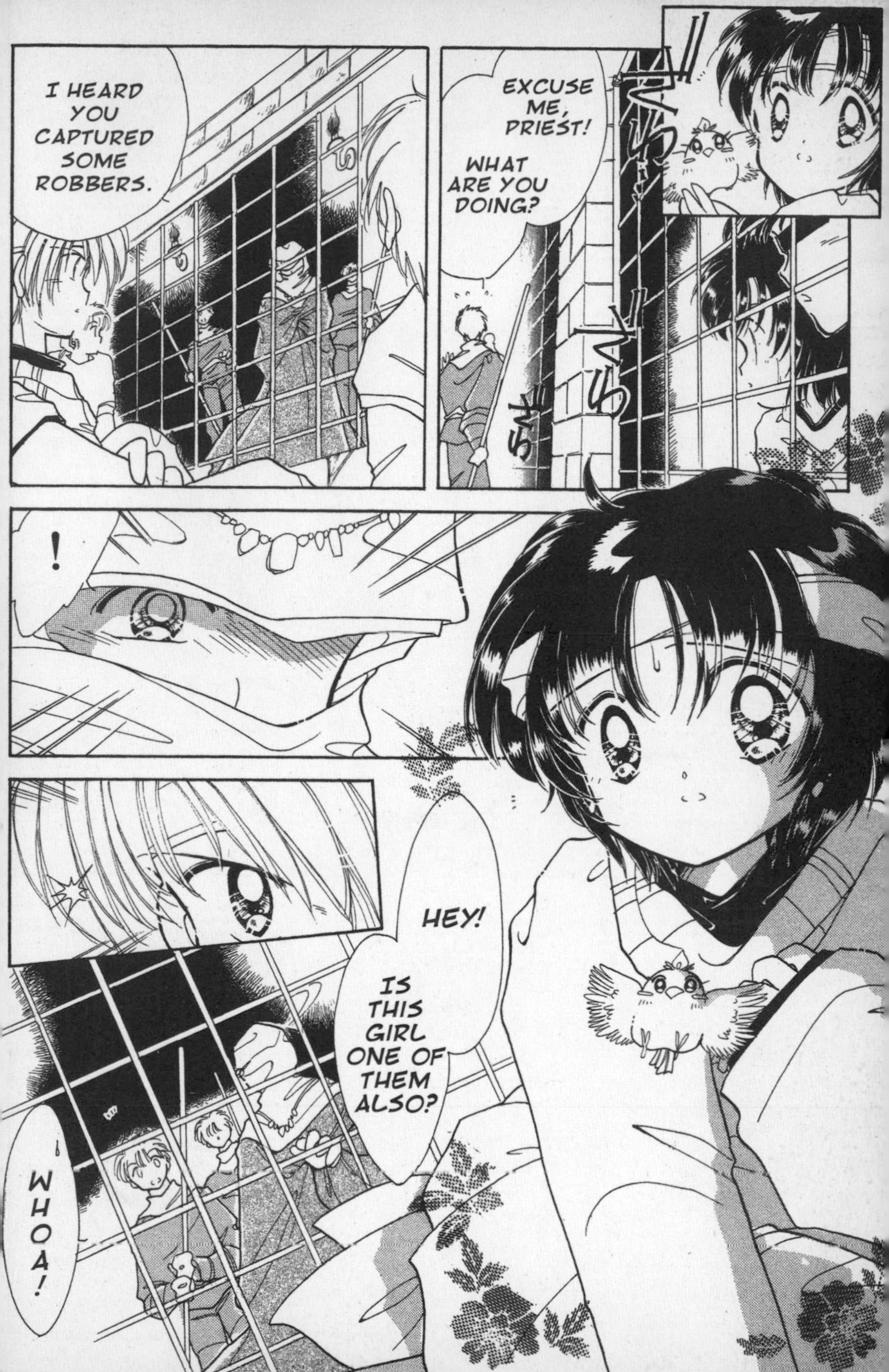
EXCUSE ME, PRIEST!
WHAT ARE YOU DOING?
I HEARD YOU CAPTURED SOME ROBBERS.
!
HEY!
IS THIS GIRL ONE OF THEM ALSO?
WHOA!

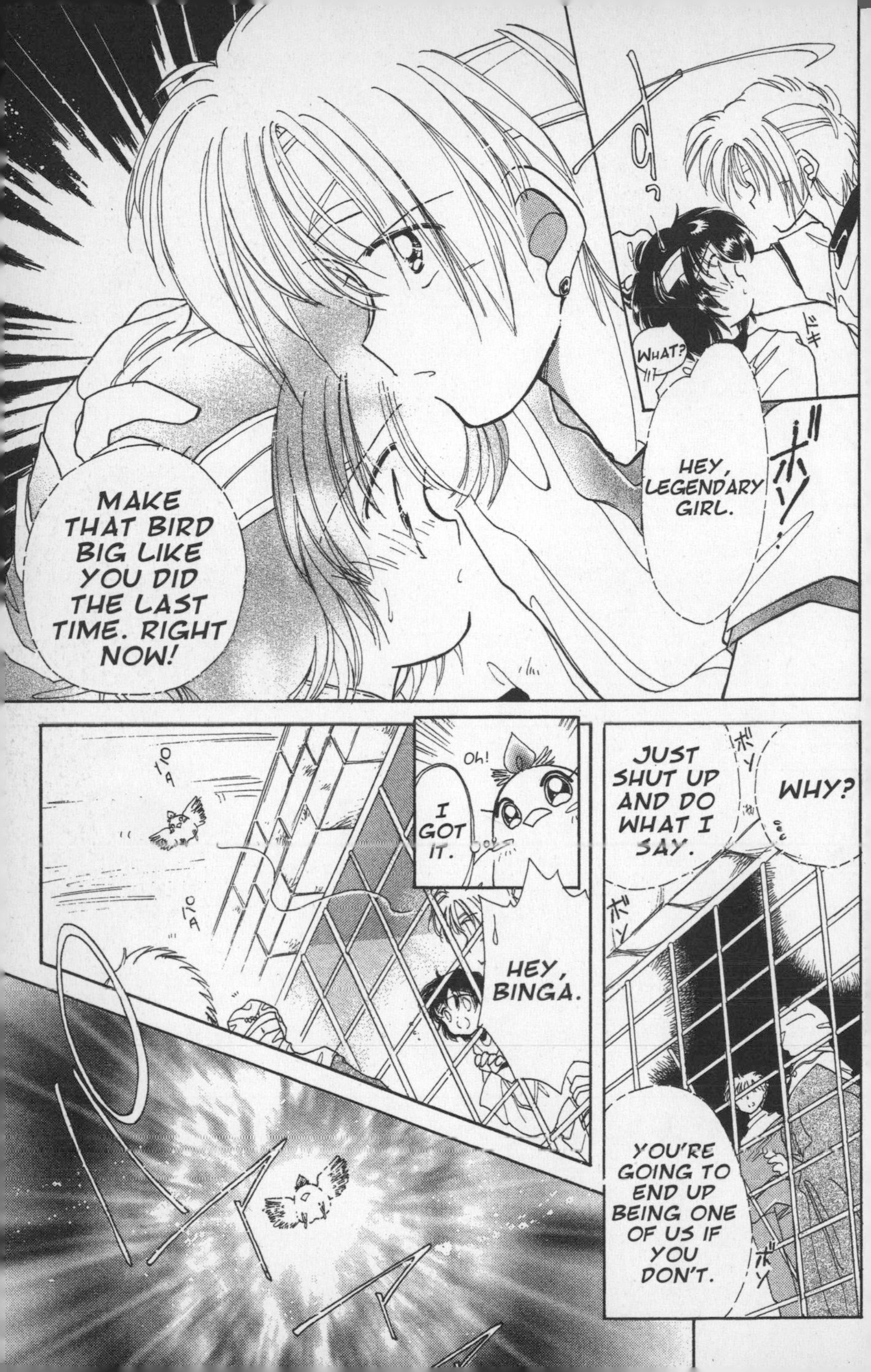
WHAT?
HEY, LEGENDARY GIRL.
MAKE THAT BIRD BIG LIKE YOU DID THE LAST TIME. RIGHT NOW!
WHY?
JUST SHUT UP AND DO WHAT I SAY.
YOU'RE GOING TO END UP BEING ONE OF US IF YOU DON'T.
Oh!
I GOT IT.
HEY, BINGA.

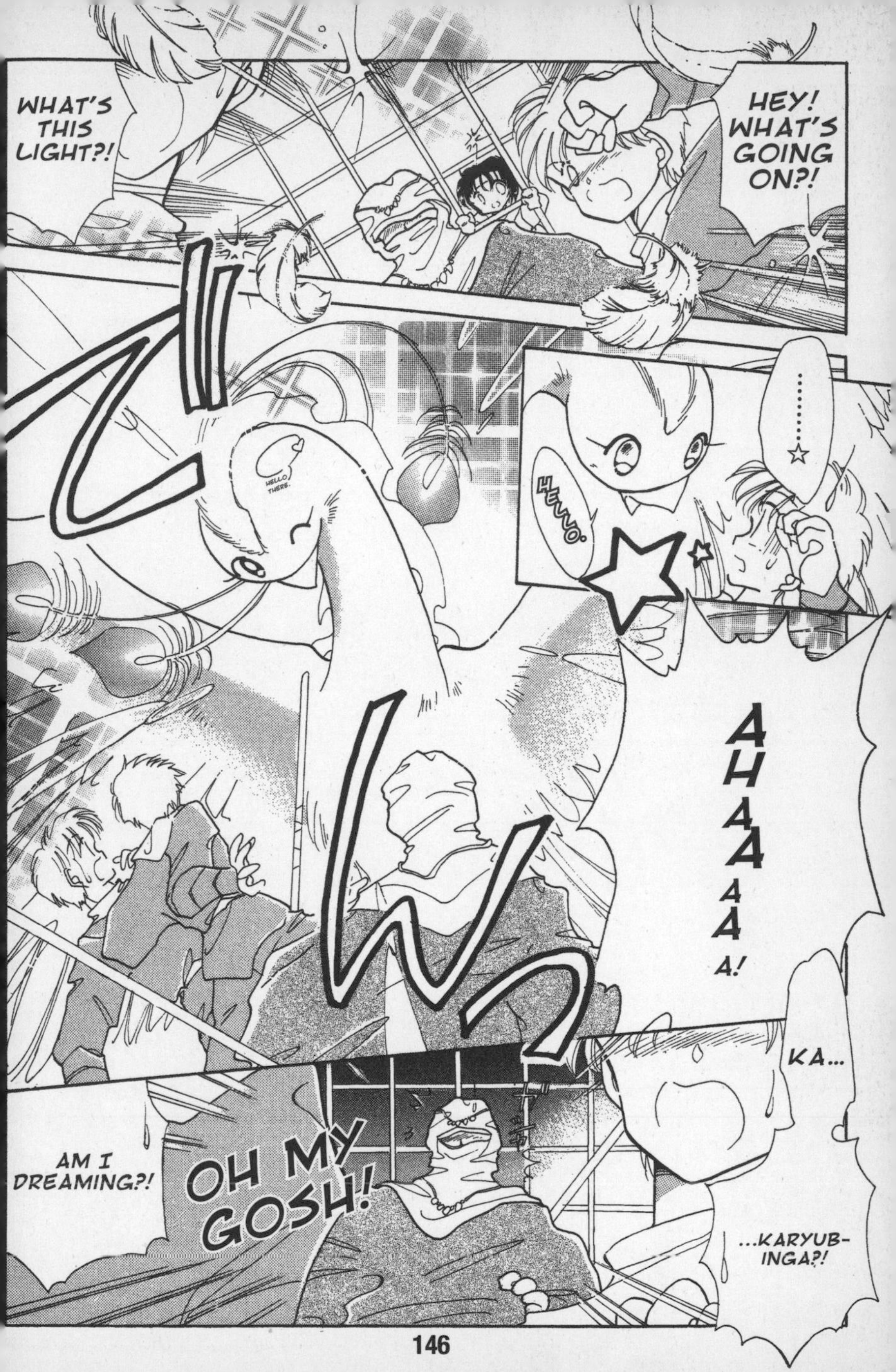
HEY! WHAT'S GOING ON?!
WHAT'S THIS LIGHT?!
......☆
HELLO.
HELLO THERE.
AHAAAAA!
KA...
...KARYUB-INGA?!
OH MY GOSH!
AM I DREAMING?!

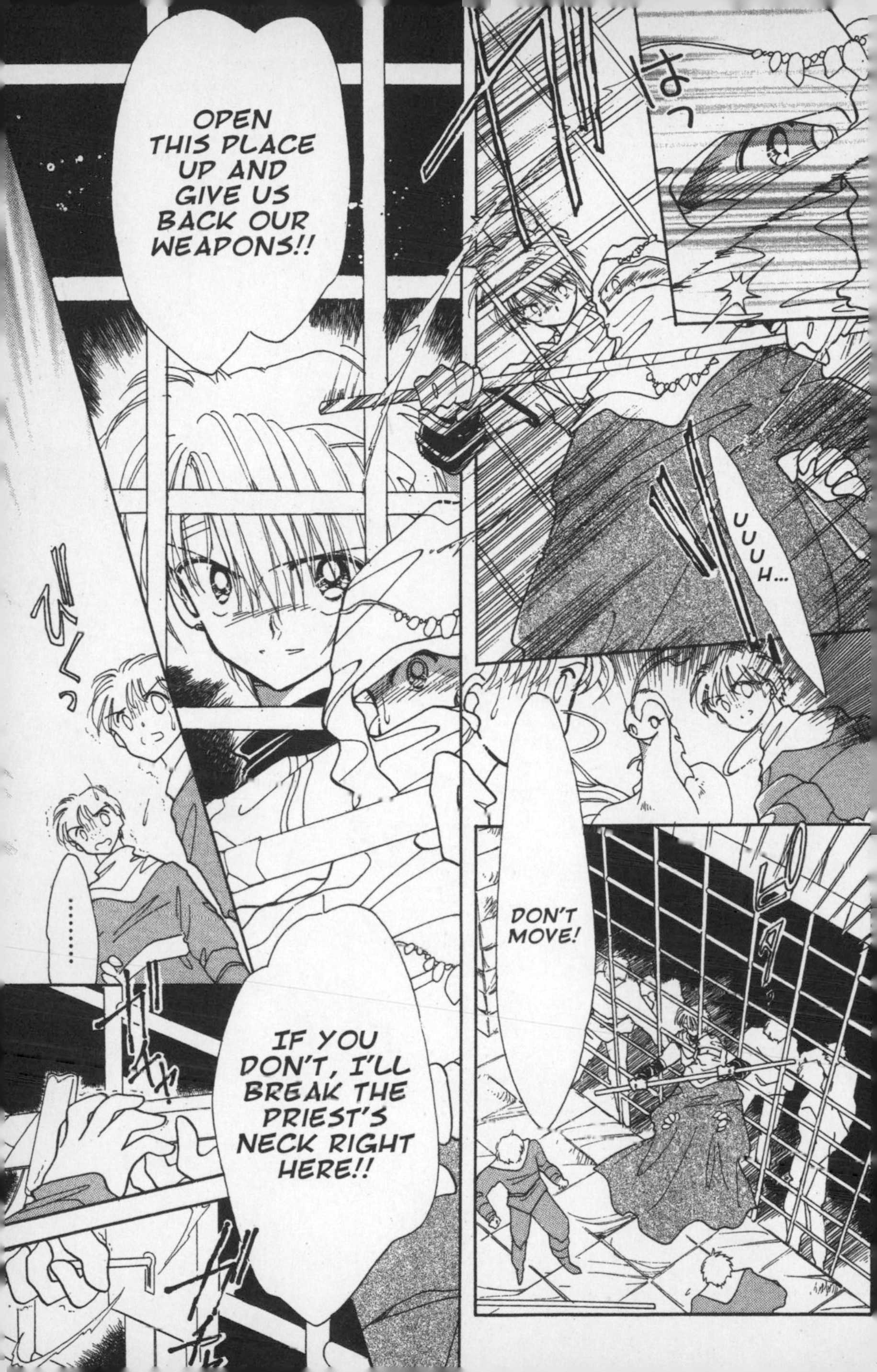
はっ
UUUH...
DON'T MOVE!
OPEN THIS PLACE UP AND GIVE US BACK OUR WEAPONS!!
......
IF YOU DON'T, I'LL BREAK THE PRIEST'S NECK RIGHT HERE!!

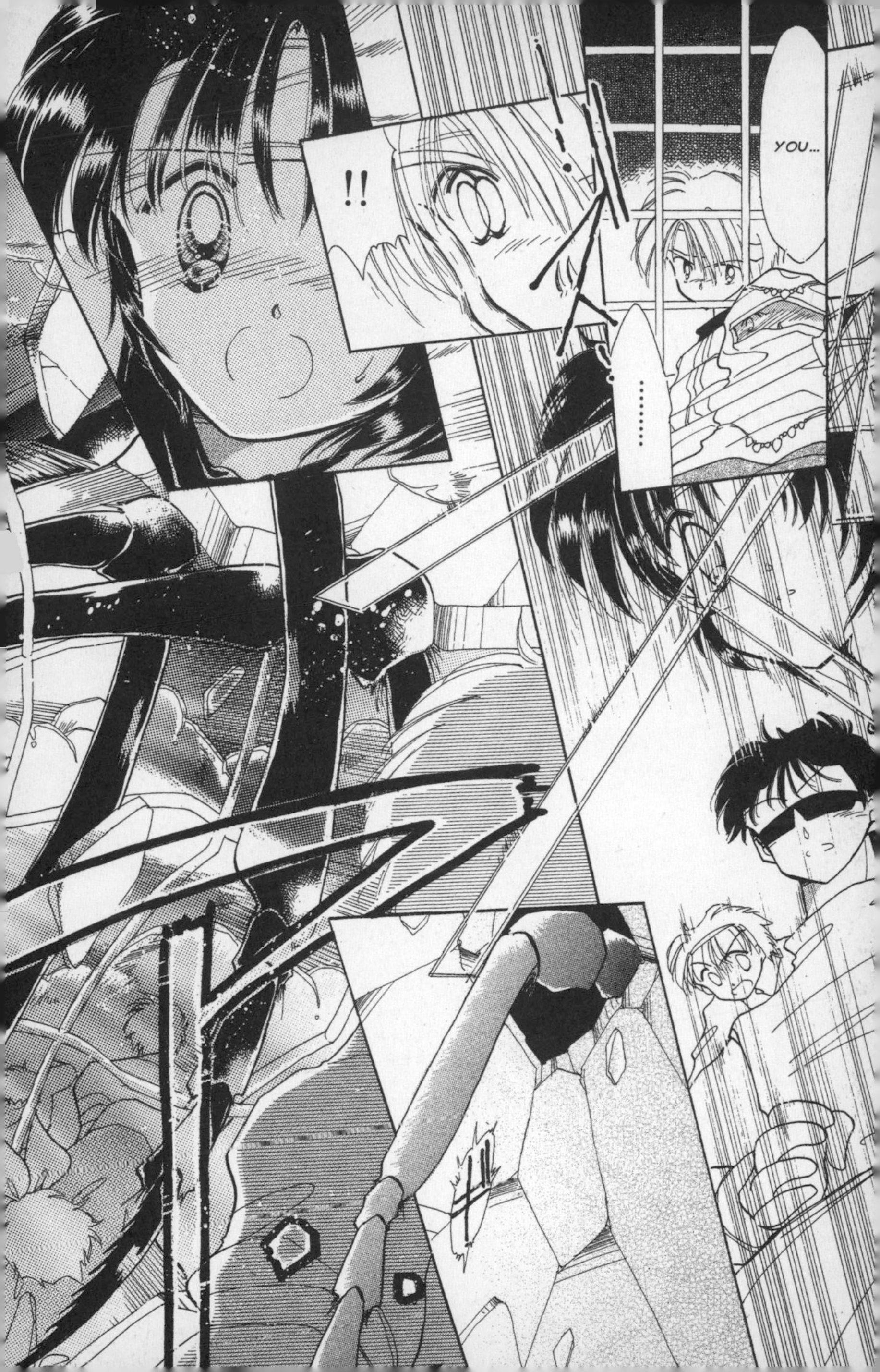
YOU...
......
!!

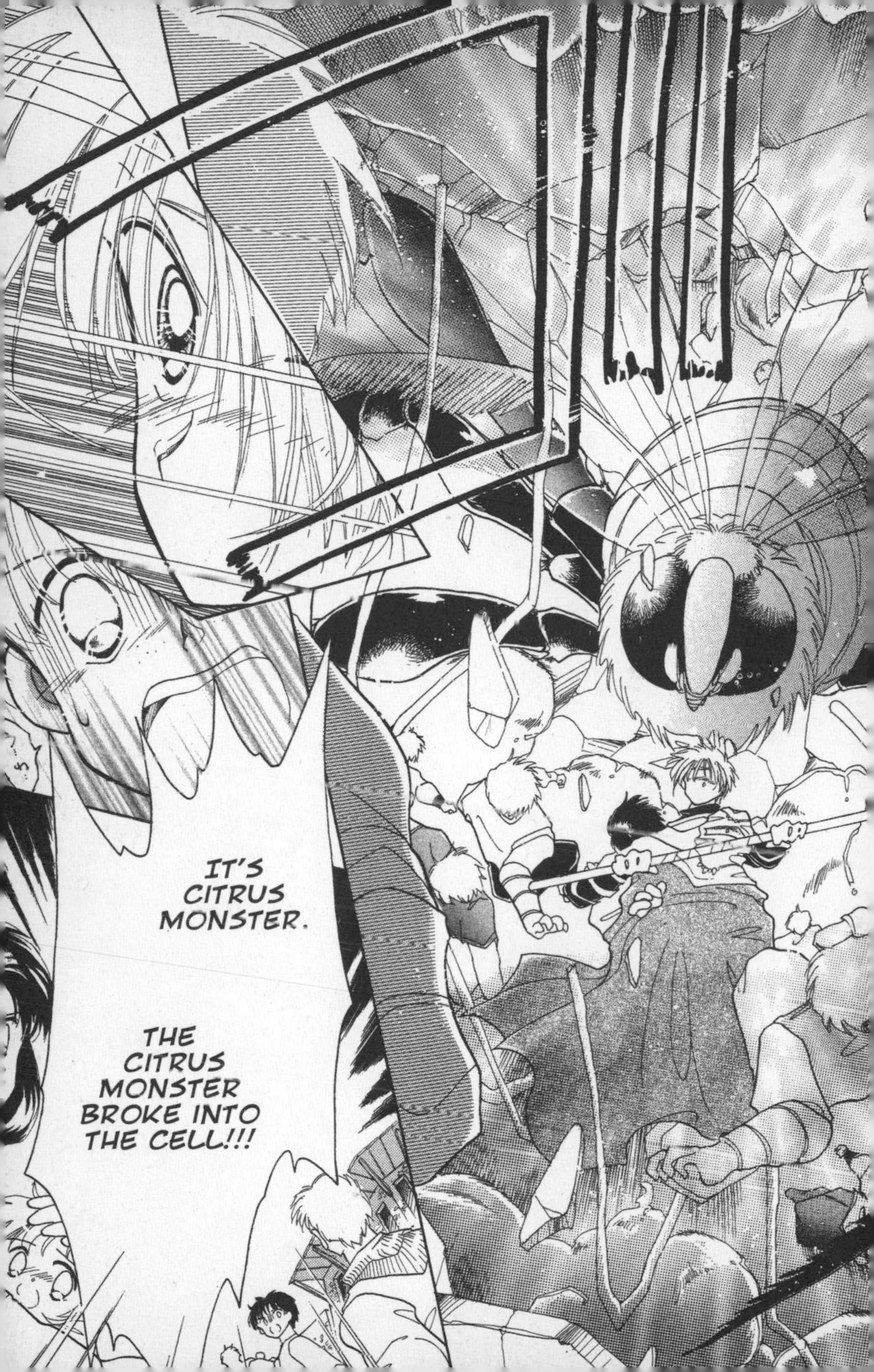
IT'S CITRUS MONSTER.
THE CITRUS MONSTER BROKE INTO THE CELL!!!

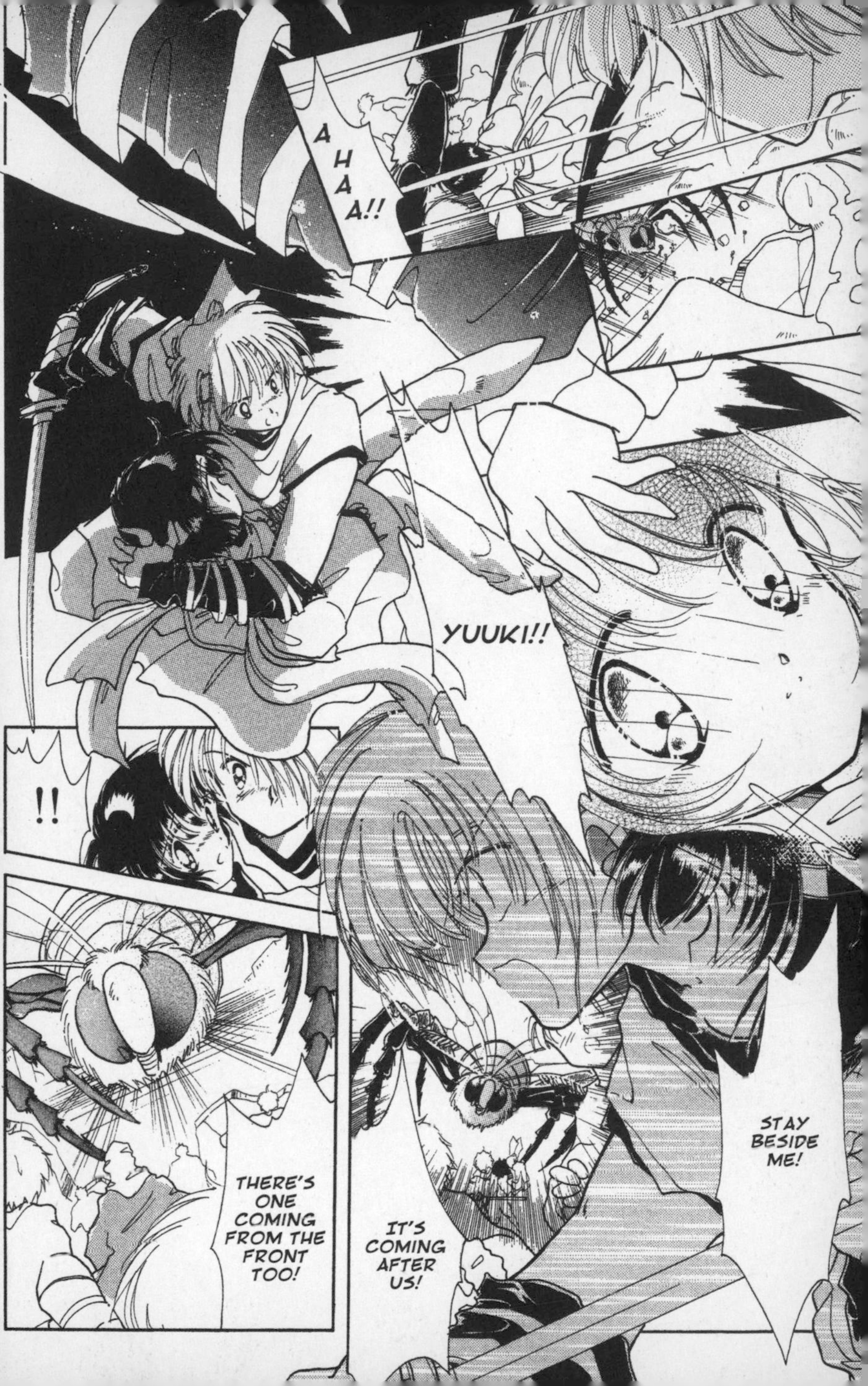
AHAA!!
YUUKI!!
!!
STAY BESIDE ME!
IT'S COMING AFTER US!
THERE'S ONE COMING FROM THE FRONT TOO!

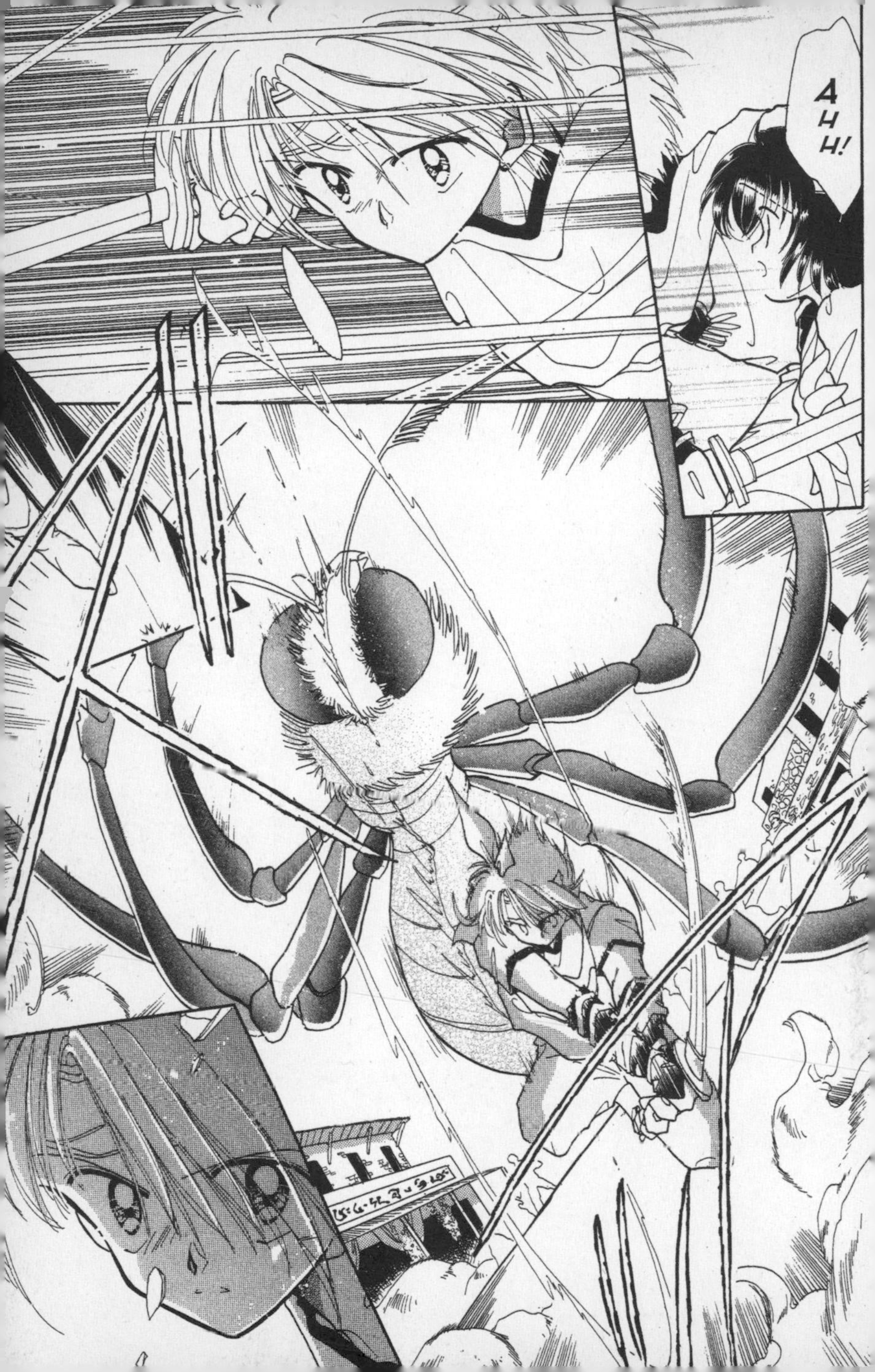
AHH!

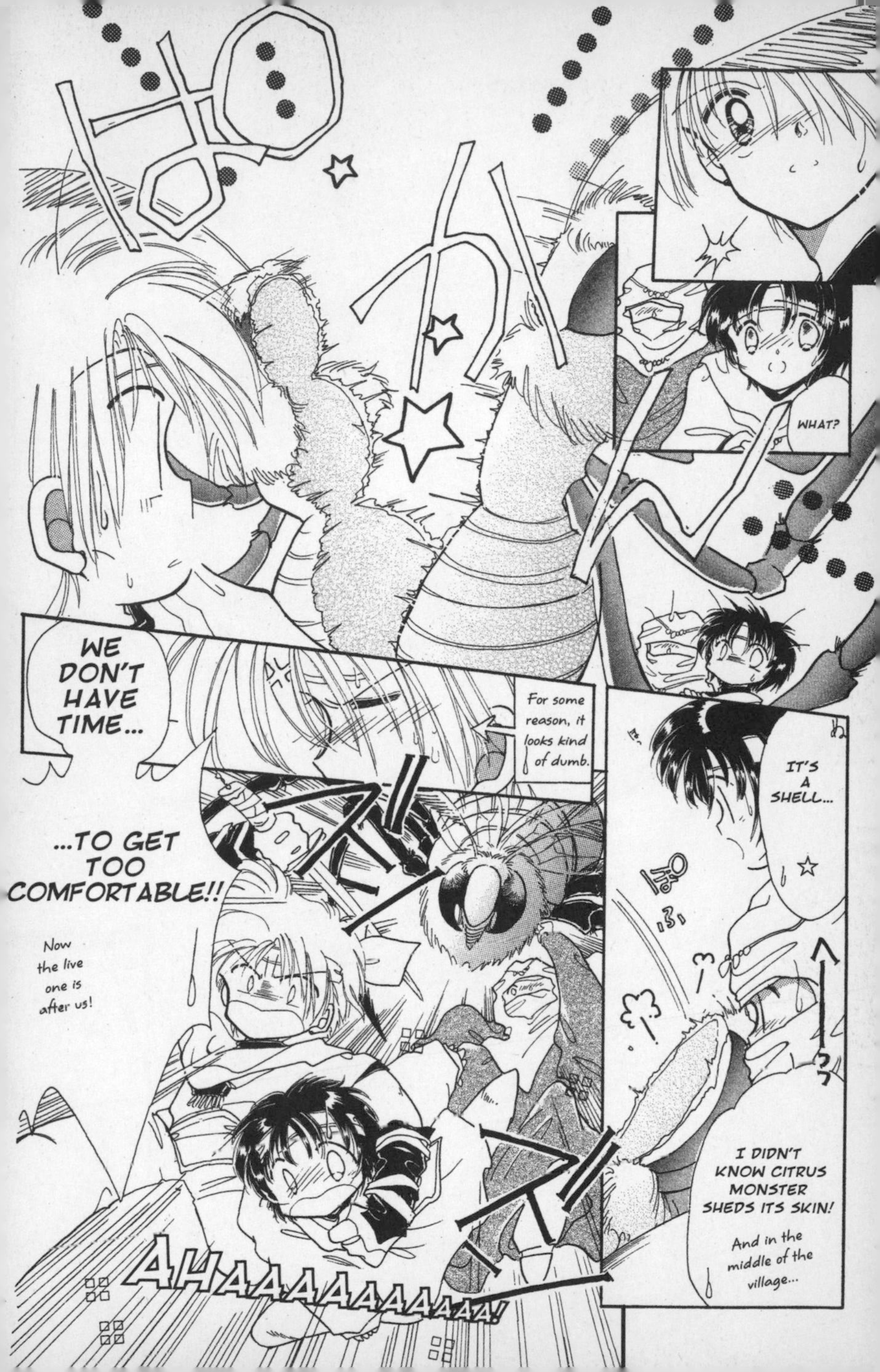

WHAT?
IT'S A SHELL...
I DIDN'T KNOW CITRUS MONSTER SHEDS ITS SKIN!
And in the middle of the village...
WE DON'T HAVE TIME...
For some reason, it looks kind of dumb.
...TO GET TOO COMFORTABLE!!
Now the live one is after us!
AHAAAAAAAAAAAA!

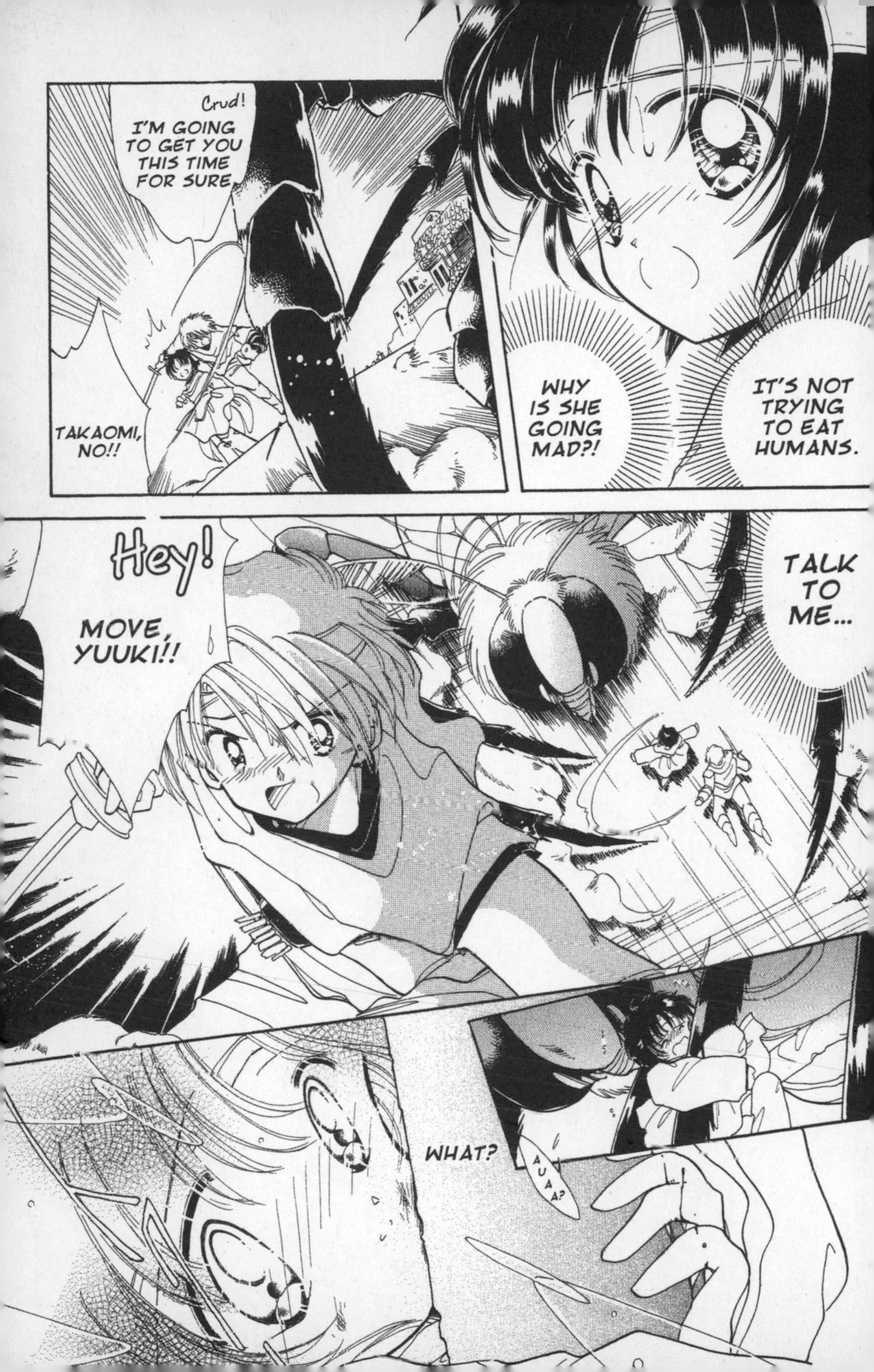
IT'S NOT TRYING TO EAT HUMANS.
WHY IS SHE GOING MAD?!
Crud!
I'M GOING TO GET YOU THIS TIME FOR SURE
TAKAOMI, NO!!
TALK TO ME...
Hey!
MOVE, YUUKI!!
AUAA?
WHAT?

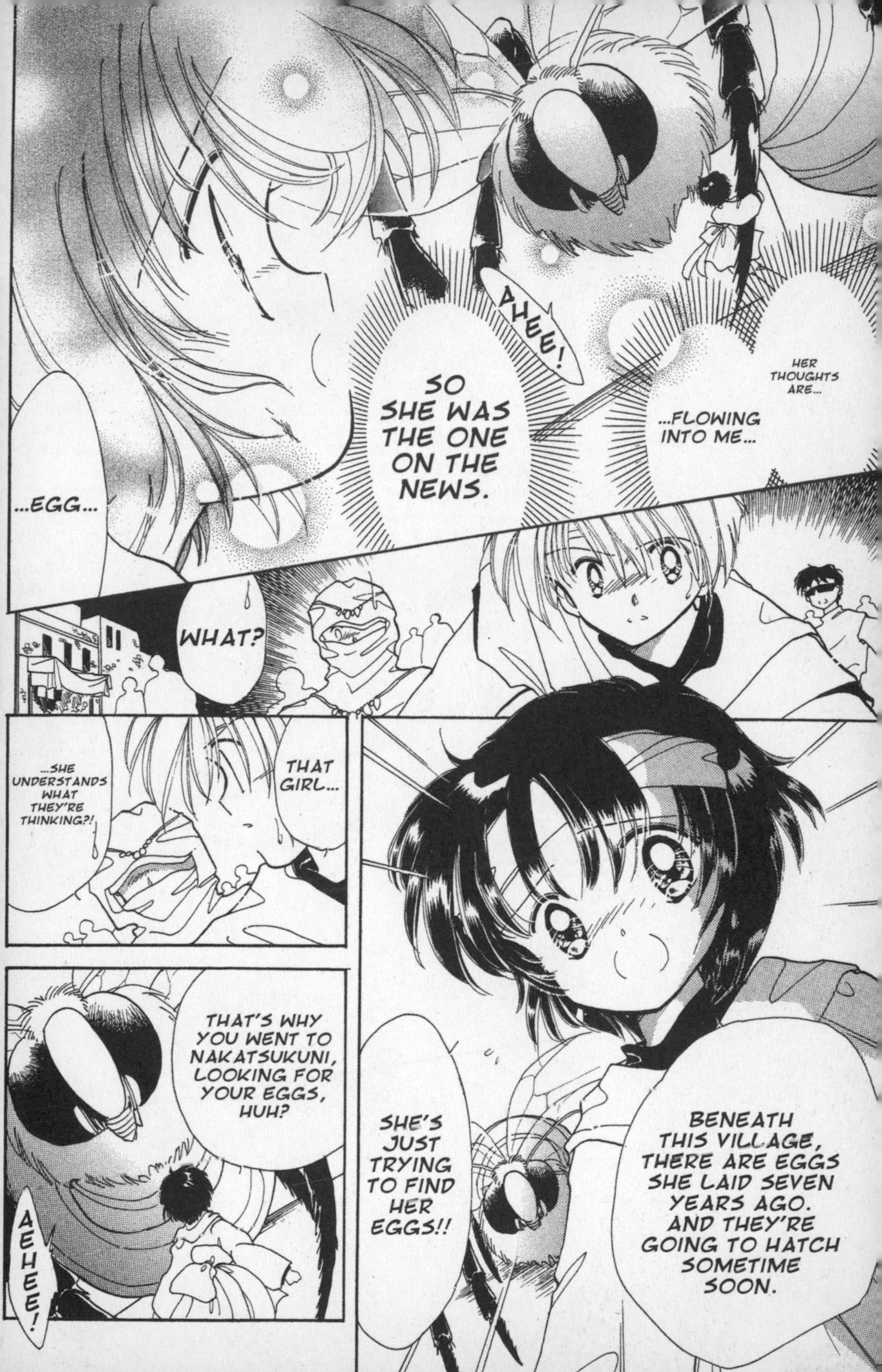
HER THOUGHTS ARE...
...FLOWING INTO ME...
AHEE!
SO SHE WAS THE ONE ON THE NEWS.
...EGG...
WHAT?
BENEATH THIS VILLAGE, THERE ARE EGGS SHE LAID SEVEN YEARS AGO. AND THEY'RE GOING TO HATCH SOMETIME SOON.
SHE'S JUST TRYING TO FIND HER EGGS!!
THAT GIRL...
...SHE UNDERSTANDS WHAT THEY'RE THINKING?!
THAT'S WHY YOU WENT TO NAKATSUKUNI, LOOKING FOR YOUR EGGS, HUH?
AEHEE!

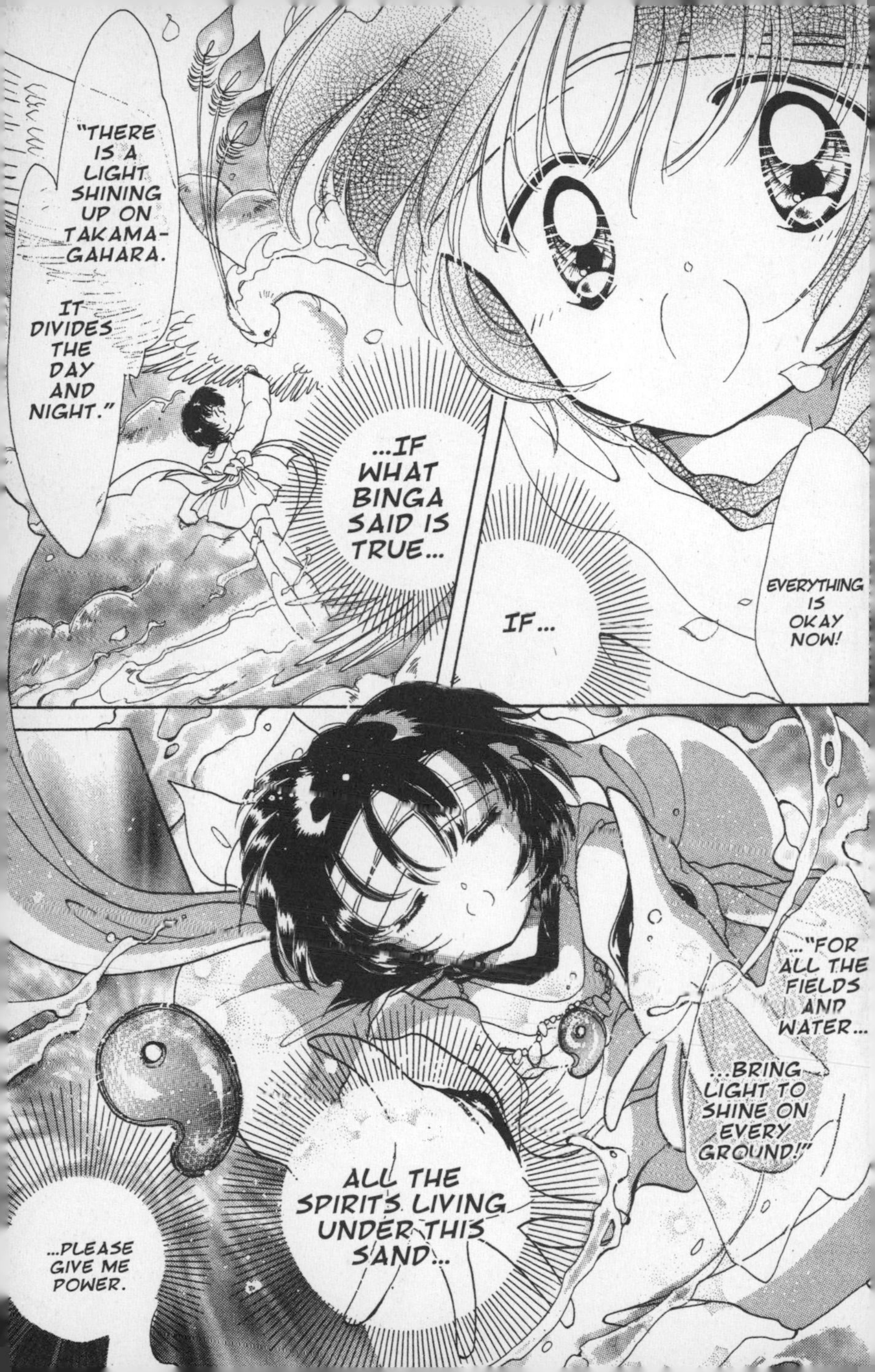
EVERYTHING IS OKAY NOW!
IF...
...IF WHAT BINGA SAID IS TRUE...
"THERE IS A LIGHT SHINING UP ON TAKAMA-GAHARA.
IT DIVIDES THE DAY AND NIGHT."
..."FOR ALL THE FIELDS AND WATER...
...BRING LIGHT TO SHINE ON EVERY GROUND!"
ALL THE SPIRITS LIVING UNDER THIS SAND...
...PLEASE GIVE ME POWER.

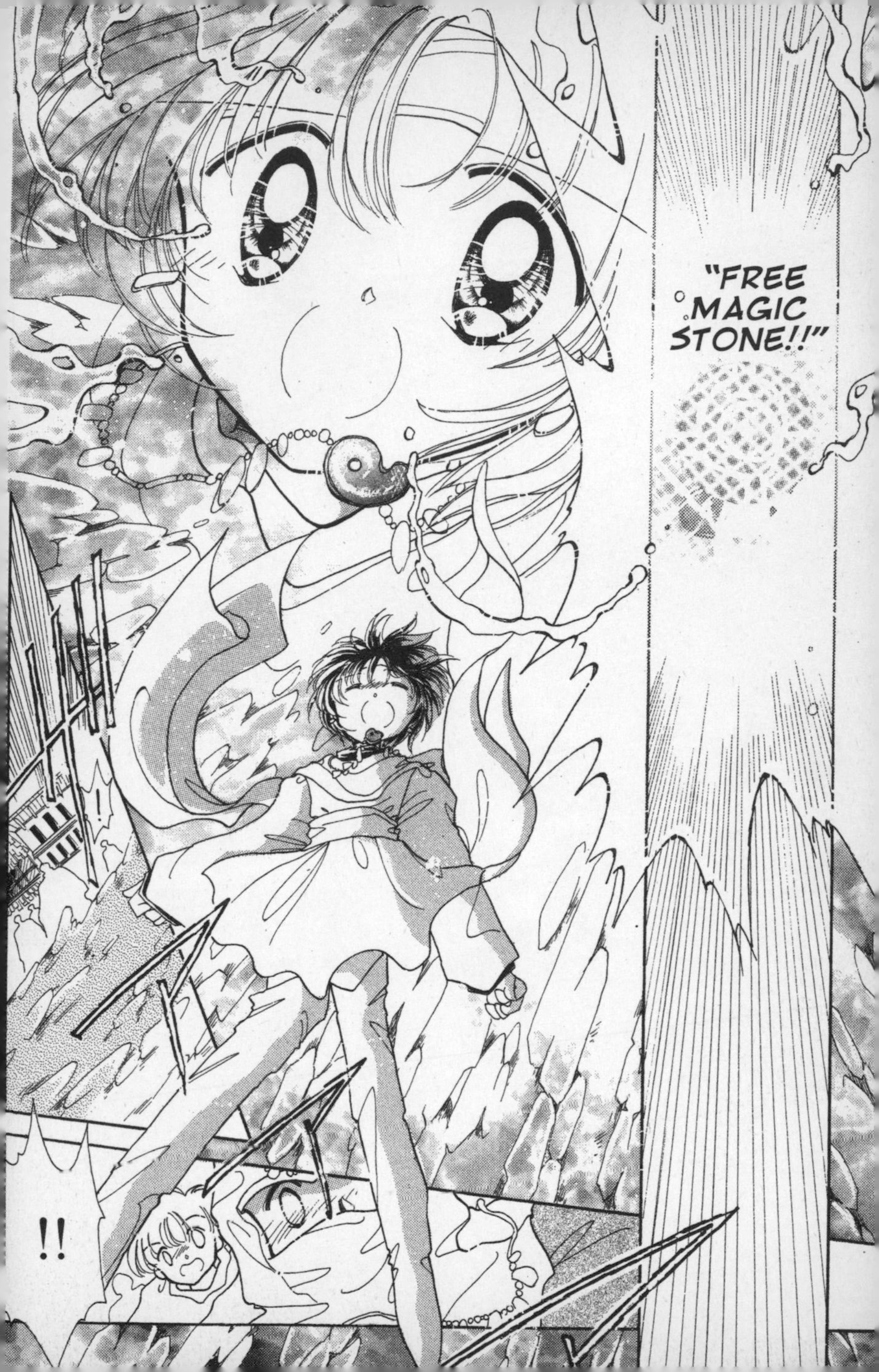
"FREE MAGIC STONE!!"
!!

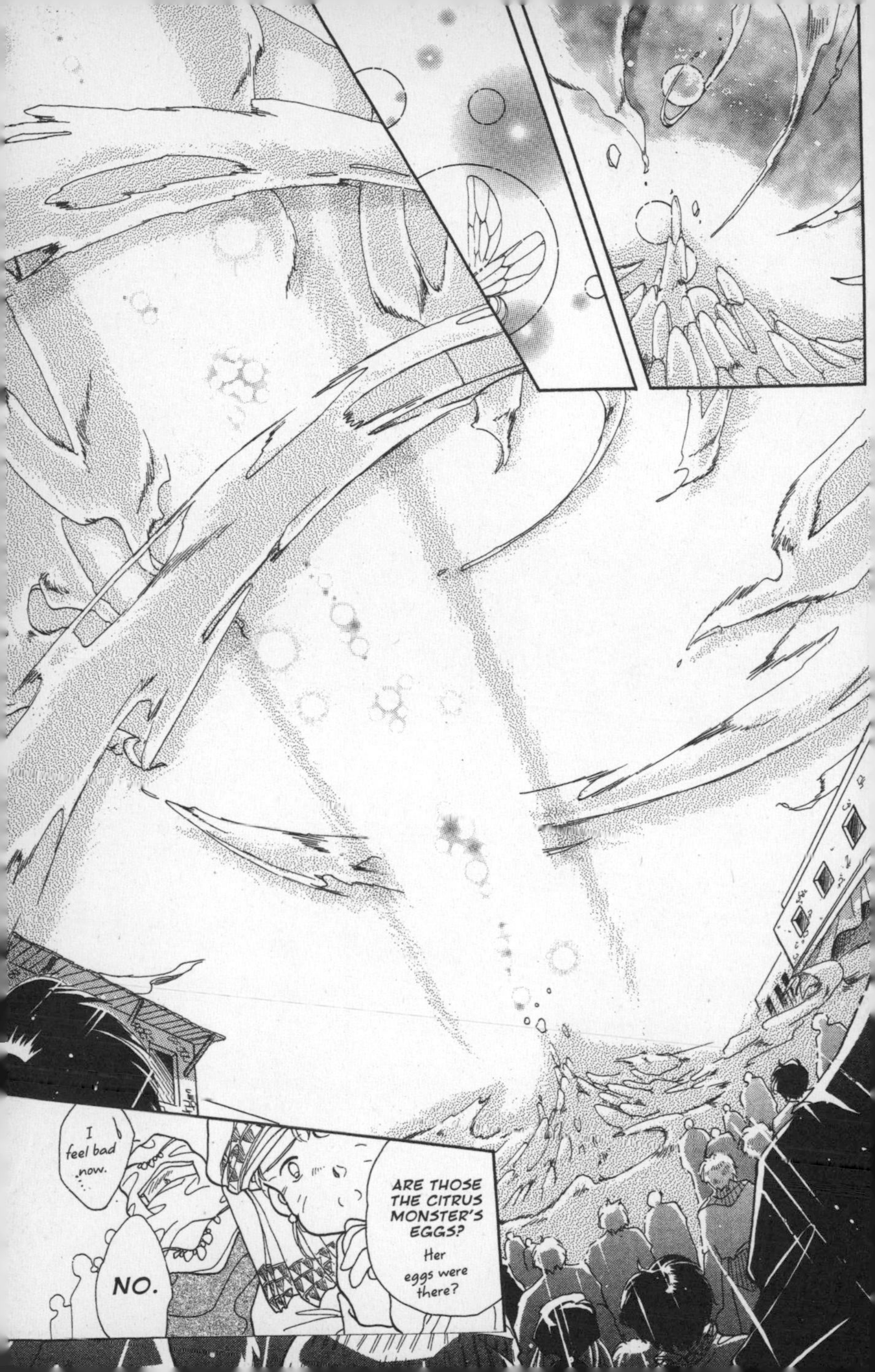
ARE THOSE THE CITRUS MONSTER'S EGGS?
Her eggs were there?
I feel bad now.
NO.

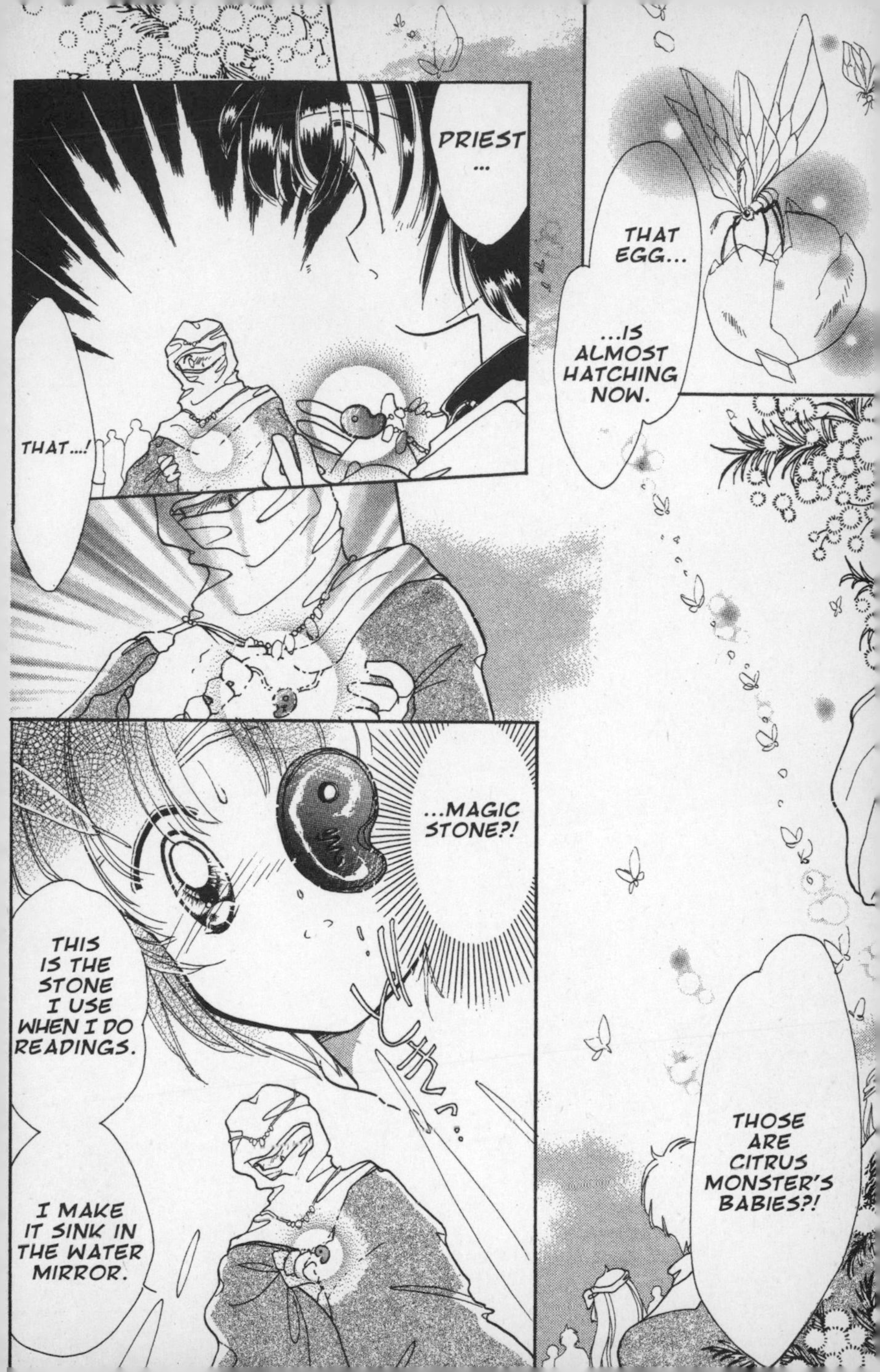
THAT EGG...
...IS ALMOST HATCHING NOW.
THOSE ARE CITRUS MONSTER'S BABIES?!
PRIEST ...
THAT...!
...MAGIC STONE?!
THIS IS THE STONE I USE WHEN I DO READINGS.
I MAKE IT SINK IN THE WATER MIRROR.

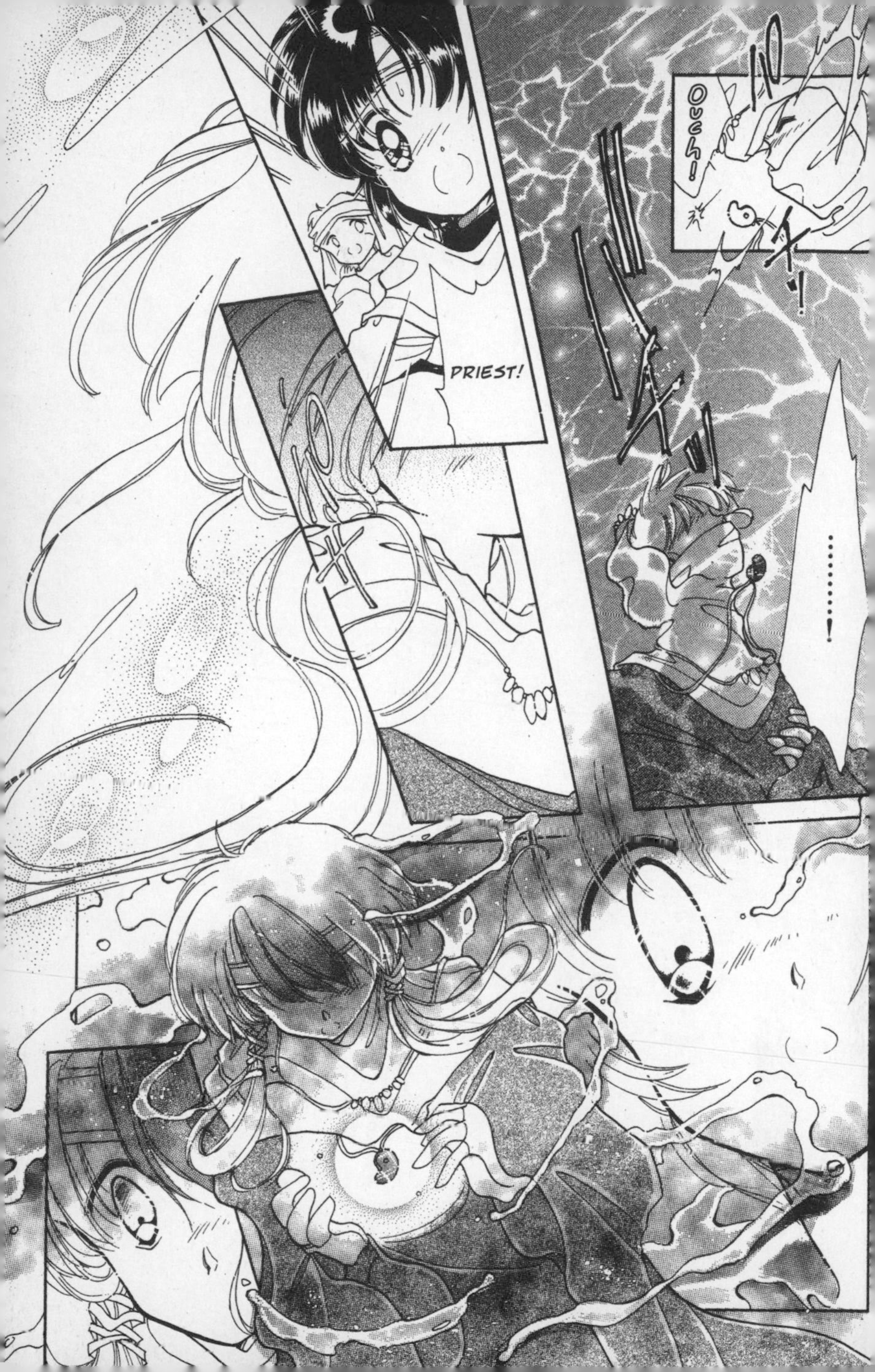
Ouch!
......!
PRIEST!

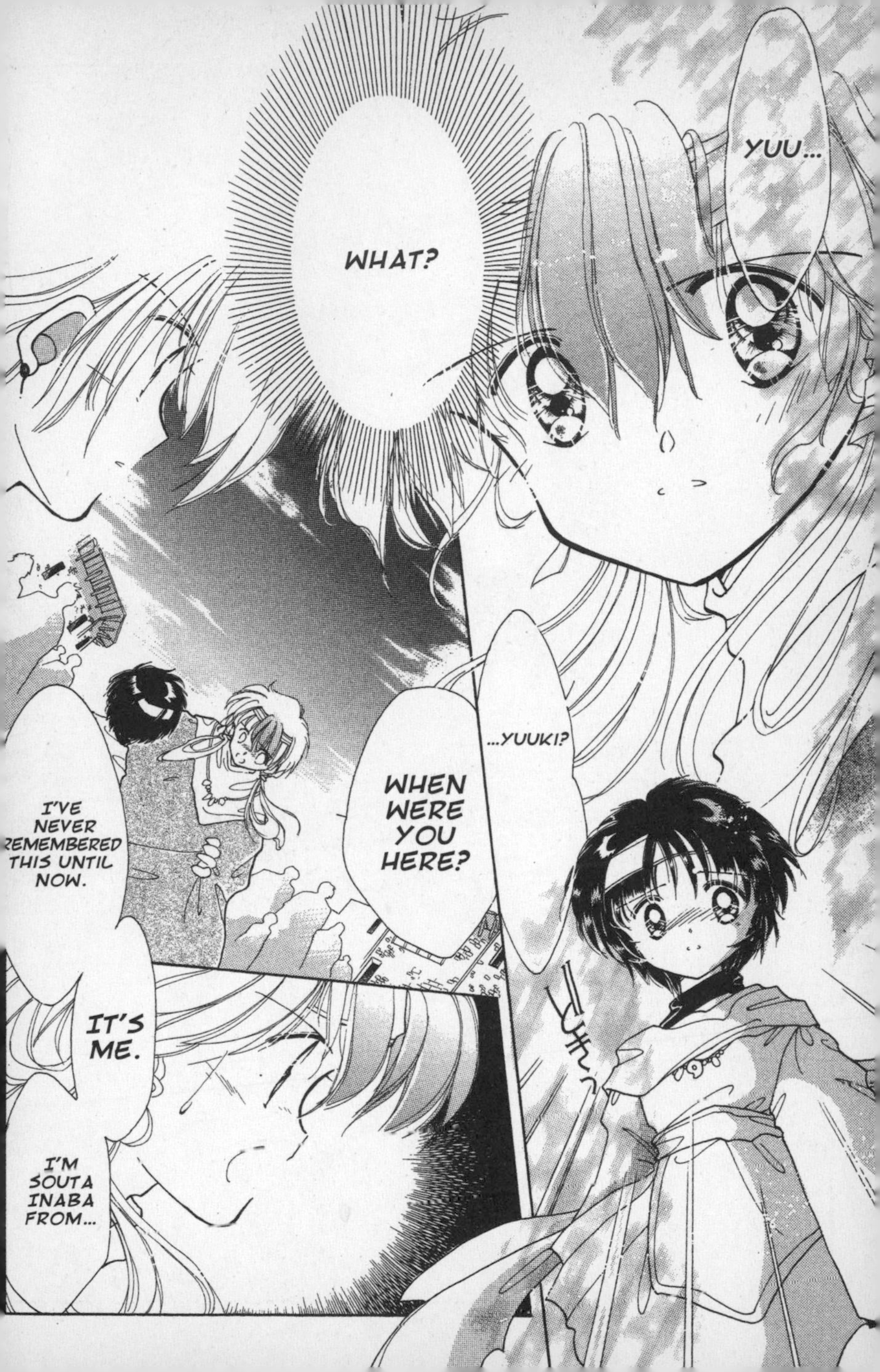
YUU...
WHAT?
...YUUKI?
WHEN WERE YOU HERE?
I'VE NEVER REMEMBERED THIS UNTIL NOW.
IT'S ME.
I'M SOUTA INABA FROM...

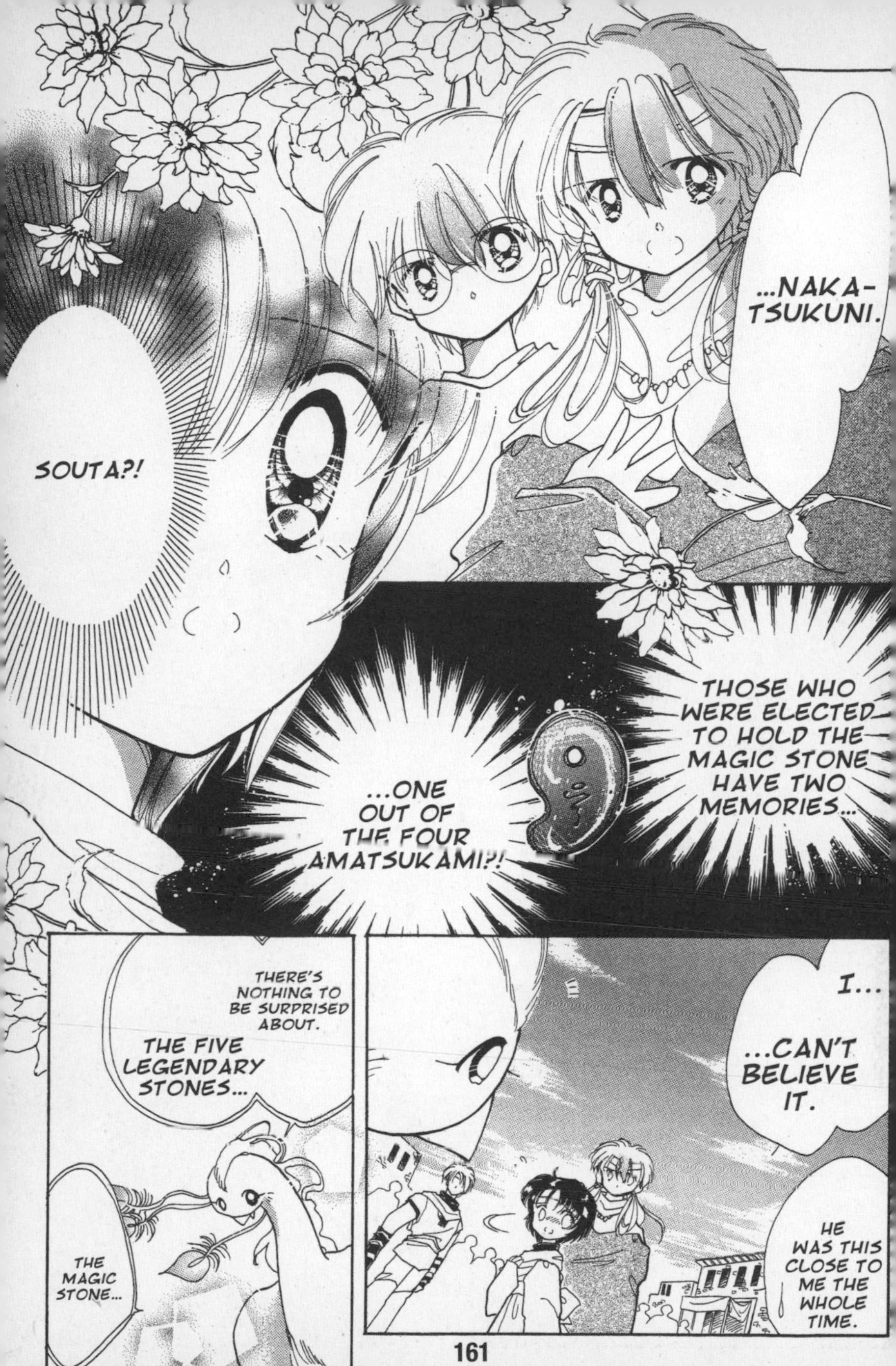
...NAKA-TSUKUNI.
SOUTA?!
THOSE WHO WERE ELECTED TO HOLD THE MAGIC STONE HAVE TWO MEMORIES...
...ONE OUT OF THE FOUR AMATSUKAMI?!
I...
...CAN'T BELIEVE IT.
HE WAS THIS CLOSE TO ME THE WHOLE TIME.
THERE'S NOTHING TO BE SURPRISED ABOUT.
THE FIVE LEGENDARY STONES...
THE MAGIC STONE...

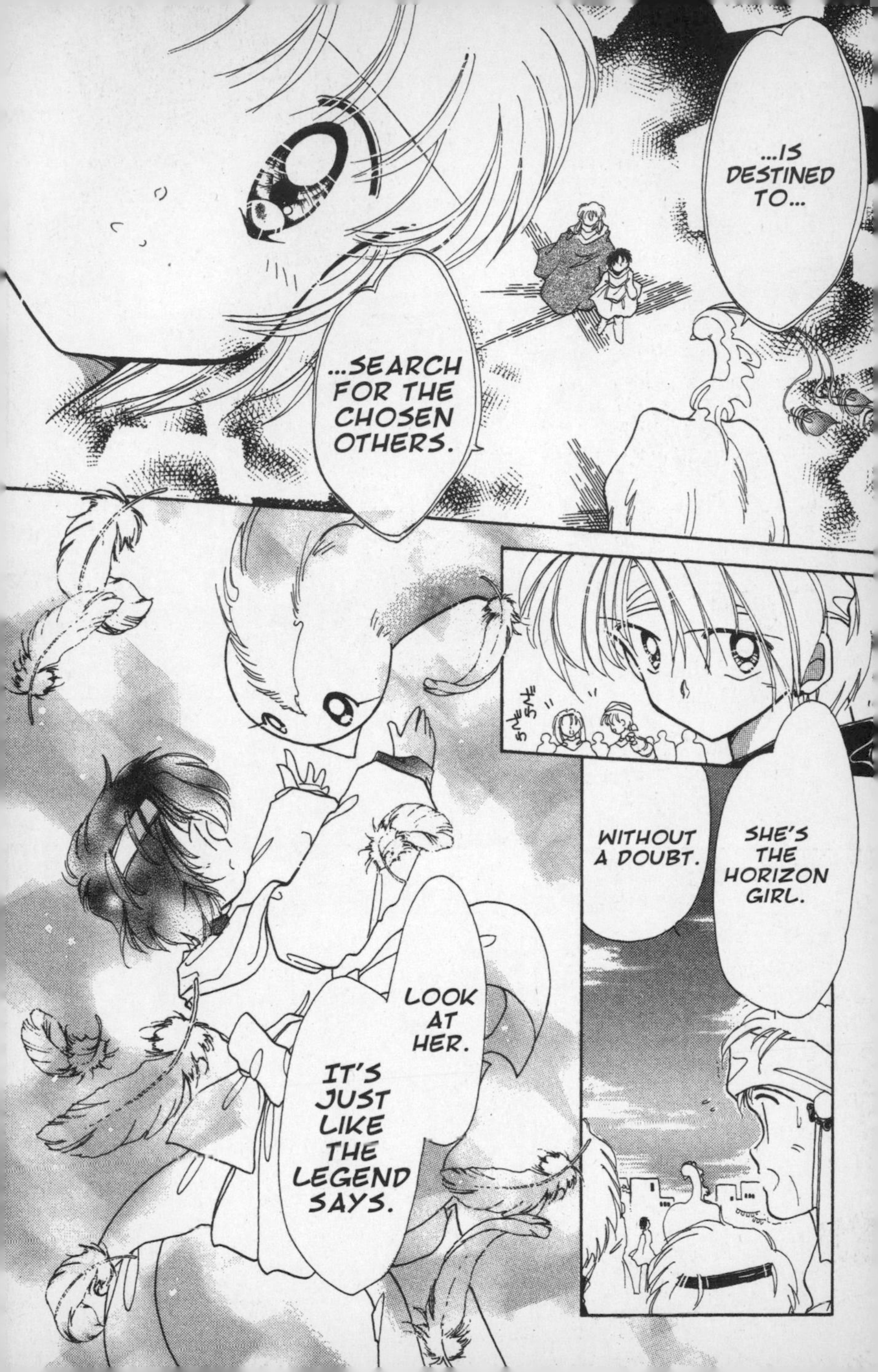
...IS DESTINED TO...
...SEARCH FOR THE CHOSEN OTHERS.
SHE'S THE HORIZON GIRL.
WITHOUT A DOUBT.
LOOK AT HER.
IT'S JUST LIKE THE LEGEND SAYS.

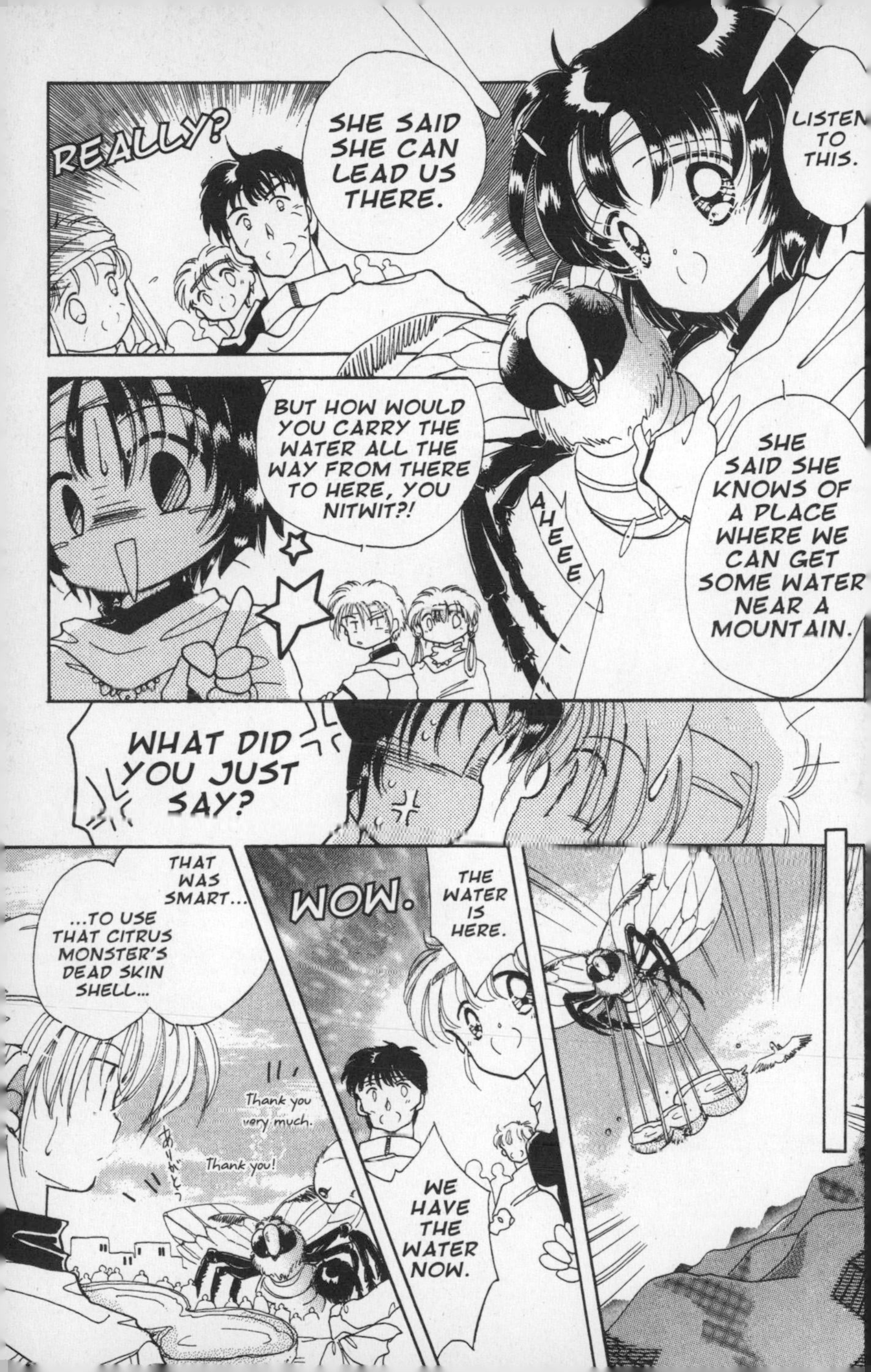

LISTEN TO THIS.
SHE SAID SHE KNOWS OF A PLACE WHERE WE CAN GET SOME WATER NEAR A MOUNTAIN.
SHE SAID SHE CAN LEAD US THERE.
REALLY?
BUT HOW WOULD YOU CARRY THE WATER ALL THE WAY FROM THERE TO HERE, YOU NITWIT?!
AHEEE
WHAT DID YOU JUST SAY?
THE WATER IS HERE.
WE HAVE THE WATER NOW.
WOW.
Thank you very much.
Thank you!
THAT WAS SMART...
...TO USE THAT CITRUS MONSTER'S DEAD SKIN SHELL...

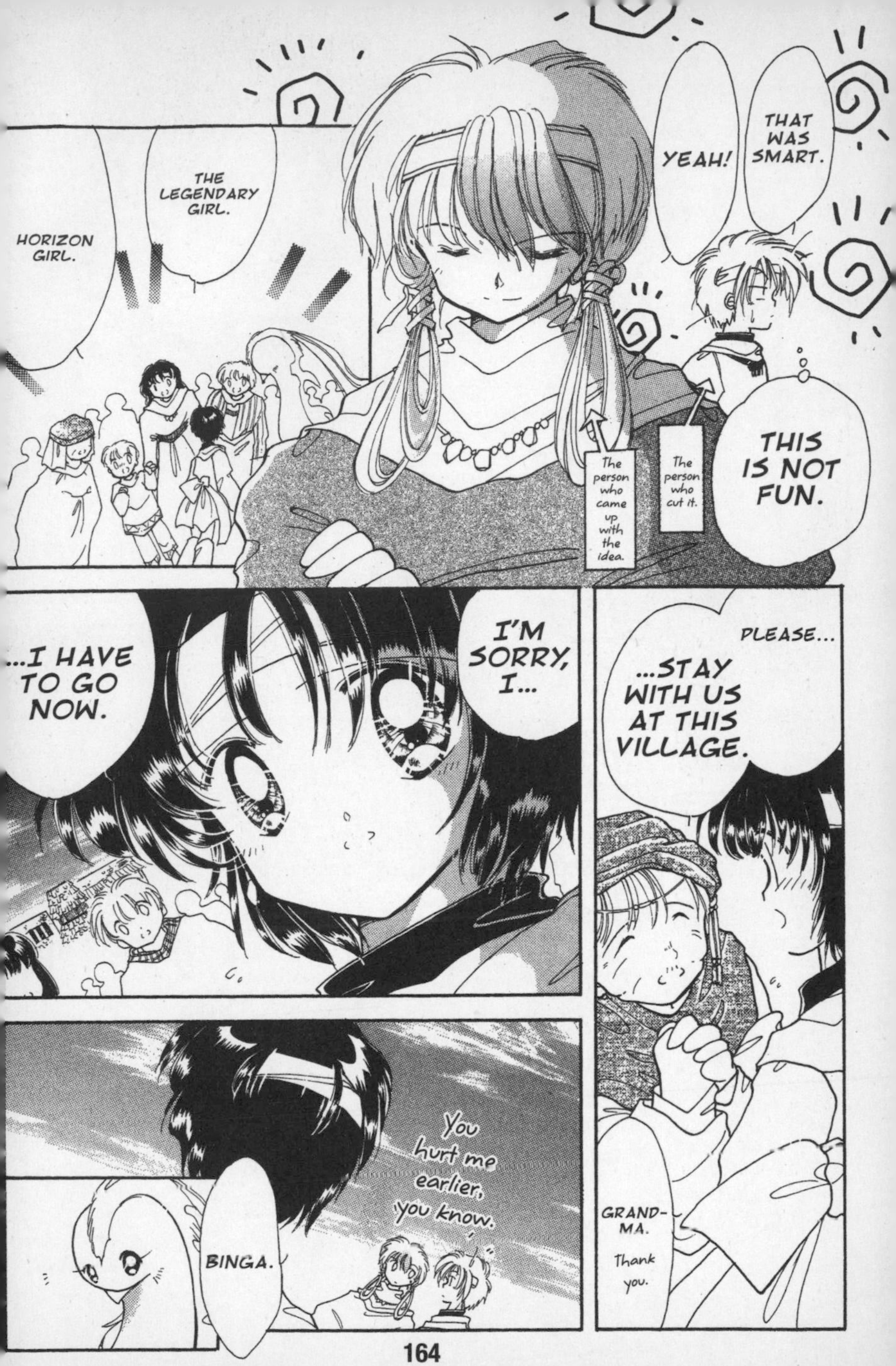
THAT WAS SMART.
YEAH!
THIS IS NOT FUN.
The person who cut it.
The person who came up with the idea.
THE LEGENDARY GIRL.
HORIZON GIRL.
PLEASE...
...STAY WITH US AT THIS VILLAGE.
GRAND-MA.
Thank you.
I'M SORRY, I...
...I HAVE TO GO NOW.
You hurt me earlier, you know.
BINGA.

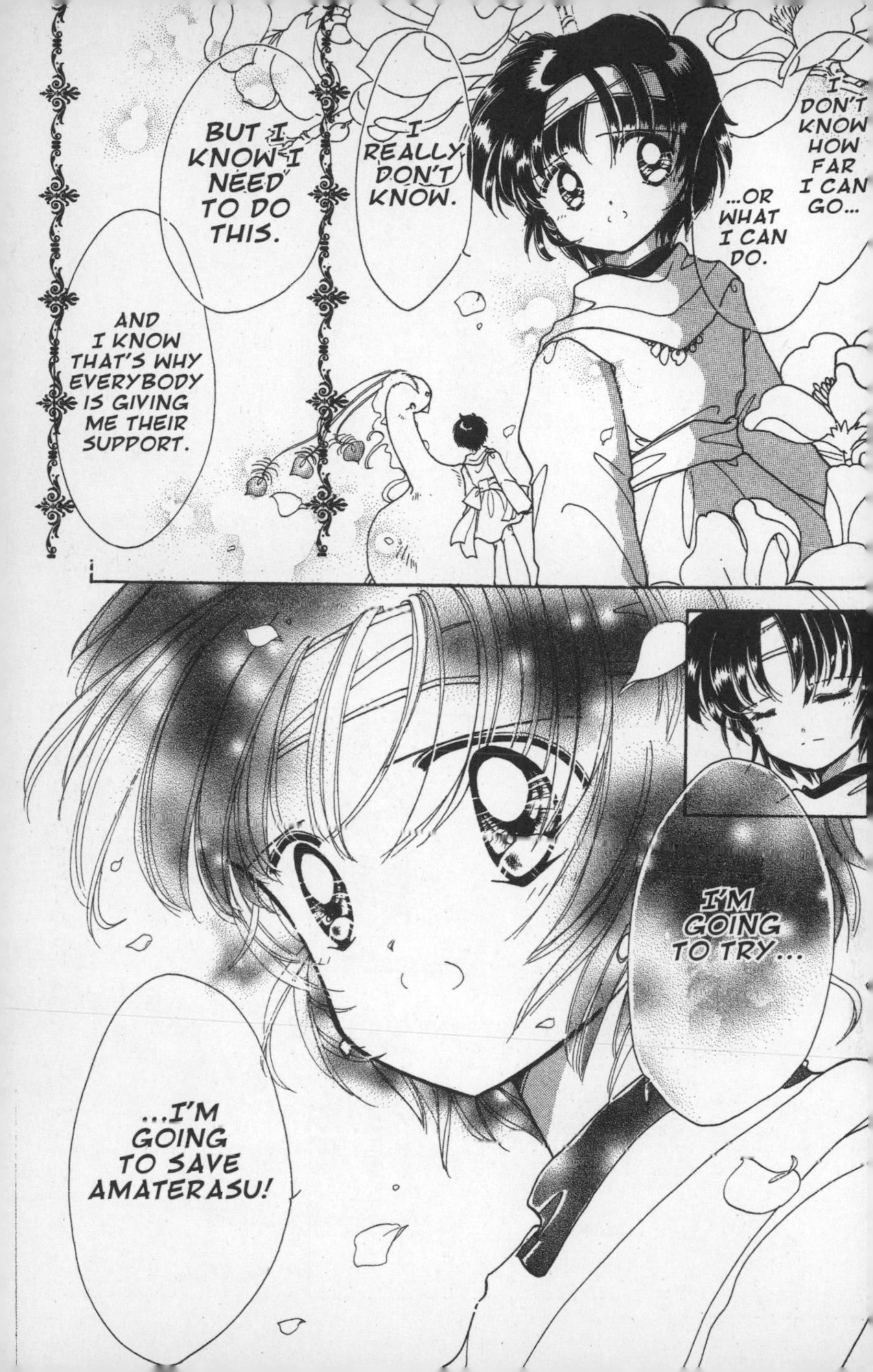
I DON'T KNOW HOW FAR I CAN GO...
...OR WHAT I CAN DO.
I REALLY DON'T KNOW.
BUT I KNOW I NEED TO DO THIS.
AND I KNOW THAT'S WHY EVERYBODY IS GIVING ME THEIR SUPPORT.
I'M GOING TO TRY...
...I'M GOING TO SAVE AMATERASU!

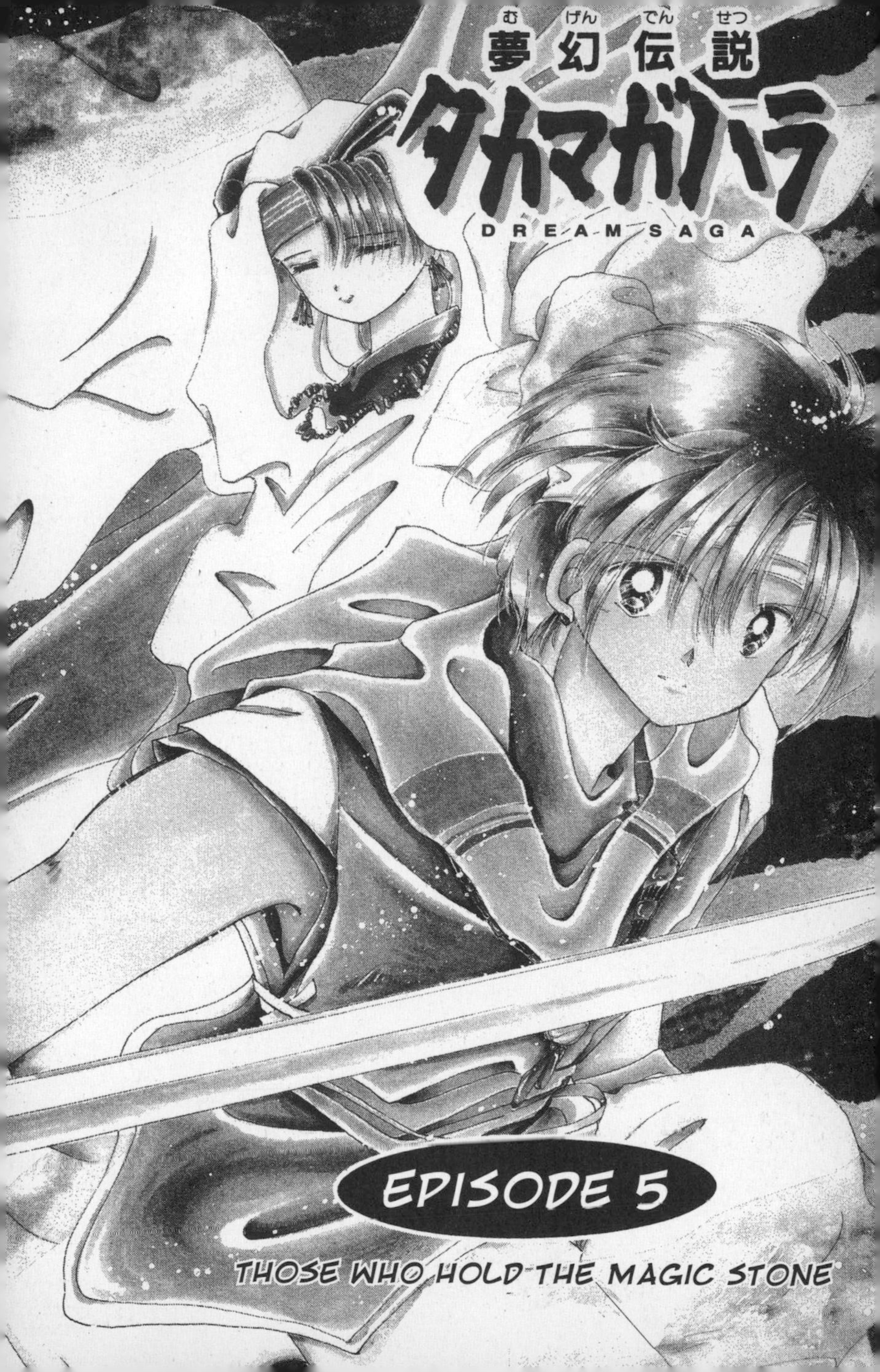
むげんでんせつ
夢幻伝説
タカマガハラ
DREAM SAGA
EPISODE 5
THOSE WHO HOLD THE MAGIC STONE

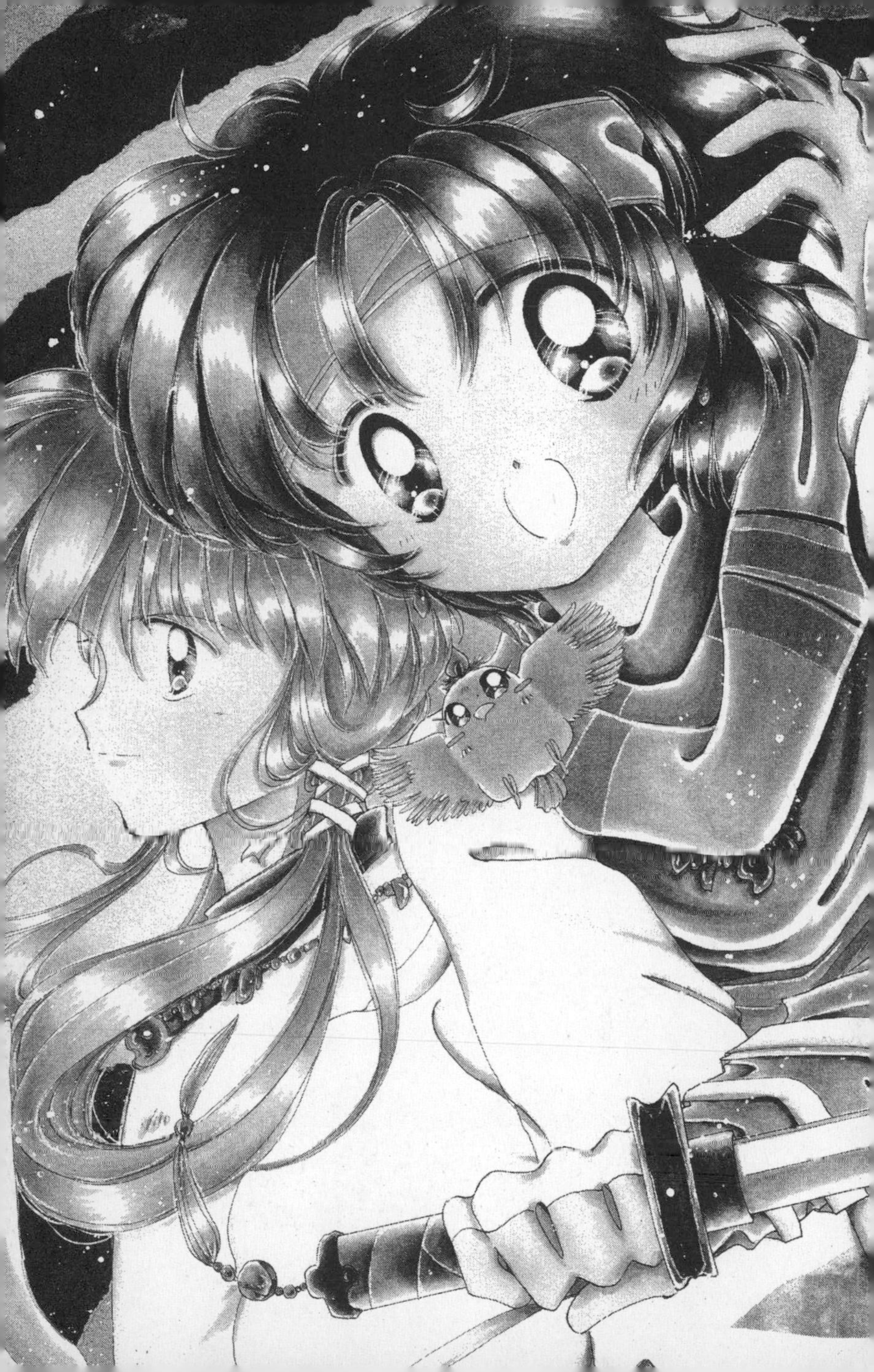

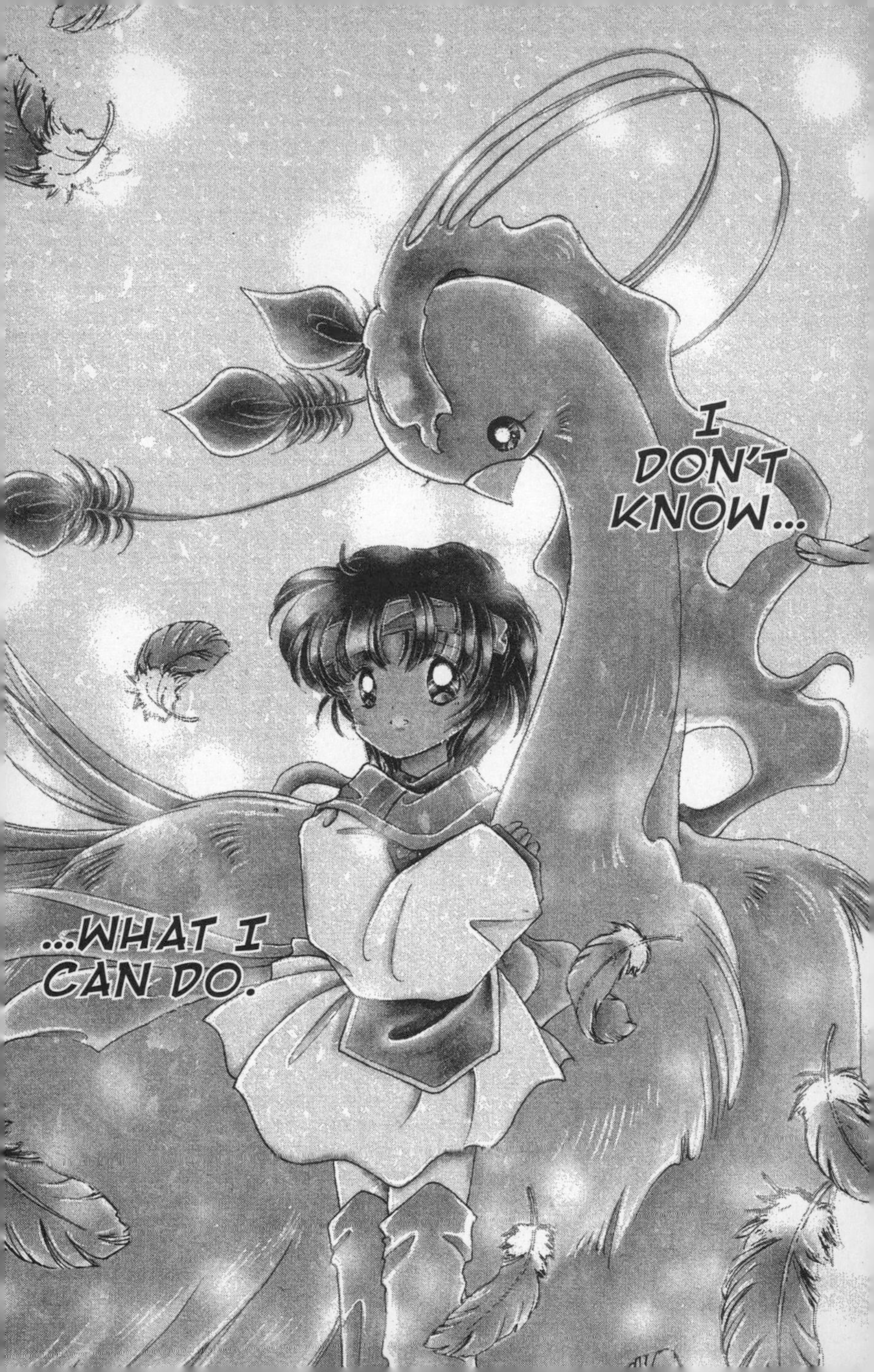
I DON'T KNOW...
...WHAT I CAN DO.

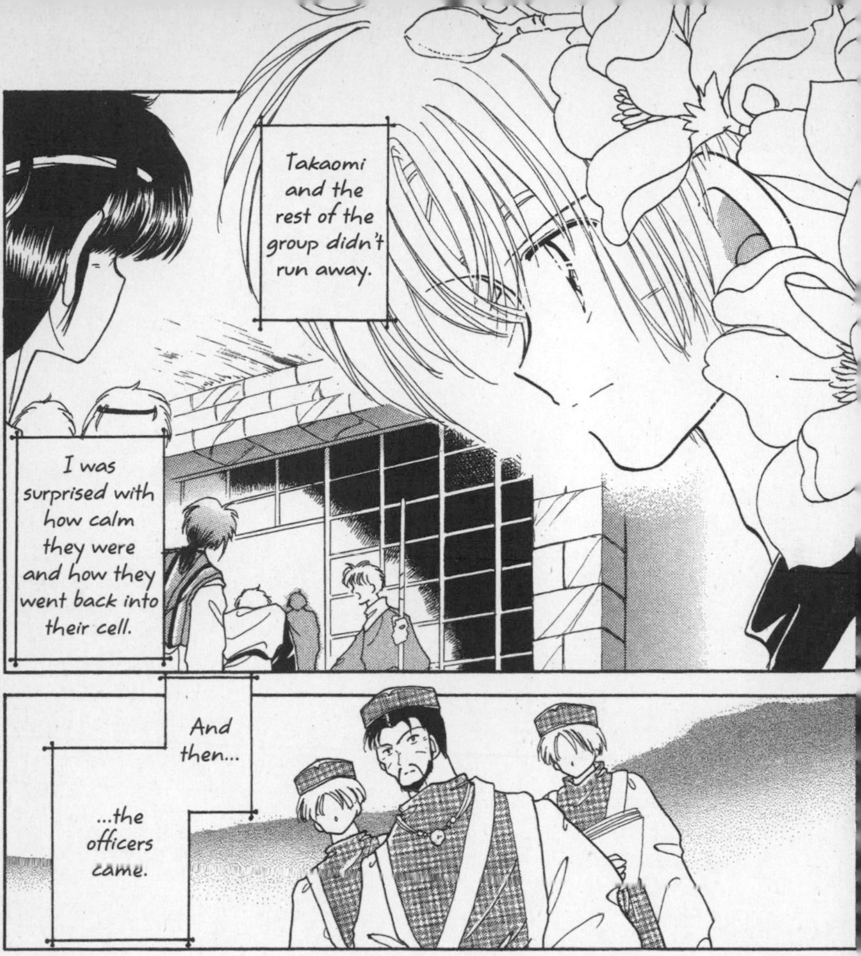
Takaomi and the rest of the group didn't run away.
I was surprised with how calm they were and how they went back into their cell.
And then...
...the officers came.

Question: When did you start drawing manga in ink? When did you start writing?

Answer: I started drawing when I was in fifth grade. I started writing manga when I was in junior high. I wrote for Nakayoshi magazine too. Then there was a period of time when I didn't write for five years, and then I started up for Nakayoshi again. I was 23 years old at the time. That was the first time I actually used screen tones. Two years after that, I made my professional debut. So even if you take your time getting into screen tones, you'll be fine!

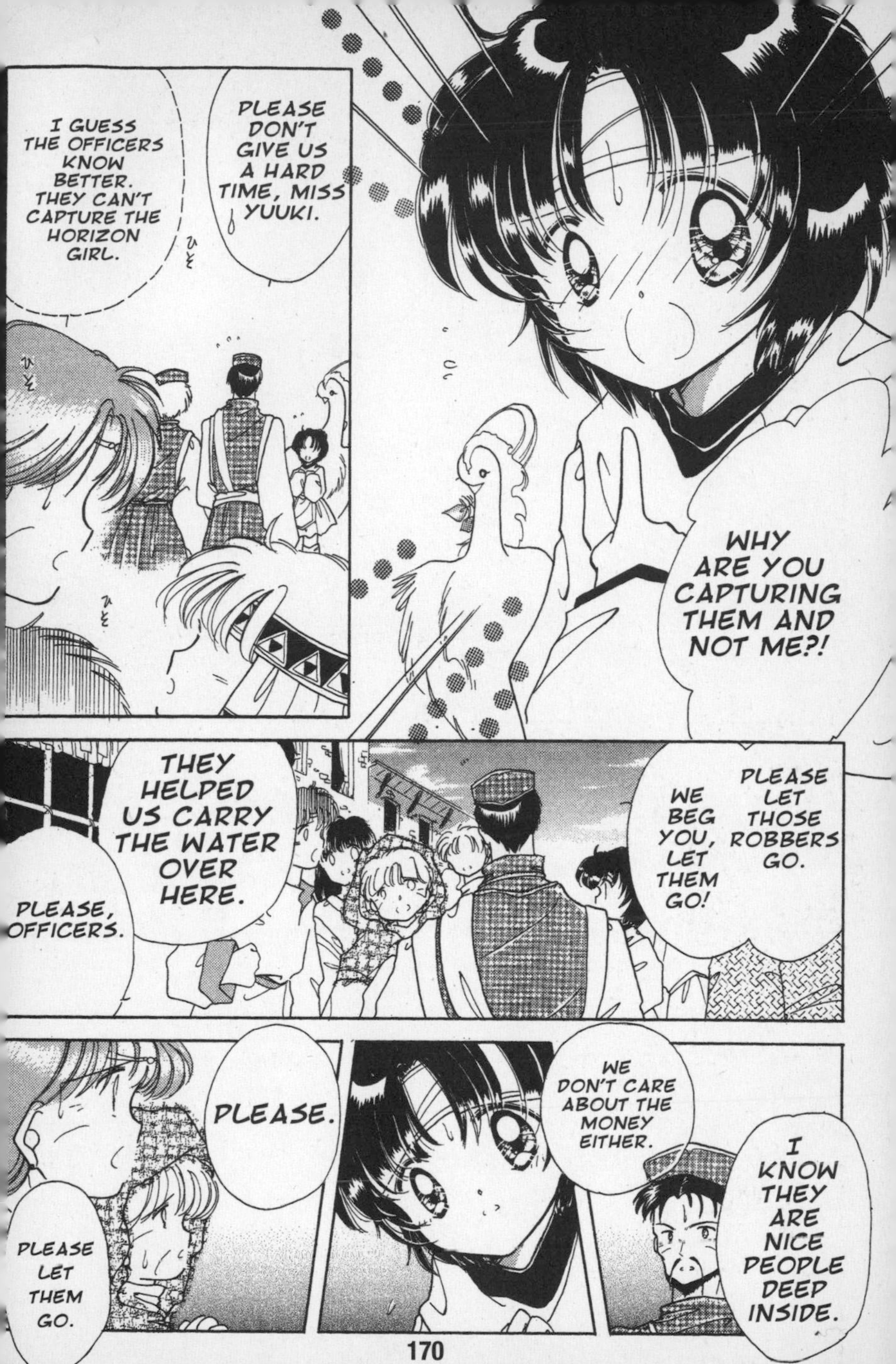
WHY ARE YOU CAPTURING THEM AND NOT ME?!
PLEASE DON'T GIVE US A HARD TIME, MISS YUUKI.
I GUESS THE OFFICERS KNOW BETTER. THEY CAN'T CAPTURE THE HORIZON GIRL.
PLEASE LET THOSE ROBBERS GO.
WE BEG YOU, LET THEM GO!
THEY HELPED US CARRY THE WATER OVER HERE.
PLEASE, OFFICERS.
I KNOW THEY ARE NICE PEOPLE DEEP INSIDE.
WE DON'T CARE ABOUT THE MONEY EITHER.
PLEASE.
PLEASE LET THEM GO.

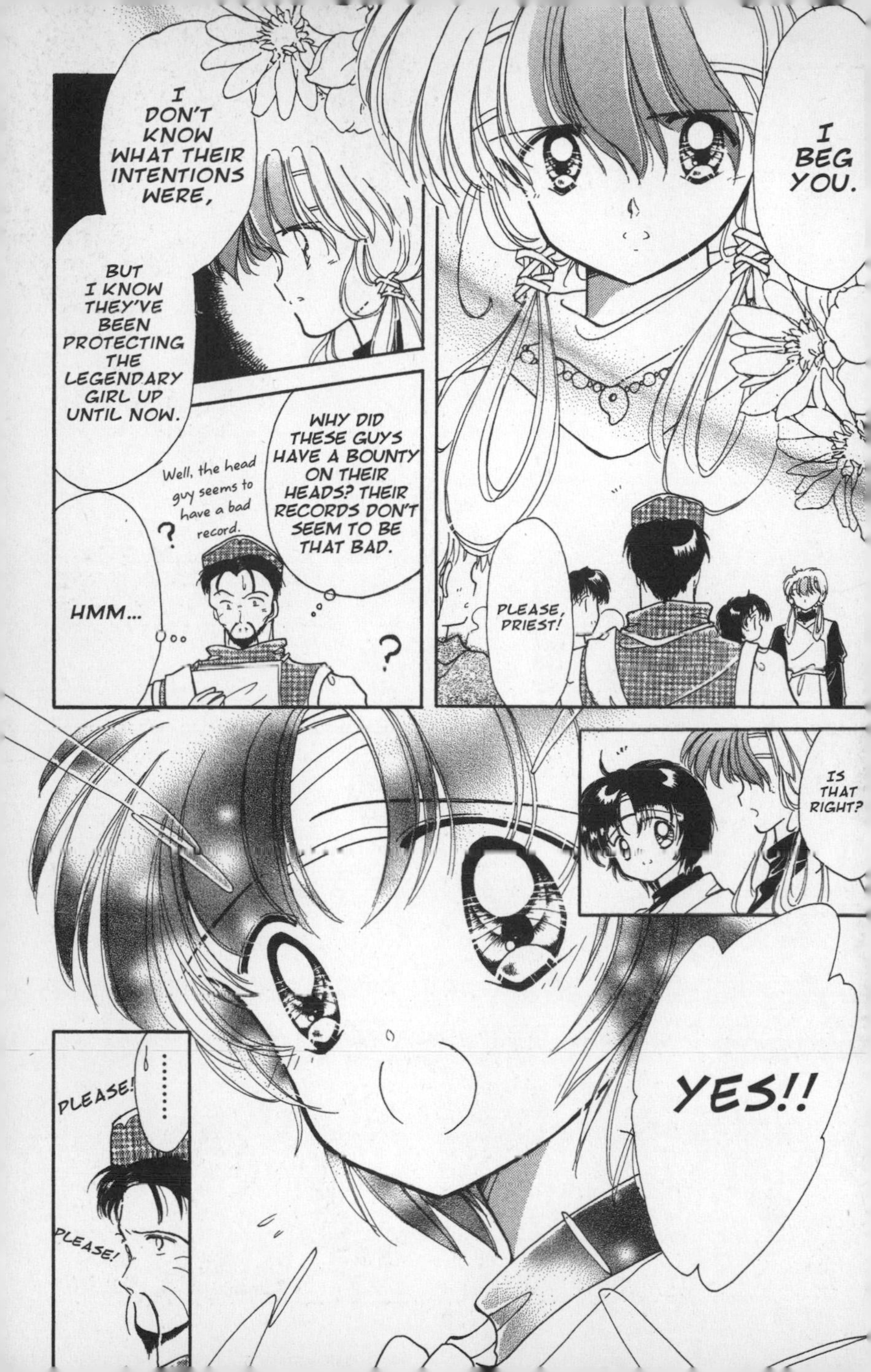
I BEG YOU.
PLEASE, PRIEST!
I DON'T KNOW WHAT THEIR INTENTIONS WERE,
BUT I KNOW THEY'VE BEEN PROTECTING THE LEGENDARY GIRL UP UNTIL NOW.
WHY DID THESE GUYS HAVE A BOUNTY ON THEIR HEADS? THEIR RECORDS DON'T SEEM TO BE THAT BAD.
Well, the head guy seems to have a bad record.
HMM...
IS THAT RIGHT?
YES!!
PLEASE!
......
PLEASE!

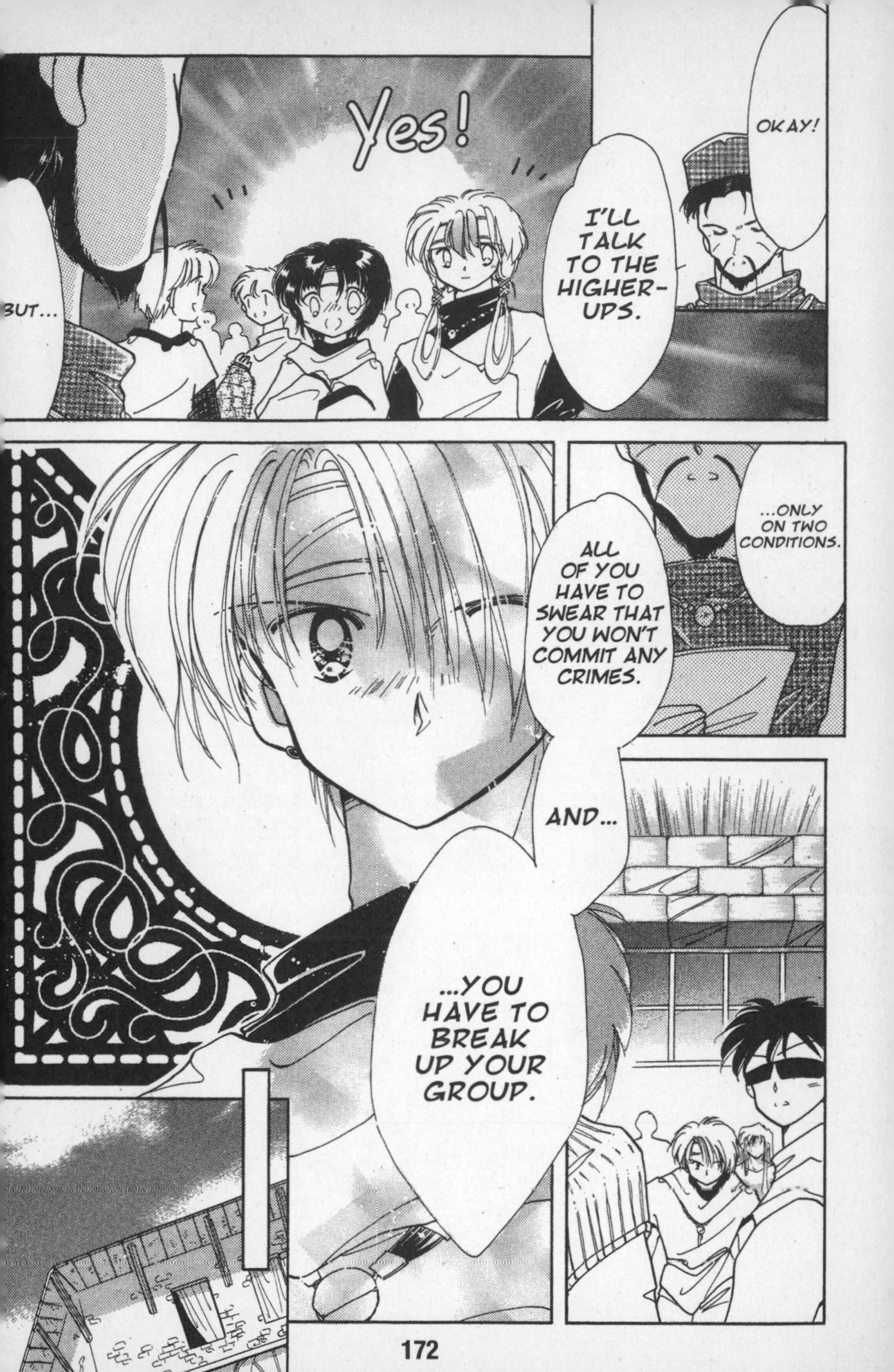
OKAY!
I'LL TALK TO THE HIGHER-UPS.
Yes!
BUT...
...ONLY ON TWO CONDITIONS.
ALL OF YOU HAVE TO SWEAR THAT YOU WON'T COMMIT ANY CRIMES.
AND...
...YOU HAVE TO BREAK UP YOUR GROUP.

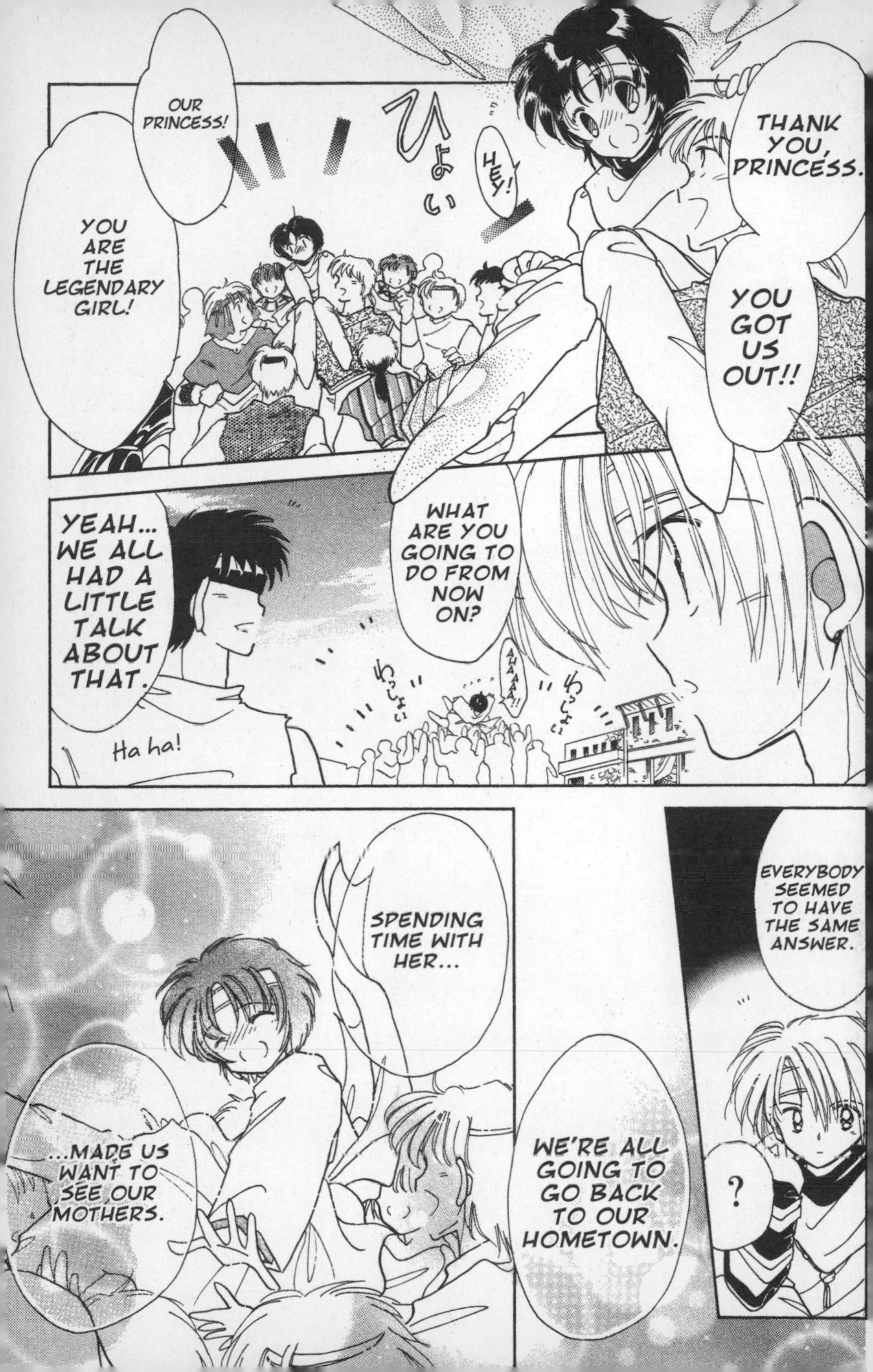
THANK YOU, PRINCESS.
YOU GOT US OUT!!
HEY!
ひょい
OUR PRINCESS!
YOU ARE THE LEGENDARY GIRL!
WHAT ARE YOU GOING TO DO FROM NOW ON?
わっしょい
わっしょい
YEAH... WE ALL HAD A LITTLE TALK ABOUT THAT.
Ha ha!
EVERYBODY SEEMED TO HAVE THE SAME ANSWER.
?
WE'RE ALL GOING TO GO BACK TO OUR HOMETOWN.
SPENDING TIME WITH HER...
...MADE US WANT TO SEE OUR MOTHERS.

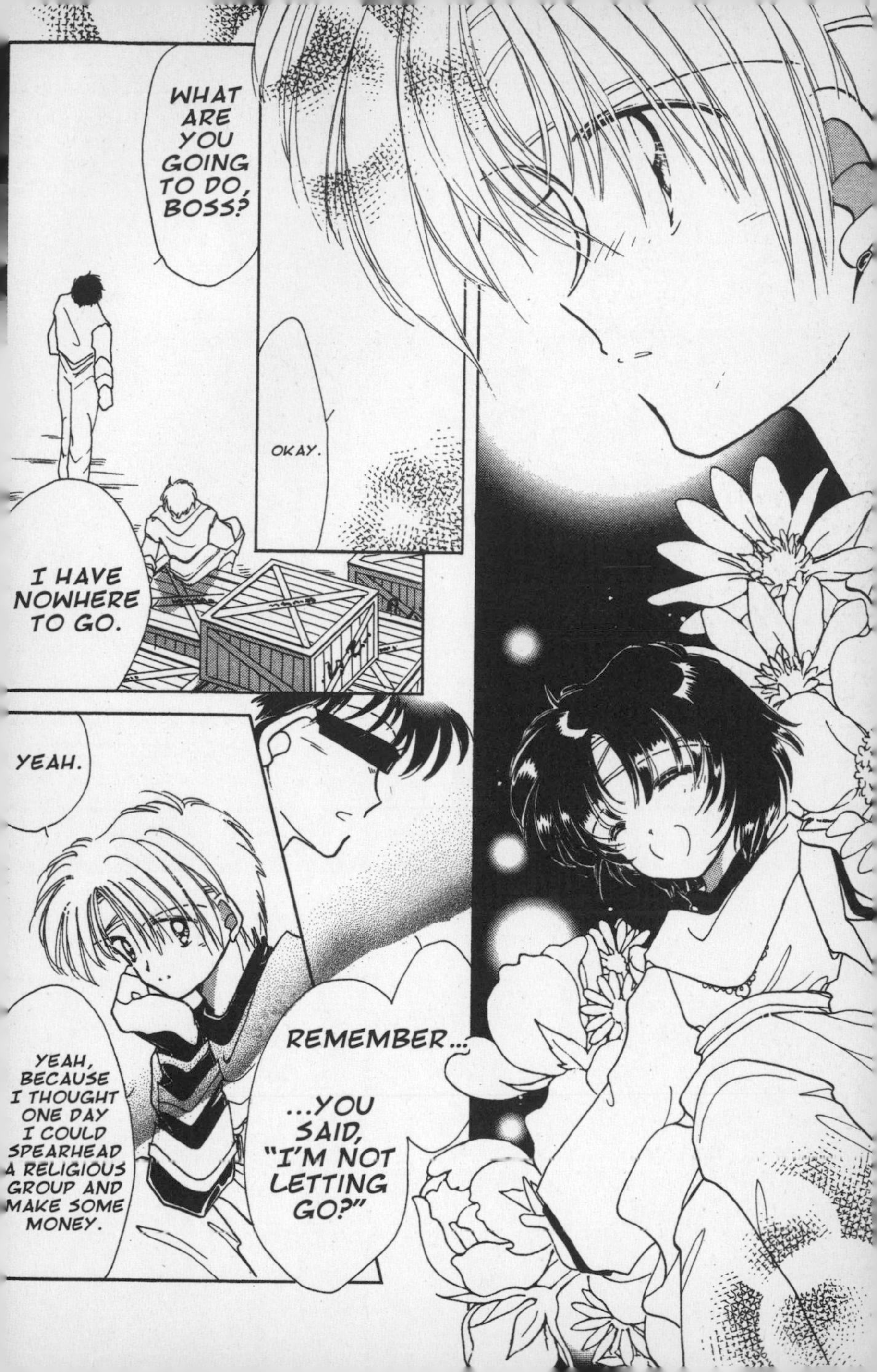
WHAT ARE YOU GOING TO DO, BOSS?
I HAVE NOWHERE TO GO.
OKAY.
REMEMBER...
...YOU SAID, "I'M NOT LETTING GO?"
YEAH.
YEAH, BECAUSE I THOUGHT ONE DAY I COULD SPEARHEAD A RELIGIOUS GROUP AND MAKE SOME MONEY.

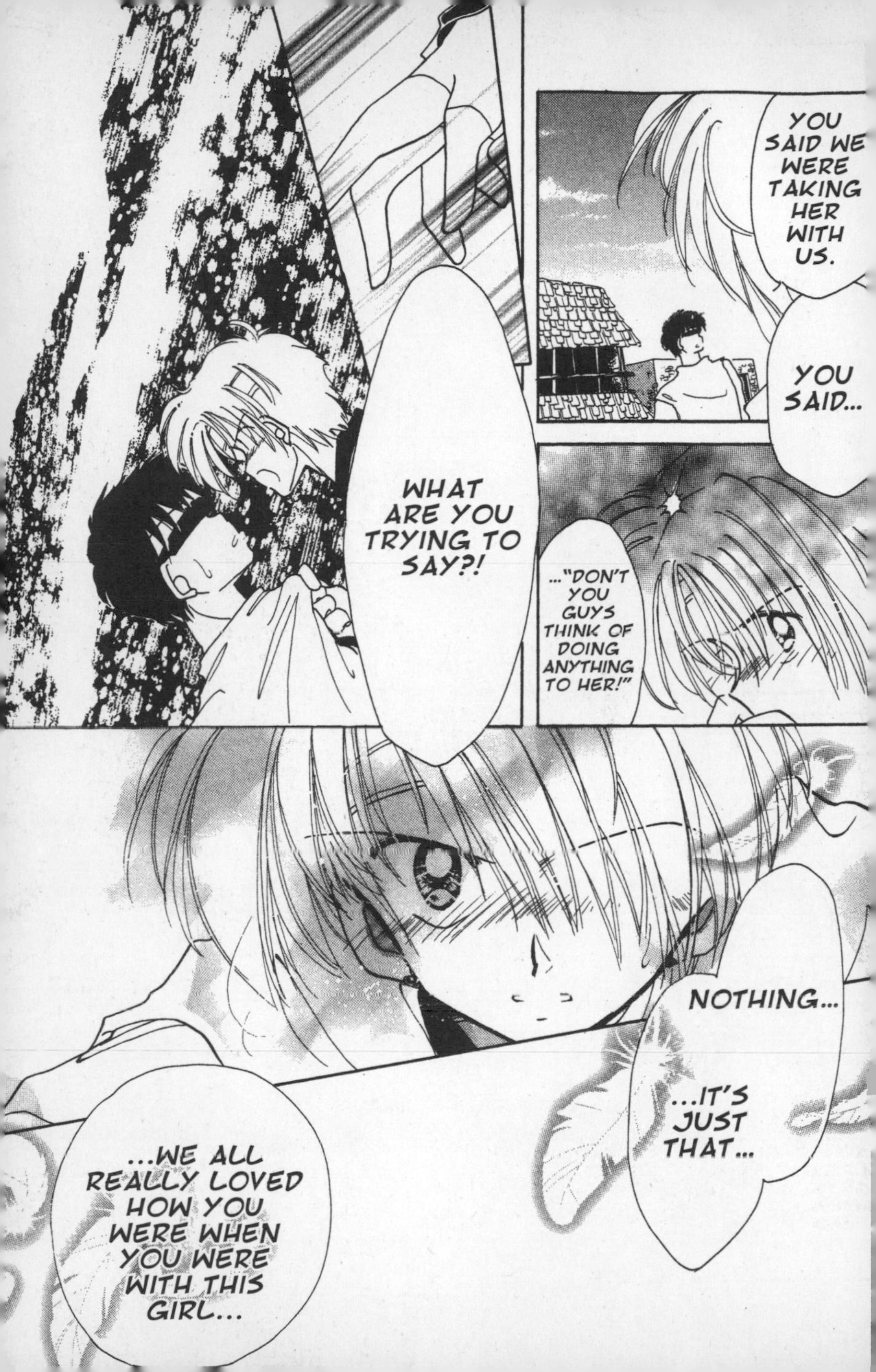
YOU SAID WE WERE TAKING HER WITH US.
YOU SAID...
..."DON'T YOU GUYS THINK OF DOING ANYTHING TO HER!"
WHAT ARE YOU TRYING TO SAY?!
NOTHING...
...IT'S JUST THAT...
...WE ALL REALLY LOVED HOW YOU WERE WHEN YOU WERE WITH THIS GIRL...

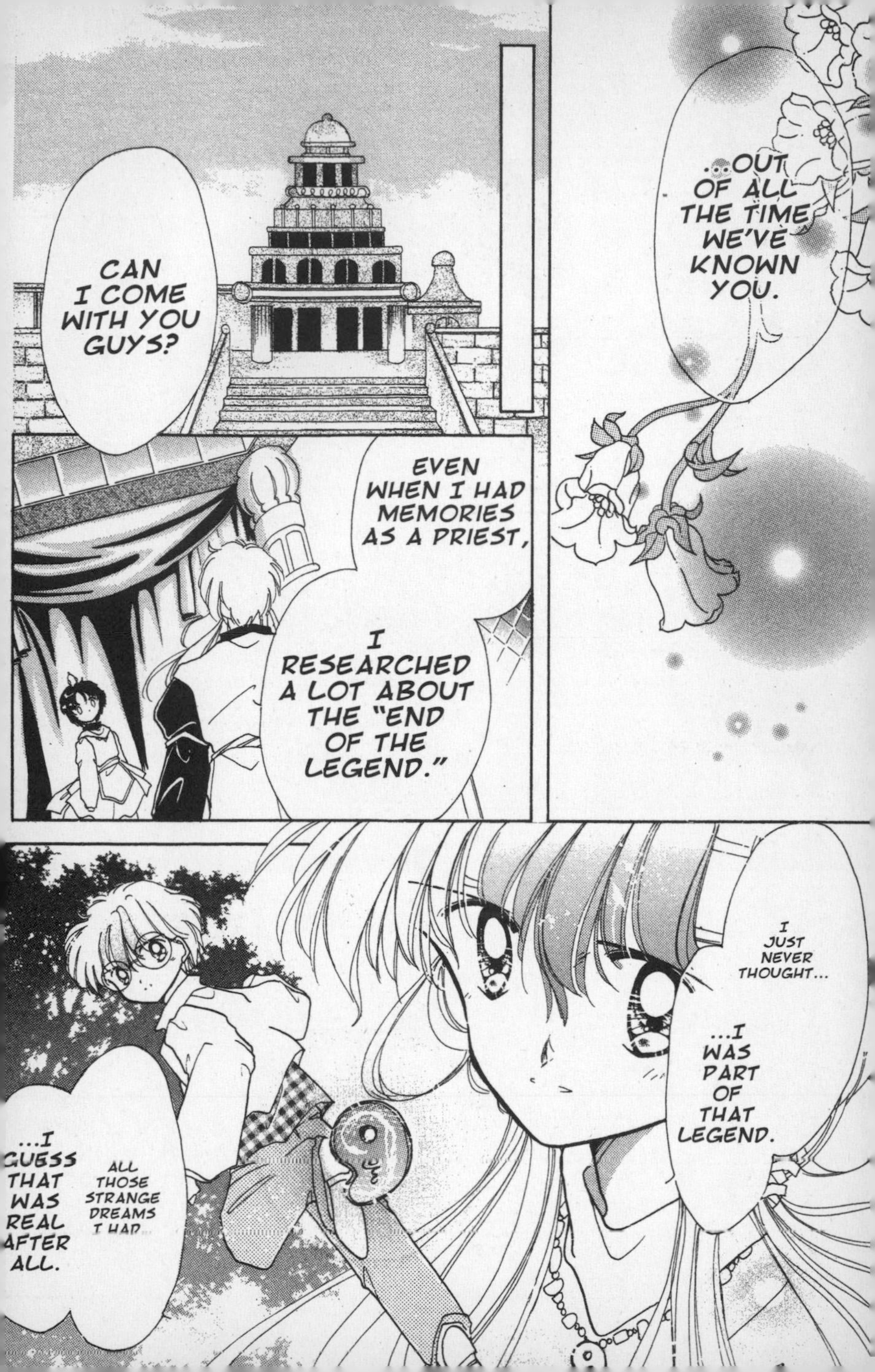
...OUT OF ALL THE TIME WE'VE KNOWN YOU.
CAN I COME WITH YOU GUYS?
EVEN WHEN I HAD MEMORIES AS A PRIEST,
I RESEARCHED A LOT ABOUT THE "END OF THE LEGEND."
I JUST NEVER THOUGHT...
...I WAS PART OF THAT LEGEND.
ALL THOSE STRANGE DREAMS I HAD...
...I GUESS THAT WAS REAL AFTER ALL.

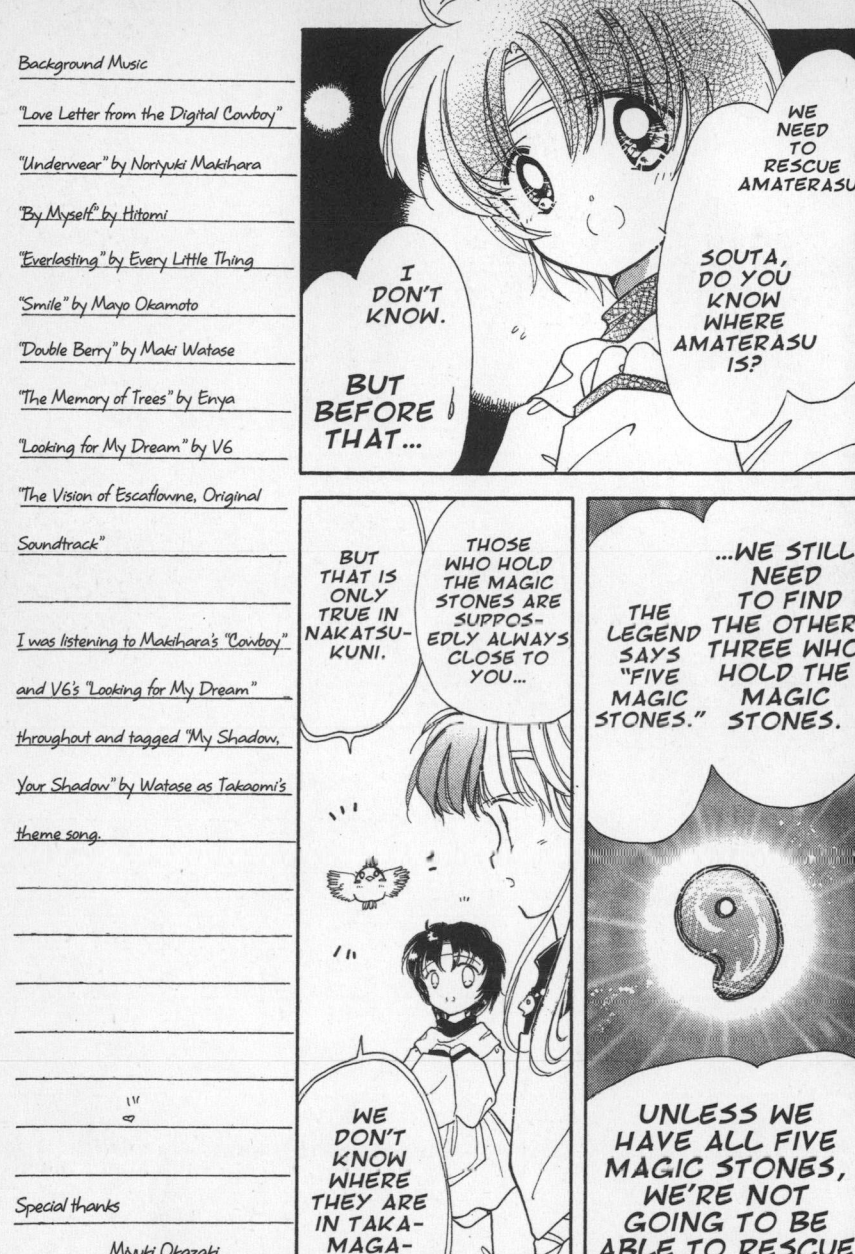

Background Music

"Love Letter from the Digital Cowboy"

"Underwear" by Noriyuki Makihara

"By Myself" by Hitomi

"Everlasting" by Every Little Thing

"Smile" by Mayo Okamoto

"Double Berry" by Maki Watase

"The Memory of Trees" by Enya

"Looking for My Dream" by V6

"The Vision of Escaflowne, Original Soundtrack"

I was listening to Makihara's "Cowboy" and V6's "Looking for My Dream" throughout and tagged "My Shadow, Your Shadow" by Watase as Takaomi's theme song.

Special thanks

Miyuki Okazaki

Miwa Isioka

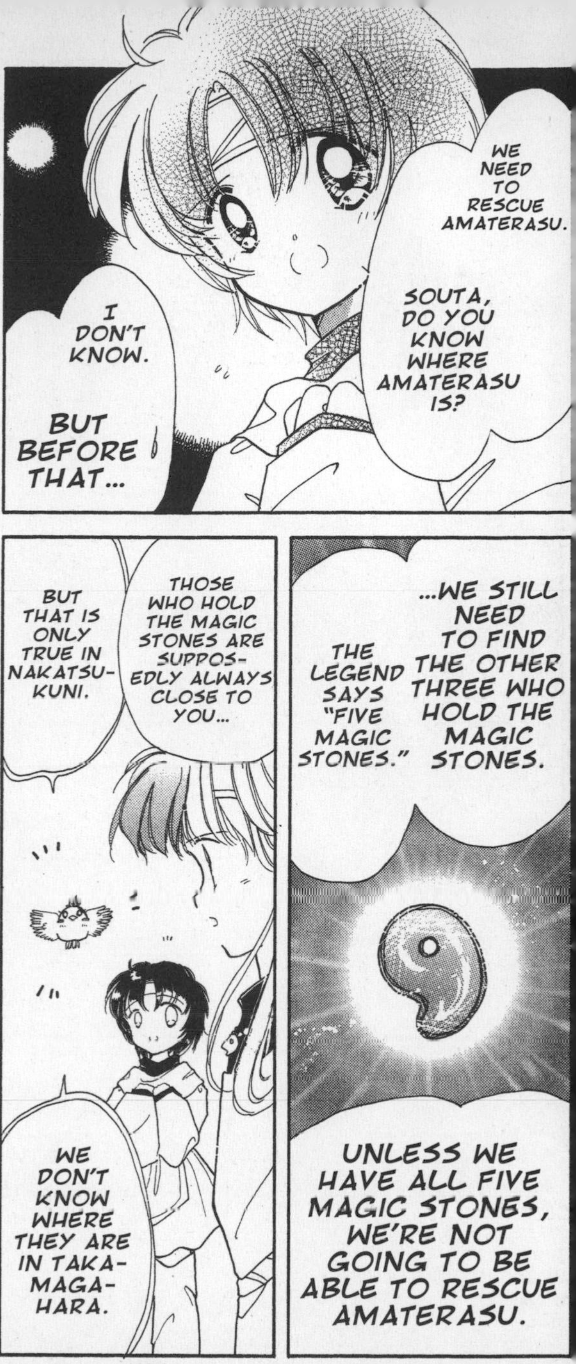
WE NEED TO RESCUE AMATERASU.
SOUTA, DO YOU KNOW WHERE AMATERASU IS?
I DON'T KNOW.
BUT BEFORE THAT...
...WE STILL NEED TO FIND THE OTHER THREE WHO HOLD THE MAGIC STONES.
THE LEGEND SAYS "FIVE MAGIC STONES."
UNLESS WE HAVE ALL FIVE MAGIC STONES, WE'RE NOT GOING TO BE ABLE TO RESCUE AMATERASU.
THOSE WHO HOLD THE MAGIC STONES ARE SUPPOS-EDLY ALWAYS CLOSE TO YOU...
BUT THAT IS ONLY TRUE IN NAKATSU-KUNI.
WE DON'T KNOW WHERE THEY ARE IN TAKA-MAGA-HARA.

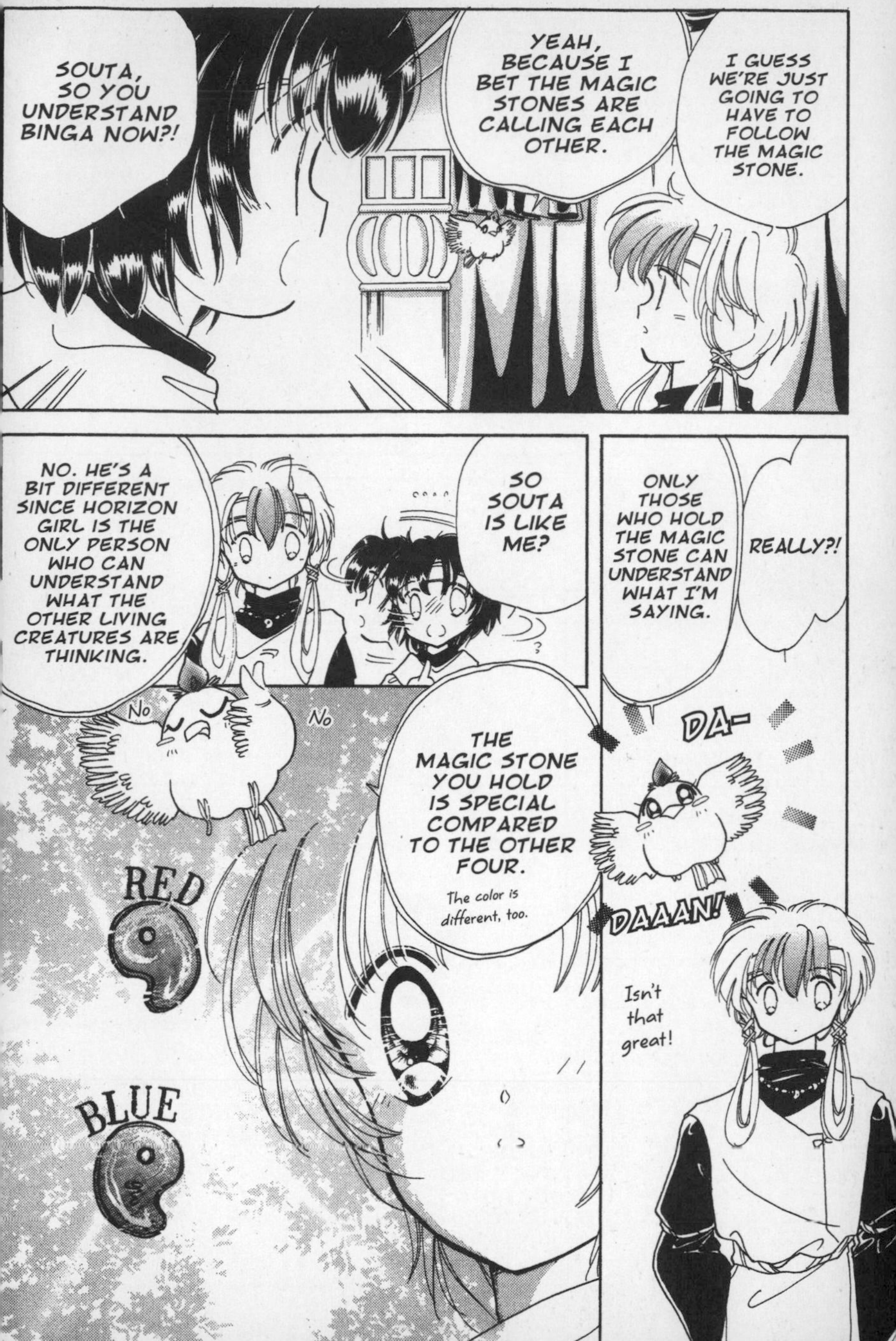
I GUESS WE'RE JUST GOING TO HAVE TO FOLLOW THE MAGIC STONE.
YEAH, BECAUSE I BET THE MAGIC STONES ARE CALLING EACH OTHER.
SOUTA, SO YOU UNDERSTAND BINGA NOW?!
REALLY?!
ONLY THOSE WHO HOLD THE MAGIC STONE CAN UNDERSTAND WHAT I'M SAYING.
DA-
DAAAN!
Isn't that great!
SO SOUTA IS LIKE ME?
NO. HE'S A BIT DIFFERENT SINCE HORIZON GIRL IS THE ONLY PERSON WHO CAN UNDERSTAND WHAT THE OTHER LIVING CREATURES ARE THINKING.
No
No
THE MAGIC STONE YOU HOLD IS SPECIAL COMPARED TO THE OTHER FOUR.
The color is different, too.
RED
BLUE

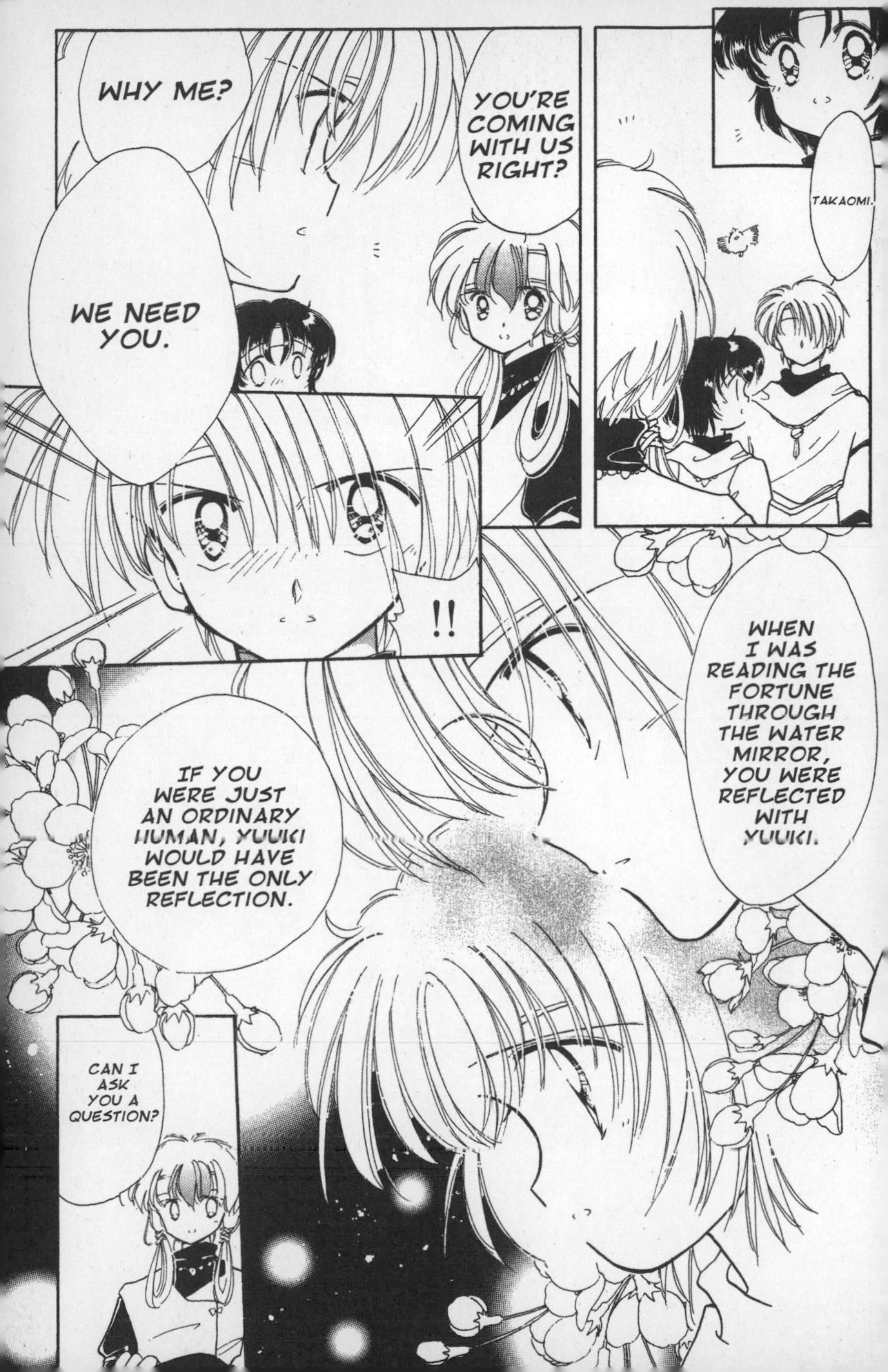
TAKAOMI.
YOU'RE COMING WITH US RIGHT?
WHY ME?
WE NEED YOU.
!!
WHEN I WAS READING THE FORTUNE THROUGH THE WATER MIRROR, YOU WERE REFLECTED WITH YUUKI.
IF YOU WERE JUST AN ORDINARY HUMAN, YUUKI WOULD HAVE BEEN THE ONLY REFLECTION.
CAN I ASK YOU A QUESTION?

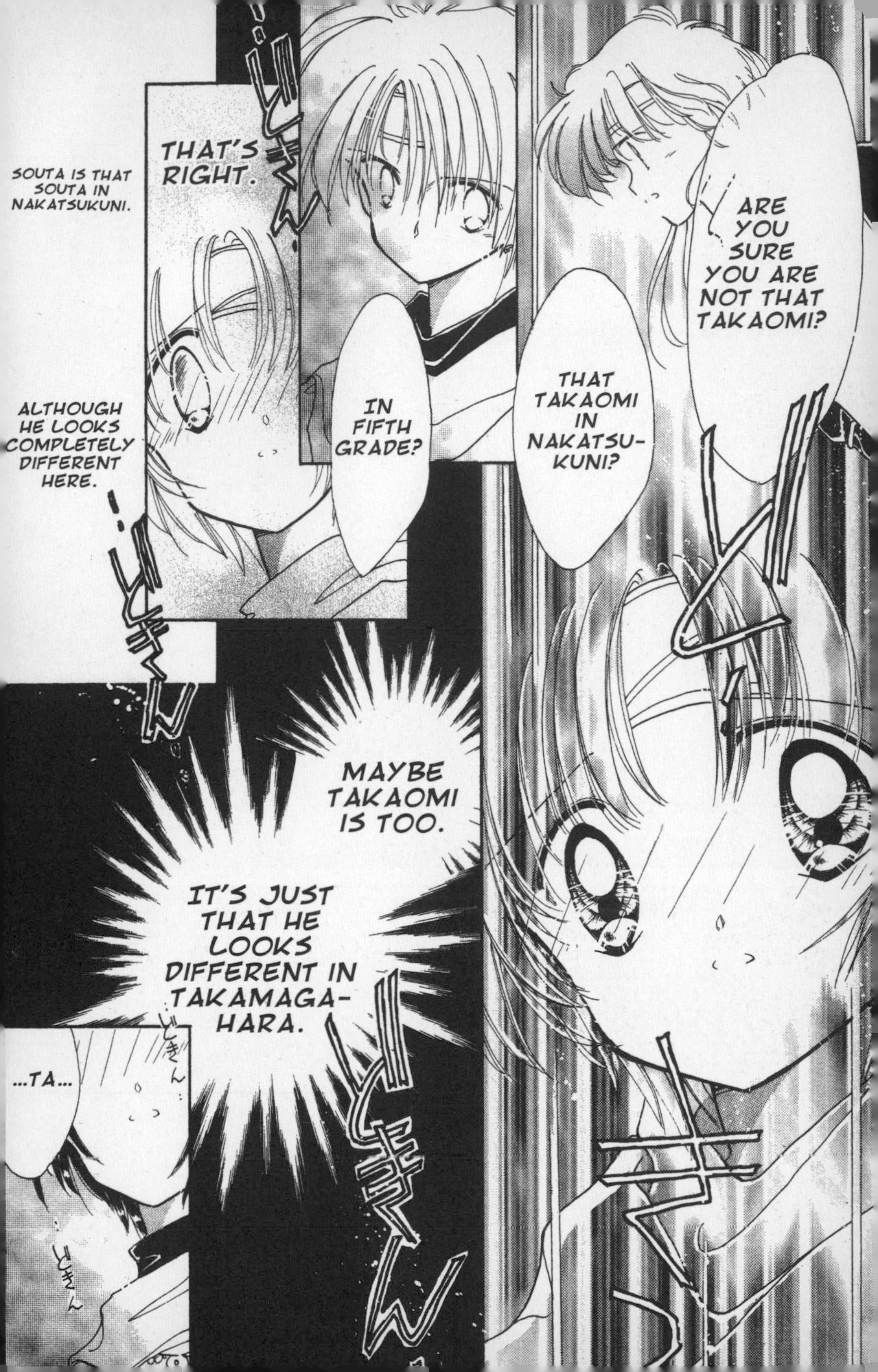
ARE YOU SURE YOU ARE NOT THAT TAKAOMI?
THAT TAKAOMI IN NAKATSU-KUNI?
IN FIFTH GRADE?
THAT'S RIGHT.
SOUTA IS THAT SOUTA IN NAKATSUKUNI.
ALTHOUGH HE LOOKS COMPLETELY DIFFERENT HERE.
MAYBE TAKAOMI IS TOO.
IT'S JUST THAT HE LOOKS DIFFERENT IN TAKAMAGA-HARA.
...TA...

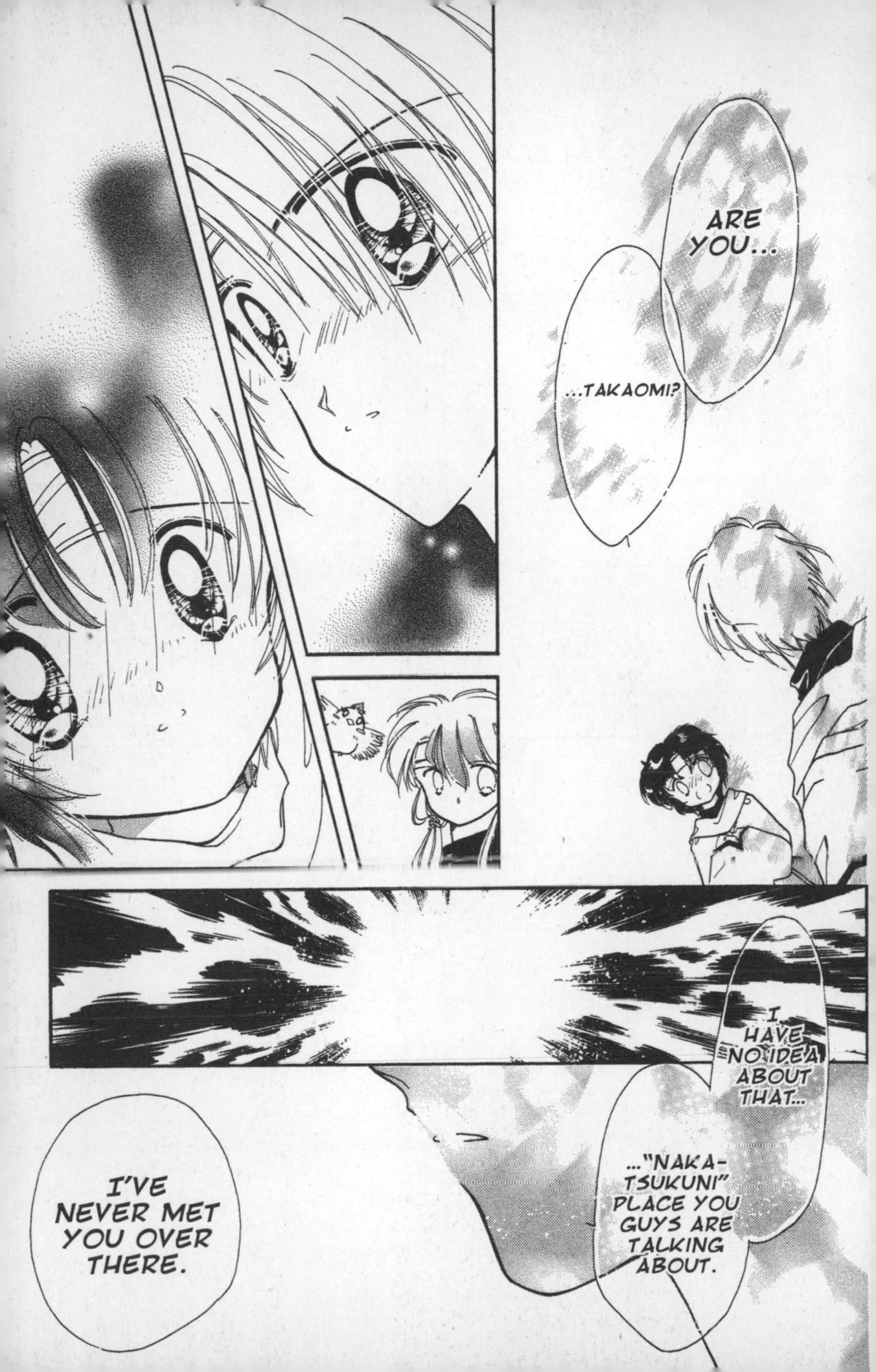
ARE YOU...
...TAKAOMI?
I HAVE NO IDEA ABOUT THAT...
..."NAKA-TSUKUNI" PLACE YOU GUYS ARE TALKING ABOUT.
I'VE NEVER MET YOU OVER THERE.

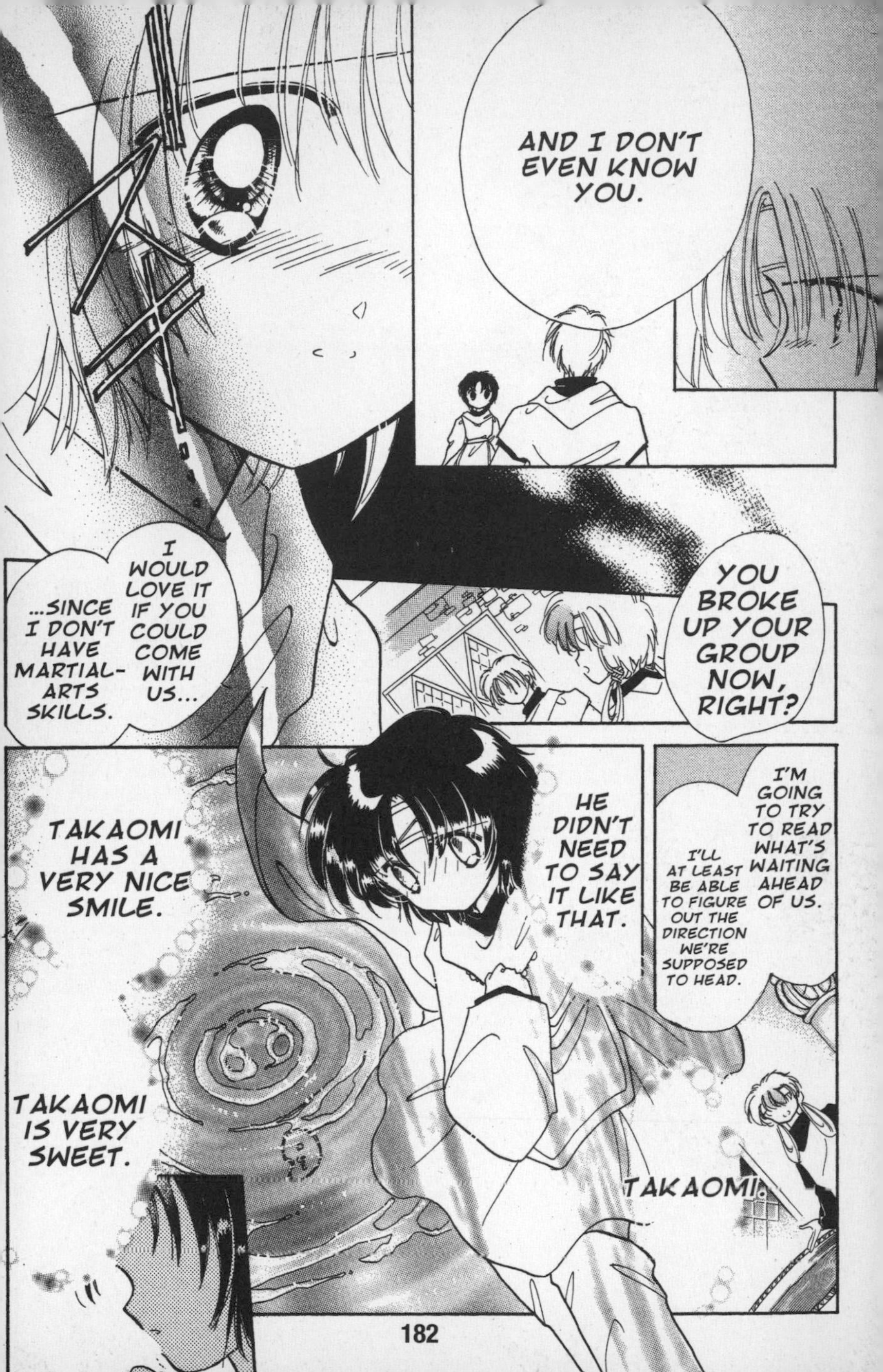
AND I DON'T EVEN KNOW YOU.
YOU BROKE UP YOUR GROUP NOW, RIGHT?
I WOULD LOVE IT IF YOU COULD COME WITH US...
...SINCE I DON'T HAVE MARTIAL-ARTS SKILLS.
I'M GOING TO TRY TO READ WHAT'S WAITING AHEAD OF US.
I'LL AT LEAST BE ABLE TO FIGURE OUT THE DIRECTION WE'RE SUPPOSED TO HEAD.
TAKAOMI.
HE DIDN'T NEED TO SAY IT LIKE THAT.
TAKAOMI HAS A VERY NICE SMILE.
TAKAOMI IS VERY SWEET.

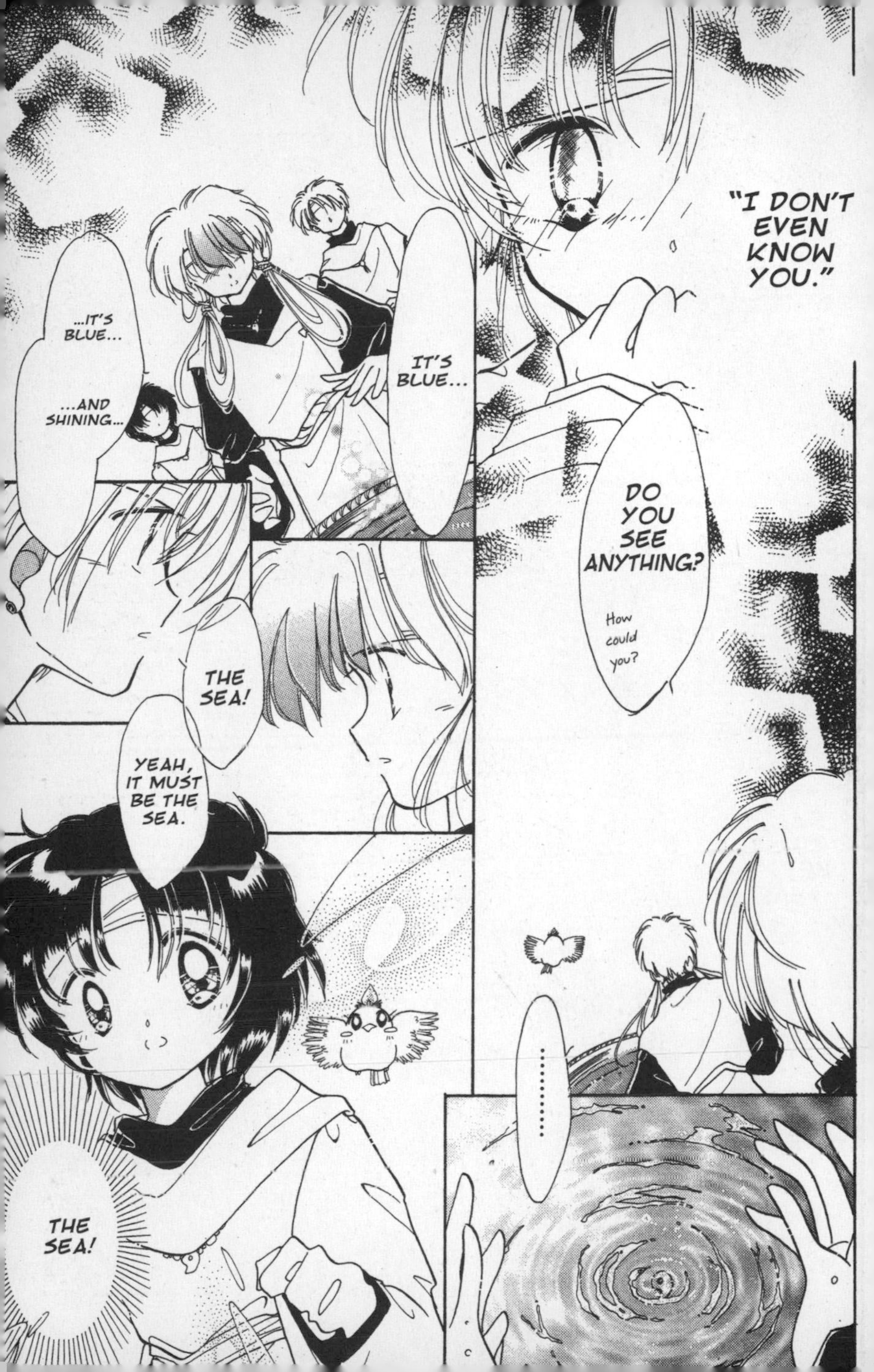

"I DON'T EVEN KNOW YOU."
DO YOU SEE ANYTHING?
How could you?
IT'S BLUE...
...IT'S BLUE...
...AND SHINING...
THE SEA!
YEAH, IT MUST BE THE SEA.
......
THE SEA!

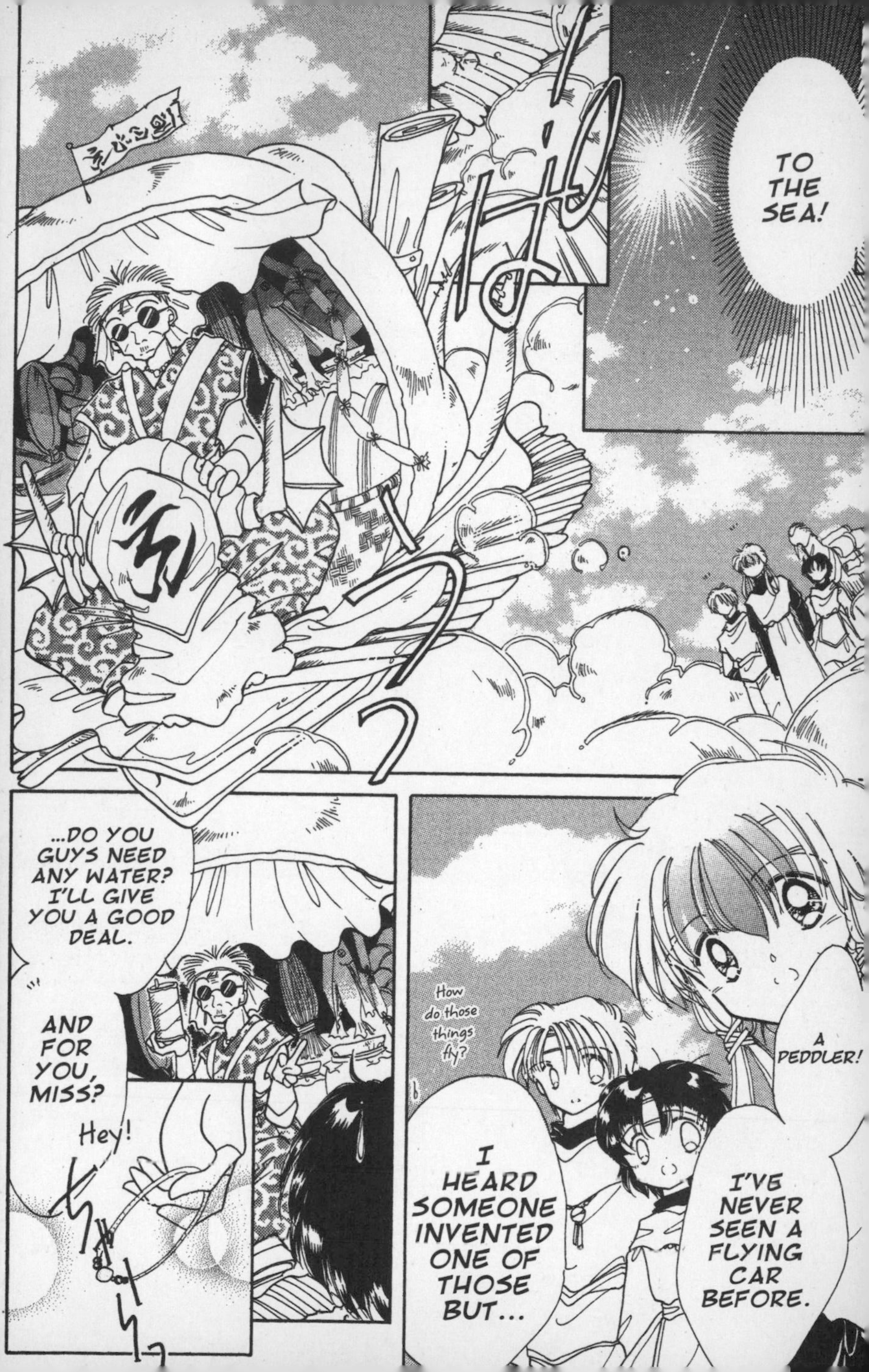
TO THE SEA!
A PEDDLER!
I'VE NEVER SEEN A FLYING CAR BEFORE.
How do those things fly?
I HEARD SOMEONE INVENTED ONE OF THOSE BUT...
...DO YOU GUYS NEED ANY WATER? I'LL GIVE YOU A GOOD DEAL.
AND FOR YOU, MISS?
Hey!

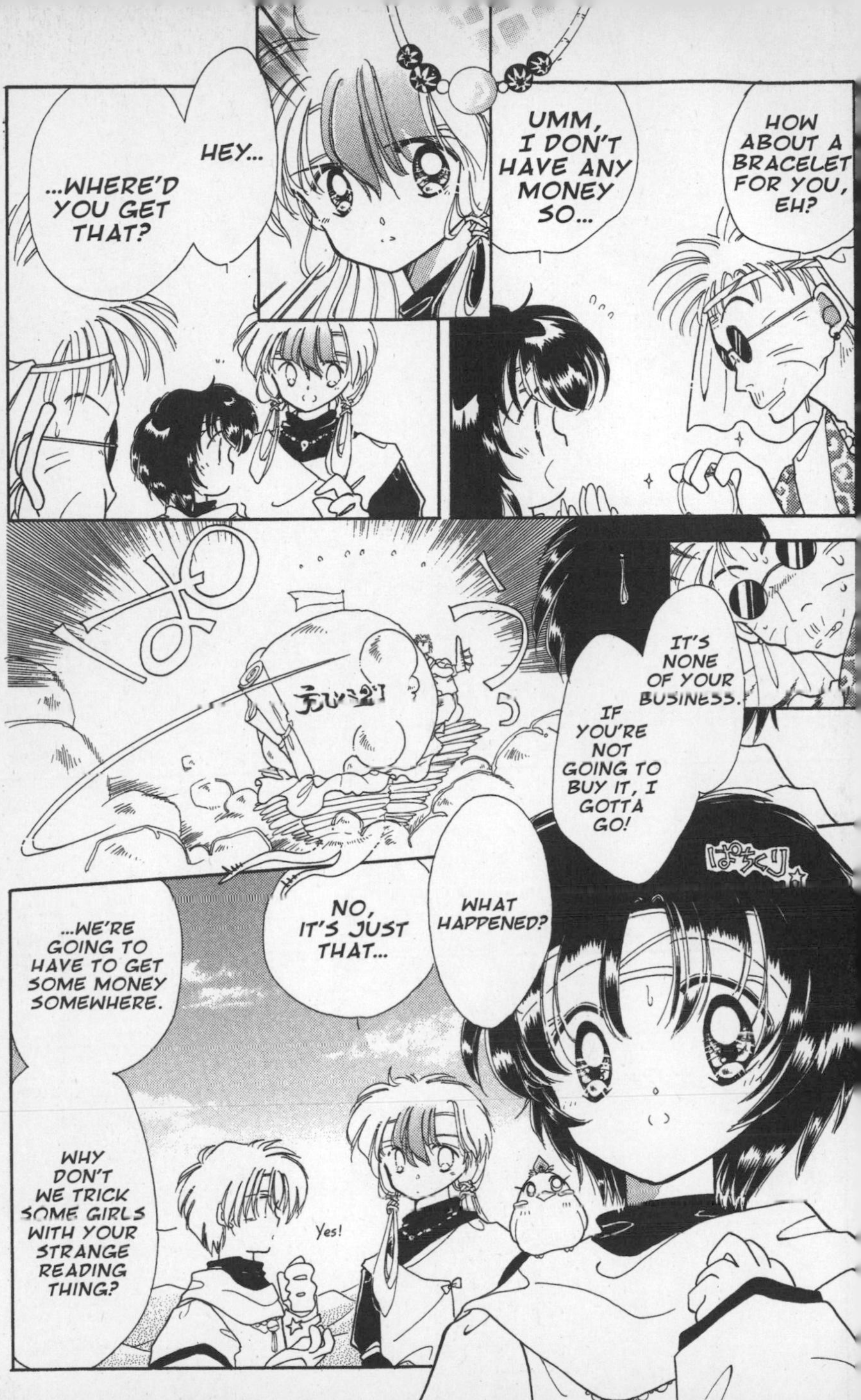
HOW ABOUT A BRACELET FOR YOU, EH?
UMM, I DON'T HAVE ANY MONEY SO...
HEY...
...WHERE'D YOU GET THAT?
IT'S NONE OF YOUR BUSINESS.
IF YOU'RE NOT GOING TO BUY IT, I GOTTA GO!
ぱちくり
WHAT HAPPENED?
NO, IT'S JUST THAT...
...WE'RE GOING TO HAVE TO GET SOME MONEY SOMEWHERE.
WHY DON'T WE TRICK SOME GIRLS WITH YOUR STRANGE READING THING?
Yes!

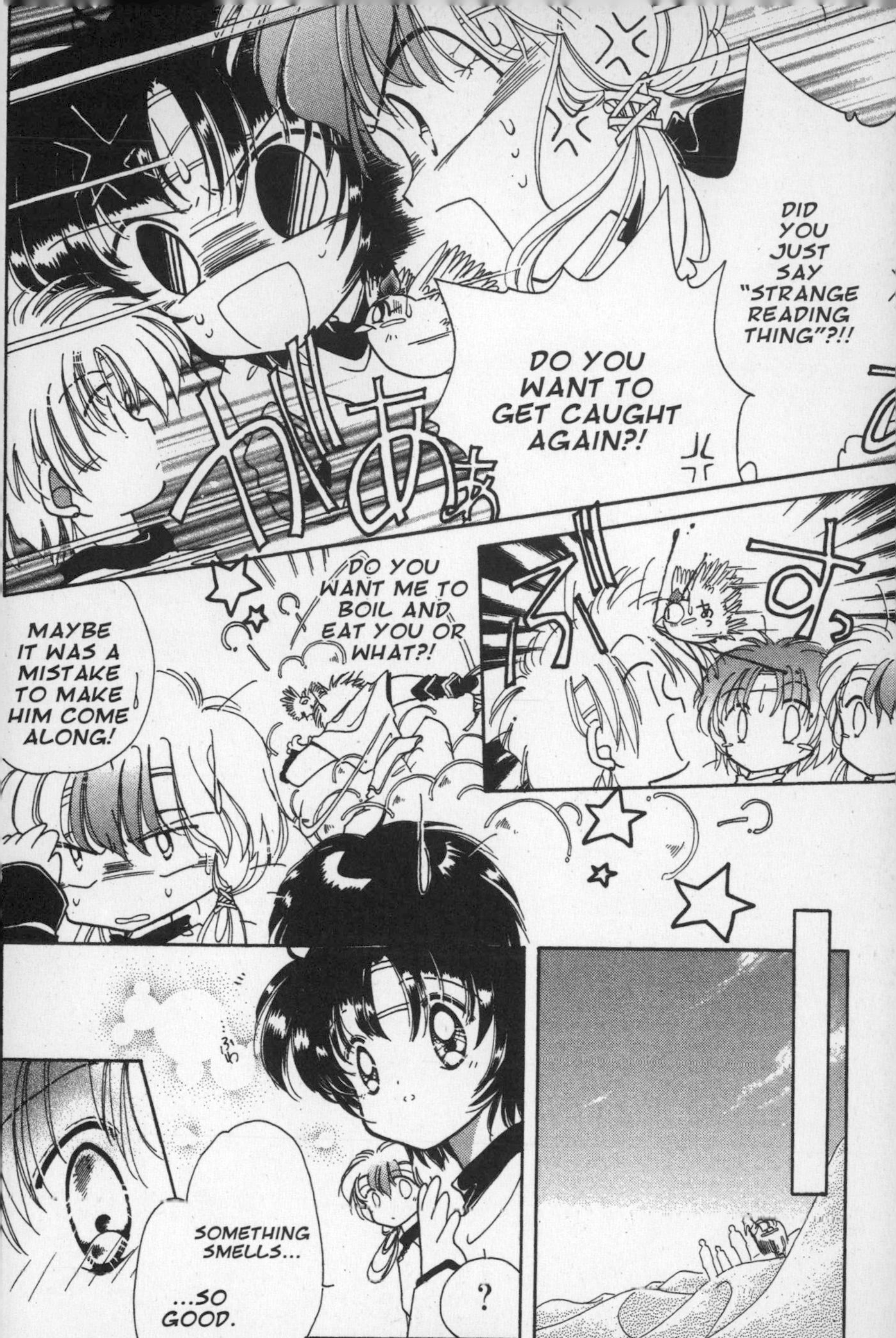
DID YOU JUST SAY "STRANGE READING THING"?!!
DO YOU WANT TO GET CAUGHT AGAIN?!
DO YOU WANT ME TO BOIL AND EAT YOU OR WHAT?!
MAYBE IT WAS A MISTAKE TO MAKE HIM COME ALONG!
?
SOMETHING SMELLS...
...SO GOOD.

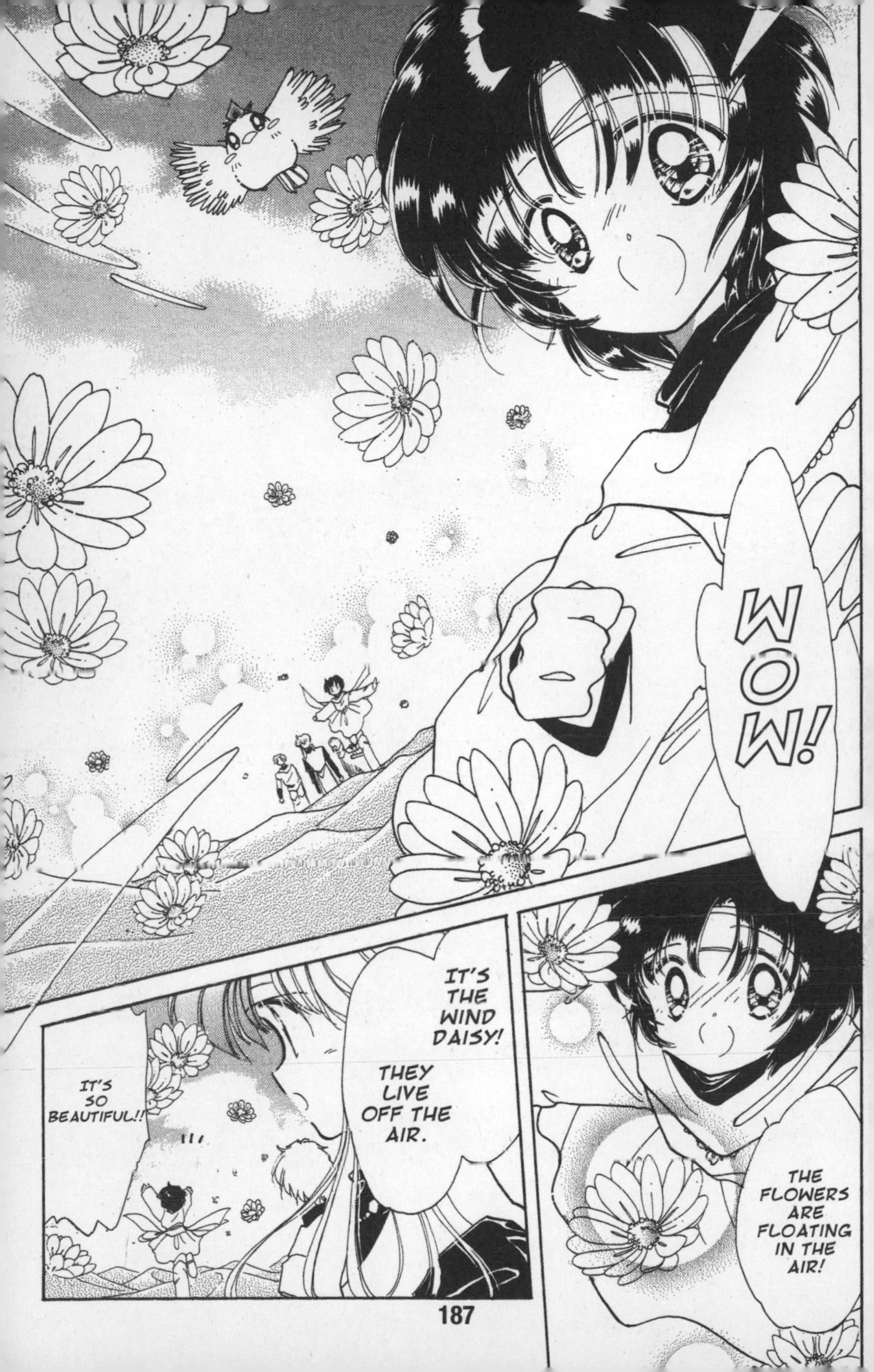
WOW!
THE FLOWERS ARE FLOATING IN THE AIR!
IT'S THE WIND DAISY!
THEY LIVE OFF THE AIR.
IT'S SO BEAUTIFUL!!

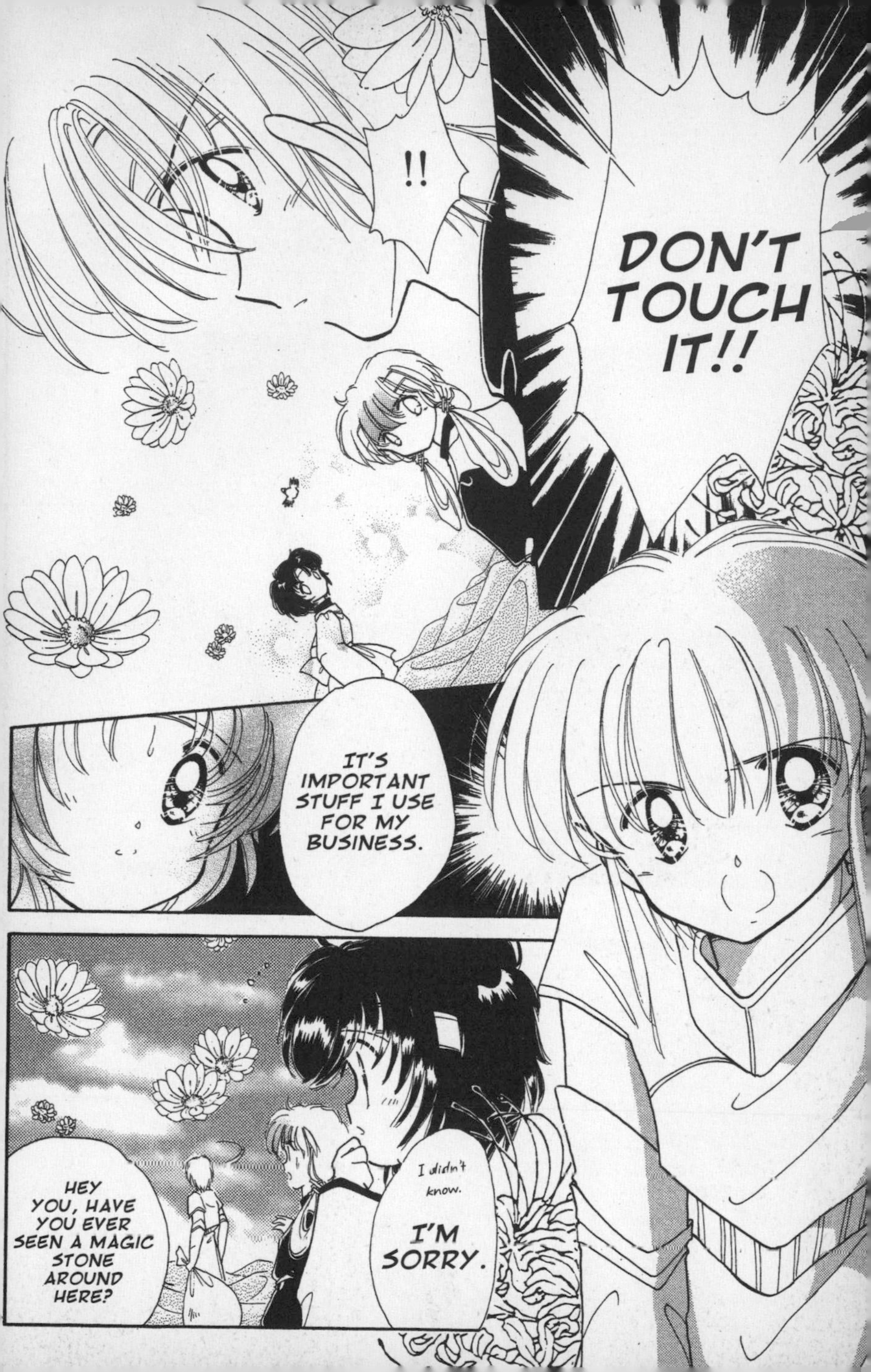

DON'T TOUCH IT!!
!!
IT'S IMPORTANT STUFF I USE FOR MY BUSINESS.
I didn't know.
I'M SORRY.
HEY YOU, HAVE YOU EVER SEEN A MAGIC STONE AROUND HERE?

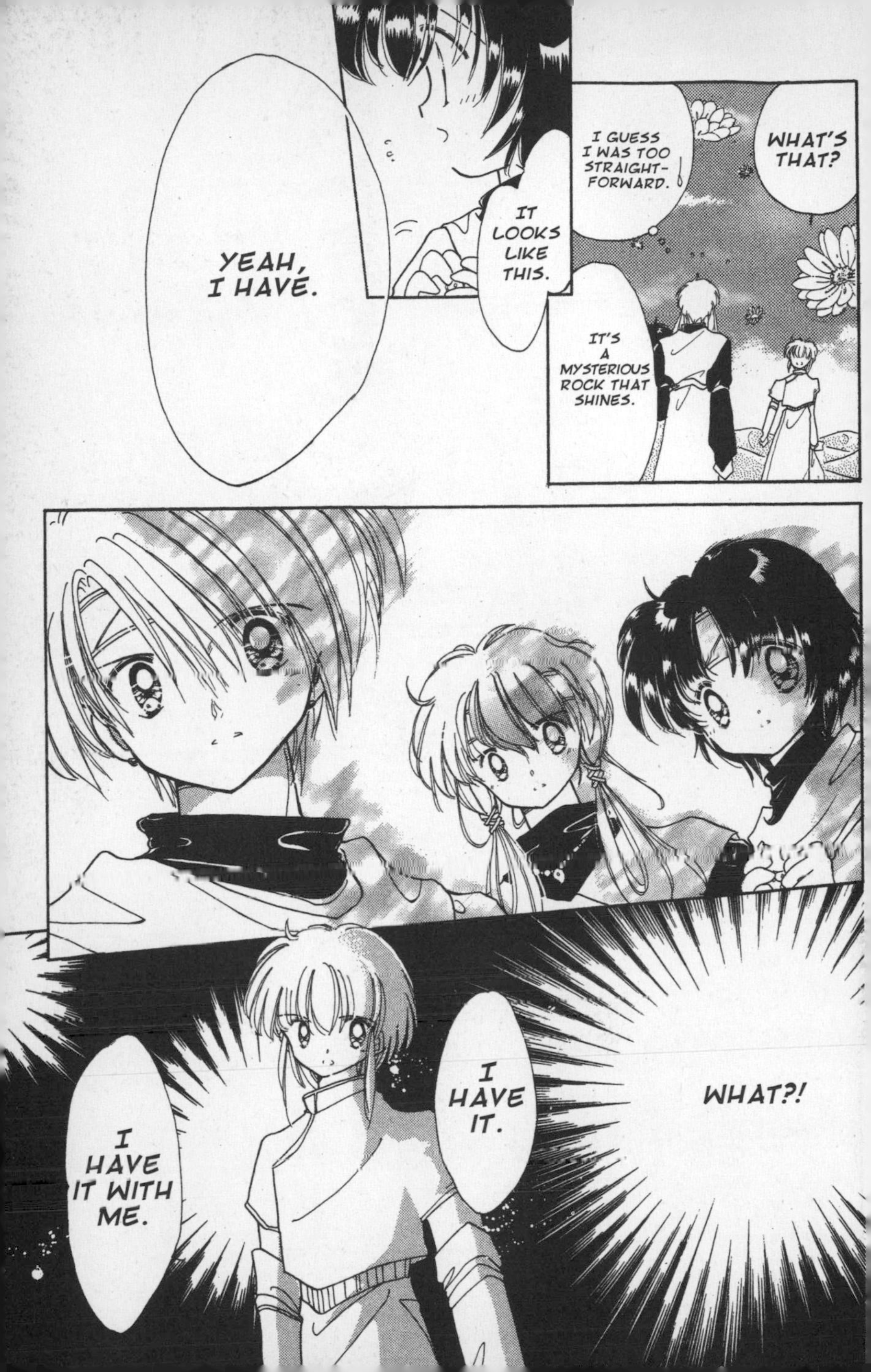
WHAT'S THAT?
I GUESS I WAS TOO STRAIGHT-FORWARD.
IT'S A MYSTERIOUS ROCK THAT SHINES.
IT LOOKS LIKE THIS.
YEAH, I HAVE.
WHAT?!
I HAVE IT.
I HAVE IT WITH ME.

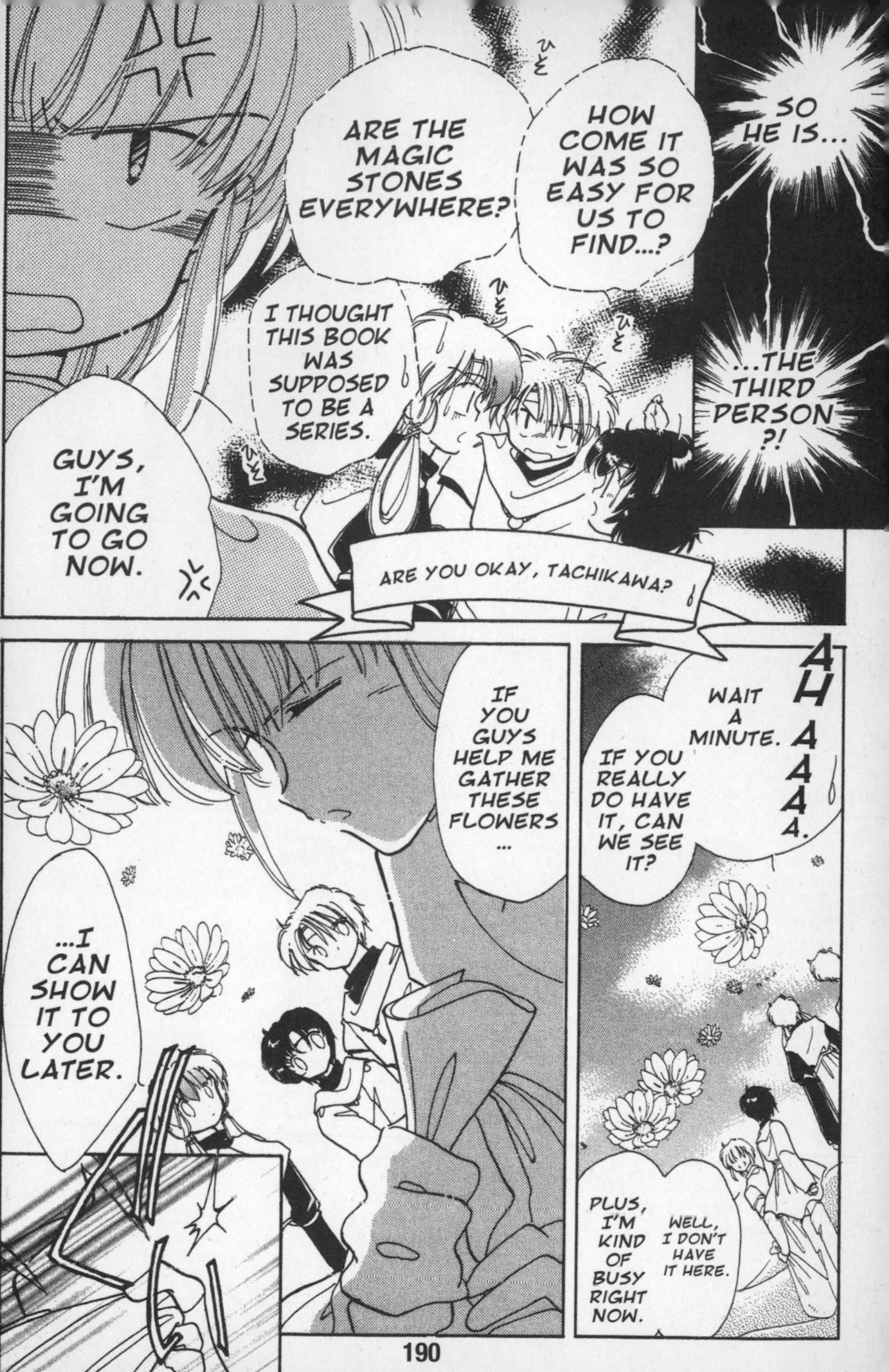
SO HE IS...
...THE THIRD PERSON?!
HOW COME IT WAS SO EASY FOR US TO FIND...?
ARE THE MAGIC STONES EVERYWHERE?
I THOUGHT THIS BOOK WAS SUPPOSED TO BE A SERIES.
GUYS, I'M GOING TO GO NOW.
ARE YOU OKAY, TACHIKAWA?
AHAAAAA.
WAIT A MINUTE.
IF YOU REALLY DO HAVE IT, CAN WE SEE IT?
WELL, I DON'T HAVE IT HERE.
PLUS, I'M KIND OF BUSY RIGHT NOW.
IF YOU GUYS HELP ME GATHER THESE FLOWERS...
...I CAN SHOW IT TO YOU LATER.

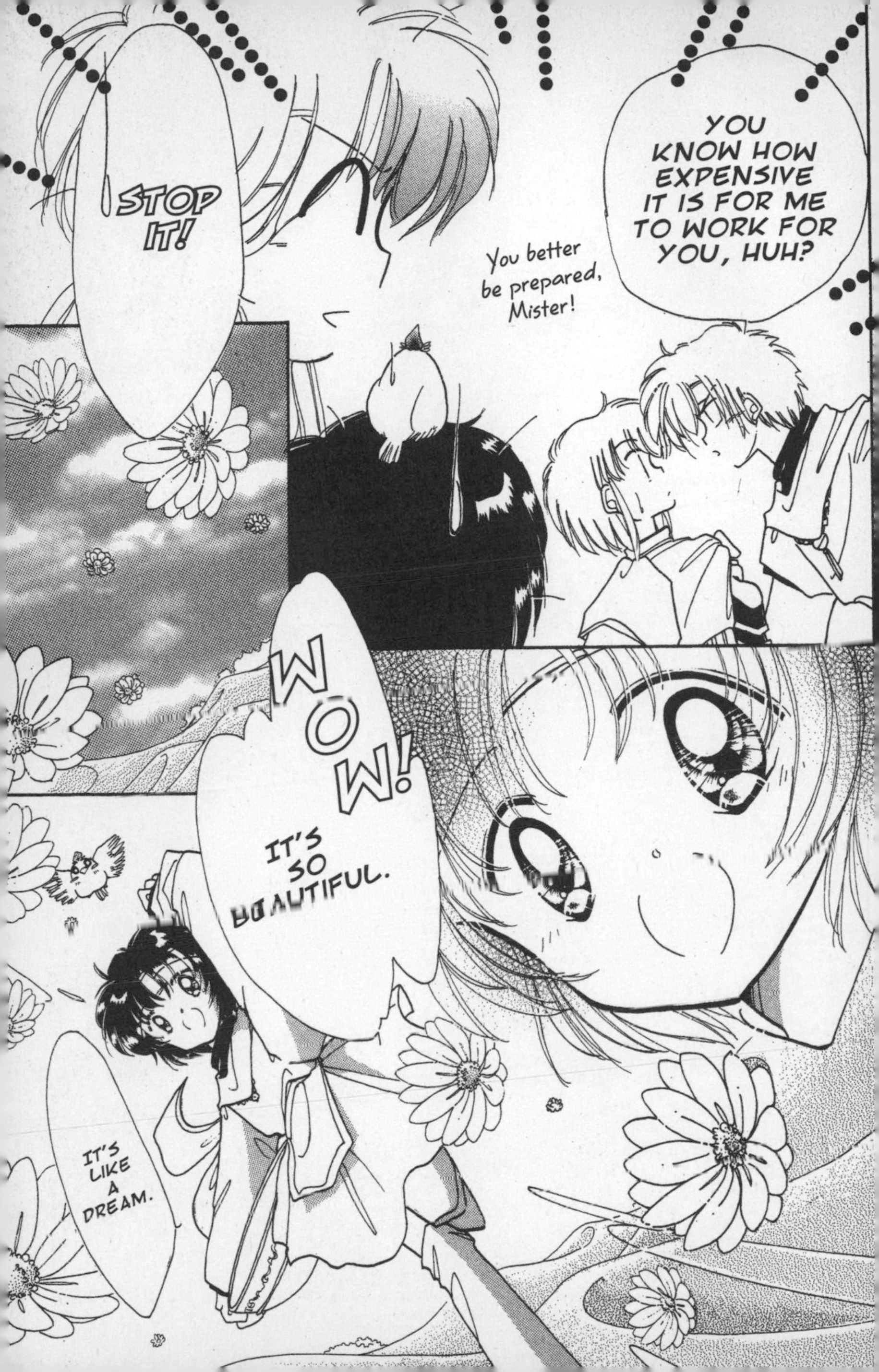
YOU KNOW HOW EXPENSIVE IT IS FOR ME TO WORK FOR YOU, HUH?
You better be prepared, Mister!
STOP IT!
WOW!
IT'S SO BEAUTIFUL.
IT'S LIKE A DREAM.

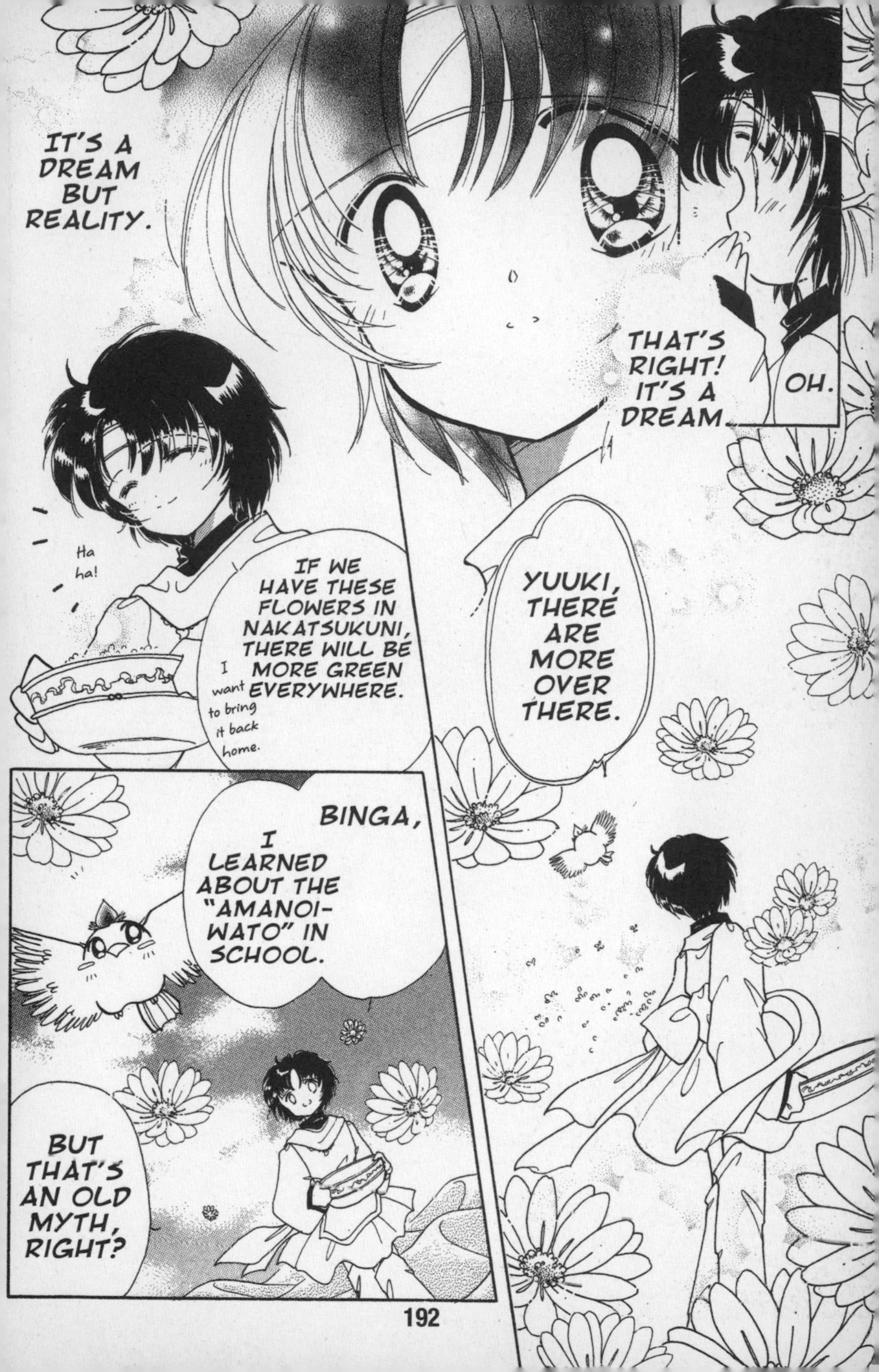
OH.
THAT'S RIGHT! IT'S A DREAM.
IT'S A DREAM BUT REALITY.
YUUKI, THERE ARE MORE OVER THERE.
IF WE HAVE THESE FLOWERS IN NAKATSUKUNI, THERE WILL BE MORE GREEN EVERYWHERE.
I want to bring it back home.
Ha ha!
BINGA, I LEARNED ABOUT THE "AMANOI-WATO" IN SCHOOL.
BUT THAT'S AN OLD MYTH, RIGHT?

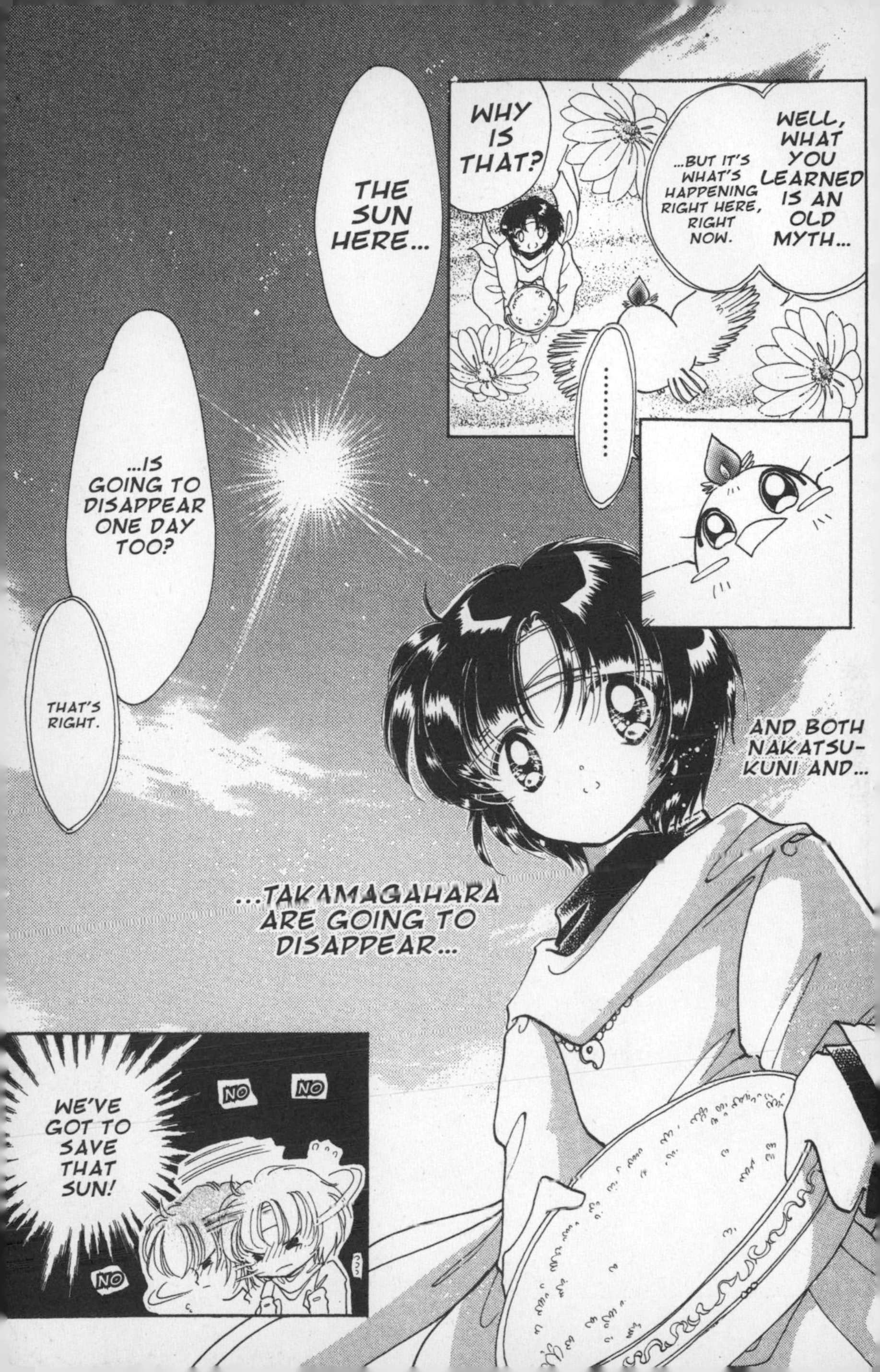
WELL, WHAT YOU LEARNED IS AN OLD MYTH...
...BUT IT'S WHAT'S HAPPENING RIGHT HERE, RIGHT NOW.
WHY IS THAT?
......
THE SUN HERE...
...IS GOING TO DISAPPEAR ONE DAY TOO?
THAT'S RIGHT.
AND BOTH NAKATSU-KUNI AND...
...TAKAMAGAHARA ARE GOING TO DISAPPEAR...
NO
NO
WE'VE GOT TO SAVE THAT SUN!
NO

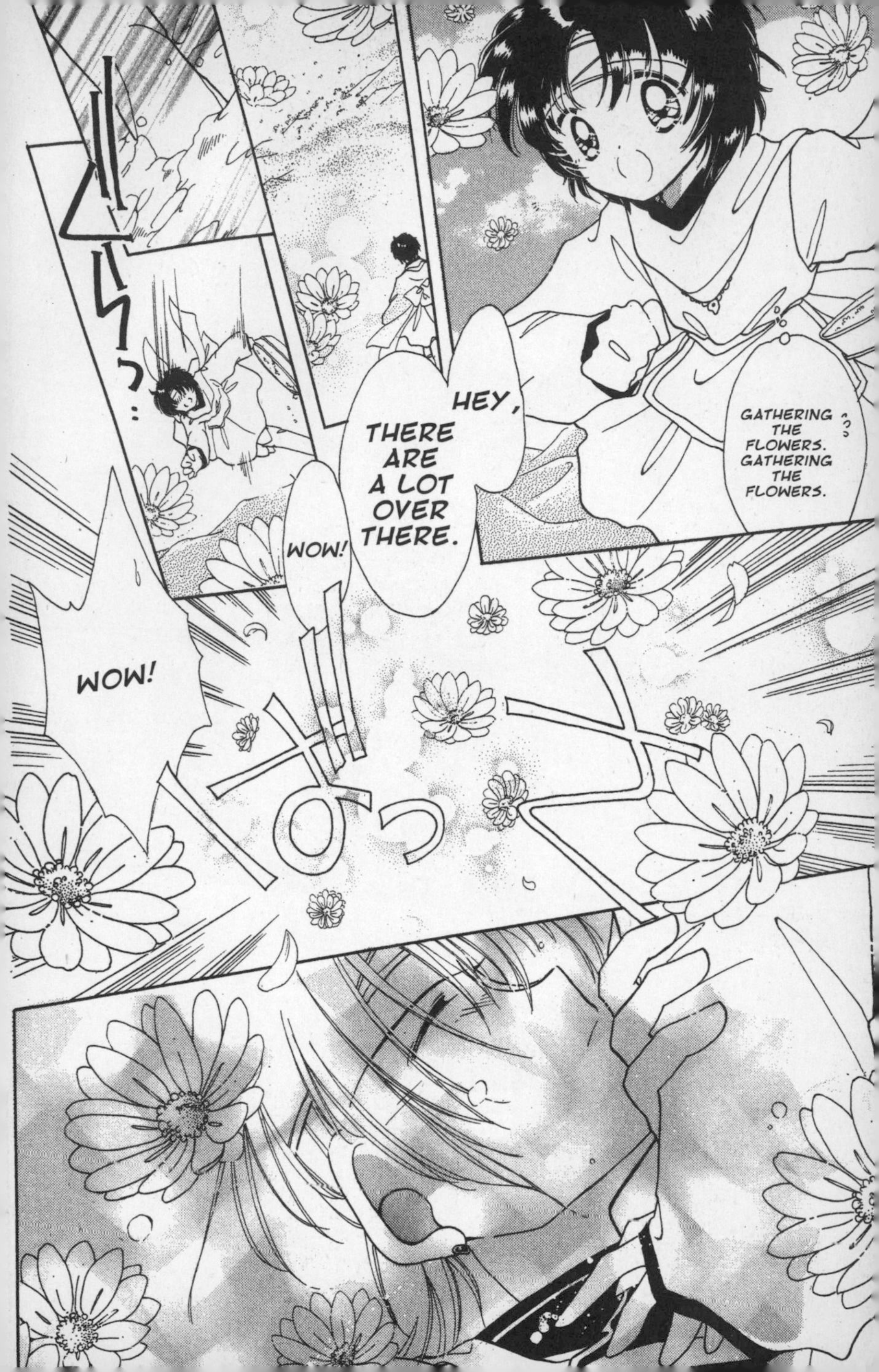
GATHERING THE FLOWERS. GATHERING THE FLOWERS.
HEY, THERE ARE A LOT OVER THERE.
WOW!
WOW!

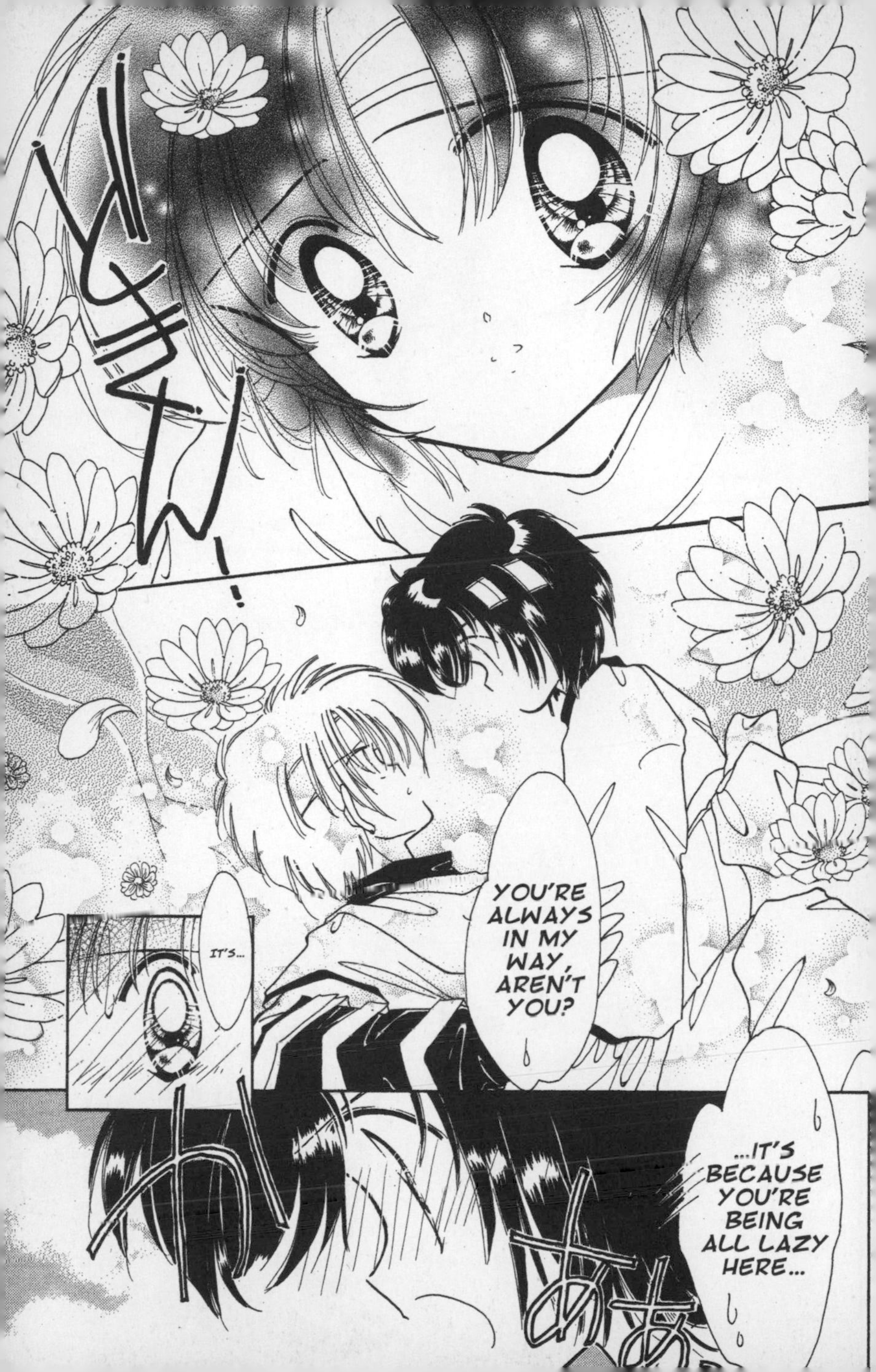
YOU'RE ALWAYS IN MY WAY, AREN'T YOU?
IT'S...
...IT'S BECAUSE YOU'RE BEING ALL LAZY HERE...

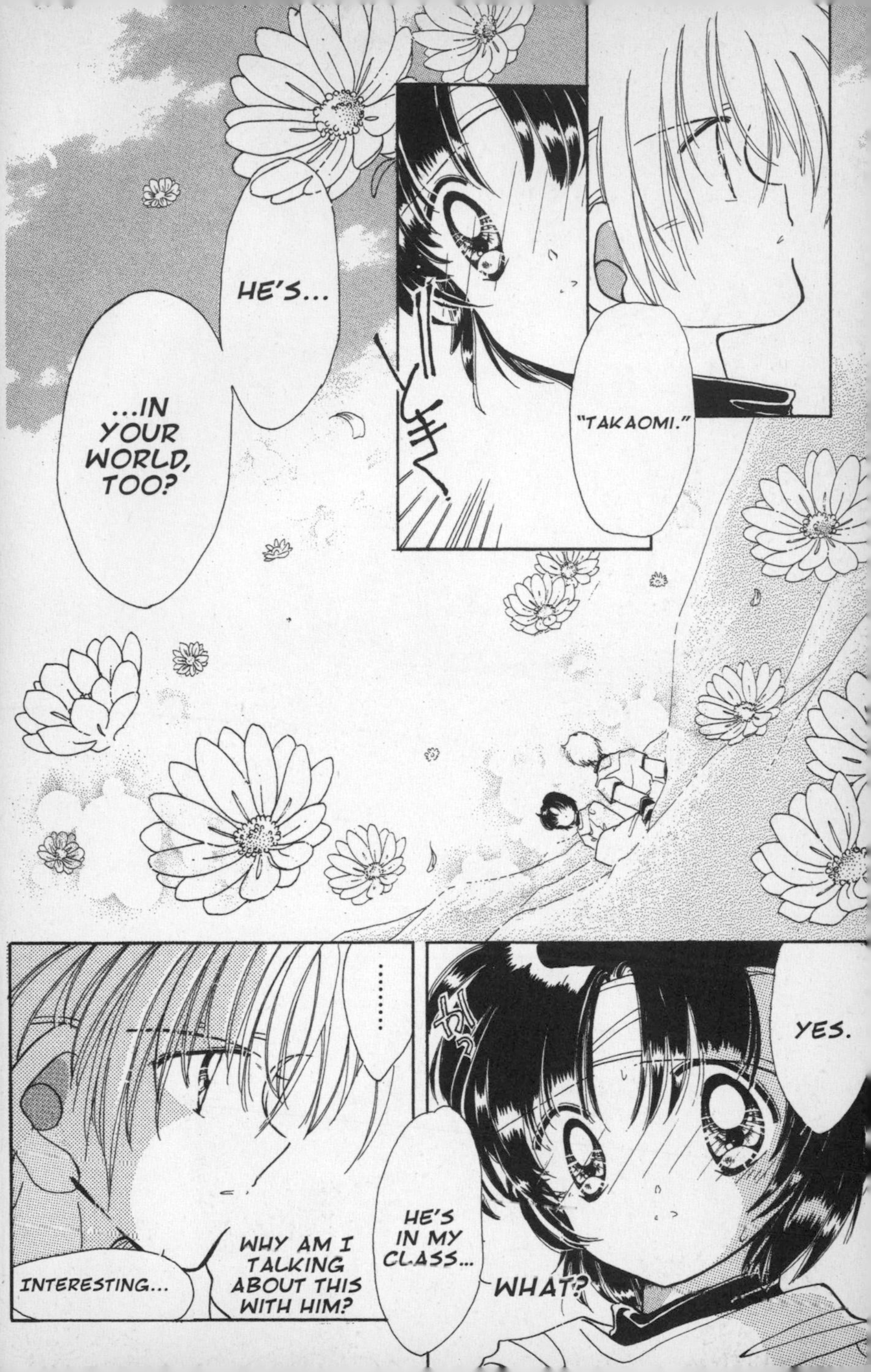
"TAKAOMI."
HE'S...
...IN YOUR WORLD, TOO?
YES.
HE'S IN MY CLASS...
WHAT?
......
WHY AM I TALKING ABOUT THIS WITH HIM?
INTERESTING...

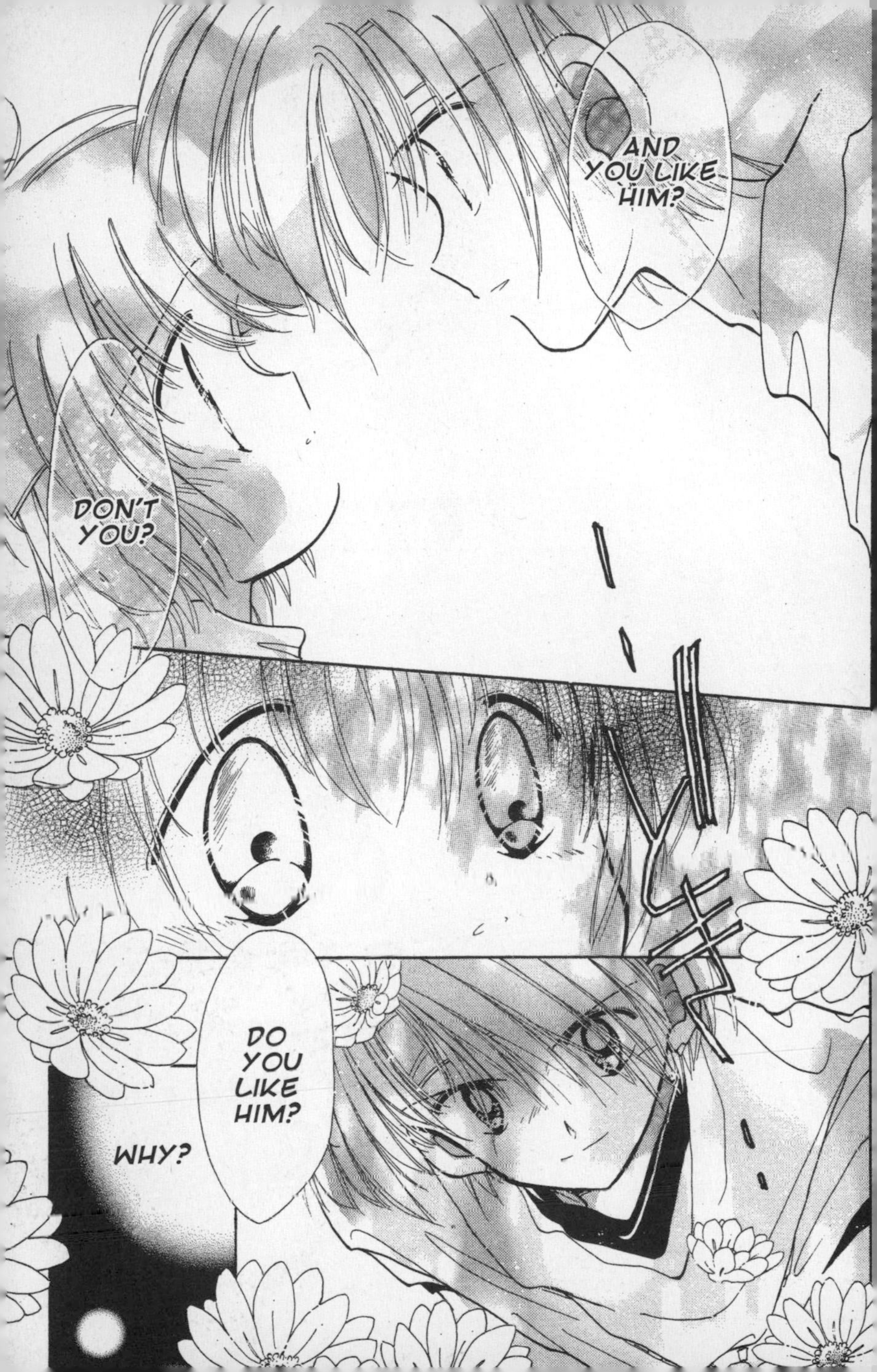
AND YOU LIKE HIM?
DON'T YOU?
DO YOU LIKE HIM?
WHY?

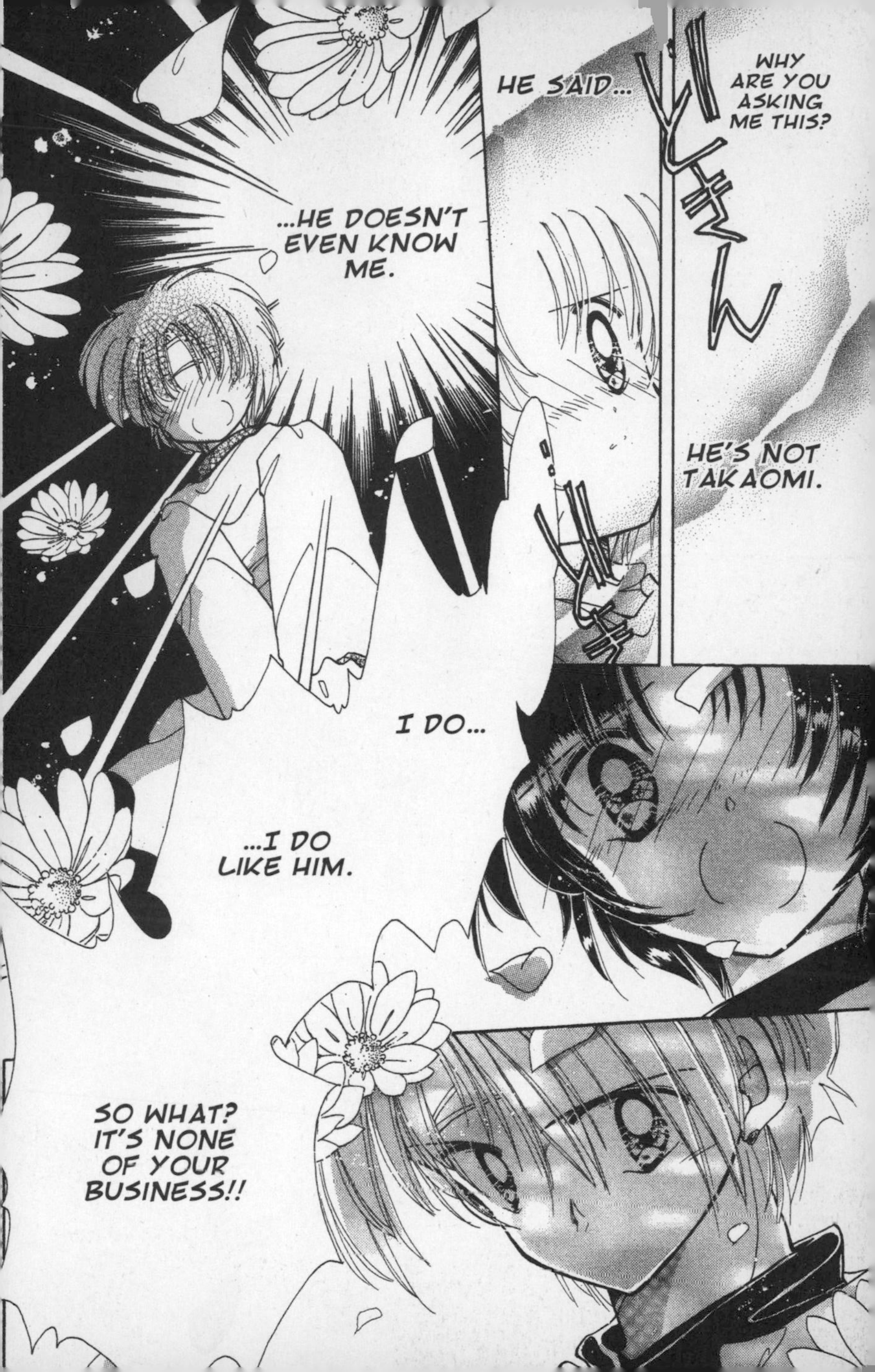
WHY ARE YOU ASKING ME THIS?
HE'S NOT TAKAOMI.
HE SAID...
...HE DOESN'T EVEN KNOW ME.
I DO...
...I DO LIKE HIM.
SO WHAT? IT'S NONE OF YOUR BUSINESS!!

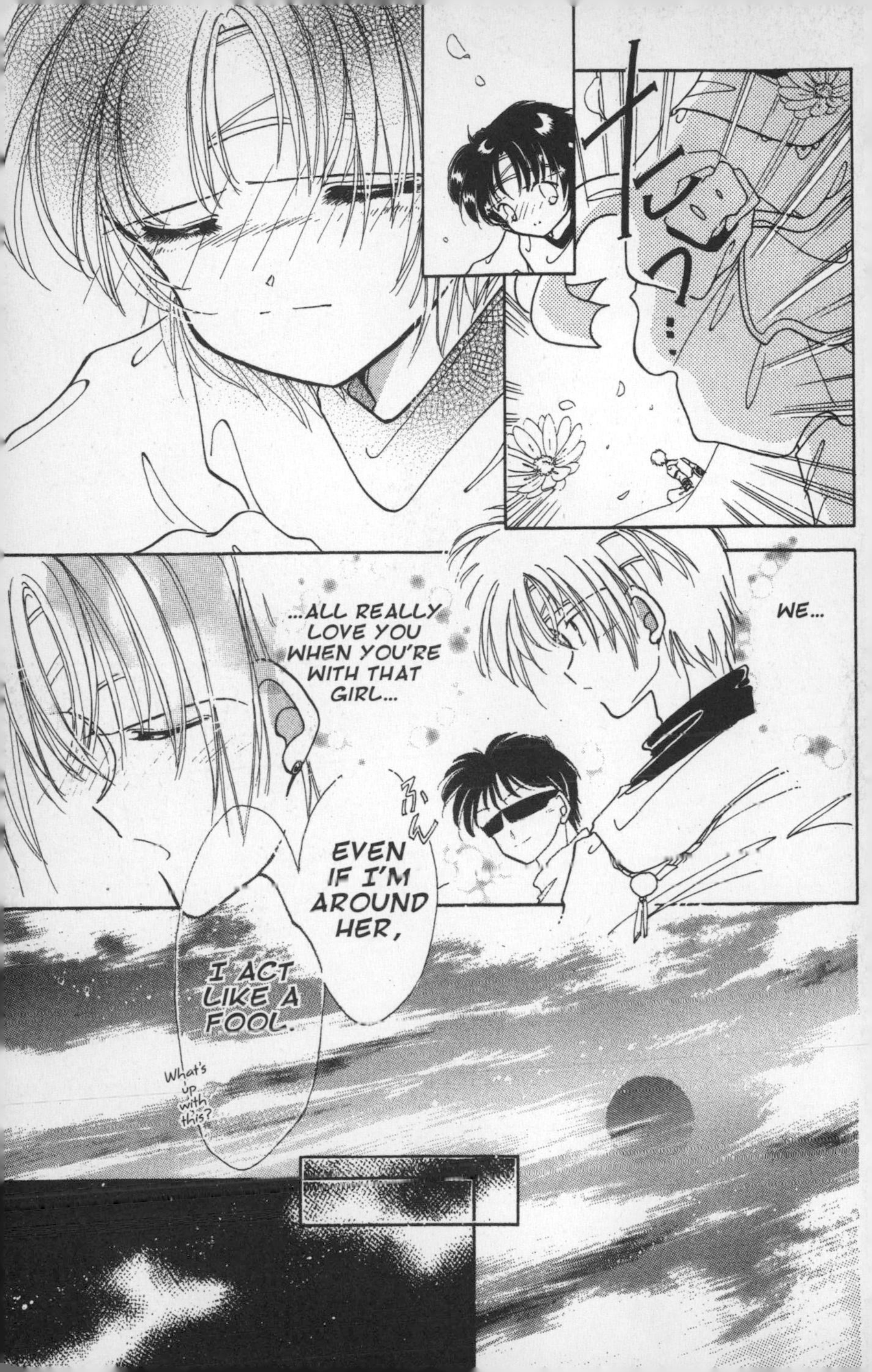
WE...
...ALL REALLY LOVE YOU WHEN YOU'RE WITH THAT GIRL...
ふん
EVEN IF I'M AROUND HER,
I ACT LIKE A FOOL.
What's up with this?

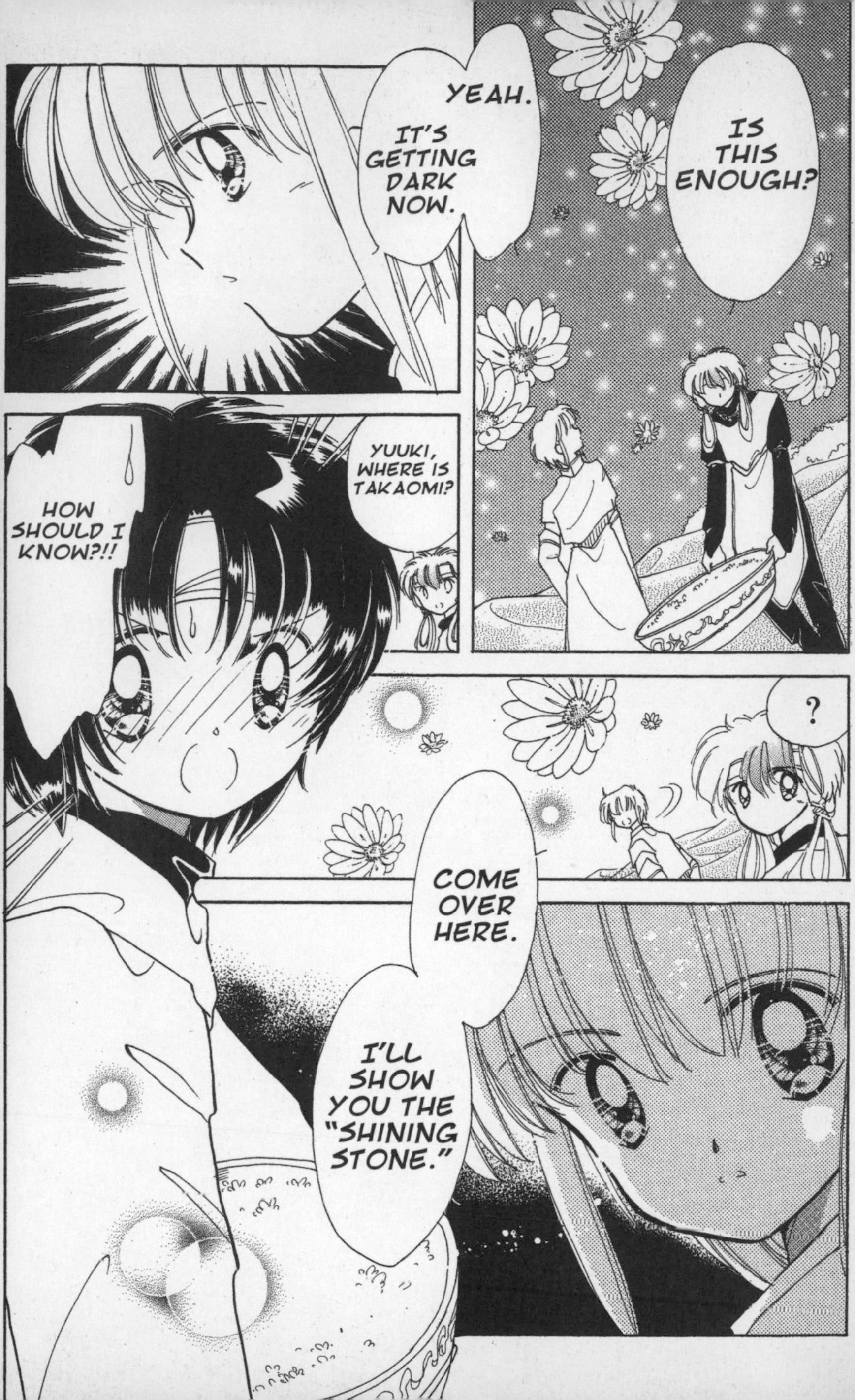
IS THIS ENOUGH?
YEAH.
IT'S GETTING DARK NOW.
YUUKI, WHERE IS TAKAOMI?
HOW SHOULD I KNOW?!!
?
COME OVER HERE.
I'LL SHOW YOU THE "SHINING STONE."

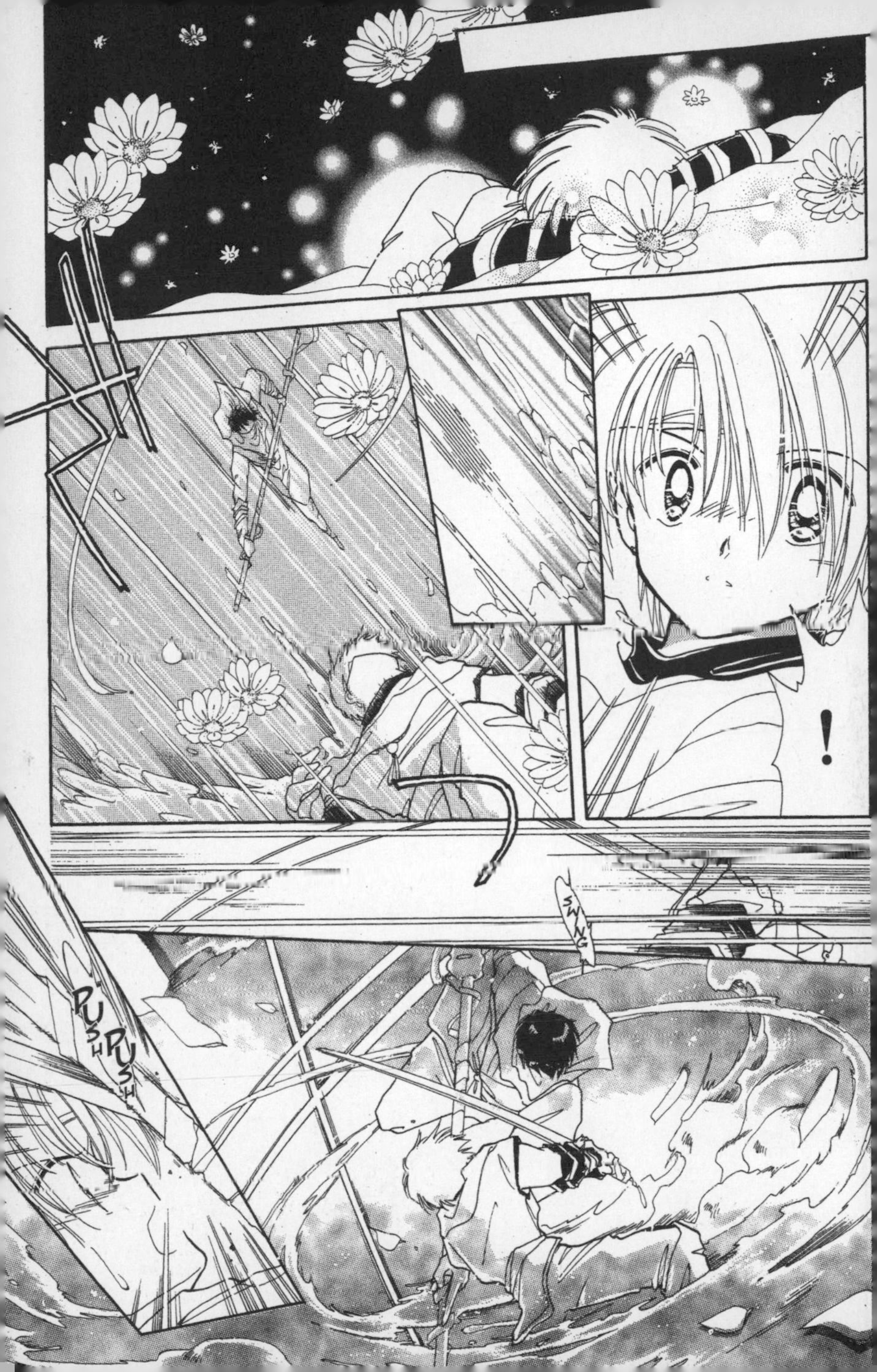
!
SWING
PUSH PUSH

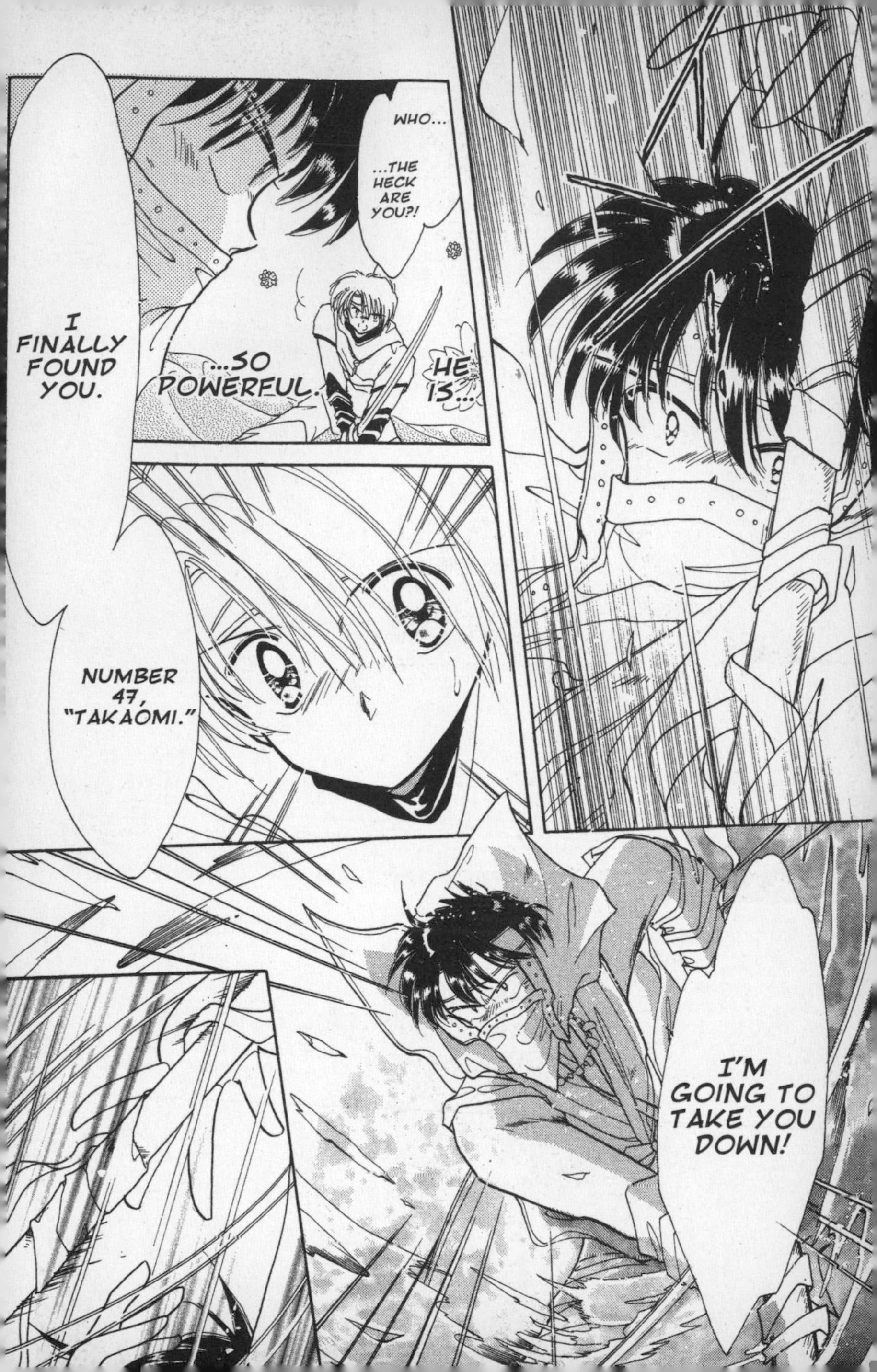
WHO...
...THE HECK ARE YOU?!
HE IS...
...SO POWERFUL.
I FINALLY FOUND YOU.
NUMBER 47, "TAKAOMI."
I'M GOING TO TAKE YOU DOWN!

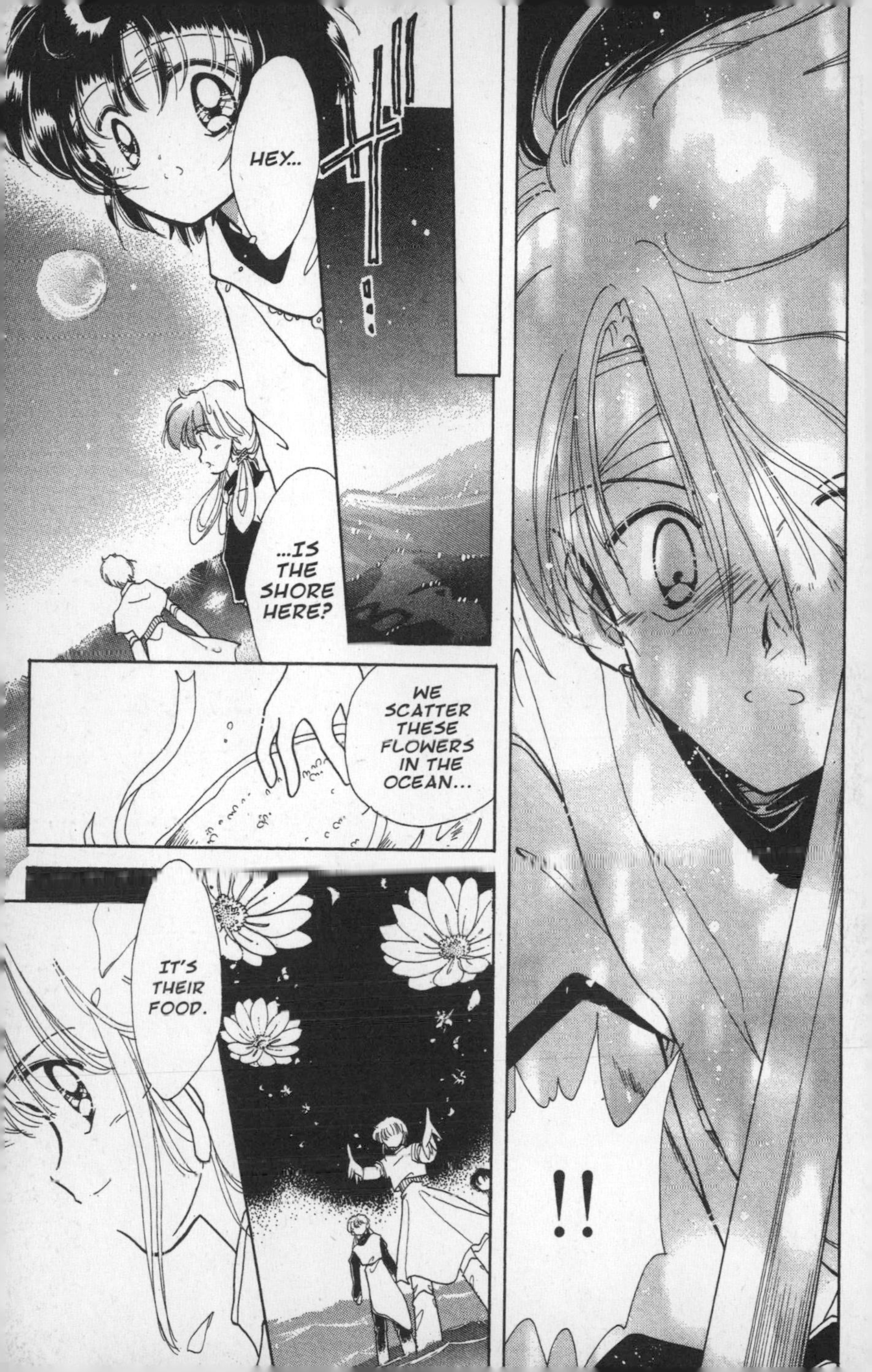
!!
HEY...
...IS THE SHORE HERE?
WE SCATTER THESE FLOWERS IN THE OCEAN...
IT'S THEIR FOOD.

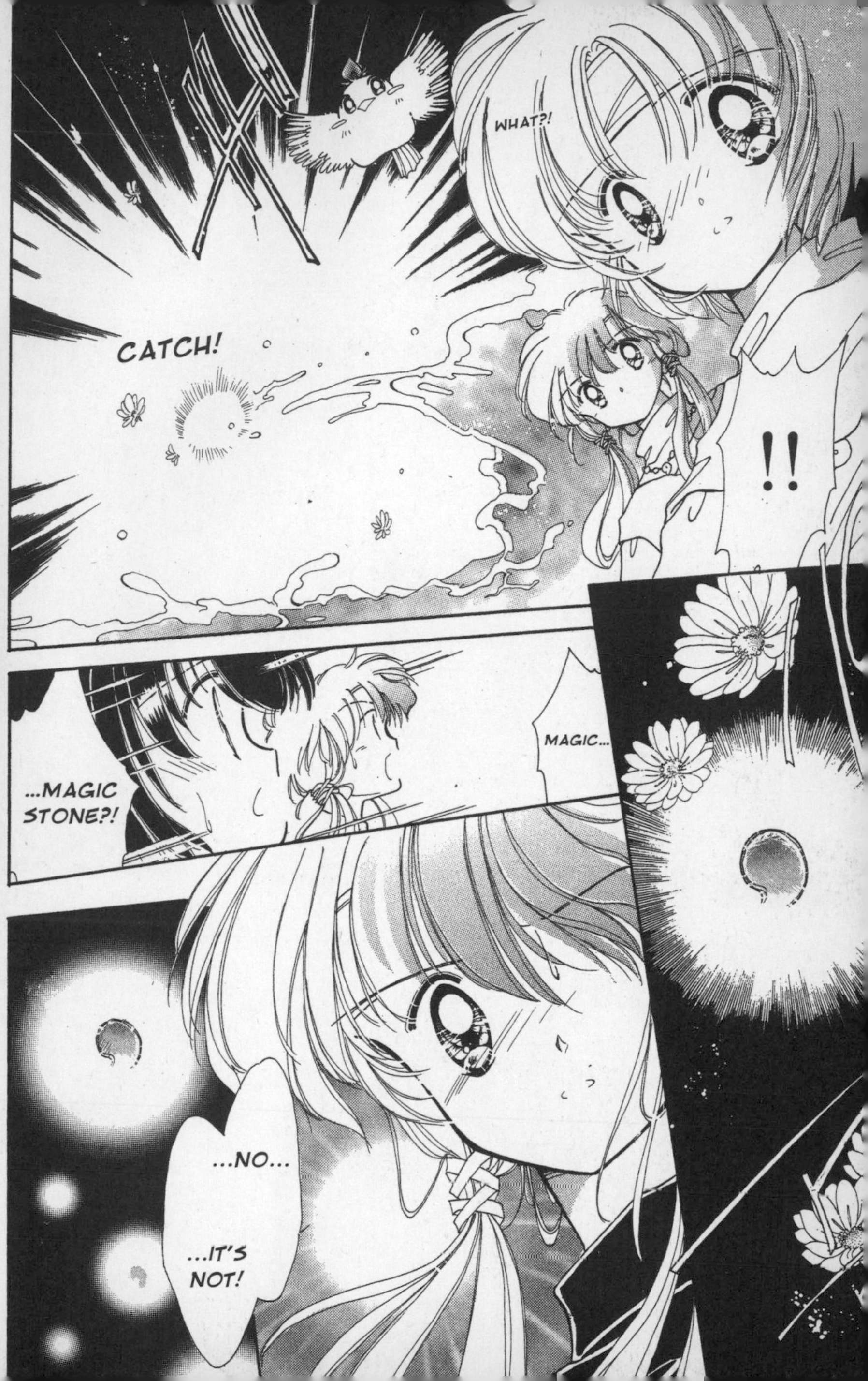
WHAT?!
!!
CATCH!
MAGIC...
...MAGIC STONE?!
...NO...
...IT'S NOT!

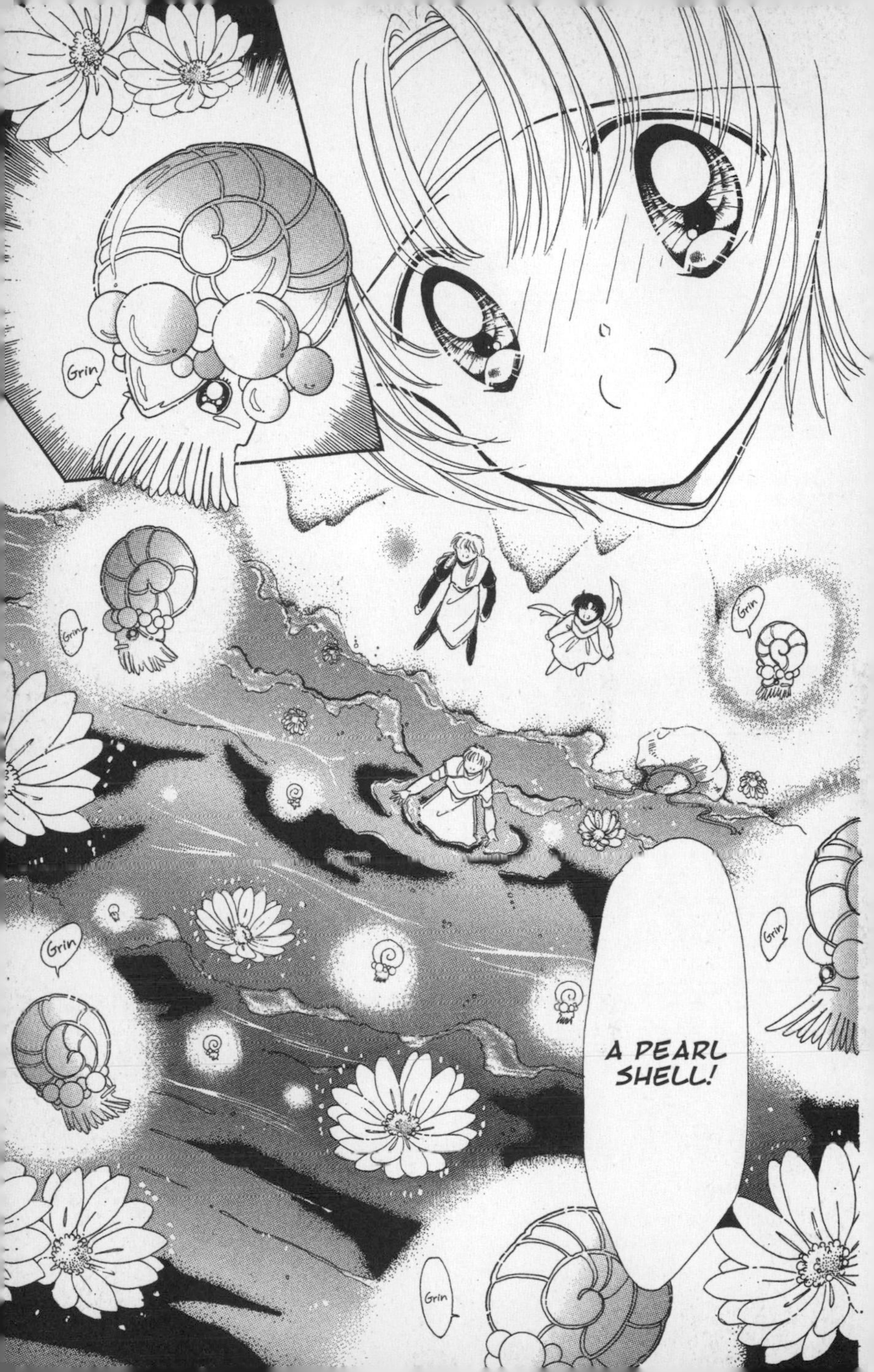
Grin
Grin
Grin
Grin
Grin
A PEARL SHELL!
Grin

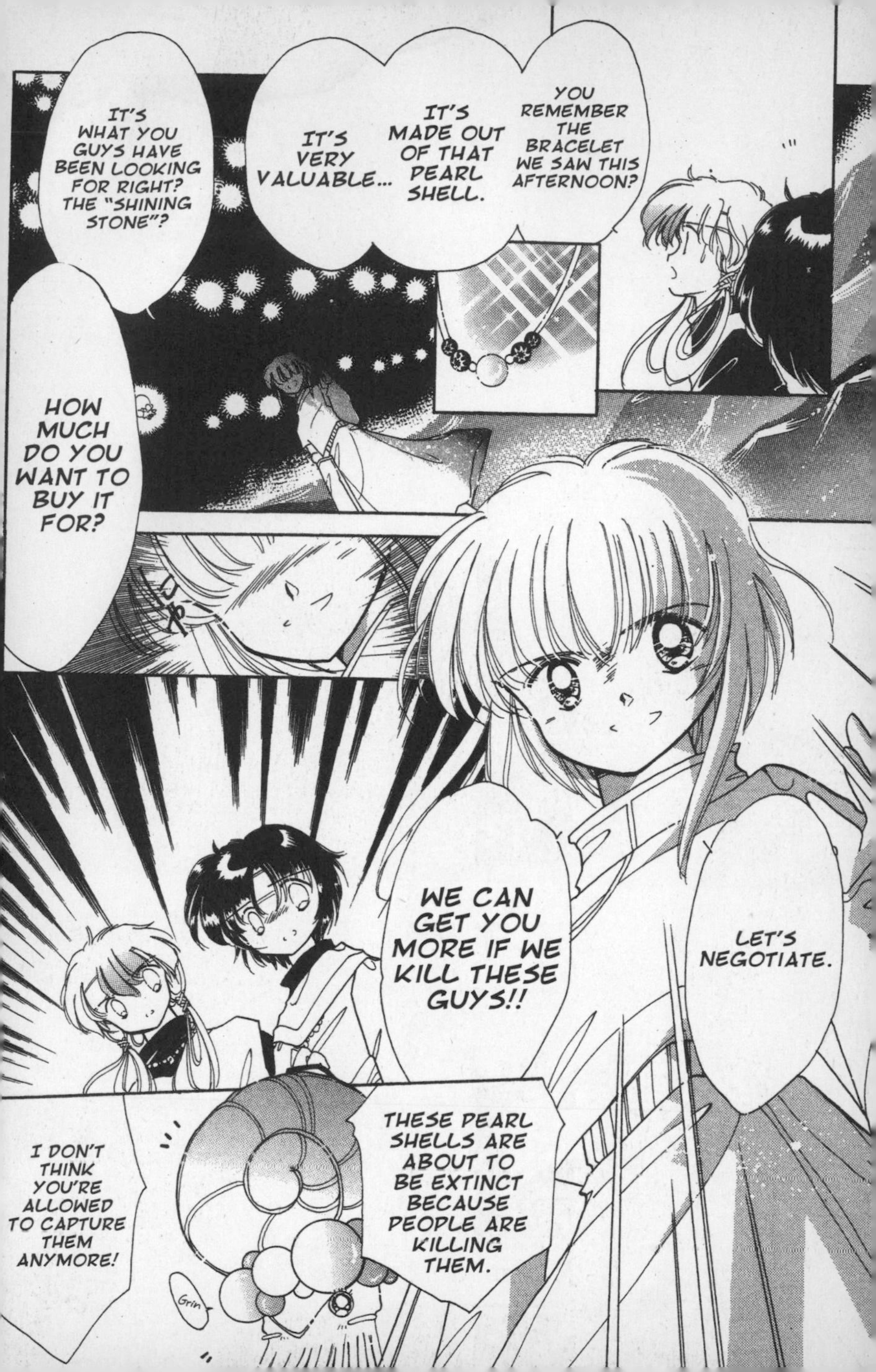
YOU REMEMBER THE BRACELET WE SAW THIS AFTERNOON?
IT'S MADE OUT OF THAT PEARL SHELL.
IT'S VERY VALUABLE...
IT'S WHAT YOU GUYS HAVE BEEN LOOKING FOR RIGHT? THE "SHINING STONE"?
HOW MUCH DO YOU WANT TO BUY IT FOR?
LET'S NEGOTIATE.
WE CAN GET YOU MORE IF WE KILL THESE GUYS!!
THESE PEARL SHELLS ARE ABOUT TO BE EXTINCT BECAUSE PEOPLE ARE KILLING THEM.
Grin
I DON'T THINK YOU'RE ALLOWED TO CAPTURE THEM ANYMORE!

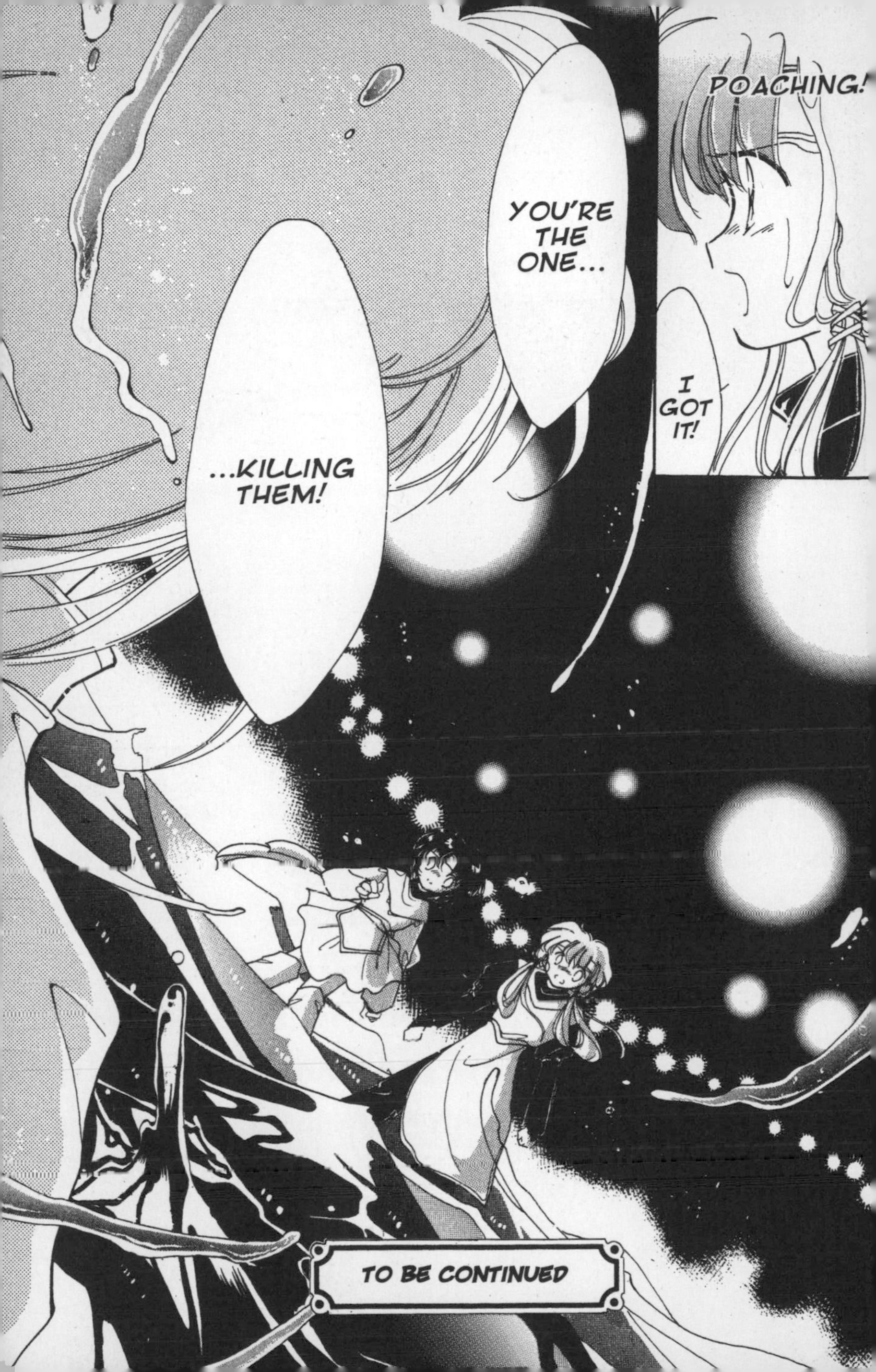
POACHING!
I GOT IT!
YOU'RE THE ONE...
...KILLING THEM!
TO BE CONTINUED

In the next volume of

DREAM SAGA

While Yuuki and her band of friends continue on their quest to save Takamagahara, the balance between the dream world and the real world is thrown into turmoil. When Japan's municipal water unexpectedly turns red, a bloody trail leads to a once-murky pond in Takamagahara, where all of the fish have gone foul. Will Yuuki's magic be enough to solve the mystery behind this crimson-colored killer?

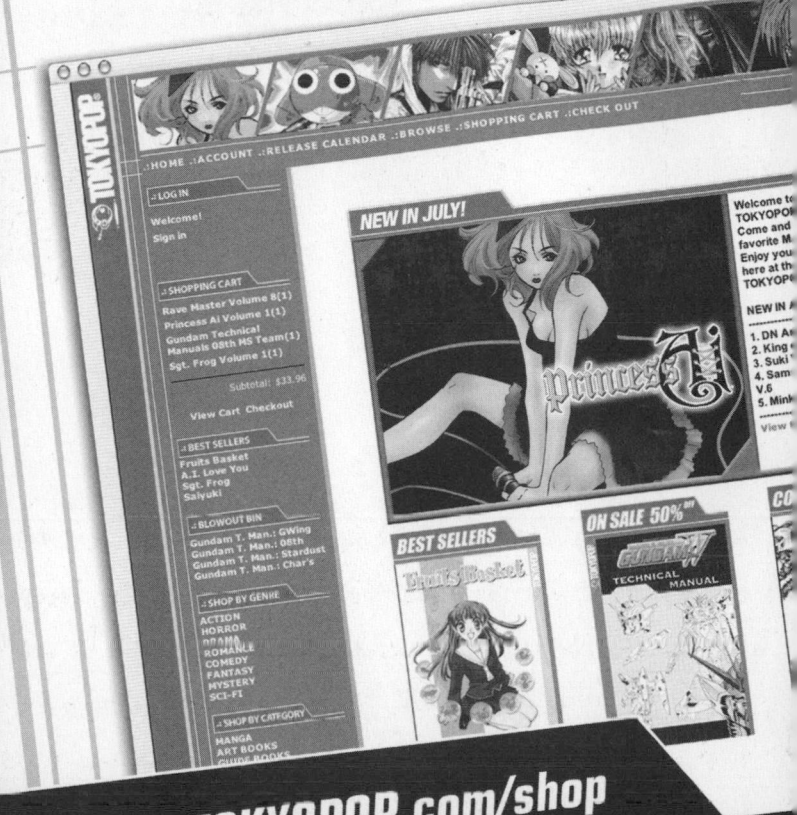

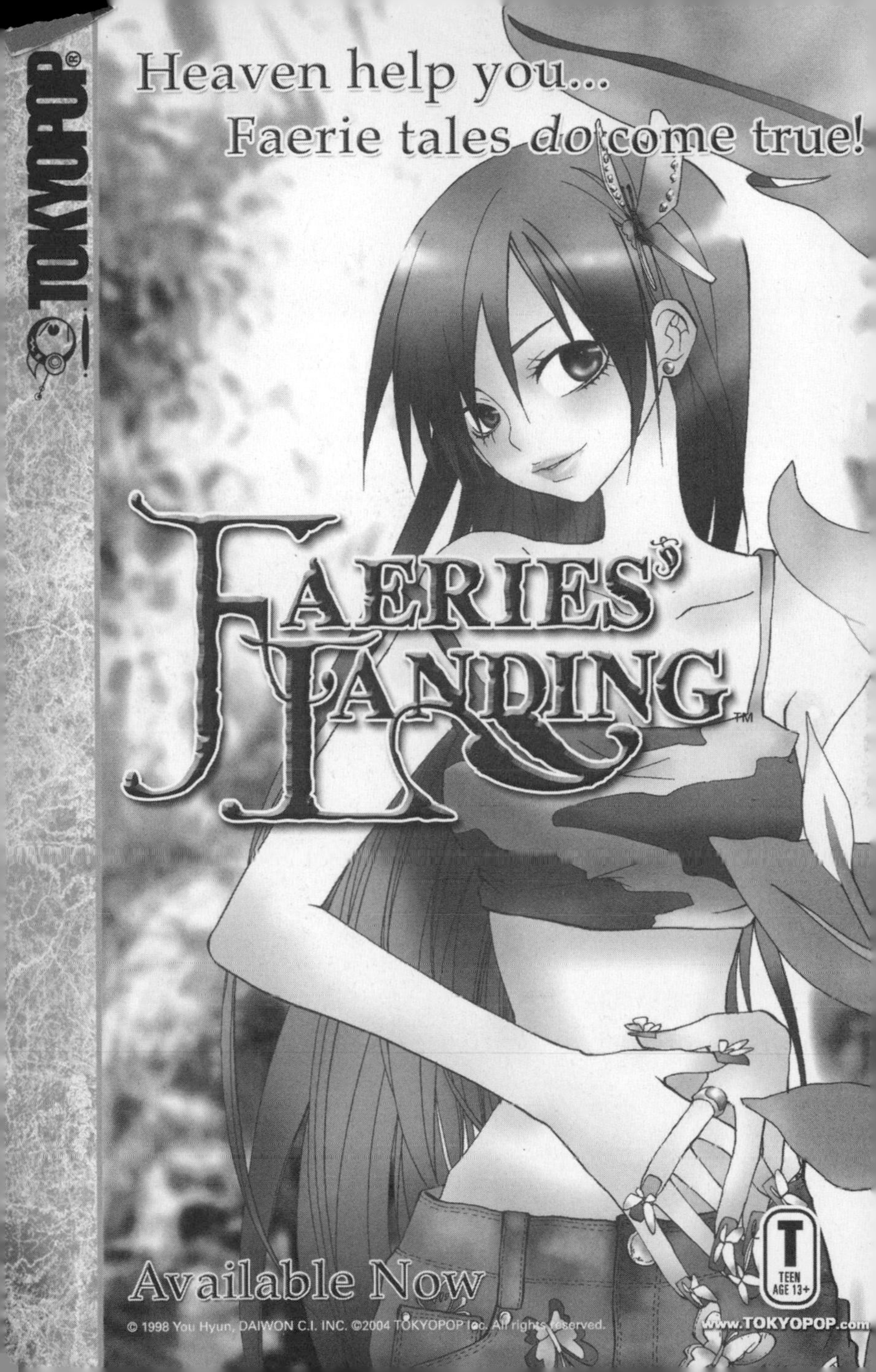
TOKYOPOP®
Heaven help you...
Faerie tales *do* come true!
FAERIES' LANDING™
Available Now
T TEEN AGE 13+
© 1998 You Hyun, DAIWON C.I. INC. ©2004 TOKYOPOP Inc. All rights reserved.
www.TOKYOPOP.com

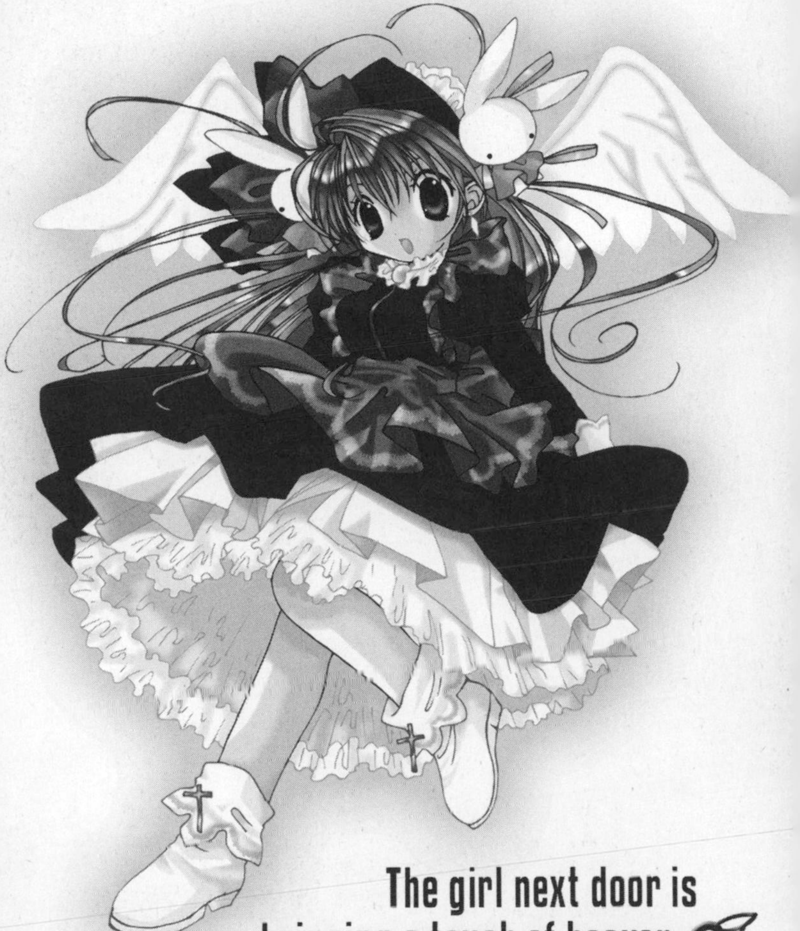

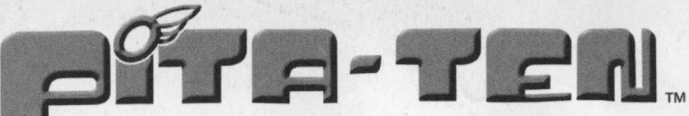

ALSO AVAILABLE FROM TOKYOPOP®

PLANET LADDER
PLANETES
PRIEST
PRINCESS AI
PSYCHIC ACADEMY
QUEEN'S KNIGHT, THE
RAGNAROK
RAVE MASTER
REALITY CHECK
REBIRTH
REBOUND
REMOTE
RISING STARS OF MANGA
SABER MARIONETTE J
SAILOR MOON
SAINT TAIL
SAIYUKI
SAMURAI DEEPER KYO
SAMURAI GIRL REAL BOUT HIGH SCHOOL
SCRYED
SEIKAI TRILOGY, THE
SGT. FROG
SHAOLIN SISTERS
SHIRAHIME-SYO: SNOW GODDESS TALES
SHUTTERBOX
SKULL MAN, THE
SNOW DROP
SORCERER HUNTERS
STONE
SUIKODEN III
SUKI
THREADS OF TIME
TOKYO BABYLON
TOKYO MEW MEW
TOKYO TRIBES
TRAMPS LIKE US
UNDER THE GLASS MOON
VAMPIRE GAME
VISION OF ESCAFLOWNE, THE
WARRIORS OF TAO
WILD ACT
WISH
WORLD OF HARTZ
X-DAY
ZODIAC P.I.

NOVELS

CLAMP SCHOOL PARANORMAL INVESTIGATORS
KARMA CLUB
SAILOR MOON
SLAYERS

ART BOOKS

ART OF CARDCAPTOR SAKURA
ART OF MAGIC KNIGHT RAYEARTH, THE
PEACH: MIWA UEDA ILLUSTRATIONS

ANIME GUIDES

COWBOY BEBOP
GUNDAM TECHNICAL MANUALS
SAILOR MOON SCOUT GUIDES

TOKYOPOP KIDS

STRAY SHEEP

CINE-MANGA™

ALADDIN
CARDCAPTORS
DUEL MASTERS
FAIRLY ODDPARENTS, THE
FAMILY GUY
FINDING NEMO
G.I. JOE SPY TROOPS
GREATEST STARS OF THE NBA
JACKIE CHAN ADVENTURES
JIMMY NEUTRON: BOY GENIUS, THE ADVENTURES OF
KIM POSSIBLE
LILO & STITCH: THE SERIES
LIZZIE MCGUIRE
LIZZIE MCGUIRE MOVIE, THE
MALCOLM IN THE MIDDLE
POWER RANGERS: DINO THUNDER
POWER RANGERS: NINJA STORM
PRINCESS DIARIES 2
RAVE MASTER
SHREK 2
SIMPLE LIFE, THE
SPONGEBOB SQUAREPANTS
SPY KIDS 2
SPY KIDS 3-D: GAME OVER
THAT'S SO RAVEN
TOTALLY SPIES
TRANSFORMERS: ARMADA
TRANSFORMERS: ENERGON

**You want it? We got it!
A full range of TOKYOPOP
products are available now at:
www.TOKYOPOP.com/shop**

05.11.04T

ALSO AVAILABLE FROM TOKYOPOP®

MANGA

.HACK//LEGEND OF THE TWILIGHT
@LARGE
ABENOBASHI: MAGICAL SHOPPING ARCADE
A.I. LOVE YOU
AI YORI AOSHI
ANGELIC LAYER
ARM OF KANNON
BABY BIRTH
BATTLE ROYALE
BATTLE VIXENS
BRAIN POWERED
BRIGADOON
B'TX
CANDIDATE FOR GODDESS, THE
CARDCAPTOR SAKURA
CARDCAPTOR SAKURA - MASTER OF THE CLOW
CHOBITS
CHRONICLES OF THE CURSED SWORD
CLAMP SCHOOL DETECTIVES
CLOVER
COMIC PARTY
CONFIDENTIAL CONFESSIONS
CORRECTOR YUI
COWBOY BEBOP
COWBOY BEBOP: SHOOTING STAR
CRAZY LOVE STORY
CRESCENT MOON
CROSS
CULDCEPT
CYBORG 009
D•N•ANGEL
DEMON DIARY
DEMON ORORON, THE
DEUS VITAE
DIABOLO
DIGIMON
DIGIMON TAMERS
DIGIMON ZERO TWO
DOLL
DRAGON HUNTER
DRAGON KNIGHTS
DRAGON VOICE
DREAM SAGA
DUKLYON: CLAMP SCHOOL DEFENDERS
EERIE QUEERIE!
ERICA SAKURAZAWA: COLLECTED WORKS
ET CETERA
ETERNITY
EVIL'S RETURN
FAERIES' LANDING
FAKE
FLCL
FLOWER OF THE DEEP SLEEP
FORBIDDEN DANCE
FRUITS BASKET
G GUNDAM

GATEKEEPERS
GETBACKERS
GIRL GOT GAME
GIRLS' EDUCATIONAL CHARTER
GRAVITATION
GTO
GUNDAM BLUE DESTINY
GUNDAM SEED ASTRAY
GUNDAM WING
GUNDAM WING: BATTLEFIELD OF PACIFISTS
GUNDAM WING: ENDLESS WALTZ
GUNDAM WING: THE LAST OUTPOST (G-UNIT)
GUYS' GUIDE TO GIRLS
HANDS OFF!
HAPPY MANIA
HARLEM BEAT
I.N.V.U.
IMMORTAL RAIN
INITIAL D
INSTANT TEEN: JUST ADD NUTS
ISLAND
JING: KING OF BANDITS
JING: KING OF BANDITS - TWILIGHT TALES
JULINE
KARE KANO
KILL ME, KISS ME
KINDAICHI CASE FILES, THE
KING OF HELL
KODOCHA: SANA'S STAGE
LAMENT OF THE LAMB
LEGAL DRUG
LEGEND OF CHUN HYANG, THE
LES BIJOUX
LOVE HINA
LUPIN III
LUPIN III: WORLD'S MOST WANTED
MAGIC KNIGHT RAYEARTH I
MAGIC KNIGHT RAYEARTH II
MAHOROMATIC: AUTOMATIC MAIDEN
MAN OF MANY FACES
MARMALADE BOY
MARS
MARS: HORSE WITH NO NAME
MINK
MIRACLE GIRLS
MIYUKI-CHAN IN WONDERLAND
MODEL
MY LOVE
NECK AND NECK
ONE
ONE I LOVE, THE
PARADISE KISS
PARASYTE
PASSION FRUIT
PEACH GIRL
PEACH GIRL: CHANGE OF HEART
PET SHOP OF HORRORS
PITA-TEN

05.11.04T

STOP!

This is the back of the book.
You wouldn't want to spoil a great ending!

This book is printed "manga-style," in the authentic Japanese right-to-left format. Since none of the artwork has been flipped or altered, readers get to experience the story just as the creator intended. You've been asking for it, so TOKYOPOP® delivered: authentic, hot-off-the-press, and far more fun!

DIRECTIONS

If this is your first time reading manga-style, here's a quick guide to help you understand how it works.

It's easy... just start in the top right panel and follow the numbers. Have fun, and look for more 100% authentic manga from TOKYOPOP®!